The Barnstorming
Hawaiian Travelers

ALSO BY JOEL S. FRANKS

Asian Pacific Americans and Baseball: A History
(McFarland, 2008)

The Barnstorming Hawaiian Travelers

A Multiethnic Baseball Team Tours the Mainland, 1912–1916

JOEL S. FRANKS

McFarland & Company, Inc., Publishers
Jefferson, North Carolina, and London

LIBRARY OF CONGRESS CATALOGING-IN-PUBLICATION DATA

Franks, Joel S.
The barnstorming Hawaiian Travelers : a multiethnic
baseball team tours the mainland, 1912–1916 / Joel S. Franks.
              p.   cm.
Includes bibliographical references and index.

ISBN 978-0-7864-6566-8
softcover : acid free paper ∞

1. Hawaiian Travelers (Baseball team)—History.
2. Baseball—Hawaii—History.
3. Baseball—United States—History.
4. Asian Americans—Sports—History.
5. Pacific Islander Americans—Sports—History.
I. Title.

GV875.H39F73   2012   796.357'64096931—dc23   2011051515

BRITISH LIBRARY CATALOGUING DATA ARE AVAILABLE

© 2012 Joel S. Franks. All rights reserved

*No part of this book may be reproduced or transmitted in any form
or by any means, electronic or mechanical, including photocopying
or recording, or by any information storage and retrieval system,
without permission in writing from the publisher.*

Front cover: In the 1900s, culturally diverse Hawaiians enthusiastically organized teams and leagues. This is a photograph of the Hawaii team, c. 1910 (courtesy of Library of Congress, Prints & Photographs Division, LC-USZ62-119529); cover design by David K. Landis (Shake It Loose Graphics)

Manufactured in the United States of America

*McFarland & Company, Inc., Publishers
Box 611, Jefferson, North Carolina 28640
www.mcfarlandpub.com*

To the memory of my brother, Jerry

Table of Contents

Acknowledgments viii

Preface 1

Introduction 5

ONE: The First Journey, 1912   27

TWO: The "Yellow Peril" at Bat, 1913   64

THREE: The Not So "All-Chinese," 1914   94

FOUR: Never the Home Team, 1915   123

FIVE: One Last Time, 1916   156

SIX: Further Travels   175

SEVEN: Buck Lai's Journeys   196

Epilogue 223

Notes 231

Bibliography 244

Index 250

Acknowledgments

In putting together this book, I have received a great deal of help from several sources. San Jose State's interlibrary loan department has provided me with much in the way of needed microfilm. All sorts of people working for the library at the University of Hawai'i, Manoa, have been helpful. The same can be said for fine folks at the Library of Congress, as well as Special Collections at the University of Arizona, Seton Hall University, Rice University, Long Island University, Occidental College, and Notre Dame University. I am grateful to Mary Lai for her memories and I am no less indebted to Andy Yamashiro, Jr., and his daughter Chris Ueno. Baseball historians Thomas Barthel and John Thorn provided advice. And to my children, Kait Franks and Spencer Franks, who performed research for their old dad, when they could have been enjoying a day in the Oahu sun: I love you both. To their mother, Cheryl, I owe more than she can ever imagine.

Preface

It was well over a decade ago that I ran across a reference to the "Chinese University of Hawaii" baseball team in *Baseball: The People's Game*, Dorothy and Harold Seymour's great book about grassroots baseball. The Seymours discussed this team in the book's chapter on American college baseball, for the understandable reason that the Hawaiians seemed to represent a legitimate college and played several college nines on their sojourns to the American mainland in the 1910s. The Seymours asserted that this team won many games on the mainland and quoted extensively from outfielder S.H. Hoe.[1]

At that time, I was early in my tenure as an Asian American studies instructor at San José State University. I also was very interested in sport history. The Chinese Hawaiian ballplayers illuminated by the Seymours piqued my curiosity and I began to research their experiences in earnest. I contacted the National Baseball Hall of Fame and ordered copies of Hawaiian newspapers from the University of Hawai'i. My family and I vacationed on the islands in the late 1990s and early 2000s and I managed to cop a few days in the University of Hawai'i's library at a microfilm machine.

I discovered that the Seymours got some of it wrong. The young ballplayers crisscrossing the Pacific to the mainland did not go to the "Chinese University of Hawaii." There was no such institution. It was a concoction by one or more of the Hawaiian promoters of the trip. The Seymours claimed that the Hawaiian ballplayers journeyed to the mainland from 1910 to 1916, whereas they actually did not begin their treks until 1912. The Hawaiians did indeed oppose and beat mainland college nines with regularity, but they also played and frequently defeated white and African American semi-professional and professional teams. I also eventually discovered that while the first team of Travelers was largely composed of players of Chinese ancestry, subsequent barnstorming nines included multicultural rosters of Chinese, Japanese, Indigenous Hawaiian, and white ballplayers.

Further research led to the finding that a few of these Hawaiian ballplayers had interesting experiences trying to enter the ranks of American organized baseball in the 1910s. Outright racism prevented Lang Akana from playing in the Pacific Coast League, one of the best baseball leagues in America outside of the major leagues. Racism, moreover, clearly stunted the advancement of Vernon Ayau, and less clearly Buck Lai and Andrew Yamashiro.

However, the young men who played for the Hawaiian Travelers were not victims. In a variety of ways, they asserted a sense of agency. That is, if for whatever reason infielder Buck Lai, whose real name was Lai Tin, could not make it into the big leagues, he still achieved an admirable career in baseball as a semi-pro player, manager, and umpire. From 1935 to 1937, he led a contingent of Hawaiian ballplayers to the mainland and worked as a major league scout. He married a European American woman and raised a family in the Philadelphia area. One of his children became a respected college coach and educator at Long Island University. Other Travelers took up careers in public service and music, as well as in coaching baseball.

This book is organized in a roughly chronological fashion. The first chapter foregrounds and then covers the inaugural trek of the Travelers to the American mainland in 1912. The second, third, fourth, and fifth chapters take up the annual journeys from 1913 through 1916. The sixth chapter focuses on the post–Traveler experiences of individuals such as Vernon Ayau, Andy Yamashiro, and Apau Kau among others, while the seventh takes a look at arguably the most famous Chinese American athlete of the early twentieth century—Buck Lai.

The hazard of organizing this book chronologically is that readers will run across a certain repetition of experiences. While this may not always make for exciting reading, it serves a purpose. History, as most of us know, does not move in a smooth, linear fashion. For example, one might think that after a fairly successful and well-publicized display of baseball talent in 1912, the Travelers would less consistently encounter stereotypical representations of Chinese people in the mainland press. Instead, those representations persisted, even though the Travelers also experienced more complicated, even respectful representations of their skills and humanity. Moreover, it is hoped that a chronological take on the Travelers will give readers a sense of movement, of traveling. Such a take can capture the journeying from town to town, college to college, and base to base that was such an essential, exciting, and sometimes dreary aspect of these young men's baseball experiences on the American mainland.

The best sources of information have been contemporary newspapers published in Honolulu as well as big and small towns on the American mainland. Of course, this information is biased. Some press accounts seem to have been written by the Travelers' promoters rather than local journalists. As for the latter, they may not always accurately report on the Travelers' experiences, but they reveal some complex truths about America in the early twentieth century.

Fortunately, the internet revolution has made more contemporary newspaper and other material available to the researcher in recent years. Living in Silicon Valley with a growing family, I have been burdened with a full-time teaching load, but not with tenure, money or fellowships. Accordingly, it would have been hard for me to journey from town to town, library to library across the mainland looking for microfilmed tidbits about the Travelers. However, through various online resources offered by libraries, genealogical societies and the Society for American Baseball Research, I was able to consult historical newspapers (from major dailies to small-town weeklies) and access archival information related to individual Travelers, including census reports, schedules, ship manifests, and draft cards. I have also put in my time perusing microfilm. Indeed, my children, Kait and Spencer, spent a sunny day at the University of Hawai'i, Manoa, doing the same at my request. Neither, by the way, wants me to forget it.

Many of the athletes mentioned in these pages went by different names. Buck Lai, for example, was known in his years as a ballplayer on the islands as Lai Tin. As he made a permanent home on the mainland, he became known as William Tin Lai, William T. Lai, and Bill Lai, as well as Buck Lai. Moreover, players with European, Hawaiian, and Japanese surnames were often given Chinese names to persuade mainlanders they were seeing genuine Chinese in action. For example, Andy Yamashiro played on the Travelers as "Andy Yim." I have tried my best to make sense of it all, but I'm not sure I always have.

The team itself was referred to in multiple ways. The Honolulu sporting pages cheered and sometimes criticized the All-Chinese as they ventured to the mainland for the first time in 1912. As the team roster included more Hawaiians of European, indigenous, and Japanese descent, they became known on the islands as the Chinese Travelers or the Hawaiian Travelers. On the mainland, as I have pointed out earlier, they were often depicted as members of a team representing the fictional Chinese University or College of Hawaii. Interestingly, as late as 1916, the mainland press described the Hawaiian ballplayers as Chinese students even when more than half of the roster possessed no Chinese ancestry. Accordingly, the name I believe best fits the team is the Hawaiian Travelers, since they were a multiethnic, multiracial team of barnstormers from Hawai'i.

Other issues related to terminology also should be exposed. When I quote press accounts, I will use Hawaii. However, out of respect for indigenous Hawaiians, I will use Hawai'i in unquoted material. I will refer to all people born and raised in Hawai'i as Hawaiians. Hawaiians of indigenous or native ancestry will be described as Native Hawaiians. I will, however, identify persons who clearly possessed European and Hawaiian backgrounds with the Hawaiian language *hapa haoles*. People who clearly possessed European ancestry will often be described as either white, European American, or haole.

I will also refer to Hawaiians of Chinese or Japanese ancestry as Chinese Hawaiians/Hawaiian Chinese or Japanese Hawaiians/Hawaiian Japanese. I am not happy with identifying Hawaiians of Chinese or Japanese ancestry as just Chinese or Japanese unless referring to Chinese or Japanese nationals. Buck Lai was born in Hawai'i in 1894. He was not legally, therefore, Chinese. Upon Hawai'i's annexation, Buck Lai automatically became a U.S. citizen. Yet it seems inaccurate to call him a Chinese American when he grew up and developed his athletic skills in Honolulu in the early twentieth century. To call him a Chinese Hawaiian seems to be more in keeping with the hybrid project in which the Travelers were engaged. Finally, I will call Hawaiian and mainland Americans who can trace their ancestry to places such as China, Japan, Korea, and the Philippines either Asian Pacific people or Asian Pacific Americans.

Introduction

The *Bennington Evening Banner* was not happy. The local team had allowed itself to be beaten in extra innings by "Chinamen," who had arrived in the New England city during the summer of 1912. Even though the "nine Chinese ballplayers" had just lost several games in Vermont, they had thrown off the burden of prior defeats and "trimmed to a frazzle our aspirants for the league championship and the state championship." Clearly, however, the inferior team had triumphed. The Bennington ballplayers would have won, the *Evening Banner* complained, if the locals had played harder and not suffered through injuries that they well could have avoided if they had taken better care of themselves.[1]

Still, the *Evening Banner* begged off from its complaints. After all, the game was well attended and though long and not always played crisply, was enjoyed thoroughly by the spectators who followed the see-saw action. The "orientals" had to come from behind to tie the locals in the eighth. Then the visitors had to once again dig themselves out of a hole by tying the game in the ninth. In the eleventh, they put the finishing touches on the home team.[2]

As it turned out, the visitors were not exactly "Chinese," but "Hawaiian-Chinese." According to the *Evening Banner*, the winning team was made up of students from the "University of Hawaii"—students who had previously graduated from various Hawaiian colleges. The victors had learned their baseball from American sailors, and they had been such apt pupils that they wound up forming the only "Chinese team" playing anywhere.[3]

Since leaving Honolulu in early spring, the *Evening Banner* told its readers, the Hawaiian ballplayers had experienced seasickness on the Pacific and California's cold weather upon their arrival. Their earlier schedule primarily consisted of college teams but then included semiprofessional contingents once the college season ended. In any event, the Hawaiians had proven their mettle by beating several college nines.[4]

Financed by Chinese merchants in Honolulu, the ballplaying tourists represented to the *Evening Banner* the modern, even revolutionary changes, transforming China in the early decades of the twentieth century. While all of the athletes were born in Hawai'i and, therefore, U.S. citizens in 1912, each reputedly supported the revolution which they hoped would disperse republican institutions throughout China.[5]

Interviews conducted with the Chinese Hawaiians indicated to the *Evening Banner* that weather was their biggest problem on the American mainland. It was too cold in the spring and had gotten much too warm in the summer. The ballplayers reported that back home in Hawai'i they experienced pleasant 78 degrees Fahrenheit weather all year round. Because of the agreeable climate on the islands, "F.L. Akana," described by the *Evening Banner* as the team "humorist," declared that Hawaiian athletes could compete in various sports "13 months a year."[6]

The visiting ballplayers had traveled extensively since arriving on the mainland, while presumably making an intriguing fashion statement to mainlanders. They maintained that they averaged 1,000 miles a week. However, the *Evening Banner* could not help but note that many of visitors wore "a curious hat woven from the feathers of Chinese pheasants."[7]

Apparently, the Hawaiians regaled the press with stories about the "University of Hawaii." Various sports such as baseball, football, rugby, soccer, tennis, and track and field were played by "University of Hawaii" students. Moreover, aquatic sports were popular. Not only did "University of Hawaii" students engage in competitive swimming, but also "surfing which consists of riding the crests of waves on a board." Among the best athletes on the team was "Lai Tin who holds down the dizzy corner," otherwise known as third base. Lai Tin was not only an accomplished ballplayer but a Hawaiian record holder in track and field.[8]

The *Evening Banner* assured readers that each visiting athlete "spoke English," but "with a sibilant softness that makes ordinary conversation sound like crude pantomime and each writes it like a copy book." The ballplayers spoke warmly about their Hawaiian home, telling the press that the island population was comprised of a quarter million people of "all races." They asserted that sanitation was excellent on the islands, while the public schools were exemplary. "The native population," the ballplayers guaranteed, "is extremely pleased with the American regime." They added that sugar and pineapples were the islands' most prominent exports and reinforced the fact by hawking the latter to curious mainlanders. One ballplayer happened to mention that the islands were volcanic and endured earthquakes. Another, however, shut him up rapidly, according to the *Evening Banner*, assuring the press that Honolulu had never fallen victim to an earthquake.[9]

While in Bennington, the visitors were shown local manufacturing plants as well as "other points of interest." The ballplayers expressed pleasure in their reception in Bennington, adding that not all communities on the mainland were so welcoming. The local team, moreover, displayed themselves as "good sports" to the Hawaiians, who unanimously declared Bennington "the most beautiful small city they have visited."[10]

Several months later, a publication designed by and for students of Chinese descent in the United States announced the arrival of the "Honolulu Chinese Baseball Team." The June 10, 1913, edition of *The Chinese Students' Monthly* reported that this team was stronger than the one that toured "the States" in 1912. Moreover, the *Monthly*'s editorial revealed that the Hawaiian ballplayers played "under an assumed name, 'Chinese University Team of Hawai'i,'" so that mainland colleges would feel justified in scheduling games against them. Perhaps these mainland colleges had regretted doing so since the Hawaiians had mowed down college opposition easily, thus far winning 37 of 38 games against university nines from Stanford, California, Colorado, Utah, Missouri, and Illinois. The Hawaiians had not been quite so dominant against semipro opponents. Still, they managed to win 12 of their first 20 games against semipros.[11]

The Chinese Students' Monthly briefly explored the history of Chinese Hawaiian baseball. In 1904, it claimed, Chinese baseball teams were formed in Honolulu. One team, the "Chinese Athletics," was particularly good, copping its share of league championships against "American, Hawaiian, Portuguese, and Japanese" opponents. Rather snidely, the monthly remarked, "Our Japanese friends were usually at the tail end of the pennant race."[12]

Indeed, the *Monthly* lingered a bit over games played between the Chinese Hawaiians and visiting Japanese teams from Waseda and Keio Universities. In 1909, the Waseda nine arrived on the islands after touring the American mainland. The Chinese Athletics, the *Monthly* reported, defeated the Japanese nine. By the time the Keio team visited Hawai'i the Chinese Athletics had merged with another Chinese team to form an even stronger unit. Accordingly, Keio lost two out of three games to the nine dubbed by the monthly as the Chinese Baseball Team of Honolulu.[13]

Between the end of the "Chinese team's" 1912 tour of the mainland and the beginning of its 1913 visit to the "states," the ballplayers had dominated Hawaiian baseball. The monthly boasted that they won 17 of 18 games against opponents in the "International League of Honolulu."[14]

"Most of the members of the team are good athletes," the *Monthly* proclaimed. The publication pointed out the athletic versatility of En Sue Pung, "the centre fielder [who] can run the 100 yards in 10⅔ seconds and broad jumps more than 21 feet." The outfielder, moreover, was described as the best baserunner in Honolulu. Right fielder Sing Hung Hoe was an expert soccer player. And "third baseman, Lai Ting, is considered the best athlete in Honolulu." The young man more accurately called Lai Tin by the *Evening Banner* held the Hawaiian records in the 50-yard dash and the broad jump. He reportedly could run the 100 yard dash in 10⅕ seconds and broad jump over 22 feet. Finally, Kan Yen Chun, depicted as both catcher and captain of the team, was apparently a good high jumper.[15]

The *Monthly* urged readers to take heart in what the "Chinese Baseball Team of Honolulu" represented. In less than a decade, Chinese in Honolulu had raised the number of baseball teams in their midst from two to 20. As for the Chinese Hawaiian team touring the American mainland, their example should inspire "Chinese students to take new interests in sports." Any individual heeding the *Monthly*'s call will not only "build up a strong body and constitution necessary for a long useful life but he will add to the prestige and fair name of the Chinese people."[16]

The *Monthly* even speculated that the Chinese Hawaiian baseball team could enhance economic relations between the U.S. and a financially strapped China. It asked readers to imagine "big American bankers" getting a chance to "see a classy game of baseball between a crack American nine and a Chinese team." Since "all true Americans are baseball fans ... it would be an immediate solution of all loan difficulties. Perhaps, these baseball-loving American bankers might not lower "the interest rates charged by the European robbers, but their good American baseball sporting instincts would not let them ask for the whole of the Chinese Empire as a security for a temporary little accommodation." Lest readers miss the point, the *Monthly* finished its editorial piece with "LONG LIVE BASEBALL!!!"[17]

Widely and mistakenly publicized as athletically-minded students of a non-existent "Chinese University of Hawaii," a team of Hawaiian baseball players, indeed, barnstormed throughout much of the American mainland from 1912 through 1916. In 1912, they even journeyed briefly into Canada with surprisingly controversial results. In 1915, they played in Cuba. These skillful ballplayers took on college, town, semiprofessional, and professional nines, as well as at least one dumbfounded high school team in California. In so doing, they frequently impressed and even stunned spectators and opponents with their mastery of America's National Pastime.

The team had been initially organized and sponsored by relatively elite members of the Chinese Hawaiian community in Honolulu. These community leaders were understandably anxious to represent people of Chinese descent to white America in a positive light. They knew well that Chinese immigrants had faced systematic racism and nativism in the United States, as well as sporadic acts of anti–Chinese violence. They were aided by the

The Travelers spent relatively little time on the West Coast of the mainland. They rather rapidly headed to the urban Midwest and East Coast. In this photograph, c. 1916, four Travelers stand outside the Indianapolis Speedway. From left to right, outfielder Yen Chin, outfielder Andy Yamashiro, infielder Lai Tin, and infielder Chinito or Jimmy Moriyama (courtesy of the Yamashiro Family).

Hawaiian Merchants and Advertisers Club, no less anxious to boost Hawai'i to the mainland as a site of investment and tourism. Since U.S. policy makers and opinion shapers justified annexation of Hawai'i as necessary because nonwhite Hawaiians could not rule themselves, the largely *haole* or white business leaders on the islands now felt the need to persuade mainlanders that Hawaiians, regardless of racial identity, were civilized enough to welcome mainland dollars.[18]

Initially, the barnstorming squad was known as the All-Chinese as well as the Chinese University of Hawaii. Subsequent barnstorming teams became more clearly representative of Hawai'i's multicultural, multiracial population, with players of not only Chinese, but Japanese, Native Hawaiian, and European descent. Meanwhile, the Honolulu press took to calling these teams the "Hawaiian Travelers," the "Chinese Travelers" or the quite cumbersome "near All-Chinese." Red McQueen, longtime sportswriter for the *Honolulu Advertiser*, stated in 1964 that while the "All-Chinese" traveling nines were not actually all Chinese, "the teams were completely international and justly represented the 'World's Greatest melting pot,' which was Hawaii even at that early date."[19]

The following pages will tell all sorts of stories about these intriguing teams that played in towns and cities throughout the American mainland, as well as the multiracial, multiethnic athletes who well represented Hawai'i from San Francisco to Maine. As a consequence, readers will hopefully gain some insight into the often complex relationship between sport and society at a time of dramatic historical changes throughout the United States and its Pacific Empire. The experiences of these multiracial, multiethnic Hawaiian athletes will not make these stories easy to recount or, for that matter, always enjoyable to learn as they reveal a great deal how sports reflect and reinforce the erection of durable social hierarchies. Yet just as strikingly, these stories also relate how sports have, albeit too briefly and infrequently, been put to democratic uses.

As the two pieces of journalism opening the introduction point out, these Hawaiian athletes were identified and identified themselves in multiple and conflicting ways. For the Hawaiian ballplayers, identity crisscrossed cultural borders just as they traversed the American mainland and its ballparks. Each no doubt had a sense of who he was — i.e. Chinese, Hawaiian, American, student, worker, male, businessman, baseball player, or Christian. However, those who watched them as fans, opponents, or journalists also entertained a sense, more or less reasonable, of who the Hawaiian ballplayers were. We will find that by examining different press accounts of the Travelers' tours, identity on the American mainland as well as Hawai'i was more fluid than fixed and perhaps often a product of the need to sell newspapers, promote tourism, extol colonialism, firm up a racial hierarchy and occasionally chip away at it.

The experiences of these Hawaiian ballplayers call to mind Jean-Paul Sartre's admonition that it is not solely important to know what is done to the historically aggrieved but also what they do about what is done to them. The experiences of the men of Asian Pacific Islander ancestry who participated on the traveling Hawaiian baseball team demonstrate that historically aggrieved people will not be easily silenced or pigeonholed. By playing baseball and playing it well, they confounded alike vicious critics of the Asian Pacific Islander presence in the U.S. and the often equally troubling, patronizing friends of that presence. They demonstrated that Hawaiians perceived as non-white were neither degraded Orientals and savage primitives, on the one hand, nor obedient Orientals and noble savages, on the other. That is, by playing baseball, these Hawaiians of Asian Pacific Islander descent disclosed to later generations their humanity in all of its complexity at a time when assertions of Asian Pacific Islander humanity were in short supply in the United States.

Many fine scholars have noted how social identity has been constructed by a variety of cultural practices and institutions. In the process, they have done us an important service by reminding us how slippery social identity can be. Newspapers, for example, identified the Hawaiian Travelers in all sorts of interesting ways. While legally U.S. citizens and not always of Chinese extraction, they were called Chinese, and at least some of the Travelers called themselves Chinese. There was nothing necessarily wrong in all this, especially since the news media often just echoed what the team's promoters wanted them to write. Still, the difficulties persist in applying the term assimilation or really any kind of theory of social relations to what the Travelers were trying to do or what was being done to the Travelers.

We can find one of the more powerful and relevant discussions of the social construction of racial identity in Michael Omi and Howard Winant's *Racial Formation in the United States*. To Omi and Winant, racial categories do not adhere to nature but are formed, altered, and eliminated. Racial categories are not objective facts but potent ways for people to maintain and contest power in a society. In the following pages, we will note efforts to racialize or essentialize the Hawaiian ballplayers — efforts to assert that they possessed an innate essence that determined their behavior on and off the playing field. We will also note how, by crossing foul lines and cultural borders, Hawaiian ballplayers seemed to baffle those efforts.[20]

Political scientist Benedict Anderson writes about nations as "invented communities" — as social constructions. People create nations as a way of bonding across natural, social, and chronological barriers. After the Civil War, America needed to reinvent itself as a nation. One way in which it was able to do this was through Pacific expansion into Hawai'i and, subsequently, the Philippines. Regional, class, and ethnic differences could perhaps be plastered over a bit in America's attempt to shoulder the white man's burden in far-off Pacific islands. But what about the people who lived in these islands? What were their roles in the reinvention of the American nation? Were they subjects or citizens? How the Hawaiian ballplayers were represented by mainland periodicals discloses an interesting ambivalence — an ambivalence enhanced by the fact that China was redefining itself as a nation based on republican institutions in the second half of the twentieth century. Accordingly, were Chinese Hawaiian ballplayers, all of whom were U.S. citizens, embraced by this national redefinition?[21]

Thus, as we get to know these Hawaiian ballplayers we should attend to the facts but also to the contemporary but varied and contradictory interpretations of those facts. Because these ballplayers and the men who managed their tours were not well known, they did not leave behind a lot of facts. We do know that many were products of a Chinese diaspora, but those that could claim Chinese parentage often descended from Native Hawaiians as well. We know also that by 1914 several of those on the team did not possess any Chinese ancestry at all and that by 1916, a few ballplayers possessed neither Asian nor Native Hawaiian ancestry — that is, they were *haoles* or white. We do know, moreover, that they were nearly all born on the islands and as native-born Hawaiians were U.S. citizens, regardless of their racial and ethnic identities.

We do know that many of the Asian Hawaiian ballplayers were proud of their Asian ancestry, but they were at least as proud of being Hawaiian. We do know that the Hawaiian ballplayers wanted to use baseball as a way of demonstrating their equality with mainland Americans but there is also evidence that they cared about demonstrating how American or, at least, how "Western" they were. In other words, they did not see necessarily see baseball as a vehicle transporting them toward assimilation into American society. They did perceive the game as a source of individual and collective pride — that Asian ethnic group members and/or Hawaiians were as good as mainland, white Americans.

The Travelers also told a tale about gender. The mid-nineteenth century proponents of baseball boasted that the sport would enhance and assert the manliness of young American males. Baseball would test their toughness and cleverness as office work and domestic life would not. It was a tough sell given baseball's historical connection to children's games, but it was a sell that many American males were willing to make and willing to buy. At the same time, Americans were encountering Chinese at home and abroad in greater numbers. To European Americans, the relatively small size of Chinese males, combined with the fact that many wore queues and labored in the domestic services, seemed to demonstrate that there was something suspiciously unmasculine about them. Consequently, the Travelers, regardless of whether they actually possessed Chinese ancestry, contested the troubling association many European Americans had made between race, nationality, and gender whenever the Hawaiians won or even lost a hard-fought ballgame on the mainland.

Perhaps the traveling Hawaiian baseball teams moved beyond their perceived Chineseness and offer us an early instance of what Hawaiians call "local culture." This "local culture" emerged out of a blending of diverse Asian, Pacific Islander, and European cultures begun in the late 1800s and early 1900s. The sugar and pineapple plantations served as primary meeting places for people of varied cultures recruited to work for these agricultural factories, as did the docks and streets of Honolulu and Maui's Laheina. The first languages of these people included Cantonese, Japanese, Portuguese, Spanish, Korean, Ilocan, and Native Hawaiian. If they were Chinese they probably harbored hostility toward the Japanese, nurtured by years of antipathy between Japan and China. If they were Korean they probably did not care much for either the Chinese or the Japanese, especially the latter once Japan colonized Korea. If they were Filipino, they were probably disliked by all of the major ethnic groups on the islands. Those running the plantations liked recruiting a multiracial, multiethnic, and multilingual work force. A divided work force was a more controllable work force, they assumed.[22]

However, Creole Hawaiian or Pidgin English worked as a powerful

Hawaiian sugar and pineapple plantation owners needed labor, and that need brought workers of Chinese, Japanese, Korean, Filipino, Spanish, Portuguese, and Puerto Rican ancestry to the islands to work under typically arduous, regimented circumstances (courtesy of Library of Congress, Prints & Photographs Division, LC-USZ62-108293).

bridge across historical divisions. The Hawaiian immigrant workers and shopkeepers may not have had much in common except the realization that they were viewed as innately or culturally inferior by a haole elite and the English that the haoles spoke to them — a simple, childlike English that the benighted Japanese plantation worker or Chinese tailor would presumably understand. Using this simplistic English as a foundation, Hawaiian immigrants would interweave their own languages with Native Hawaiian to form a living, dynamic language — the language of Hawaiian local culture. Through Creole Hawaiian, immigrants and their offspring could socialize, organize athletic teams, date, and lay the groundwork for relatively effective anti-racist political and labor movements after World War II.[23]

The Hawaiian elite's relative tolerance of immigration fed the development of local culture. Indeed, for plantation owners immigration was vital. For workers, Hawai'i was not exactly an island paradise. Laboring in a hot Hawaiian sun six days a week for comparatively meager wages was not something that people dreamed about. Thus, recruiting and maintaining the needed work force was always a problem for plantation owners. When the plantation emerged as Hawai'i's primary economic institution in the middle of the nineteenth century, indigenous Hawaiians were expected to comprise its work force. But the common Hawaiian people did not embrace the drudgery of plantation work designed to enrich haoles and the *ali'i*, Native Hawaiian nobles. Accordingly, Native Hawaiians proved unsatisfactory plantation workers, although they could well prove handy as crew members of merchant ships or whalers. Even if they had more zealously cut sugar cane from sunrise to sunset, Native Hawaiians were apparently dying out due largely to their possession of immune systems that could not fend off the germs brought to the islands by outsiders, let alone the poverty many experienced as the nineteenth century proceeded.[24]

Accordingly, plantations depended upon immigrants — Chinese, Japanese, and then Korean and Filipino — as field hands and Portuguese and Spanish to supervise as *lunas*. The haole plantation owners might have welcomed U.S. annexation but they did not necessarily welcome all the talk of mainlanders about immigration restriction and subsequent laws restricting immigration such as the Chinese Exclusion Law of 1882. Indeed, the Hawaiian economic elite not only generally encouraged the immigration of workers to the islands but welcomed their families as well. Haole employers figured that families rooted workers to the islands. Such workers were less likely to return to their homelands or head off to the mainland, where wages were higher even if racism was more vociferous. Employers also figured that workers were less likely to strike if they had their families with them. At any rate, spouses and children could do agricultural work. Women could be paid less than men and the young children did not have to be paid at all.[25]

The Hawaiian haole elite rendered the islands more tolerant of interracial marriage than most places on the American mainland. This tolerance was somewhat self-serving as it allowed haole males to marry indigenous Hawaiian women. But it also permitted Chinese immigrant males to marry indigenous Hawaiian women as well, Portuguese immigrant males to marry Chinese women, and so on. Hawaiian locals became less interested in assimilating into a dominant culture than developing a blend of diverse cultures, including that of the haole elite. Like Hawaiian local culture, the island ballplayers who trekked to the American mainland frustrated racial, ethnic, and national conventions even if they could not abolish them.[26]

At the same time, the Travelers represented the fascinating interactions of race, ethnicity, nationality, and culture prevalent in the early twentieth century, which witnessed the powerful rise of a consumer culture largely centered in the United States but encompassing other industrializing and urbanizing capitalist societies. Numerous historians have pointed out that while the consumer culture was scarcely new in the early twentieth century, it became more vital and certainly more widely applauded by the powerful since convincing people to buy things, even unnecessary things, was and remains a key to capitalism's success.[27]

Industrialization and urbanization aided the development of the consumer culture in multiple ways. Industrialization meant that many working persons were getting paid more, and mechanization meant they had greater time to spend that money. This was not just a matter of industrial capitalism's generosity or desire to manipulate. The American labor movement was often effective at assuring workers better pay and fewer hours on the job. Urbanization meant that more and more Americans did not have the geographical space to grow their own food, make their own clothes, or play ball in the public square any time they pleased. At the same time, urbanization meant there would be saloons, movie theatres, ballparks, amusement parks, race tracks, opera houses, and museums in their cities. Meanwhile, transit companies gladly conveyed people to various places of amusement.[28]

Geographic expansion of American capitalism should not escape attention. One factor favoring pushing American economic and political institutions westward beyond the Mississippi and then beyond the Pacific Coast was the desire to find and expand consumer, investment, and labor markets. As new American towns and cities were founded west of the Mississippi River, they vied with one another to lure permanent residents and tourists as long as they had sufficient money in their pockets and appeared sufficiently white. Boosterism practically created urban Los Angeles. Would Honolulu, once Uncle Sam gained sovereignty of it, be far behind?

The commercialized baseball park during the early 1900s serves as a useful representation of the ambiguities of the consumer culture. From Lewiston, Maine, to Honolulu, it stood as a source of neighborhood and civic pride. Most assuredly, its presence gave joy to baseball fans throughout the United States and its empire. However, the baseball park's defining purpose was to make money for those who invested in commercialized baseball, directly through the sales of admission tickets and indirectly through the merchandising of programs, souvenirs, food, and drink. Privately owned transit companies often operated trains to ballparks and counted upon baseball to fatten their profit margins. Indeed, transit companies frequently owned a part or all of the commercialized ballparks. Neighboring restaurants and bars counted even more upon well-attended games, as did shops selling baseball and other athletic equipment.

The key was to get people in the park. A town or a city with a popular or semiprofessional baseball team playing regularly in that park had a leg up on the problem. However, the local professional nine would typically have to play half of its league games someplace else, leaving the ball park empty of spectators, as well as trains, restaurants, bars, and shops too close to being empty. The regular baseball season, moreover, usually lasted from April to early October at the latest. From a capitalist perspective, the ballpark could well be seen as an irritating waste.

However, baseball and sports entrepreneurs found ways to get folks into the local ballparks when the local team was on the road or when the league season was not underway. Ballparks even then could be multi-purpose. They could host boxing matches, bicycle races, or even circuses. Moreover, they could host games not played by the local team. And ballparks in warmer climates could become venues for winter leagues.

Those in charge of college athletics in the United States might portray themselves as far removed from this entire money making hubbub. Calling their athletes amateurs and insisting upon the purity of their educational missions, college administrators were probably more successful at fooling themselves than anybody else as "King Football" ruled from New Haven to Palo Alto by the turn-of-the twentieth century.[29]

School coffers and school spirit demanded, and supporters of college athletics maintained, filled seats for football games. Those responsible for American football then might strike us today as quaint innocents wandering through the market place. They honestly thought the football season should largely be confined to the months of September through the first week of January at the latest. This meant that for six months of the academic year college sports might not be making money or nurturing loyalty to the old alma mater. Basketball could help take up the slack, but in the spring track and field and baseball were widely considered as more valuable economically to colleges than James Naismith's recently invented sport. Thus, it became useful, if not imperative, to make baseball a paying proposition on American college campuses.

The existence of something called organized baseball worked for and against the exigencies of the consumer culture. Among perhaps the more trivial byproducts of what historian Robert Wiebe called America's "search for order" after the Civil War, organized baseball was a top-down effort to effectively structure professional baseball. By 1903, the National Commission was set up to rule the two major leagues and the several minor leagues that had cropped up throughout the U.S. Many excellent baseball histories have explored the emergence of organized baseball as a way of disciplining players and capping their salary demands, as well as insuring that the minor leagues would serve the needs of big league owners.[30]

On the one hand, organized baseball seemed to supply fans with a reliable product. That is, players could not just "revolve" from team to team depending upon who paid the most. Leagues were mandated to come up with strictly adhered-to schedules, and umpires were endowed with the power to temper unruly players, managers, and spectators, while guaranteeing that only luck could thwart the better team from winning on a given day.

Organized baseball, on the other hand, was wondrously hypocritical since like many economic monopolies it hailed the free market economy while denying employees and business rivals the opportunity to take advantage of it. Moreover, by the early 1900s it sometimes silently and always insidiously enforced Jim Crow practices while breathlessly pronouncing itself an icon of American democracy.

However, if organized baseball was a monopoly, it was not a very good one in the early 1900s. Its hold on professional baseball was constantly challenged by individual players, entrepreneurs, and leagues. It met many of the most serious challenges effectively until the Black Sox scandal. Yet the appearance of countless teams, defiantly independent of the National Commission, and even more semiprofessional nines throughout much of North America suggested that many Americans entertained the notion that the product manufactured by organized baseball was all very good but not quite enough to satisfy them.

Organized baseball liked to claim that it had cornered the market on America's most talented players and managers. In reality, there was no denying that Ty Cobb, Honus Wagner, and Walter Johnson offered the public a great deal of skill and excitement. However, there were very talented players and managers who performed beyond the realm of organized baseball. Some did so out of choice. They or their families favored steady incomes that would not disappear as they got older. These ballplayers might prefer playing weekends for semipro teams. Rightly or wrongly, others might not like the discipline imposed on players by organized baseball. These ballplayers might prefer performing for independent or traveling barnstorming aggregations. Finally, there were ballplayers that had no choice. Because of racial identity or gender, they would have to play outside of organized baseball.

Barnstormers could, despite the querulous attitude of organized baseball, often fit well the needs of consumer culture. Barnstormers proved handy in luring people into the city, town, or college ballpark. In baseball, barnstormers were usually professional or semiprofessional teams independent of the official American major and minor league organizations. They might travel in certain regions or throughout North America, playing professional, semiprofessional, or amateur opponents. Like traveling theatre groups, they typically employed a booking agent who would negotiate for an advance and/or a share of the gate money. Thus they had to be marketable. That is, since a barnstorming team did not represent a rival college, town or city, there had to be something about its players that could captivate potential customers.

Teams comprised of well-known professionals from various major league organizations would draw well in the off-season. Southern Californians did not get a chance to see Ty Cobb play during the spring and summer. But if he was on a team that barnstormed the region during winter, then they could not only catch the vibrant Cobb in action but maybe other renowned ballplayers from the New York Giants, Pittsburgh Pirates, and Philadelphia Athletics as well.

Teams that entrepreneurs might effectively promote as "colorful" could find bookings. Before and even during the time the Negro Leagues emerged, somewhat stabilized African American teams such as the Chicago American Giants looked for and played games from one coast to another. It helped, of course, that the Chicago nine could give white and other African American teams more than they could handle competitively, but that they were black made it possible for paying fans to see them as unique attractions in places like Stockton or Santa Cruz, California.

Thus, despite the reverence organized baseball had generally developed for racial exclusion in the early 1900s, non-whiteness was marketable in the sport. Non-white teams or teams featuring players that were non-white enticed fans into ballparks. Promoters merchandised these teams and players as colorful, as novelty acts that helped make baseball consumable nearly year-round.

Aiding these promotional efforts was the notion that exoticism, primitivism and orientalism significantly constructed non-whiteness as fashionably marketable in early twentieth century America. This is not to say that middle and upper class European Americans wanted to live as primitives or orientals. But, for a variety of reasons we will discuss, many of them wanted a taste of something different — an occasional liberation from what was experienced as the restrictions of Western Civilization. They wanted to transcend, if but for a little while, Victorian conventions and the materialism and stress nurtured by modernity. And even if they did not especially long for at least a turn at "going native," they were, as P.T. Barnum, Buffalo Bill Cody, and James Dole knew very well, curious about the exotic and willing to pay good money to see the exotic on display in dime museums, Wild West Shows, World Fairs, or grocery stores.[31]

In sports, the marketing of Duke Kahanamoku furnishes a useful and pertinent example. A Native Hawaiian, Kahanamoku developed into the world's fastest swimmer, winning a gold medal at the 1912 Olympiad. Though he was not a professional athlete, promoters could still make money off of his athletic prowess not only as a competitive swimmer but as a master of other water sports such as, of course, surfing. Kahanamoku was often represented as a poi-eating, hula-dancing, dark-skinned child of the Pacific who excelled in modern competitive sports because of his exoticism. Kahanamoku, moreover, proved useful as a marketing tool for Hawai'i's growing tourist industry in the early twentieth century. To many mainlanders, Kahanamoku seemed a soothing reminder that even though thousands of non-white indigenous people inhabited the islands, they were happy to show off their culture to haole tourists desiring to experience the "simple life" and get in touch with their "primitive roots" if but for a couple of weeks.[32]

We need to note the continuing fascination into the twentieth century with dark-faced theatrical and athletic performances that were sustained even after the minstrel shows themselves had been eclipsed by vaudeville and then the movies. Many of America's leading entertainers performed in blackface during the early decades of the twentieth century. Singer Al Jolson was widely considered as America's greatest live performer during the first third of the twentieth century. Much of Jolson's act revolved around him singing and dancing in blackface. Other popular entertainers such as Sophie Tucker and Eddie Cantor also performed in blackface. Unlike many of the blackfaced minstrel shows of the early nineteenth century, these entertainers did not necessarily intend to insult African Americans. However, they seemed to have agreed that performing in blackface afforded them the license to sing and dance with the kind of abandon that reputable white people were not expected to exhibit. African American entertainers such as Bert Williams were also counted upon to perform in blackface and reinforce prevailing stereotypes of black men as ignorant and shiftless. To his dismay, Williams learned that racial stereotypes sold tickets to theaters and helped make him one of the best-paid live performers of his era.[33]

In prize fighting, something similar took place. The sport had long promoted racial and ethnic stereotypes to attract paying customers. Everyone seemed to acknowledge in 1900 that the Irish were great fighters. Thus, Italian-American boxers changed their names and became known as Irish-American boxers to get fights. On the East Coast, a couple of professional boxers were so anxious to get into the ring that they assumed Chinese names in order to at least achieve bouts as exotic novelties. These boxers would appear in "Yellowface"—wearing make-up which they hoped would convince promoters and spectators they were Chinese.[34]

Audiences could experience exoticism by way of Al Jolson masquerading as an exotic or by way of an "authentic" exotic such as Duke Kahanamoku. Orientalism, meanwhile, became a potent expression of "Civilization's" flirtation with the exotic. In the late 1970s, the controversial scholar Edward Said argued that Orientalism arose out of the West's need to not only demarcate the peoples of the world east of Europe as distinct, but as fit targets of Western imperialism. Orientalism did not always attribute negative features to so-called Orientals, who could be represented in popular literature and silent films as generous, brave, obedient, and wise, on the one hand, or lustful, treacherous, and cruel, on the other. However, Orientalism did emphasize that Orientals were strange and exotic. The word "Celestial" was consistently applied to people of Chinese ancestry to stress their presumed other-worldly character, although it should also be stressed that the term derived from the Chinese political elite referring to their nation as the "Celestial Empire."[35]

Orientalism, as P.T. Barnum understood, sold in antebellum America. He exhibited a "Chinese family," members of which were not actually related but who Barnum believed piqued the public's interest in the Orient. During the first six days they were displayed in 1850, 20,000 people were lured to Barnum's exhibit. Previously, Barnum had worked with the famous Siamese twins, Chang and Eng Bunker, as they toured Europe.[36]

In the early twentieth century, popular novels and movies displayed and sensationalized Orientalism. In 1913, *The Mystery of Dr. Fu Manchu* was published. The English author was Arthur Henry Ward, who wrote the novel under the name Sax Rohmer. Fu Manchu represented the dark, lurid side of Orientalism. Cruel, deceptive, and brilliant, Fu Manchu ruthlessly pursued world domination. He played upon the fears of readers that the "Yellow Peril" was real, that Asians would not quietly bow to the West and were hell-bent instead on its demise. The fictional character of Charlie Chan represented the other side of the Orientalist coin. Created by Earl Biggers, Charlie Chan was based on a real Chinese Hawaiian police detective active in the early twentieth century. Unlike Fu Manchu, Chan was a hero who called upon the wisdom of the Orient to solve crimes.[37]

More inclined to a darker use of Orientalism, many mainland Americans believed a "Yellow Peril" had arisen from Asia to threaten Western Civilization in the early 1900s. However, while the Chinese and Japanese signified two different versions of this "Yellow Peril," the American mainland responded to each in roughly similar ways—that is, immigration restriction, exclusion, and even mob violence.[38]

Flaring most viciously during periods of economic distress, the anti–Chinese movement, for instance, was abetted on the American mainland by a contradictory racial ideology that claimed Chinese immigrants possessed characteristics that rendered them "unassimilable" in American society. They were, that is, corrupt, violent, deceptive, and lustful, but submissive and childlike. To some degree, however, this racial ideology bore a class bias as Chinese possessing upper class backgrounds frequently sidestepped the more virulent forms of anti–Chinese racism. Regardless of class, however, the anti–Chinese movement on the mainland noted what its adherents perceived as the unmanly qualities of Chinese males, who, significantly, comprised the greater proportion of Chinese immigrants to the U.S. mainland. That many of these Chinese men, usually smaller than European American males, wore their hair braided in a queue did not help matters. The fact that the Chinese government mandated that Chinese men sport queues failed to register with the anti–Chinese movement, which often all too happily pointed out that in the United States only girls wore pigtails. Moreover, the presence of Chinese immigrant males in domestic service trades reinforced the emerging stereotype of Chinese males as effeminate and servile.[39]

The anti–Chinese movement retained an energetic stranglehold on California and Pacific Coast politics and scored occasional victories in the late 1860s and 1870s. Chinese immigrants in West Coast communities were subject to a series of humiliating laws, as well as violence. In 1870, Congress modified America's naturalization laws that had previously declared that only white immigrants were eligible for naturalization. Consequently, immigrants of African ancestry became eligible for citizenship, but Congress pointedly excluded "Mongolian" immigrants from citizenship. The anti–Chinese movement developed into more of a national power by the 1880s thanks, in part, to major economic depressions during the 1870s and California's skill at promoting the crusade.

In 1882 Congress passed the Chinese Exclusion Act, which sought to arrest the immigration of Chinese laborers into the U.S. The Chinese Exclusion Act, moreover, reinforced prior naturalization laws by declaring that Chinese immigrants, regardless of class, were ineligible for citizenship. The Act was subject for renewal in ten years. Chinese immigrants, who apparently overstayed their welcome in towns and cities in the West, often faced unbridled violence rarely checked by legal authorities.[40]

From 1882 to 1892, Congress conscientiously strengthened the Chinese Exclusion Act. For example, under the original act, Chinese immigrants could migrate to the U.S. if they possessed Hawaiian passports. By 1892, they were no longer allowed to do this. In 1892, Congress passed the Geary Act, extending the Chinese Exclusion Act for another ten years. In 1902, Congress once again extended the Chinese Exclusion Act. By this time, the act was clearly working to the extent that the Chinese population on the American mainland had dropped in both absolute and relative terms. The act, furthermore, was widely popular, although Hawaiian planters voiced some serious reservations about a law that would derail their search for labor. Still, Congress, in 1904, decided to make Chinese Exclusion permanent.[41]

While anti–Asian nativists turned to Japanese immigration, more Chinese were trying to get into the U.S. The San Francisco Earthquake had destroyed federal immigrant records. Desperate Chinese wanting to come into the U.S. or wanting relatives to enter the U.S. could use forged documents, claiming that individuals were legally eligible to enter America. In response, the federal government set up an immigrant detention center on Angels Island in San Francisco Bay. In former army barracks, the government confined legal and illegal Chinese immigrants pending a frequently humiliating and deliberate investigation of their claims.[42]

The situation for Asian immigrants and their offspring proved somewhat different in Hawai'i than on the mainland even though American missionaries, merchants, sailors, and military personnel had established a firm link between the islands and the United States by the mid-nineteenth century. Native Hawaiians, regardless of class, lost control of the government by the end of the century. That the United States had become a primary market for Hawaiian sugar was a blessing but it could also prove a curse if Washington, D.C. enacted onerous sugar tariffs. From the perspective of haoles of American descent, one good way around the problem was for Hawai'i to become a part of the United States.[43]

Meanwhile, the United States grew more interested in nurturing a global presence that would rival that of the great European powers. Gaining access to Asian Pacific markets and guarding that access with a watchful and powerful military excited influential Americans such as the youthful Theodore Roosevelt. One problem was that Native Hawaiians did not want to salute the Stars and Stripes. Another problem was that many Americans nurtured a healthy skepticism of imperial ventures and an even healthier skepticism of making the Stars and Stripes responsible for more people of color.

In the mid–1870s, David Kalakaua became the Hawaiian monarch. Seen as friendly to American interests, Kalakaua was Hawaiian nationalist enough to find American haoles just a little too pushy for his taste. Called the "merrie monarch," Kalakaua encouraged a renaissance in Hawaiian cultural traditions. Some haoles were offended that the decades of work done by white missionaries was being undone. Wiser haoles recognized that the Hawaiian cultural renaissance was not only relatively harmless, but hula dancing and surfboarding could help white Hawaiians cash in on a growing global tourist industry. More seriously, however, Kalakaua was negotiating with Japanese diplomats at a time when the U.S. was beginning to consider Japan a grave rival for Pacific power.[44]

In the late 1880s, the United States was set to enact a disturbing sugar tariff. Action was needed and Kalakaua gave in to a U.S. naval station at Pearl Harbor in exchange for Uncle Sam keeping his door open to sugar grown on the islands. Moreover, with U.S. military presence expanding, haoles with American connections pressured Kalakaua into agreeing to the "Bayonet Constitution"—a constitution which both diluted the power of the monarch and the suffrage rights of indigenous Hawaiians.[45]

In 1891, Kalakaua died while seeking medical help in San Francisco. His sister, Liliuokalani, assumed the Hawaiian throne. A remarkable poet, musician, and composer, Liliuokalani possessed a greater fervor for Hawaiian nationalism than her brother. Insulted by the new constitution, she sought to have it rescinded and the old constitution restored. Rather than wait for Liliuokalani to make her move, influential American haoles, with the help of U.S. military personnel stationed in Honolulu, made theirs. They staged a coup, removing Liliuokalani from power and placing her under house arrest. The republic of Hawai'i was declared and many haoles joyfully anticipated American annexation.[46]

They were, however, to be disappointed. Democrats were in power in Washington, D.C. Less supportive of imperialism than their Republican counterparts, Democrats called on Americans to remember their nation's anticolonial beginnings. They also, however, called on Americans to remember that Hawaiians were largely non-white and that America had quite enough non-white people within its already vast borders.[47]

By the end of the 1890s, the Republican Party had taken back the White House and Congress. In the wake of the Spanish-American War and persistent pleadings about the "white man's burden," the U.S. government agreed to declare Hawai'i a territory and its Hawaiian-born residents U.S. citizens. The latter meant that Asian Pacific Islanders born in Hawai'i could be citizens. However, as African Americans already knew, citizenship did not guarantee equality.[48]

As the twentieth century dawned, white America had not quite made up its mind what to do about people of color in the United States and around the globe. Rudyard Kipling had urged America to take up the white man's burden in its pursuit of global conquests. Just as the darker-skinned folks of Asia and Africa needed the firm but fair hand of white England to show them the way, so Filipinos and, by extension, Hawaiians needed white America to pull them kicking and screaming toward civilization. Not that early twentieth century European Americans always required that much prompting to treat people of color as members of childlike races requiring a firm push up the evolutionary ladder. For decades, well-intentioned European Americans had set up missionary and secular schools to "uplift" supposedly benighted Hawaiians, Native Americans, and African Americans.[49]

Meanwhile, such venues as Wild West Shows and World Fairs exhibited people of color throughout the United States. As indigenous people were conquered in North America and throughout the world during what historian Eric Hobsbawm called the "Age of Empire," they found themselves riding horses at Wild West Shows and climbing trees at World Fairs. Hawaiian musicians and hula dancers, moreover, performed on the American mainland as early as 1893 at the Chicago World Fair. They were marketed as exotic and perhaps at least a little ridiculous. These performances may have helped make indigenous people less threatening to native-born European Americans than African Americans and many European immigrants were. But they scarcely erased perceptions that indigenous people were racially or culturally inferior to whites, especially of the Anglo-Saxon variety.[50]

As in the case of Duke Kahanamoku, racial performances were frequently athletic. Significantly, Duke Kahanamoku's achievements at the 1912 Olympiad were more than matched by Jim Thorpe, who won gold medals in the Decathlon and Pentathlon. If Kahanamoku was the world's greatest athlete on the water, Thorpe was the world's greatest athlete on the land. Possessing Sauk and Fox ancestry, Thorpe gained national attention as the star of the Carlisle Institute's famed football team.

Playing many of the best college football teams in the land, Carlisle gridders won far more often than they lost in the early 1900s. Usually smaller than their opponents, Carlisle elevens often resorted to speed and intelligence to win games. They even helped propel the popularity of the forward pass at a time when most powerful college teams were satisfied with an offense based on dreary line plunges.

White observers were not sure what to make of it all. To Teddy Roosevelt, American football was supposed to allow young men identified as descended from the finest European stock to excel in competitive sports. American football seemed to demand the kind of blend of brains, bravery, and brawn Roosevelt admired in White Anglo-Saxon Protestant masculinity. Accordingly, some simply emphasized that the Native American gridders succeeded because they resorted to the kind of deception that had doomed poor Custer. In other words, Indians were not capable of playing or fighting fair. Others expressed surprised admiration that Native Americans could compete effectively against the Ivy League and military school powerhouses even if they employed an occasional forward pass or trick play. In any event, there was no getting around the fact that Jim Thorpe was stronger and faster than nearly every college football player he faced.[51]

If white America had to nimbly process the ability of Jim Thorpe and Duke Kahanamoku to defeat European American opponents, it was harshly stung by the triumphs of Jack Johnson. In America's world of sports, the heavyweight boxing championship was the most vaunted title of them all. People of color in general, and African Americans in particular, were not expected to possess the racial traits needed to reign as world heavyweight champions. The heavyweight champion was a source of white male pride in America. He exemplified strength, intelligence, and courage. African Americans could, it was widely suspected, be strong, but they lacked the brains and heart to go round after round with a white opponent determined to knock them into bloody pulps. To be sure, European Americans might look the other way while African Americans and other non-white prize fighters won lower weight division bouts. But the heavyweight division was another thing entirely. Jack Johnson, a Texas-born African American heavyweight, changed all that when he won the heavyweight championship in 1908. Even before white sports fans understood Jack Johnson's indifference to racial conventions, writer Jack London called for a "great white hope" to restore European American prestige. The pro-Klan movie *Birth of a Nation* and the subsequent renaissance of the Ku Klux Klan itself reaffirmed the "great white hope" that African Americans and many other non-whites would be well advised to recognize their subordinate place in America's racial hierarchy.[52]

The America encountered by the Hawaiian Travelers, therefore, was a troubled place but a place that perhaps possessed some democratic possibilities. To be sure, it had embraced Jim Crow, alien land laws, imperialism, and race riots much too warmly. It also, however, embraced the different and cultural border-crossing syncopations of ragtime and Hawaiian music. However whitened by Tin Pan Alley, ragtime and Hawaiian music originated among non-white people who pushed and pulled American culture in a way that surprised if not subverted conventional thinking on race and colonialism. Thus as these young Hawaiians traveled basepaths and the American mainland, American culture traveled as well — pushed and pulled by shifting racial and cultural identities, ambiguous colonial experiences, and an enveloping, conflictive consumer culture. And this consumer culture called upon them to perform — as athletes and entertainers — as representatives of Hawai'i, overseas Chinese, and an American Empire dominated by those that often saw them, regardless of nativity and citizenship status, as foreigners, invaders, "Yellow Perils" and strangers.

ONE

The First Journey, 1912

Honolulu's Chinatown mocked the desires of Hawai'i's haole elite to control the islands' non-white residents. Its population was too largely comprised of former plantation workers who thought they could and very often did do better economically in the islands' biggest city. Indeed, the Hawaiian legislature had sought to bar Chinese from certain non-agricultural jobs. But Honolulu's Chinatown endured. It endured, in fact, even when catastrophe struck it in the late 1890s.[1]

In 1894, bubonic plague was discovered in Canton and Hong Kong. In San Francisco, Chinese and Japanese arrivals were quarantined. In 1899, two cases of the terrible disease were discovered in Honolulu's Chinatown. Several thousand of its residents were evacuated and their homes were burned.[2]

Still, Honolulu's Chinese revived their Chinatown. One area in which this could be seen was in their attention to organizations devoted to physical development and sports. As we will see, the community established athletic organizations and was represented by talented all-around athletes. By the twentieth century, Chinese Hawaiians had been playing baseball. The future president of the Chinese Republic, Sun Yat Sen, reportedly took up the game as a Hawaiian student in 1883. In the mid-1890s, two Chinese Hawaiian players were recruited by St. John's University of Shanghai to coach its first baseball team.[3]

Chinese Hawaiians and, for that matter, future Travelers were very active in Honolulu baseball in the early 1900s. In 1905, En Sue Pung played for the Honolulu Athletic Club nine. "Ensue," according to a *Honolulu Independent* poet-sportswriter, was such an admired "sprinter, he'd beat Hatter." En Sue Pung and "Lo-On, a speedy Chinese boy" were members of a Hawaiian team dispatched to Japan in 1905. This team represented St. Louis College, which was actually a Catholic secondary school in Honolulu. In 1906, a team called the Kauluwehas fielded future Traveler star F.L. Akana at second. In a Riverside

To most mainlanders, Honolulu was a far-off, exotic place. To Honolulans in the early twentieth century, it was little different from cities in the U.S.—a place to live, work, and watch or play baseball. This is a photograph of Honolulu's Fort Street, c. 1900 (courtesy of Library of Congress, Prints & Photographs Division, LC-USZ62-104480).

League game, the Chinese Athletics slaughtered a team called the Hawaiian Independents, 14–4. Within a week, the Independents beat the Chinese Alohas at Aala Park, 6–2. That same day, the Chinese Athletics took the measure of the Palamas, 7–2. A few days later, En Sue Pung slugged a home run and played third base for the Athletics, representing the Chinese Athletic Club. In the process, he helped his team beat the Waipahus.[4]

In September of 1906, the Chinese Athletics won the Riverside League championship by beating the Palamas. According to the *Pacific Commercial Advertiser*, "the game was witnessed by a large and enthusiastic Chinese delegation sporting flags, colors, brooms, ribbons and honors. They seem to have a hunch that their representatives would win and the hunch made good."[5]

Largely assuming that their readers would be surprised by such information, mainland newspapers reported on the presence of Chinese ballplayers in and from Hawai'i in the early 1900s. In February 1906, the *New York Tribune* published a photograph of the "Chinese Baseball Team of Honolulu." The accompanying story focused on the progress Chinese Hawaiians were making as athletes on the islands. It purported, "The Chinaman is not abused in Hawaii simply because he is a Chinaman." Titled "Chinese Can Play Ball," a brief article in *Sporting Life* maintained that the Chinese Alohas had defeated the U.S. Twentieth Infantry Nine on July 4, 1907. Also in 1907, the *Decatur Review* published a piece that asserted, "Although Chinese baseball players are mighty scarce in this country, over in Honolulu there is a team composed exclusively of Chinese, and they play good baseball. The team is called the Chinese Alohas." The Alohas had beaten, according to the article, a contingent representing the Hawaiian Hotel. Later in the year, the *Reno Evening Gazette* reprinted a *Newark News* story, claiming that in Hawai'i a "Chinese baseball team" had defeated a team of Americans. It added, "The yellow peril seems to be more real than some of us thought." Perhaps sarcastically raising the issue of colonialism, the *Washington Herald* informed readers that a "measly Chinese team simply walloped the life of a Honolulu team.... And still there are growlers and grumblers who object to our maintaining a strong naval outfit in the Pacific."[6]

Mainland accounts of Chinese Hawaiian baseball continued in 1908 and 1909. In February 1908, readers of the *Philadelphia Inquirer* learned that the Chinese Athletic Club nine had lost to the Kaala Athletic Club. Ah Pau, perhaps the Apau Kau who would star as a hurler for the Travelers, lost the game thanks, in part, to the errors committed by teammates. The next month, the *Washington Post* noted, "The batting order in that recent Chinese game in Honolulu looked like the police roster of the captured in a tong riot." During the summer of 1908, the *San Jose Mercury* reported on the experiences of the Santa Clara College baseball team as it trekked to Hawai'i in order to play island and Japanese national nines. The daily declared that the California team had found out that "the Island teams are made up of Chinese, Japs, Americans, and Hawaiians." That same year, the *Los Angeles Times* acknowledged the presence of a Chinese Hawaiian who not only played for the nearby Pomona Preparatory team but also served as captain. Under the title, "Chinese Baseball Wonder," the *Times* depicted Henry Pan Hoe as a "Chinese student from the Hawaiian Islands." Hoe had learned America's national pastime on the islands, the *Times* told readers who might have wondered how a person of Chinese ancestry could master baseball. The daily added that the "Celestial" had become a good infielder as well as a pitcher. In 1909, several mainland newspapers ran a wire story reporting on a Chinese Baseball League in Honolulu. Fans of this league reportedly set off firecrackers to "scare hoodoo."[7]

In 1911, readers of the *Washington Post* learned of a somewhat disturbing

event when the Keio University team took on "the local team composed of Chinese." In a story dispatched from Honolulu on July 26, readers were told that Keio had beaten the Chinese Hawaiian nine in the first game of a series. In the process of losing the second game, the Keio players were enflamed by what they considered unfair umpire decisions. They decided to quit the game, and a riot involving players and fans ensued. After the melee, Honolulu's Chinese and Japanese merchants were consulted about what to do next, and they advised that the series between the Chinese Hawaiian and the Keio nines be terminated. Their advice was taken and an army nine replaced the Chinese Hawaiian team.[8]

In September 1911, the *Worcester Telegram* announced the imminent arrival in the U.S. of a Chinese baseball team organized in Hawai'i. It suspected it was all a publicity stunt to make overseas Chinese look better in European American eyes. In December, the *Washington Post* ran a brief article titled "Chinese Nine to Invade" and subtitled "Is From Honolulu and Composed of Players of Hawaiian College." The news item was datelined Chicago and announced that Robert Yap, a resident of the Windy City, intended to bring a team of Chinese Hawaiians to the American mainland. This team would represent the Chinese Athletic Club and consist of students and former students of Hawaiian colleges. The article purported that Hawaiian residents had donated $6,000 to transport the Chinese Hawaiian team to the mainland. Yap, meanwhile, attained guidance from the University of Chicago's baseball coach, Pat Page, who had previously supervised a trip of Japanese collegian ballplayers to the U.S. The ambitious Yap intended to book the team throughout the mainland. In what must have seemed even in 1911 a lame attempt at ethnic humor, the *Los Angeles Times* notified readers in December that "[a] Chinese baseball team will invade the United States this coming season. There are quite a number of chop suey pitchers among them."[9]

The idea of skilled, athletic young men of Chinese descent struck at least some mainlanders as absurd. Much of the contempt for Chinese athleticism was based on the widespread belief that effeminate Chinese men were contemptuous of physical exercise. Early in the 1900s, Price Collier claimed in *Outing* that because of their distaste for physical exercise, Chinese men "can scarcely be driven to fight, even for their own country, and their lack of decision and their pulpy condition of dependence are now all too manifest." Casper Whitney agreed that the Chinese were "non-athletic."[10]

The very athletic En Sue Pung, however, inspired at least some interest

Opposite: In the 1900s, culturally diverse Hawaiians enthusiastically organized teams and leagues. This is a photograph of the Hawaii team, c. 1910 (courtesy of Library of Congress, Prints & Photographs Division, LC-USZ62-119529).

in organized baseball on the mainland. Late in 1906, the San Francisco Seals of the Pacific Coast League reportedly signed two Hawaiian ballplayers — En Sue Pung and Barney Joy. The *San Francisco Call*, in October 1906, published a photograph of both athletes, adding that $100 a month plus expenses would be offered to the two "stars of the Hawaiian Athletic Club." According to an article published in the *Washington Post*, Pung and Joy were "two Chinese players [and] the best men on the Honolulu Athletics team. The offers have been accepted." While En Sue Pung was, in fact, a Chinese Hawaiian, Barney Joy apparently possessed both indigenous Hawaiian and European ancestors. Indeed, according to the 1930 census, Joy was listed as a Caucasian-Hawaiian, a category enumerators in Hawai'i employed as a means of saying a Hawaiian resident possessed a blend of European and indigenous ancestry. Joy's father was born in Nova Scotia, while his mother was born on the islands. En Sue Pung's ancestry may explain, however, why he did not show up at the Seals' training camp the next spring, while Joy did. The Seals may have been desirous of attracting fan attention in the wake of the 1906 earthquake that nearly destroyed the franchise as well as other Pacific Coast League franchises. However, the Seals may not have been desirous of offending fans and players living in the anti–Chinese capital of America. En Sue Pung, in the meantime, may have had his own very good reasons for wanting to remain on the islands.[11]

Joy's tryout with the Seals was a triumph. He not only made it onto a high-level minor league roster but the "husky brown skid lad" piqued major league interest. In early September, the *Washington Post* told readers that the Pittsburgh Pirates wanted the Hawaiian, but the Boston Braves signed him. Tellingly, although Joy was a U.S. citizen by virtue of his Hawaiian birth, the *Post* referred to him as a "foreigner."[12]

Joy failed to climb or was kept from climbing onto the highest rung of American baseball's ladder. Apparently, he never returned to the mainland to pitch professionally, presumably with the complicity of the Boston Braves. After the Braves signed him, rumors swirled that Joy was actually African American and, if not, at least too dark-skinned to be welcomed into the National League. At the same time, Joy was accused of possessing an exaggerated sense of his own talents, demanding too much in compensation for his southpaw pitching skills. In 1912, a minor league franchise in Spokane bought his contract from Boston. Yet Joy decided to remain in Hawai'i that spring as opposed to reporting to Spokane. The riled Spokane owner promised to seek Joy's expulsion from organized baseball for breaking his contract. Whether he succeeded or not is unclear. However, Joy stayed in Hawai'i rather than pursue a dimming major league career.[13]

Covering the trip of Pacific Coast Leaguers to the islands in the winter of 1907–1908, sportswriter H.L. Lowery claimed a lack of enthusiasm for the way Hawaiians such as Barney Joy played baseball. Lowery asserted that Joy had cost the Seals the PCL pennant. Joy wanted to be a good pitcher and could perhaps be, but "he is like the rest of the Hawaiians too crude to carry" on a team in a tight pennant race. Of the Hawaiians he saw in action, Lowery conceded that "En Sue" was one of the few worth acknowledging. A "Chinaman," En Sue had impressed the professional ballplayers as "the most remarkable player of the Hawaiian teams." He was a good infielder and could sprint to first base faster than anyone they had ever seen.[14]

In 1908, Frank Chance, who was a player-manager of the powerful Chicago Cubs, declared he wanted to sign a "Chinese ballplayer." Writing from Hawai'i, Chance asserted to the mainland press that "if a Mongolian goes south with the famous Chicago 'Cubs' he will certainly add zest to the training period." Chance had his eyes trained on En Sue Pung, whom he described as the most remarkable Hawaiian ballplayer of all. At the time, En Sue Pung was guarding third base for St. Louis College. Chance maintained that other mainland professional franchises had sought the Chinese Hawaiian's services, but negotiations had fallen through. However, the optimistic Chance believed that En Sue Pung would not turn down the Cubs, one of the greatest teams of the early 1900s. En Sue Pung's long suit, according to Chance, was baserunning, but he had mastered all facets of the game. Chance's correspondence ended by crediting Hawaiians with an impressive command of baseball: "The small boy, be he Chinese, Japanese, or Hawaiian or the result of a mixture of several of these races, takes to baseball as naturally as does the American small boy, whose forebears have played the game since it started." Despite Chance's apparent enthusiasm, En Sue Pung remained on the islands until he joined the Hawaiian Travelers in 1912.[15]

Furthermore, En Sue Pung's versatile athleticism won recognition from the mainland press. The *Portland Oregonian* even deemed it useful to inform readers in 1908 that he had set a Hawaiian record for the 50-yard dash with a time of 5⅕ seconds. The performance had taken place at a Chinese New Year's event, staged by Honolulu's Chinese community and patronized by the Chinese consul. The article added that the sprinter was Hawai'i's best third baseman and baserunner.[16]

By 1911, John B. Williams was pitching minor league baseball on the mainland. The 1930 census manuscript depicts "Honolulu Johnnie" as a "Caucasian-Hawaiian." His father was born in England, while his mother was Hawaiian. In 1911, he made his pitching debut for Sacramento of the Pacific Coast League in a game against Vernon. After the game, Williams was sent down the minor league ladder to a franchise in Victoria, British Columbia, for more seasoning. In 1912, Williams, "the Hawaiian tosser," became a fixture on the Sacramento pitching staff. Regardless of his Anglo father, he was described in the *Sacramento Bee* as "dusky" — a term generally referring to African Americans.[17]

Williams did well for Sacramento, leading the PCL in victories in 1912 and gaining a chance to pitch in the major leagues for the Detroit Tigers in 1914. Williams, moreover, apparently attracted PCL fans as Joy had earlier. In San Francisco, in particular, people wanted to see a real live Native Hawaiian in action. When he reported to the Tigers, Williams proved a big draw whenever he pitched in Spring Training exhibition games.[18]

Williams did not set the major league baseball world afire. As a Tiger, he failed to win a game and lost two. He was soon dispatched to the PCL and never returned to the big leagues. Nevertheless, before departing from Detroit, Williams taught manager Hughie Jennings enough Hawaiian that he could coach Tigers base runners in Williams' native language.[19]

While Williams was heading to a brief major league encounter, a team of Hawaiians barnstormed the American Midwest under the management of Guy Green, who had previously operated the barnstorming, all-Native American Nebraska Indians. Largely comprised of prominent Hawaiian ballplayers of indigenous ancestry, the team toured the Midwest. Led by the Desha brothers and Johnny Williams' brother, Willie, the Hawaiian barnstormers might play a town team in Nebraska or Kansas and then appear at a nearby theater to entertain the locals with Hawaiian songs and dances. According to William Desha, who corresponded with the *Honolulu Star-Bulletin*, the team was a big hit on and off the field, but not as big a hit as the Hawaiian team that initially journeyed throughout much of the mainland a year earlier.[20]

The visits of Japanese baseball teams to the American mainland in 1905 and 1911 helped set the stage for the Hawaiian Travelers baseball team's initial journey in 1912. In 1905, a contingent from Waseda University traveled eastward to the United States. Under the headline of "Japs as Ballplayers," the *Washington Post* told readers that Waseda's trip to America had enhanced baseball's popularity in Japan as well as "future international contests between the universities of the Pacific Coast and the Orient." The Japanese nine, moreover, had improved its play during its stay on the mainland. Waseda offered relatively little competition to Stanford, Cal, and St. Mary's nines. But in Southern California, the Japanese contingent played better.[21]

Indeed, in Southern California, the Waseda nine managed to take part in the first baseball game played on the American mainland between two teams representing different non-white racial groups. At a Los Angeles ballpark, Waseda encountered a team from Sherman's Institute, a Riverside County boarding school for Native Americans. Waseda beat the Sherman Institute nine, which included John Tortez, a talented Cahuilla Indian athlete who became better known as "Chief" Meyers, a solid catcher for the New

York Giants. Waseda also defeated a Los Angeles High School nine and, more impressively, a team representing the University of Southern California. In all, according to the Seymours, Waseda won seven of 26 games in the U.S.[22]

In 1911, the Waseda nine returned to the American mainland, as did a team from Keio. These Japanese ballplayers from Waseda had a hard time with Stanford but impressed observers. The *Daily Palo Alto* saw them as both skilled athletes and racialized exotics: "The Japanese proved their reputation for sportsmanlike playing.... They are a nine of small men and they have to work for everything they get. Their native smallness handicaps them in their playing, but what they lose in size is made up in quickness, and in their taking advantage of every opening offered by the opposing nine."[23]

The next year the "Chinese Traveling Team" left the islands for the U.S. mainland with the blessings of Honolulu's Chinese community and haole business interests. The team, affiliated with Honolulu's Chinese Athletic Club, had raised, according to the *Hawaiian Star*, $6,000 for the trip. Fortuitously, the notion of sending a team of Chinese Hawaiians to the American mainland brought together Honolulu's Chinese and non–Chinese commercial interests. The former wanted to divert white mainlanders from their frequently zealous support of anti–Chinese legislation. The latter wanted to entice mainland tourists and investment. The fact that Japanese teams had toured the American mainland in 1905 and again in 1911 with some success and apparently without any major incidents suggested that the logistics of sending a Chinese Hawaiian nine westward were secure and manageable.[24]

Of course, no one wanted to ship off a contingent of incompetents to mainland baseball diamonds. But Honolulu's small baseball world knew of a number of very good Chinese Hawaiian ballplayers — ballplayers that would be seen as surprisingly skilled curiosities by many mainlanders. Scattered on various Honolulu teams, players such as En Sue Pung, Lai Tin, and infielder Alex Asam were assembled into an All–Chinese nine just in time to greet the Keio University team when it came to the islands in 1911.[25]

Before taking on the Keio nine, the All-Chinese team easily defeated the best team in the Oahu League, the Hawaiis, 8–2. The *Pacific Commercial Advertiser* bemoaned the inability of the "Celestials" to enter a team in the Oahu League. As it was, fans were surprised that the league champion could fall so readily to the Chinese Hawaiians.[26]

Meanwhile, many Japanese and Chinese Hawaiians were excited about the Keio-All-Chinese game scheduled for July 12, 1911. The *Pacific Commercial Advertiser* lamented that the game between Keio and the All-Chinese was scheduled for mid-week. Accordingly, Japanese and Chinese Hawaiian working people, as well as other Hawaiian baseball fans, would be prevented from attending. Nevertheless, the game was slated for late in the afternoon and most Honolulu baseball fans, except for Honolulu's Nikkei population, seemed to back the local team.[27]

A relatively huge crowd arrived for the Keio-All-Chinese match-up. Apparently, feelings ran high. According to the *Advertiser*, spectators were warned in English, Japanese, and Chinese to refrain from fighting, a warning which was supposedly heeded. The Japanese team won, 6–3. However, a rematch was arranged and the *Advertiser* speculated on a possible victory this time for the Chinese Hawaiians. "It will be a great feather in the caps of the Chinese team if they can pull a victory from the Japanese players, and the rejoicing in the Chinese community will beat any Fourth of July and Chinese New Year rolled into one that Honolulu has ever seen." Meanwhile, Chinese Hawaiian baseball fans persisted in attending and rooting against the Keio nine as the Japanese ballplayers opposed Honolulu's various multi-ethnic teams.[28]

In the rematch, the Chinese Hawaiians proved too much for the visitors. According to the *Advertiser*, Apau Kau, "the burly, good natured Chinese ... pitched the game of his life." The score was 5–2 to the advantage of the locals when the Keio players left the field to protest an umpire's decision. The *Advertiser* surmised as well that violence was simmering between the Japanese and Chinese spectators. However, "the mounted and foot police came in on the lope and stopped the little 'tea party.'"[29]

Things had gotten too exciting for all concerned. A rubber match between the All-Chinese and Keio was, indeed, cancelled. Moreover, at least the *Advertiser* seemed concerned about Asian Pacific athletes assuming a prominent place in Hawaiian baseball. "Aliens" were hurting the sport on the islands, according to the daily, "and the sooner the Europeans and their descendants get busy, and start the best game on earth going like it used to be, years ago, the better for the peace of mind of the Honolulu people." In truth, the *Advertiser* appeared most distressed over the behavior of those Nikkei baseball fans determined to boycott all games between Keio and Hawaiian nines because they believed the Japanese ballplayers got a raw deal in the second game against the All-Chinese.[30]

In August, the *Advertiser* announced plans for a mainland tour of Chinese Hawaiian ballplayers, many of whom indicated to the press that they could draw just as well in North America as the Keio and Waseda nines. These ballplayers, the *Advertiser* pointed out, would all be Hawaiian-born, had learned well "the American National game" on the islands, and would promote Hawai'i to mainlanders. Moreover, "The Chinese of Honolulu are a good, clean lot of boys, and they have always set a good example to the athletes of this city. In baseball, track meets and all other branches of athletics, the Chinese have made good, and they are much admired by the followers of sport."[31]

Waseda University twice dispatched baseball teams from Japan to the U.S. in the early 1900s. The relative success of the team in playing competitively and attracting fans encouraged Hawaiian promoters to send the Travelers to the U.S. mainland in 1912. This photograph c. 1911, shows a Waseda player posing with a University of Chicago opponent (courtesy of Library of Congress, Prints & Photographs Division, LC-USZ62-119534).

The Chinese Athletic Club (CAC) had indeed assembled a formidable contingent. In mid–January of 1912, the CAC nine fielded a top-notch team that included some of the finest Chinese Hawaiian ballplayers such as En Sue Pung, Lai Tin, and Vernon Ayau. The team beat a navy nine from the U.S.S. West Virginia — a nine that supposedly held the championship of the Pacific Fleet. Playing for the Chinese Red Cross, the two teams drew 900 spectators, producing a "fine sum" of proceeds. The CAC nine won, 6–3, with Apau Kau in the box. According to the *Advertiser*, "the shifty little fellows fairly stole away the game, their base running being something to conjure with." The *Advertiser* added, "The Chinese team is easily one of the best in Honolulu, and is known as one of the best drawing cards."[32]

As the date of the team's departure for the mainland drew nearer, Hawaiian promoters of the trip seemed fixed upon turning the ballplayers into island boosters. In February 1912, the *Advertiser* announced that E.K.C. Yap would manage the team's trek and that Sam Hop, who also was a notable Chinese Hawaiian athlete, would accompany the CAC barnstormers as a trainer. At this stage of the planning process, the team was expected to tender evening performances at the various mainland stops — performances that would be directed by outfielder Lang Akana who had previously acquired stage experience as a singer. The *Advertiser* added, "The evening performances will hopefully add to gate receipts. Hopefully islands scenes can be shown on film. Sam Hop will give boxing exhibitions. There will be lectures and some music. Thus the islands will be boosted."[33]

But while "boosting" Hawai'i, the CAC ballplayers were also supposed to perform Orientalism. According to the *Advertiser*, the players would parade through mainland towns and cities. These American citizens were expected to march through the streets wearing "the orthodox blouse and trousers of *their country* [italics mine], as well as regulation caps to which will be attached false queues." While they played baseball, the *Advertiser* assured readers, the Chinese Hawaiians would wear typical baseball gear.[34]

The CAC awaited word from Robert Yap, E.K.C.'s brother, as to the ballplayers' mainland schedule. Yet it seemed clear at the time that colleges and other educational institutions would offer most of the opposition. However, by March, Robert Yap, described as a musician working and living in Chicago in the 1910 manuscript census, had worked out a fairly complete schedule and sent it to Honolulu.[35]

The *Hawaiian Star*, meanwhile, expressed displeasure with the departing Chinese Hawaiian ballplayers. Under the title "Chinks Failed To Show Up," the *Star* explained to readers that the "All-Chinese" nine was slated to oppose a team of American sailors stationed on the U.S.S. California. However, the "All-Chinese" did not appear. Revealing an ongoing resentment against the CAC contingent, the *Star* added, "as usual they played fast and loose with the fans who are getting disgusted with the antics of the Celestial outfit." Several days before the "All-Chinese" departed, the *Star* announced:

> Next Sunday at the Athletic Park there will be a double-header for the benefit of the All-Chinese team, who never seem to have enough money, no matter how many benefits the public falls for.... On Saturday night there will be a benefit at the Young Hotel and it is announced that the proceeds will be devoted to buying overcoats and suit cases for the trippers.

The following day *Star* readers learned that the All-Chinese manager, E.K.C. Yap, "feels pained that the newspapers have criticized the non-attendance of members of the team at scheduled games." Yap reported that for the U.S.S. California game one All-Chinese player, Sing Hung Hoe, was on business on Maui, while another, Hong Chack, was on a sales trip to the Big Island. Many players, moreover, had heard that Athletic Park was going to be used by a Japanese bicycle meet that day. In any event, Yap maintained, it was raining and players were concerned about incurring injuries on the eve of the team's important trip to the mainland. The *Star* warned that the CAC nine tried the patience of Honolulu baseball fans. It pointed out, "It would be well for the sake of the good graces of the fans, for the entire Chinese team to be present at the next scheduled game."[36]

The *Star*'s March 5 edition underscored a prime factor motivating the All-Chinese trek across the Pacific — to promote the Islands to potential mainland tourists and investors. The *Star* asserted, "It is hoped that the Chinese baseball nine on its tour of the mainland will be served by a more communicative press agent than the phenomenally reticent individual who is chaperoning the Hawaiian swimming expedition." The *Star* referred to the "expedition" to the mainland by Hawaiian swimmers Duke Kahanamoku and Vincent Genovese — an excursion, the Hawaiian sporting community hoped, that would lead to one or both swimmers joining the U.S. swim team in the 1912 Olympiad, which, in turn, would promote Hawai'i. Clearly, the *Star* did not consider the swimmers' manager, Lew Henderson, a sufficiently enthusiastic booster of the Hawaiian Islands.[37]

The *Star*'s March 13 edition published a report on a problem that would

By the time the Travelers reached the mainland for the first time in 1912, the American sports world was becoming better acquainted with the athletic talents of Hawaiians. In the spring of 1912, Hawaiian swimmers Vincent Genovese, second from the left, and Duke Kahanamoku, second from the right, were vying for places on the U.S. Olympic swim team. Genovese would fail but Kahanamoku would not only make the team but begin a legendary career as a swimmer, surfer, and symbol of Hawaii. At the far left is Lew G. Henderson, who served as the swimmers' manager and, in so doing, provoked the ire of Honolulu newspapers who believed he was not doing enough to promote either his athletes or Hawai'i (courtesy of Library of Congress, Prints & Photographs Division, LC-B2-1281-8).

continue to haunt the Hawaiian nine — which Hawaiian ballplayers were adequately Chinese to join? W. Espinda was a ballplayer well known in Hawaiian circles and apparently quite good, because he was dubbed the "King of Spain" by the *Star* and considered by the CAC as a possible member of its barnstorming team. The *Star* reported that Espinda declared he was "of partial Chinese extraction and with the assistance of some bosom friends tried to attach himself to the Chinese team." However, the CAC turned Espinda down and when he learned he was not sufficiently Chinese for the traveling team he declared, according to the *Star*, "he wouldn't be a Chinaman if he could."[38]

Still, the matter of fielding an effective, representative team of Chinese Hawaiians inspired concern. For one thing, the team's management feared that pitching would be weak. The team's management also sought talent residing on the mainland. For example, the *Advertiser* reported that once the Hawaiian aggregation hit the East Coast, a Yale student named Mon Yin would join the roster.[39]

The Chinese Hawaiian nine seemingly needed the help. Swift outfielder En Sue Pung announced that he would have to stay behind. An undisclosed illness to one of his children reportedly prompted his intended stay in Honolulu. Exerting pressure on the situation was that much money had been invested in the team. The Chinese Athletic Club had incorporated, and several prominent members of Honolulu's Chinatown held stock. The CAC expected a return on its initial $6,000 investment as well as the money spent on various benefit baseball games and dances. It hoped, indeed, to dispatch a team to the mainland for at least another ten years. Thus most if not all of the investors had to have been disappointed to hear of En Sue Pung's intentions.[40]

The *Advertiser* struck an optimistic note as the team made last-minute preparations for the trip. The daily predicted that "the Chinese should make a hit on the mainland" and that they would play competitively. It claimed that only college nines had thus far been scheduled and added that there remained some hope that the team could add engagements in Los Angeles and San Diego to the previous schedule. The *Advertiser* quite mistakenly speculated that the Hawaiians would then take the "southern route" to the "Old South" so that they could compete there in the spring and then summer in the North.[41]

On March 20, the *Hawaiian Star* reported that "a large crowd of friends and well wishers of the Oriental athletes was on hand to wish them aloha and God speed. Leis were greatly in evidence and the band put the finishing touches on the occasion." It added that En Sue Pung, who could not leave due to "domestic matters," would probably catch up to the team in a few weeks. As the steamer carrying the athletes eastward headed out of Honolulu harbor, the ballplayers were heard chanting their club cheer, which to the *Star* reporter's ears sounded like this: "Hi, Hi, hi-hi-yah. Sharks, fins smashu, rah, rah, rah, haul in haul in, che-che-fa, chop suey, konohl, Aloha."[42]

The 1912 tour began in San Francisco. Yet even before they set foot on the U.S. mainland, the Hawaiian ballplayers had been subjected to mainland newspaper scrutiny. In early March, the *Boston Daily Globe* notified readers that "a Chinese baseball team is on the way to this country to show us what the Yellow Peril can do to us in the National game." Alluding to "Chief" Bender, the Philadelphia Athletics' star hurler, the daily added, "The captain's name is Yap and the center fielder is Pung, but we think that it will be a case of three strikes and out if they face the aboriginal Mr. Bender."[43]

The April edition of *Baseball Magazine* ran a piece on the traveling ballplayers titled "A New Feature of the Yellow Peril." The magazine linked the tour with the emergence of a republican form of government in China even though all the players were U.S. citizens. It argued that the Chinese people had become interested in things "occidental," including baseball. The evidence, according to the *Monthly*, was the imminent tour of the mainland by "native Chinese ballplayers." The *Monthly* described the visiting nine as a "picked club of Chinese students educated for the most part in Honolulu." The *Monthly* hoped that the tour would proceed for the "good of the game" and prove baseball's "civilizing mission." Still, it had picked up on distressing rumors of financial problems besetting the tour at its outset and that players were reluctant to leave home for such as extended journey with little expectation of making money.[44]

The *Hawaiian Star*, meanwhile, hoped things would go well for the Chinese Hawaiian ballplayers on the mainland. It pointed out that the team had received considerable advance publicity in the "college towns where games have been scheduled." The *Star* predicted that "the Chinese will undoubtedly create a big impression." However, it feared that some mainland college nines would present too much of a challenge for the Hawaiians. The *Star*, meanwhile, was saddened that the local league seemed weakened by the departure of top flight ballplayers such as Lai Tin, catcher Kan Yen Chun, and Apau Kau.[45]

Upon arrival in San Francisco, the Hawaiian ballplayers were greeted with a considerable amount of attention from the national press. *Sporting Life's* March 16 edition proclaimed the Hawaiian ballplayers did not constitute a "Yellow Peril." To be sure, the weekly promised readers a "Chinese invasion of the United States," but no blood would be shed. Rather the struggles for superiority would be waged on assorted baseball diamonds around the country. In addition, the "Chinese in Hawaii are good ballplayers," having beaten several white military contingents on the islands. Indeed, "the Chinese boys" took delight in overcoming white teams, according to the weekly. Representing the CAC, the players came from various schools on the islands, *Sporting Life* accurately maintained. On March 16, the *South Carolina State* ran a short, not so respectful announcement of the Travelers' tour. The headline read, "Ching at Bat" and the text explained that the "Chinese" would be unable to use a wash tub as a bat.[46]

San Francisco reporter and *Sporting Life* correspondent Abe Kemp wrote that the Chinese Hawaiian ballplayers were all young men, from 18 to 24 years old. Kemp described Lai Tin as one of the best players on the team, as well as one of the fastest Hawaiian track sprinters. Kemp also told readers about Lang Akana, another team standout. Like Lai Tin, Akana was more than just a baseball player. He was a talented singer known as "the Hawaiian nightingale."[47]

The *San Francisco Call* observed the Hawaiian team's arrival by publishing a photograph of the players on the Lurline. There was nothing exotic about the young men in the photograph. The players wore sweaters emblazoned with the letter C, which more than likely stood for Chinese. In the front row, a couple of them carried a pennant imprinted with "All Chinese." Seemingly confused in its handling of ethnic stereotypes, the text that accompanied the photo was titled, "'Hawaii's Crack Chinese Ball Nine Here in Search of Scalps." The *Call* declared the nine "the pride of the territory of Hawaii" and asserted that each player was a "full-blooded Chinese." Nevertheless, they were "born in Hawaii" and wanted mainlanders to know that "they all speak 'United States.'" The *Call* also noted that the ballplayers maintained "the Hawaiian love of music." Manager Yap told the press upon the team's arrival that his team's purpose on the mainland was simple: "We want to show the fans of America that we know something about the game. We will do our best to win, but whether we win or not, I think that our tour will show the United States that we thoroughly understand the game."[48]

The *Call* continued to cover the Hawaiian ballplayers through their game with the University of California nine. A few days after their arrival, the *Call* asserted that the "Chinese Tossers Are Seal Rooters." The San Francisco Seals were going to open their season the next Tuesday and the Hawaiians, according to the daily, planned on attending the game "The oriental stars never have seen a real big league game, and the prospect of witnessing this treat ... has had the effect of smoking them all up in a marked degree." The Hawaiians explained that they hoped they would learn more about baseball by watching skilled professionals at work. A few days later, the *Call* told readers that the "Chinese Nine" was about to oppose the Cal contingent. "The Celestial champions of Hawaii" would not embarrass themselves, the *Call* insisted. They "should be able to hold their own with the college teams in this country."[49]

Soon after their arrival, the Hawaiian barnstormers attracted Asian Pacific American communities on the U.S. mainland. After they got off the Lurline, a delegation from San Francisco's Chinatown met the ballplayers and accompanied them to a nearby hotel. Announcing the team's appearance in California's Central Valley, the *Sacramento Bee* headlined an article claiming, "Orientals Await Opening Game." According to the *Bee*, Sacramento's Young Chinese Association was organizing a large reception for their "countrymen." The *Bee* predicted that "all of Chinatown" would attend the game. Moreover, Sacramento's Japanese community would appear as well, because its members wanted to see the team that beat the Waseda and Keio University nines. The next day, the *Bee* published a photo of Lai Tin, depicting him in the caption as a star third baseman and track performer. The *Bee* mentioned as well that manager Yap had informed the press that the fictional University of Hawaii had given the players a fictional four-month leave of absence to barnstorm the American mainland.[50]

The Hawaiians lost their first game of the tour against Cal. The *San Francisco Examiner* claimed in an article headlined "California Defeats Hawaiian Chinese Team" that "international baseball was the order of the day" when the "Chinese baseball team of Hawaii" met the Cal nine. The Hearst daily declared, "The celestials surprised the collegians with the kind of ball they played, but poor fielding prevented their outscoring the Blue and Gold players." The *San Francisco Chronicle* somewhat contradicted its rival by claiming that the Hawaiians "surprised the spectators by their fast fielding and heavy hitting ability" upon losing to the University of California nine.[51]

The *San Francisco Call* expressed admiration as well, identifying the players with the anti-dynasty forces in China. In an article headlined, "Chinese .900 in Baseball Slang," the *Call* purported that the Chinese Hawaiians "treat[ed] the Ump like a Manchu." The *Call* declared, "The Celestials displayed an astonishing knowledge of the game." In particular, the Hawaiians articulated a notable command of baseball slang and etiquette: "'On your toes, boys,' 'peaches and cream,' 'good night' and numerous other kindred phrases were frequently used to the great delight of the fans." Moreover, "the Chinese unlike the Japanese who visited this country last year, are very quick to assert their rights, and several times it looked as though [umpire] big Joe Nealon would reverse his decisions."[52]

Other newspaper accounts of the Hawaiian nine's early adventures in Northern California deserve mention. While its article on the Cal game was similar to other stories, the *Oakland Tribune* printed a headline reading, "Chinese Players Show Little On Diamond." Baseball columnist James Nealon of the *San Francisco Chronicle* revealed slight enthusiasm for the Chinese Hawaiian contingent. He conceded that the "Celestial combination" performed better than the Japanese who had previously visited the Bay Area. However, "like all foreigners who adopt the game, they play mechanically and display little knowledge of the inside game." Bob Dunbar, a nationally syndicated sportswriter, observed in light of the Cal game that "the yellow peril of the Chinese baseball team of Hawaii exploded."[53]

The Hawaiian ballplayers apparently enjoyed "a big time" during their early days of the mainland tour, according to Sam Hop. The team trainer wrote the *Pacific Commercial Advertiser* that the Hawaiian ballplayers "like the theaters, which they call the 'night shows,' and are treated royally by the Coast baseball managements, having been repeatedly their guests at the baseball games."[54]

The *Advertiser* also published what it claimed was a "logbook" of one "All-Chinese" player. While in the San Francisco Bay Area, this athlete reported, the team headed to Berkeley from San Francisco on "the ferry Claremont, which is the fastest on the river and very steady, considering its speed." He added, perhaps to the discomfort of some of the parents of the Chinese Hawaiian contingent, "The boys are all enjoying themselves at every spare minute, surveying the streets and taking in the night shows." Still, the "boys were all in perfect health" and were about to take in a Pacific Coast League game and then another night show. Interestingly, the players had not yet seen San Francisco's Chinatown, but the writer declared that "Chinatown" had visited them at their hotel.[55]

The *Advertiser*, however, found odd some of the publicity the Hawaiian team had attracted on the Pacific Coast. The logbook pages it received included a clipping from a "Coast newspaper" describing the All-Chinese team as representatives of a non-existent University of Hawaii. In addition, this clipping claimed that Apau Kau had pitched a 17-inning perfect game in Hawai'i, which was apparently news to the *Advertiser*. The *Advertiser* also criticized the team's "routing agent" for not booking the Hawaiians enough dates in San Francisco.[56]

Noting that the Travelers opposed a Sacramento nine representing a real estate company a week after the Cal game, the *Advertiser* continued to express doubts about the team's schedule. It maintained that playing one game a week would not make money for the Hawaiians. Thus, the routing agent, who was presumably Robert Yap, should show more initiative and schedule more games. A few days later, the *Advertiser* complained that while the Hawaiian ballplayers were achieving "good press" on the Coast, they were not bringing in "good receipts."[57]

Journeying eastward after finding few games to play in California, the Chinese Hawaiians had their hitting shoes on when they opposed the University of Utah nine in mid–April. Before the Hawaiians arrived in Salt Lake

City, a local paper promoted the series between the Hawaiians and the University of Utah squad as a battle between "China and Utah" and between "China and the United States." Sportswriter Tommy Fitzgerald of the *Salt Lake Herald Republican* expected large crowds to watch "the little men from China." Fitzgerald speculated that many local Chinese would attend since "500 Japs" had showed up to watch Waseda University play the University Utah nine the previous year. Manager Yap, according to Fitzgerald, had already arrived in Salt Lake City. He told the press that the "boys are in good shape." Fitzgerald speculated that "the little brown men have a good team this year, and expect to trim the majority of opponents in this country." Rain, unfortunately, halted the first game in Salt Lake City after six innings. The *Salt Lake Herald Republican* said that the "Chinese did not hit their stride" and could not overcome the Utah lead before the rains came.[58]

Bill Yates, in the *Salt Lake City Evening Telegram*, was a little less understanding of the Hawaiians' defeat. His article was revealingly headlined: "Utah Defeats the 'Chink' Aggregation." Finding "Apau, the giant twirler for the Chinese," an easy mark, the Utah team jumped ahead to a 10–0 lead. Worried that rain might call the lopsided affair, the Utah coach apparently ordered his team to take it easy on the Hawaiian pitchers in order to let the game advance through the halfway mark and, therefore, become official. "The Chinamen," according to Yates, did not offer much of a challenge to Utah. However, "the vaunted ... Chinks moved and worked the ball like ballplayers." Perhaps the altitude and the inclement weather hurt them, Yates suggested, but perhaps not.[59]

On April 14, the Hawaiians outslugged the Utah nine, 22–15. Moreover, according to Fitzpatrick, the pitching of the local boys was not only "easy meat for the Orientals" but the "Hawaiians outguessed them on the basepaths," as well. The Utah nine had jumped out to another supposedly insurmountable ten-run lead. The confident crowd "joshed" the local nine for unnecessary cruelty to the visitors. Then the Hawaiian bats woke up. Lai Tin wielded the most potent piece of wood for the Hawaiians, hitting two grand slams to lead his team to a come-from-behind victory. Apau Kau apparently did not fool the locals but reliever Alex Asam kept a lid on the Utah offense. Observers were impressed with the Hawaiian outfield, especially the work of right fielder "Sing Hung," and also praised Lai Tin's job at catcher and Vernon Ayau's work at shortstop.[60]

As the Hawaiian squad made their way into Chicago, the *Advertiser* marked the close of the western portion of the team's trek. Thus far, the *Advertiser* maintained, the team had achieved "varying success." Correspondence from team members, according to the daily, indicated dissatisfaction with the financial rewards the tour reaped west of the Mississippi. "They complain of poor management and poor booking arrangements," the *Advertiser* declared. Still, the young athletes seemed to enjoy their journey.[61]

The national weekly *Sporting Life* publicized the Chinese Hawaiian ballplayers' excursion across U.S. mainland. Late in April, it reported that "the Chinese boys" heading eastward from California were showing "Americans" the "athletic ability of Chinese." In May, the weekly proclaimed in a headline: "The Chinese Team: The Colorful Visitors from Hawaii Superior to Japs Who Visited in 1911—Their General Work Causes Astonishment." In praising the Hawaiians, the Orientalist text, like the headline, stressed the foreignness of the visitors. It was not just that they came from the Hawaiian Islands that rendered them strange but that they were Chinese, despite their U.S. citizenship status. *Sporting Life*, at the same time, declared that the Chinese Hawaiians had transcended their Orientalism in mastering American slang. While exploding into a hitting binge against the University of Chicago, "the Chinese players shouted through large megaphones, 'Everybody's doing it now' and added still more to the demoralization of the Chicago pitcher.[62]

While in the Midwest, the Hawaiian ballplayers elicited both admiration and wonder. Upon arrival in the Windy City, the Hawaiians were greeted by the *Chicago Tribune* coverage. "Maroon," the apparent University of Chicago correspondent to the *Tribune*, described the visitors as members of the "College of Hawaii" team. "Maroon" said that prior to the game members of the University of Chicago freshman track team would compete against Hawaiians Lai Tin, Albert and Lang Akana, and Sing Hung Hoe. The Hawaiians had been granted the opportunity to practice on the Maroons' baseball field and "Maroon" asserted that they looked good. Despite grabbing an early lead, the Hawaiians wound up losing to the University of Chicago, 6–3. However, the *Chicago Tribune* insisted, "The Chinese played a remarkable fielding game, several of the catches in the outer gardens robbing the local men of hits." Before the game, Lai Tin lost a 50-yard sprint match against a University of Chicago freshman named S.H. Lanyon. Any other races that might have taken place went unreported by the *Tribune*. Under the headline "Celestial Beaten In Sprint," the *Tribune* explained that the race was close until the 40-yard mark and then the mainlander pulled away.[63]

After leaving Chicago, some of the Hawaiian ballplayers dropped in on Wisconsin. In Waukesha on April 29, they beat the St. John's Military Academy nine, 11–3. Then the "Hawaiian Celestials" were edged by University of Wisconsin team, 8–7, before 2,000 spectators. Despite the loss, the *Advertiser* mentioned that "the Chinese baseball players wrote that they were more or less lionized by the co-eds at Wisconsin University. They add naively that they think Wisconsin probably is the greatest university of them all. No wonder! The co-eds scrambled for a chance to dance with the visitors from

Hawaii." All in call, a curious piece of evidence that racial/sexual shibboleths were not all they were cracked up to be in ragtime America. The *Advertiser*, moreover, advised readers that the team was somewhat better off financially, but it is not clear why the whole ball club did not appear in Wisconsin with their dancing shoes on. In early May, Beloit College in Wisconsin defeated the "Chinese student club of the Hawaiian Islands." A Midwestern newspaper titled the account of the game "Beloit Shades the Celestials." Apparently about 2,600 people watched the "hotly contested" game.[64]

From Ohio, Sam Hop corresponded to the *Advertiser* that the Hawaiians lost to the University of Cincinnati due to sloppy fielding, evidenced by nine errors, and poor hitting. Hop wrote that Alex Asam, "our crack second baseman," had been doing well as a base stealer and pitcher, adding that "he is known here as Ty Cobb." The team had been provisioned with season passes to major league games and had taken advantage of them — especially when it came to National League contests. Hop predicted that the team would journey east and then return to Chicago around June 15. Showing off his Hawaiian identity, Hop added, "After that our schedule with universities and colleges we will be *pau* [italics added] and we will play semiprofessional teams."[65]

The *Advertiser*, meanwhile, found more to celebrate in the Travelers' schedule. It predicted that games would come "fast and thick" once the team crossed into the eastern section of the mainland. Still, it bemoaned the fact that the Hawaiians had been beaten by a Cincinnati semipro nine called the Shamrocks, 4–0. "The boys" were suffering from injured ankles but overall, the *Advertiser* assured readers, they were in good spirits and physical health.[66]

On the East Coast, the *Washington Post* promoted the upcoming game between the Hawaiians and the Georgetown University nine. In the process, the Washington daily largely stressed the ballplayers' foreignness. Describing the visitors as the "Hawaiian Nine" from the "College of Hawaii," the *Post* told readers, "This will be second time that Washington baseballdom has been afforded the opportunity of witnessing a foreign interpretation of our national game." The first time occurred in 1911 when the Keio University team toured the U.S. The Japanese nine stirred excitement and the *Post* expected more of the same from the Hawaiians since "the visiting ball tossers have defeated the Keio sluggers in a series of games and the merits of the team are somewhat attested to in view of such a victory." Indeed, according to the *Post*, the impending game was "attracting an unusual amount of interest in this vicinity, and it is expected that many foreign nations will be represented when the festivities begin." As for the Hawaiian ballplayers themselves, "nearly every man on the squad is a sprinter and the base-running of the Hawaiians is said to be of the sensational order." As the *Post* predicted, the game was thrilling with the Georgetown nine winning, 6–5, in extra innings.[67]

The *Post's* W.P. Hotel generally approved of the Hawaiians' performance. He maintained:

> Outside of a tendency to throw poorly, the visitors played on a par with Americans, showing a fine knowledge of the game. They ran bases particularly well. Their fielding was all that could be asked for, [in] gathering in flies and gobbling up grounders with ease and neatness; but they seemed to get no direction in their heaving, the catchers being particularly weak in this respect.

According to Hotel, Lai Tin's throwing error proved costly as it not only brought in the winning run but was preceded by another muff by the otherwise talented "Chinese ball tosser" and third baseman — a muff which put home team baserunners in scoring position. Hotel praised the relief pitching of Alex Asam and declared that the game was not only the longest staged on Georgetown's "hilltop diamond" but the most thrilling.[68]

The next day, the *Post's* sporting section featured a cartoon displaying stereotypical Chinese images of the Hawaiian team watching a Washington Senators-Cleveland Indians game. The *Post's* Joe S. Jackson noted, "All of the members of the College of Hawaii team, the Chinese nine that gave Georgetown a great battle on Monday were in attendance at the game. They watched the work of the professionals closely, and stayed until the last man was out."[69]

Back in Honolulu, the *Advertiser* protested on May 30, 1912, that it had heard little from the "CAC boys." The team appeared to "have a pressless press agent if one judges form the frequent spells of silence which seem to mark their errant trail." The *Advertiser* caught whiffs of the ventures of the Hawaiian ballplayers in the nation's capital. The "boys were having another time of their lives." The Hawaiian delegate to the U.S. Congress feted them, since, after all, the ballplayers were all voters or prospective voters. The Chinese ambassador also threw a banquet for them. The *Advertiser* advised readers that the team would probably come home in a month. Financial matters had not actually improved, "but still the boys have managed to get along without appeals for further Honolulu help."[70]

In New York City, the Hawaiian ballplayers found something of a home away from home. In the latter part of May, the Chinese Hawaiians played their first game in New York City, opposing a Fordham University team at the upper Manhattan citadel of baseball — the Polo Grounds. A few days before the game, Columbia University's Chinese students had staged a play called "From Monarchy to Republic." Attending the play were distinguished New Yorkers and also the Chinese Hawaiian ballplayers, who entertained theater goers with ensemble singing, accompanied by guitar. The day before the Fordham game, the *New York Times* announced that the Chinese consul would throw out the first ball. Moreover, "the visiting team is composed entirely of Chinese students and is the first of that race to play the National Game in

New York City's Chinese community seemingly took a liking to the Travelers when they arrived in the city in 1912. This photograph of the city's Chinatown, taken in or around 1911, shows the Chinese Revolutionary headquarters, bearing both the U.S. and the Chinese flags. Significantly, the Travelers in 1912 were identified with the hopes of overseas Chinese for an end to the Qing dynasty and a more democratic China (courtesy of Library of Congress, Prints & Photographs Division, LOT 7178).

this city." The visitors, according to the *Times*, had beaten several of America's best college and semipro teams.[71]

After the game, *Sporting Life* pointed out that the Fordham contingent posed "an enigma to the invading Yellow Peril," winning, 3–0. The *Times* titled its account of the game, "Chinese in Baseball" with the subtitle reading "Orientals Play 'Melican' Game Well and Fast But Lose to Fordham." The *Times* claimed that at the game "the familiar diet of peanuts and almond bars was passed up for chop suey and chow mein." The reason was that "the visitors were full-blooded Chinamen — every one of 'em — but they played baseball far better than many Americans who fill the uniforms of several colleges of high standing in baseball." Fordham could have lost the game had it not been for pitcher Luck Yee's wildness and an unexplained, "slight miscue by the umpire."[72]

The *Times* estimated that about 500 people appeared at the Polo Grounds, driven by "curiosity to see the Orientals perform." They expected the New

York nine to win easily but "were agreeably disappointed." The *Times* had good words to say about the Hawaiians' fielding, especially the infield work, Luck Yee's pitching, and catcher's Kan Yen Chun's ability to gun down Fordham base stealers. But the sportswriter was most impressed with Lai Tin, who was called "the star of the aggregation." At third base, Lai Tin "grabbed hard bounders of the most puzzling variety just as handily as [big league stars] Jimmy Collins and Arthur Devlin used to grab 'em." The *Times* sportswriter was also pleased with the behavior of "the little Orientals." That is, "they played ball every minute and wasted no time disputing with the umpires." There were a few decisions that would have evoked anger from "American players." However, "the Chinamen passed them up." According to the *Times*, "the game brought out a large crowd of Chinese residents."[73]

The *New York Sun* noted, as well, the attendance of members of New York's Chinese community at the Polo Grounds. Not very subtly, it informed readers that "an amusing accessory of the visitors was their cheering section, which poured out a continual stream of wash talk and laundry advice to their undersized diamond heroes."[74]

Within a few days, the Hawaiians met a semipro team in Brooklyn before a reportedly record-breaking crowd of 12,000. The headlines of the *New York Sun*'s coverage of the game read, "Chinese Lose to Ridgewood" and "Occidentals Take Kindly to Oriental Slants." The Hawaiians went through their "Oriental paces," according to the *Sun*, and lost, 11–5. *Sun* readers learned that the visitors were better fielders than hitters. Still, Lai Tin and Apau Kau managed to hit home runs. Moreover, since the Brooklyn major league team was not doing well at the time, the *Sun* pointed out, "It is believed the Chinese experts from Hawaii would give them a battle." The *Brooklyn Eagle* chimed in that the Hawaiians played a "snappy," smart game that excited fans at Wallace Grounds in Ridgewood. The *Eagle* added, "The Orientals conducted themselves with dignity and by their gentlemanly bearing and sportsmanlike playing won the friendship of all."[75]

The Hawaiians also ventured into New Jersey to play Seton Hall at Newark's International League Park. The *New York Sun* reported that a large crowd arrived, attracted "by the reputation of the Orientals that had preceded them to Newark." Seton Hall edged the visitors, 2–1. The *Sun* insisted that the spectators "derived much amusement from the antics of the Mongolians, particularly the celestial coachers." The Hawaiians, at the very least, failed at bat since they whiffed 15 times. Outfielder Sing Hung Hoe did manage to "amaze" the crowd, stealing second, third, and home for the Hawaiians' only run. At the same time, catcher Kan Yen Chun's throwing error let in the winning run for Seton Hall in the 11th inning. Still, the *Advertiser* celebrated the Newark fans' enthusiastic reception of the "Mid-Pacific chaps."[76]

Indeed, the Hawaiians' visit to Newark did not escape attention from Jersey's baseball followers. Prior to the Seton Hall game, the *Newark News* told readers, "The Chinese Nine to Play Here." It referred to the visitors as members of the "University of Hawaii" team and "Orientals [who] are experts" at baseball. While U.S. citizens, their colonial heritage was called into play by the assertion that the Hawaiians' skills "demonstrate ... very clearly that baseball follows the flag." The visitors, according to the *News*, were good fielders and fast baserunners, but relatively weak at bat. Hawaiian pitcher "Lucky Yee" had amazed New York City fans with his command of fastballs and curves against Fordham. Thus, while Seton Hall would go with its ace, future major league infielder Joe Peploski, fans should expect the Hawaiian ballplayers to acquit themselves well.[77]

The Seton Hall game cost 25 cents for a general admission ticket and at least the local press thought it was worth it. After the game, one local newspaper maintained that the "Celestials" proved their mastery of baseball, arguing that their fielding was as good as any college team on the mainland. This was especially amazing since the Hawaiians supposedly had little experience. However, the visitors' hitting was "lamentably" bad as Peploski not only struck out 15 Hawaiian batters but gave up only two hits. Still, the "marvelous work" of the "Chinamen" deserved praise, particularly the exciting baserunning of Sing Hung Hoe, whose daring steal of home scored the Hawaiians' only run.[78]

The skills the visitors displayed in Newark encouraged the *Newark News* to reiterate its claim that the "baseball surely follows the flag." It pointed out that the stars and stripes flourished over the grandstand, but below it waved the flag of the new Chinese Republic, which was saluted "by the mongolians in attendance." The daily told readers that Seton Hall's opponent was comprised of "a team of Chinese students from the University of Hawaii, every one an American subject." The Seton Hall nine reportedly expected an easy victory, but the *News* insisted that the New Jersey ballplayers had to work hard for their eventual triumph. The crowd was relatively small, the *News* asserted. However, "Newark Chinese" attended. Some of these fans were apparently ignorant of baseball, but the "Americanized Celestials" cheered loudly when they had the opportunity and the *News* maintained that they had more than a few such opportunities.[79]

Seton Hall students had also attended the game and the *News* asserted that they tried "to rattle the Chinese" with their cheers. Yet "the Chinese had a yell of their own, which was sprung before and after the game. Just what the language the cry was written in was a question yet it was about as intelligible as those used by other schools."[80]

The *News* expected continued improvement from the Hawaiian players. It falsely claimed that annexation had lured American baseball to the islands.

Thus, Hawaiian ballplayers had gotten off to a late start. Thus, too, the Hawaiian ballplayers were especially impressive since they were relative novices. Indeed, "every trick of the game is known to the Chinese and the ability of the celestials to take advantage of every opportunity made them dangerous baseball rivals." Helping matters was that the "Chinese coaches" used "the choicest of the very best of English" when guiding baserunners. Asam at second and "L. Tin" at third merited compliments for their fielding, as did the entire "Chinese infield." To be sure, Peplosky had the Hawaiians baffled, but the Seton Hall ace had dominated other teams as well. The Hawaiian pitcher, Apau Kau, was good, too. He had command of several pitches, the *News* insisted, including the spitter.[81]

On May 29, the Hawaiians were in Syracuse, where they got clobbered. The *Syracuse Daily Journal* told readers that the Syracuse University encounter with the "Chinese Players" was the most interesting match-up on the university nine's schedule. It declared, moreover, that "the drawing power of the team from over the ocean will be great." Curious fans were abundant, lured by a desire to see a team that performed well based on expert fielding and swift baserunning. The visitors' hitting, the *Daily Journal* conceded, left something to be desired but had improved as they experienced front-line mainland pitching. Nevertheless, errors apparently did the barnstormers in against the Syracuse nine as did poor pitching. Indeed, the *Syracuse Herald* expressed disappointment in the Travelers' performance — especially that of "Apan the 'Chink' twirler." Lang Akana, however, managed to slug a homer for the "almond-eyed" team.[82]

All in all, the *Advertiser* seemed pleased with the tour as of early June. It insisted that East Coast papers were full of "interesting accounts of the team and the playing of the Chinese lads." The daily asserted, moreover, that the Keio and Waseda nines had not gotten as positive a press reception as the "Honolulu Chinese baseball team."[83]

Outfielder Lang Akana, meanwhile, thought he needed to educate mainlanders a little more about Hawaiian baseball. In a wire story datelined Philadelphia, Akana was described as a member of the "Chinese-Hawaiian" team. The Hawaiian complained that mainlanders entertained a misconception about Honolulu as "an ancient town with coconut trees standing in the streets. Instead, Honolulu was a modern metropolis in which folks could not live without baseball." Akana announced that weekday games in Honolulu consistently drew crowds of 2,000, while several thousand more might appear for weekend games. The biggest draws, according to Akana, were games arranged between the Chinese and the Japanese. Such games, Akana conceded, were rare because authorities wanted to limit the emotions they incited. Indeed, Akana was quoted as wondering why China and Japan did not go to war over these games. "Rabid fans," in any event, would wait for hours for seats and make things miserable for the umpires who officiated at the games. A sympathetic Akana called such umpires the bravest of those connected to Honolulu baseball.[84]

The mainland press did not always seem impressed by Akana and his teammates. A syndicated sports writer named Tommy Clark was less than enamored with the ethics displayed by the Travelers on the baseball diamond—ethics that were, in fact, integral to the success of nearly every successful baseball team at the time. Clark insisted, "Nothing about the heathen Chinese is more peculiar than his dark ways and vain tricks in baseball." He reported that the "laundryman" Ayau was especially adept at duping innocent European American ballplayers. Ayau would, it appears, plant himself three feet or so from second while gathering in a thrown ball from the catcher or one of the outfielders. He would then intentionally bobble the ball in order to entice white baserunners to second where he would immediately tag them out. In other words, just as Carlisle gridders could not beat whites, some critics insisted, without resorting to trickery, the same was said of the Travelers' ability to vanquish many white nines.[85]

In early and mid–June, upstate New York publications traced the journeys of the Hawaiian nine. On June 6, the *Auburn Citizen* announced the imminent arrival of the "Chinese University team" to oppose the town nine at Cold Springs diamond. The visitors, the *Citizen* added, had demonstrated that baseball was more than "America's national game." In any event, Auburn's baseball fans would be treated with a "half-holiday" so that they could experience in person the baseball "novelty." The game itself ended badly for the Travelers as they were outslugged, 14–10. An astonishing ten errors and poor pitching combined to subdue the visitors. However, the *Auburn Citizen* appraised the Hawaiians generously.[86]

According to the *Citizen,* the crowd of 500 cheered loudly "the appearance of the Chinese players of America's national game." Moreover, the fans were "surprised by the appearance of the men from the Far East as they were sturdy of build and had the appearance and actions of the kind of ball players that delight the fan." While the visitors' fielding proved disappointing, they showed they could hit, "connect[ing] with the sphere in a way that sent delight into the heart of the sound of oak meeting leather." While not flawless defenders, "the Chinese were up on the first points of the game and pulled off several fast fielding plays that brought them many rounds of applause, as did their clever base running."[87]

The Auburn newspaper pointedly portrayed the visitors as capable of speaking English well. It added, however, that spectators were "amused" upon hearing the Hawaiians coach "in their native tongue." Moreover, one of the

Hawaiian pitchers used "the Chinese language" in disagreeing with Kan Yen Chun's pitch calls.[88]

Moving on to Middletown, New York, the Chinese Hawaiians beat a local nine, 9–7, before an estimated 800 curious fans. Prior to the game, the *Middletown Daily-Times Press* announced the impending arrival of "the famous Chinese club of the University of Hawaii." The newspaper added that the visitors constituted the only "Chinese team" in America. Middletown readers were told that the visitors could throw and field well, but were inadequate hitters. Advised that they could witness the first "international" game ever played in Middletown, these readers were also informed that the clever Nat Strong had become the Hawaiian team's "American" representative. After the game, the Middletown daily published a photo of the visiting team on the bench and declared the contest "fast and exciting." The visitors were "gentlemen" and a "classy bunch of players" who, despite predictions, hit the ball hard. The *Daily-Times-Press* was particularly taken with Lang Akana's hitting and "petty larceny" on the basepaths.[89]

The Middletown fans seemed surprised at how well the Chinese Hawaiians played baseball. Still, admiration and ridicule combined to shadow the team. The *New London Day* declared on June 21 that the management of the New London nine had received a letter from Nat Strong maintaining that the "Chinks can't pole. They're all right on fielding but they're tramps with the lumber." The *Day* maintained that Strong was wrong, that "the Chinks were there with a slap and nearly got the verdict." The Hawaiians got eight hits and might have taken the game if not for Akana's misplay of a fly ball in left field—a misplay that would not have happened "if the Chink left fielder hadn't thought he was a Turk instead of a Chink and kissed the ground with his back to the sun in the fifth inning." In July, another sportswriter claimed that "the Chinese baseball team visiting in our midst is not likely to break into the world's series. There is not a Ti Cobb or a Si Yung in the whole outfit." Furthermore, while the "Chinese ballplayers" were not very good, "their language gives them a great advantage over their American brethren in jawing at the umpire."[90]

The *Honolulu Star-Bulletin* divulged the contents of a letter from Sam Hop on July 13. Hop reported that the Hawaiians had been doing well on the field, despite what he claimed were "punk decisions" made by various umpires. The team, Hop added, was financially all right. Consequently, according to the Chinese Hawaiian athlete and entrepreneur, the players were not even thinking about returning to Hawai'i.[91]

On July 23, the *Honolulu Star-Bulletin* asserted that the ball team's visit to the mainland reinforced the positive image of the islands inspired by Duke Kahanamoku's stunning aquatic skills in making the U.S. Olympic team.

However, the daily was puzzled as to why the mainland press kept bringing up the "College of Hawaii" when publicizing the traveling contingent.[92]

If the Hawaiian ballplayers defied common assumptions about people of Chinese ancestry, some publications dredged up interesting fragments of orientalism. For example, in promoting a game in upstate Amsterdam, New York, a local daily insisted that fans would see "a snappy bunch of players" and "the Mikados representatives of our national sport in this country." This was probably not the first time and certainly would not be the last that ballplayers of Chinese ancestry would be confused for Japanese nationals, or vice versa. In any event, the Hawaiians defeated the Empires of Amsterdam, prompting an *Evening Recorder* headline that read "Chinese Understand Uncle Sam's Game." In a subheadline, the daily announced, "Aggregation of ball tossers from the Native Haunts of Laundrymen" beat the locals. The *Evening Recorder* concluded that it was no disgrace for the locals to lose since the "Orientals" constituted a talented outfit.[93]

The Hawaiians managed to stir unwelcome controversy crossing over the "Great Divide." The *Star-Bulletin* complained that the "all-Chinese" nine had gotten Honolulu "in bad with the good people of Canada." In so doing, the ballplayers "advertis[ed Hawaii] as a land of howling savages and ungodly heathens." Evoking a definition of nationality transcending citizenship status, the daily continued, "Even their own countrymen in Montreal have turned from the Chinese ball-tossers in holy horror." The ball team's transgression was that it had scheduled a game with a Montreal nine on a Sunday and aggravated matters by departing the city on the same day.[94]

Sporting Life revealed that the Travelers had taken on Montreal of the high-level International League. They lost to the professionals, even though the Hawaiians outhit the home team. Unfortunately, Hawaiian pitchers found home plate much too hard to locate and handed the home team a perhaps undeserved victory. Earlier, according to *Sporting Life*, the Travelers encountered trouble with Canadian immigration authorities. Canada, too, excluded Chinese and demanded $500 per player before the authorities allowed the Travelers to cross the border. The owner of the Montreal team balked at such as sum, but eventually a compromise was worked out and the Travelers crossed into Canada.[95]

While on the East Coast, the Hawaiians were challenged by the African American Lincoln Giants professional nine. Readers of the *Decatur Review* learned the following in late July under the headline "Chinese Draw Color Line":

> The color line has been drawn in a great many cases but this one may be tied, but not beaten. The Chinese baseball team that came over here with a great reputation was challenged by the Lincoln Giants of New York recently. The

answer came back from the yellow boys that they drew the color line and would not mingle.

The Hawaiians' own racial prejudice may have figured in the decision. However, it also should be said that under African American ownership, the Lincoln Giants had resisted Nat Strong's efforts to monopolize black baseball in New York City. Thus Strong, who had taken over the booking of the Travelers, may have been key in making or influencing the decision to spurn the Giants. In the future, however, the Hawaiian barnstormers would play African American professional teams, including the Lincoln Giants.[96]

The Chinese Hawaiians, according to *Sporting Life*, got something of a taste of what African Americans habitually experienced on the mainland. Late in August, the weekly asserted that for the first time since it landed in the "United States ... the Chinese base ball team from the University of Hawaii" was denied hotel accommodations. Occurring in Franklin, Pennsylvania, such discrimination was accorded the ball players despite the fact that they were "well-educated and have been entertained by some of the best people." An apparently aroused Hawaiian nine then proceeded to trounce the local team, 14–4, and successfully sought accommodations in nearby Oil City.[97]

Returning to the Midwest in the late summer, the Hawaiians garnered an intriguing press treatment by Ohio newspapers. On August 19, the *Cleveland Plain-Dealer* published photographs of three Travelers, identified as "Long" Akana, "Apan Kan," and Mon Yen Chung. The accompanying story was titled, "Chinamen Defeat Ball Team Here" and subtitled, "Cleveland Players Dazed by Coaching in Five Languages." The *Plain-Dealer* asserted that the locals were rattled by their opponents' "orientalized coaching"— coaching in what seemed to the Cleveland journalist little but gibberish, "grunts, yelps, and howlings." Still, by winning easily, the visitors demonstrated that just as Bret Harte's "heathen Chinee" mastered poker, they had mastered another American pastime—baseball.[98]

In other words, the *Plain Dealer*, testified, "Our little straight haired brothers from our island possession across the Pacific made the Cleveland boys look like a chicken in a chop suey kitchen." Scoring in double digits, the visitors inspired the *Plain Dealer* to concede that "the team of Mongolians ... were familiar "with the swat stick as well as the chop stick." And while demolishing the Cleveland nine, "they would dance and gesticulate like a lot of monkeys, all the while talking in Chinese, Japanese, Portuguese, Hawaiian, and English, all of which ... they use with equal facility.[99]

Not only were the visitors more talented than their opponents, but they used the "hypnotic wiles of the oriental" to subdue the semipro, Tellings nine. The *Plain-Dealer* pointed out that in the sixth inning the Travelers had two men on base, presumably on first and second, with one out. Alex Asam, however, got thrown out at second for the second out. Then, as if in a trance the Tellings players ran off the field, thinking there were three outs, and "the Chinamen" runners ran home.[100]

The *Plain Dealer* interviewed Mon Yen Chung, whom it described as a Yale graduate, left fielder, and base coach. The ballplayer, who had joined the Travelers in the summer and seemed to play rarely, condemned the Chinese Exclusion Law as being enforced unfairly. In particular, he lamented, students of Chinese ancestry were having problems in getting into the United States even though the law did not bar their entry. Betraying a class bias, Mon Yen Chung articulated the hope that the Travelers would show white America that not everyone of Chinese ancestry worked in laundries.[101]

On August 17, 1912, the *Elyria Evening Telegram* printed an advertisement promoting the "All Chinese Team of University of Hawaii vs. Elyria" game on August 21. On August 19, 1912, the paper announced "Chinese Team To Play Here Wednesday." The Ohio newspaper's readers were informed that the "Mongolian Baseball Players ... Play Fine Ball." The *Evening Telegram* promised, "Elyria baseball fans will be treated to a brand new experience Wednesday when the baseball team of the Chinese University of Hawaii will come here to play the local team at Athletic Park. The 'chinks' played ... in Cleveland, Sunday, and demonstrated that they are some ball players by taking the long end of a 10 to 6 score." The "Chinese" team, according to the Ohio daily, was not just fascinating because of its talented ballplayers. "The members of the team all speak, beside their native tongue, Japanese, Portuguese and the conglomerate languages of the Hawaiian Islands. What they do to those on the coaching lines is simply shameful and no team is said to be able to withstand the bombardment of gutturals and exclamations." The *Evening Telegram* understood that there was a political reason behind the support the Chinese Hawaiian nine got from Chinatown merchants in Honolulu and that the players did not actually represent the Chinese University of Hawaii. These merchants wanted to show the "people of the United States that all Chinamen are not laundrymen or cooks." Thus "every member of the team is a graduate of either an American or a Hawaiian school or college and all speak English, in addition to the four other languages which are commonly heard on the Hawaiian Islands as fluently as they play baseball."[102]

A few days later, the Hawaiians barely lost in Michigan to a professional Grand Rapids team. Loose fielding almost did the home team in as the game attracted teams from the Erie and Central League. The *Fort Wayne News* reported on the game with "Chinks" and quoted a local manager saying, "You're right those Chinamen can play ball.... Grand Rapids was the luckiest club in the world beating those Chinks."[103]

The Travelers seemed to have been pretty busy in Michigan. The *Marshall*

Evening Chronicle announced that "the famous Chinese team" was about to visit nearby Tekonsha on September 12. The Hawaiians, the *Evening Chronicle* declared, comprised "one of the best traveling teams on the road." The Tekonsha manager had to put up his largest guarantee ever to lure the Travelers. A big crowd was expected for the 3:15 P.M. game. Ten cents would get a seat in the grandstands, while 25 cents would purchase a better view of the proceedings.[104]

Eventually, the team departed from Chicago for the West Coast. Hong Quon received a cable in Honolulu from his son and utility player, Hong Chack. From San Francisco, the ballplayer informed his father that the team would remain in the Bay Area to rustle up a few more ballgames before taking a ship to Honolulu. The *Advertiser* looked forward to the team's return. "Hopefully the boys will stay intact and play our stay-at-home nines. We love our Oahu League teams, but, oh you travelers."[105]

Meanwhile, team captain Albert Akana and Sam Hop had returned early to Honolulu. Noting their arrival, the *Advertiser* hailed the record the Travelers had achieved on the mainland. From April 1 to September 3, the "Honolulu Chinese" ball club won 53 games, while losing 44 and tying three. It also praised Hop as "the premier Honolulu baseball and general sports fan of the Chinese colony." Hop declared to the press that the "boys all played great ball," while he enjoyed the crowds. He boasted that the team drew 14,000 to a game in the Bronx. He added, according to the *Advertiser*, "Some doings, I tell you. And talk about education! Look at me. You see, I now speak in an American way." Hop did complain that some of the semipro teams the Travelers opposed brought in "ringers" to help them defeat the visitors. Still, Hop maintained, baseball was a great sport that had already warmed relations between the United States and the newly minted Republic of China. Appearing to identify with Chinese nationals, Hop naively stated, "The great American cousins of ours always enjoy us and we enjoy them. This way we always come out square and ahead." On a more practical matter, Hop promised that the team would head back to the mainland in 1913. He assured the press that bookings posed no problem, claiming that the Hawaiians could play 500 games on the mainland if they had the time and the energy.[106]

Despite the relatively pleasant publicity surrounding the Hawaiian ball club's debut on the U.S. mainland, the team's financial status had indeed proven problematic. Years later, sportswriter Red McQueen maintained that the annual treks across the Pacific never made much money for the ballplayers. Playing college teams as presumptive collegiate amateurs meant they would typically leave college towns with empty pockets. Other games, against semi-professional and professional nines, meant that the 12 to 14 Hawaiian players would divide $100 here and there. However, in 1912, the team got stranded in New York City mainly, according to McQueen, because of the poor work of their agent—the unnamed Robert Yap. Once in New York City, Red McQueen wrote in the 1960s, the financially straitened ballplayers scraped together enough to buy food, while team trainer "Sam Hop, celebrated local Chinese chef," helped through "astute buying and fine cooking." McQueen asserted that things got better when Hop, subsequently, took over the team management and Nat Strong became team agent.[107]

Nat Strong's career illustrates that the business of American baseball was in a state of considerable flux in the early 1900s and that the structured, hierarchical entity known as organized baseball had to struggle to achieve and maintain its supremacy in the National Pastime. Strong operated outside of organized baseball, knowing well that supremely talented baseball players competed beyond its boundaries. Strong's career as a baseball entrepreneur began in the 1890s. New York City embraced a wide assortment of semiprofessional teams that played on fields such as Dexter Park, which straddled the Queens-Brooklyn border. Strong recognized that these nines played well and attracted loyal followings that often matched and even surpassed those inspired by major league franchises. He, therefore, eventually assumed control of Dexter Park and other New York City ballparks and rented them out to white and black teams. By the early 1900s, according to Jules Tygiel, Strong had built something of a baseball empire on the East Coast—an empire profiting from the play of teams outside organized baseball's command. In 1905, Strong founded the National Association of Colored Professional Clubs of the United States and Cuba. This league included many of the best African American nines on the East Coast.[108]

Strong subsequently sought to maintain monopolistic control over African American baseball on the East Coast. In the process, he aroused considerable resentment from black baseball promoters and players. It is not clear how much power Strong tried to assert over the Hawaiian team but he no doubt pocketed at least ten percent of the gate money enticed by the Travelers. Still, the Hawaiians were in the hands of an energetic and well-connected promoter who was not in the least bit squeamish about marketing non-white teams as long as they played by his rules.[109]

The *Star-Bulletin* praised Strong's work on behalf of the Hawaiian barnstormers in 1912. It told readers that "Mr. Strong handled the bookings of the All-Chinese ball team during the greater part of the its tour in the states, and did well by the local boys." Strong's work perhaps encouraged a press notice published in a mainland newspaper in November 1912. The notice solemnly informed readers that the faculty and board of directors of the Chinese University of Hawaii authorized another journey to the mainland by the imaginary university's baseball team. Nat Strong, furthermore, had received the go-ahead to firm up the schedule for the 1913 season.[110]

Hawaiians warmly greeted the return of their "All-Chinese" ballplayers. In mid–October, the team arrived in Honolulu on the Sierra. Only Ah Toon, "the speedy right fielder of the organization," remained on the mainland, presumably to work in San Francisco. The *Star-Bulletin* described the scene of "a crowd of enthusiastic rooters [who] lined the rails of two launches and gave cheer after cheer for the clever players who did such good publicity work for Hawaii." After leaving the boat, the ballplayers were shepherded to waiting cars which drove around Honolulu before ending up in Waikiki. Admiringly and perhaps reassuringly, the *Star-Bulletin* pointed out that the returning athletes had played 119 games in North America "and when the mileage made is taken into consideration, it is apparent that the Honolulu boys had little time for anything but ball playing." It also informed readers that the team had brought home "two splendid loving cups," one of which was a gift from the "Chinese residents of Chicago" and the other from former Honolulu Chinese living in San Francisco. Manager Yap told the press that the team enjoyed its journey to the mainland and would be willing to return. But the ballplayers were still Hawaiians. That is, they also enjoyed, Yap pointed out, seeing Diamond Head again and spending time at home. "Half a year is a long time to be away from Honolulu," Yap asserted. Local Chinese merchants treated the returning ballplayers to a banquet at Honolulu's Notley Hall. The *Star-Bulletin* claimed the celebration was a success. Kim Tong Ho served as toastmaster, while various team members offered personal accounts of their trek across the mainland. The aforementioned trophies were also displayed.[111]

The *Star-Bulletin* speculated that the players would enjoy little rest during their stay in Hawai'i. They were expected to don their uniforms and exhibit their talents to Hawaiian baseball fans. The daily insisted that "Honolulu fans [were] clamoring to see the team in action." In particular, Hawaiian baseball lovers sought proof that the journey had improved the Travelers' skills. According to the *Star-Bulletin*, "The Chinese made a fine record on their trip and undoubtedly they have come up many notches in their playing ability."[112]

The *Star-Bulletin* considered it strange that the local Oahu League management had not arranged games pitting league members against the "Chinese team." Fans wanted to see the contests, especially "the whole Chinese community which has been behind the team financially." The *Star-Bulletin*, moreover, feared that the layoff since their last mainland game on September 25 would erode the Travelers' skills the longer it continued. Oahu League teams responded that they wanted to take on the Chinese Hawaiians. However, scheduling proved problematic since Oahu League games were played on Sunday. Saturday games were possible, but they drew fewer paying fans.[113]

The Travelers' first game back was against the Hawaiis, whom they beat handily before 1,000 Saturday afternoon fans. The *Advertiser* complimented the victors. The Travelers had shown, it declared, that by playing together constantly over the previous several months, individual players had clearly progressed. Several months earlier any team in the Oahu League could have defeated the Travelers, the *Advertiser* declared. But in October 1912, that was no longer possible. The *Advertiser* asserted, "The team as a whole played like stars, the team-work was of the best and every member showed he knew the value of the big-stick, when it came to the hitting feature of the game."[114]

In early November, the *Advertiser* promoted an upcoming game between the Travelers and the Japanese Athletic Club. Somewhat cynically the *Advertiser* announced that Sam Hop had become a "champion" of the youthful baseball fans, promising free admission to children under 12. Actually carrying few ballplayers of Japanese ancestry, the JAC was set to start future Traveler Foster Robinson in the box, a Maui native of mixed Chinese, haole, and indigenous background.[115]

It seemed fairly clear to at least some of the major participants in Honolulu baseball that the regular Oahu League teams had fallen behind the Travelers. Accordingly, "Picked Nines" were organized, comprised of some of the best Hawaiian ballplayers outside the Travelers' fold. One game between an all-star contingent headed by Barney Joy and the Travelers was arranged — a game for which the famed Royal Hawaiian Band was scheduled to play. Sam Hop, however, called off the contest, giving the appearance that the financial inducement was insufficiently satisfying. Joy insisted that he was not disappointed, because Hop demanded too high a split of the gate. One fan not only agreed with Joy, according to the *Advertiser,* but asserted that the former Pacific Coast League pitcher could lure Honolulu baseball fans just as effectively as the Travelers.[116]

Military teams on Oahu sought contests with the Travelers. Interestingly, the *Advertiser* in early November publicized a game between the Schofield Barracks nine and the Travelers as an "international contest." It would pit "Uncle Sam's Boys" who were out "to whip [the] Chinese." The soldiers were confident they would beat "the Oriental team." Furthermore, Schofield's officers promised to bring along their wives so they could "see how the Chinese youngsters handle themselves in the great American game." The soldiers in general planned on occupying one section of the stand to enhance the volume of their cheering in unison. Captain Albert Akana of "the Chinese boys" promised to use "spit-ball artist Apau Kau." Subsequently, Albert Akana seemed to want to take the box himself against the Schofield nine. Noting Akana's "Indian features," the *Advertiser* said they would "probably be sufficient to scare the lives out of the brave soldiers of Uncle Sam."[117]

The All-Chinese nine and its new head, Sam Hop, sparked increasing controversy in Honolulu sporting circles. The *Advertiser* protested, in late

November, that the nine had missed two engagements to play at Schofield Barracks, provoking the soldiers stationed there. Additionally, the Oahu League in general was upset that Hop demanded — win or lose — 60 percent of the gate every time one of its teams played the Travelers. Hop was quoted comparing the Travelers to Jack Johnson. The great heavyweight would not fight unless he was guaranteed a majority of the gate, Hop maintained, and neither would the Chinese Hawaiian nine. One critic pointed out that the comparison between the Hawaiian team and the world champion did not hold water as "the All-Chinese baseball nine is as far from reaching that station, as the north is from the south pole, if not a little further."[118]

In early December, the Chinese Hawaiians finally trekked over to Schofield Barracks to play the military nine. They beat the soldiers, 4–1. But the *Advertiser* seemed pleased. "The Chinks made a hit with the crowd by their clean and fast playing and the good will they exhibited when [two of the soldiers] were hurt. The rooters treated them kindly. It was the best game of the year at this post and everybody left in good humor."[119]

Within a week, Hop refused another challenge from a "Picked Nine" of Honolulu's best players. Hop, according to the *Advertiser*, declared that the All-Chinese would play the Oahu League champion before settling for a game against the Picked Nine. He confided to the press, "If we play the champions and we lick them, then we are the champions of Hawaii, ourselves." The *Advertiser* was persuaded that Hop would have turned down the Picked Nine's offer anyway since it did not guarantee the All-Chinese 60 percent of the gate, win or lose.[120]

Hop's alleged greed provoked criticism from one Honolulu fan, who complained to the *Advertiser* that "since the mainland tour, [the All-Chinese] think they are everything here in baseball." The collective ego of the All-Chinese had gotten a little too big, according to the fan, and "that swelling should be rubbed down right away quick." To be sure, the fan conceded, the All-Chinese had improved but not to the extent that they should expect 60 percent of the gate, win or lose. More bluntly, another fan remarked, "I like the idea of the All-Chinese, not." A veteran ballplayer insisted that Hop's aggregation "stood out for the hog's measure" of the gate receipts. Loitering perhaps a bit too much in nostalgic reveries, he insisted that he and his comrades played baseball for the sake of sport. If money exchanged hands, he added, that was fine and good, but it was not essential.[121]

On the positive side, the swift outfielder En Sue Pung earned plaudits from the *Advertiser*, which described the former track star as "the premier Chinese athlete" and the best all-around athlete on the islands. Deception and speed defined En Sue Pung's game. The *Advertiser* wryly observed, "He should have been arrested quite a number of times, but the police claim they are powerless as the laws of the country do not cover base stealing." Vernon Ayau, in the meantime, seemingly received more than just local commendations. While with the Travelers in Michigan, Ayau had impressed the Michigan Central League officials, who were reportedly willing to sign the shortstop for the 1913 season.[122]

Meanwhile, Sam Hop had confided by mail to Nat Strong that the Travelers were generally having their way with other Hawaiian teams. Strong wrote back that he was pleased that the nine was doing well and looked forward to the Hawaiians' return to the mainland the next year. Strong advised Hop to make sure he put together the best team possible even if it meant provoking the ire of local fans. While Strong was "tickled to see that the boys upheld their reputation as ball players in Hawaii," Hop needed to assemble a good pitching staff.[123]

For baseball fans, *Spalding's Official College Baseball Annual, 1913*, offered an interesting summary and critique of the Travelers' inaugural journey to the mainland. The fact that the Hawaiian team was explored in a publication devoted to college baseball proves how well mainlanders bought in to the ruse that the Travelers represented an actual Hawaiian university. The *Annual*, in any event, declared that the Hawaiians "were treated with courtesy and respect wherever they appeared." Moreover, their play improved as their length of stay on the mainland was extended.[124]

The *Annual* focused, unsurprisingly, on the Fordham game. It purported that a large crowd showed up at the Polo Grounds, anticipating a "rather farcical exhibition of the National Game." Instead, spectators witnessed an excellent college game that "illustrated the ability of the Chinese to play baseball of a high caliber." Celebrating baseball's growing global presence, the *Annual* quoted in one baseball expert, who, after watching the Fordham game, insisted, "The way [the Travelers] play is one more proof that base ball's popularity is reaching the international stage." As far as this expert was concerned, "There isn't much to choose between this rather unique team, for it is the first Chinese college team that has ever played in this country, and the average American university nine."[125]

TWO

The "Yellow Peril" at Bat, 1913

As the New Year turned, Sam Hop continued to attract criticism from the local press. On New Year's Day of 1913, the *Star-Bulletin* published a panel of cartoons showing various local athletic personalities. For Sam Hop, the daily made a New Year's resolution, proclaiming, "I will not ask Yale to give the All-Chinese ball team, 95 per cent, win or lose." Still, the *Star-Bulletin* had to admit that the Travelers delighted Honolulu fans and played better than other local clubs, perhaps because of their long stay on the mainland.[1]

Since no single club in Honolulu typically could take on the All-Chinese and expect a victory, "all-star" teams were organized to match up with the Travelers. During the second half of January, a team of former and present "school boy" stars were assembled to play the All-Chinese. A few of these young men would eventually compete for the Travelers. Formerly of Punahou and presently attending Oahu College, Fred Markham served as team captain. The *Star-Bulletin* praised Markham, called Denny by the local press, as a "big leaguer of some experience." T. Moriyama was another all-star who hailed from St. Louis College. A brother of another fine Japanese Hawaiian ballplayer, "the famous Chinito," T. Moriyama was called "a clever player" by the *Star-Bulletin*. Foster Robinson, who also went to St. Louis, would take the box for the "All-Students."[2]

Around 2,500 fans were drawn to the game, won by the All-Chinese. It was clear to the *Star-Bulletin* reporter in attendance that the All-Students had little experience playing with one another, "while the Chinese, as usual, played like a well-oiled machine." Robinson did well, inspiring the *Star-Bulletin* to linger over his "double life" as an All-Students starter and a future hurler for the Travelers. Since he would journey to the mainland with Sam Hop and company, Robinson's last name, the daily predicted, would undergo a change since it "has anything but an Oriental sound." The *Star-Bulletin* speculated incorrectly that he would pitch in Chicago and New York City as "Loo Sun," while assuring readers that since he was "part-Chinese," Robinson was eligible for the Travelers.³

Interestingly, the *Honolulu Star-Bulletin* reported that a prominent Chinese Honolulan, Kim Tong Ho, had assumed the management of the traveling team. Perhaps so, but the Travelers remained very much an operation in Sam Hop's hands. Kim Tong Ho, according to the *Star-Bulletin*, had attended Oahu College before heading to the mainland to attend the University of Wisconsin. Ho, in any event, headed up a team called the "Simon Pures" in an inter-squad game against the Long Runs, run by Sam Hop. In honor of the Chinese New Year in early February, the game pitted Foster Robinson, who would often be called Ah Heong on the mainland, against the veteran All-Chinese ace, Luck Yee. The game also showcased Hawaiians wishing to make the traveling team. Robinson, pitching for Hop's nine, got the better of the match-up as the Long Runs won, 4–1. Lai Tin, described as "the speedy third baseman of the All-Chinese," hurt his ankle and knee while trying to make "his famous hook slide" into second. His injury meant that he could no longer run track for McKinley High School.⁴

Lai Tin must have gotten better fairly quickly, because he sought to enter an AAU sanctioned track meet in Honolulu, along with Travelers teammates En Sue Pung and S.H. Hoe. However, the three athletes were barred from the meet because, according to the local AAU, they were actually professional athletes who earned money playing for the Travelers. The three denied the charge, claiming they played baseball out of love for the sport rather than for any money. Hoe, in particular, resented the AAU's action. He protested to the press that none of the ballplayers received salaries for playing on the mainland, although Hoe conceded that they got $25 a month for what he termed "incidentals." Hoe, moreover, accused the AAU of hypocrisy, pointing out that other Honolulu ballplayers had played games locally for gate receipts and were allowed to participate in the meet. Hoe said he just wanted a "square deal." As it turned out, neither he nor Lai Tin nor En Sue got that "square deal."⁵

Lai Tin was one of the most popular players on the 1913 All-Chinese squad, according to the *Pacific Commercial Advertiser*. The daily published on March 11, 1913, a photograph of the teenage ballplayer with a caption, "Al third baseman of the All-Chinese baseball team." Accompanying the photograph was an article which declared, "Among the crack players of the All-Chinese baseball team, now on the eve of a second trip to the mainland, there is probably no one better liked by the fans and fanettes who have made Athletic Park their Sunday afternoon home than Lai Tin, third baseman and all around athlete." The article went on to describe Lai Tin as unaffected and calm under the duress of playing third base. The *Advertiser* maintained, "All good sports doff their baseball caps to Lai. May the Tin never grow thinner."[6]

The All-African American 25th regiment, stationed in Honolulu, was represented by one baseball team that could give the Travelers a run for their money. On March 10, the 25th edged the Travelers, 2–1. Unfortunately, the game was tainted by controversy. Late in the contest, En Sue Pung laid down a bunt fielded by Waterhouse, the pitcher for the 25th. Waterhouse overthrew first but the ball was knocked down by the field umpire before it could get out of reach. The first baseman then threw out En Sue Pung out as he scampered to third. The Travelers and their supporters complained that the umpire, who happened to be a member of the 25th contingent, had allowed his bias to subvert the game's outcome. The *Star-Bulletin* argued that the umpire's actions may have been instinctive, but did not rule out the possibility of partiality. The stormy ending to the game was regrettable to the daily, which maintained that the 25th played well enough to win and comported themselves admirably. Yet it doubted if the 25th would get another game at Athletic Park and was certain that the "Chinese" would not play the "colored ball tossers" again. The offending umpire, William Patterson, proclaimed his innocence. He dubiously protested that he had no need to protect the 25th because the African American ballplayers were clearly the superior team that day.[7]

Not exactly mollified, Albert Akana told the press that the Travelers had encountered bad umpires on the mainland, mostly in small towns where the arbiters were determined to make sure the locals would not lose to a team of non-whites. However, he declared that what happened in the game against the 25th was the "worst robbery we have been up against." Blaming the 25th for what happened near first base and not all that much aware of the irony of what he was saying, Akana swore that his team would never take on the African American nine again even if offered $1,000 to do so.[8]

The *Star-Bulletin*'s sports editor, Lawrence Reddington, declared that the controversial game was "one of the prettiest" he had ever witnessed. To be sure, Reddington added, the umpire in question had blundered. But the 25th ball team need not be blamed. Indeed, Reddington thought the military ballplayers were disturbed by the field umpire's refusal to listen to the All-Chinese complaints.[9]

Honolulu base fans in general clamored for a rematch between the 25th and the Travelers. The 25th's ballplayers were willing to oppose the Travelers again and the team manager, Lieutenant Saunders, said the Chinese Hawaiians could name their umpires. The *Star-Bulletin* repeated that the Chinese Hawaiian team ought not to discredit the 25th nine for the actions of an African American umpire, maintaining that "even the Chinese themselves must admit these soldiers play a fair, clean, and thoroughly sportsmanlike game." Honolulu's baseball world deserved a rematch, the daily added. The game would make money, so Hop's nine ought to be interested since "nobody is accusing the Chinese of being slack in the box office." Moreover, if the All-Chinese departed for the mainland without playing the 25th, speculation would rise that the Chinese Hawaiians were afraid of the African American ballplayers.[10]

On March 17, a St. Patrick's Day game was scheduled between the All-Chinese and the 25th. The *Star-Bulletin* enthused, "Cosmopolitan Hawaii fittingly celebrated the Irish national holiday with an exhibition of the American national game, given by an All-Chinese team. About seventeen other nationalities witnessed the contest. Truly it was a representative gathering of the nations." The Chinese managed only three hits, but still won, 7–1, thanks to the wildness of the 25th's pitchers. In contrast, Foster Robinson did well as Ah Heong. En Sue Pung backed him up by covering a lot of ground in center field. Hapa haole Fred Markham made some errors at second base but showed promise. The game drew well, even though it was played during midweek. The umpiring by Captain Norris Stayton, a European American attached to the Coast Artillery Corps, earned praise from the *Star-Bulletin*.[11]

As the team prepared to depart, the *Star-Bulletin* urged readers to give the Travelers a good send-off by attending their last games in Honolulu for several months. The Travelers deserved respect, the daily asserted, because they had shown a better brand of baseball than had been seen on the islands in a long time. Honolulu baseball fans especially should make sure to say good-bye to Luck Yee as the "handsome" pitcher intended to attend an Eastern college after the Travelers' tour ended, although he wound up going to the College of Hawai'i instead.[12]

Before the largely Chinese Hawaiian contingent left for the mainland, Honolulu newspapers published a letter of appreciation to the baseball fans of the islands' biggest city for their support. The letter was signed by the team and individually by assistant captain, Apau Kau, and team manager Sam Hop. While referring to themselves as the "All-Chinese Baseball Team" despite Markham's presence on the roster, the letter writers apparently wanted readers to think of them as Hawaiian rather than just Chinese. They promised, "While we are in the States for the next few months, we will do our very best to uphold the fair name of dear old Hawaii." They regretted that team captain Albert Akana was not able to make the trip and added, "Although we are going to be far away from you, we will always remember the good people of Hawaii. As time does not permit, we will simply have to say Aloha Nuui now."[13]

In the hours before departure, the Travelers looked like they were going to leave without not only Albert Akana but also Vernon Ayau. The *Star-Bulletin* feared for the "perfection of team work that made the Orientals such a dangerous combination." Hopefully, Markham would fill the void left by Ayau's absence. Admittedly, "there's nothing Chinese about Markham," but he could take over third handily while Lai Tin moved to shortstop. Akana, however, would be tough to replace. The *Star-Bulletin* praised his cool leadership, expecting either Kan Yen Chun or Lai Tin to assume the duties of team captain. As it turned out, Ayau made the trek at the last minute, thus encouraging the *Star-Bulletin* to predict that the Travelers were at least 50 percent better than their 1912 counterparts.[14]

Meanwhile, the *Advertiser* published a photograph of the barnstorming ballplayers. Notably, the caption told readers that players with Anglicized names would be known on the mainland by Chinese names. Not only would pitcher Foster Robinson be called Ah Heong, but Markham would be called Ah Pawaa. In addition, outfielder Henry Kuali would play on the mainland as Ah Lee. As it turned out, Markham would generally be listed in box scores as "Mark."[15]

A Hawaiian-based publication expected the team to do very well on the mainland. The April 1913 edition of the *Paradise of the Pacific* bragged about the "Chinese team" heading to the "American continent" and "making a clean sweep of victories." The publication proved only slightly wrong, as the team won much more than half of its scheduled games.[16]

Sporting Life prepared mainland baseball fans for the return of the Hawaiian barnstormers. Early in February, *Sporting Life* observed that the "Chinese" were coming back to the mainland. It commended the visiting team for "put[ting] up a classy article of our national game last year in this country." The March 8 edition quoted Captain "Ankana" that the visitors would constitute a "strong" nine.[17]

The Hawaiian nine started the tour off well and kept winning throughout its journey across the mainland. The Pacific Mail Steamship Company identified the following as making the trek across the Pacific to the U.S. mainland: F.L. Akana, C. Asong Akina, V.L. Ayau, Chun Kwan Yuen, Ho Sin Hung, Kau Tin Pau, Kuali, Lai Tin, Lau Luck Yee, D. Markham, Pung En Sue, F. Robinson, and Wong Mow Yep, otherwise known as Sam Hop. Subsequently, the *San Francisco Chronicle* noted the arrival of the Hawaiian ballplayers in its city. It told readers that while heading to the U.S. mainland on *The China*, Lang Akana and his teammates entertained passengers with their singing and musicianship. They performed, according to the *Chronicle*, "plaintive Hawaiian airs and on occasion some lively rag for the dancing coterie." The *Chronicle* also announced that the Hawaiian nine expected to tour the U.S. mainland for eight months, while the ballplayers expressed confidence "that they could show their white brothers of this country a new wrinkle or two in baseball." The *Chronicle* pointed out that the Hawaiian ballplayers were "sprightly Chinese [who] are said to be sure fielders and can use their 'chop sticks' to good advantage."[18]

Oakland newspapers acknowledged the Travelers' arrival. To the *Oakland Enquirer*, the Hawaiians athletes were "Oriental Ball Tossers" and "Mongolian exponents of our national game." To the *Oakland Tribune*, the visitors were "slant-eyed boys." In any event, the *Tribune* cautioned, opponents would have to "look to their laurels" if the "Oriental baseball team" was as good as advertised.[19]

The *San Francisco Call* ran a photo of the team in jackets and ties on board *The China*. The title to the photo and the accompanying article read: "Chinese Baseball Team In Our Midst." The *Call* declared:

> That our national pastime is creeping around the world is shown by the fact the game is being played in various parts of the world. The latest arrivals to show what they have done in mastering the great game is a team of Chinese under the guidance of Sam Hop. They are real Chinks, though not from China. They come from the Chinese University of Hawaii and are natives of the islands. They reached our shores yesterday on the liner China.... From reports the slant-eyed athletes have mastered the game in a surprising manner.... It is not many years ago since the first American baseball team invaded Hawaii and the far orient. Now comes a team to show the originators of the game how they have learned the sport. The University of Hawaii team should prove a good attraction while here.[20]

In the San Francisco Bay Area, the Hawaiians beat Stanford, 7–3, after the first scheduled game against Cal was cancelled due to inclement weather. The next day the *San Francisco Chronicle* announced, "Suppers were late on the Stanford campus and in Palo Alto due to culinary celebration and kitchen fannings over the Chinese victory." Under the headline of "Hawaii Chinese Down Stanford in Baseball," the campus newspaper declared that the "Chinese baseball team" was helped by the "Oriental delivery of Aheong," otherwise known as Foster Robinson. "The Mongolians had a fast infield and put up a good snappy brand of ball," the *Daily Palo Alto* maintained. S.H. Hoe subsequently claimed that Stanford pled it was at a disadvantage because its best pitcher was not in the box. Noting the victory in Palo Alto, the *Racine Journal-News* in Wisconsin asserted that "passing out the white wash is an inherent trait of the Chinks we presume."[21]

Staying in the Bay Area, the Hawaiians defeated Oakland's St. Mary's nine. Before the game started, the *Oakland Tribune* counseled fans that "the Orientals are a fast bunch of tossers and have mastered the difficult and inside tricks of baseball until they are as adept as many of our Coast Leaguers." The game ended in the Hawaiians' favor, 12–11, but, according to the *San Francisco Call's* Bob Strand, the game would not have been so close "had Sam Hop and his aggregation of ball tossers from the Chinese University of Hawaii not started to kid the St. Mary's College team."[22]

Not providing much in the way of details, Strand continued in an article titled "Chinese Prove Handy With The Bat," "The slant-eyed athletes gathered the spoils ... but they had the St. Mary's lads buffaloed until they became too sure of victory and started a lot of funny stuff. The Oakland students resented being kidded, and they came back with a rally in the ninth inning which almost brought them victory."[23]

Strand assured readers that there was nothing freakish about what happened at the Oak- land ballpark. "The Chinese know how to play ball. They are fast as lightning on the bases and toss in bunches of inside ball. They have the delayed steal and the double steal down pat and they know how to acquire base hits when such things are necessary." Foster Robinson impressed Strand as a pitcher. He wrote, "The Hawaiian heaver had the Oaklanders breaking their backs trying to connect with the curves." However, the "Celestial" starter tired and gave way to Apau Kau, who had less luck keeping the now aroused St. Mary's bats quiet. En Sue Pung and Lai Tin also struck Strand with their athleticism. "Ensue," Strand declared, "the center fielder of the Chinese team is about the fastest piece of humanity seen on a local lot in many a day. [He] showed his speed yesterday by stealing five bases and scoring three runs. He also swung in with a couple of safe clouts." As for Lai Tin, he was "another speed burner who runs like a deer." Despite the offense the Travelers displayed, S.H. Hoe remembered that the team played like "they still had their sea legs" against St. Mary's.[24]

Moving across the Sierras, the Hawaiians played in Colorado and Utah. Hoe recalled that the cold bothered the island visitors, some of whom had never seen snow. Arriving in Colorado Springs, a local newspaper described the Travelers as a team possessing speed and plenty of good hitters. Just prior to their arrival, the *Colorado Springs Gazette* reported, the Travelers in general and En Sue Pung, in particular, thrilled "Mormon" fans in Salt Lake City. Unfortunately, snow prevented Colorado Springs fans from enjoying the same opportunity.[25]

The Hawaiians performed well before crossing the Mississippi. In Utah, the "All-Chinese team of Honolulu" ran into and over an Ogden-based semi-professional team, 7–2. Prior to the game, the *Ogden Examiner* reported Sam Hop's confidence in his traveling nine. Hop ostensibly maintained that the 1913 Travelers were "thousands of times" better than they were in 1912. To Hop the primary area of progress was in hitting, but he disclosed that the pitching had improved as well. Still, a pitiful attendance of 100 showed up in Ogden to watch the Hawaiians rap out 15 hits, while Luck Yee surrendered only two hits. Readers of the *Advertiser* learned that foul weather kept attendance down. Still, the shivering fans saw some "sensational" baseball. An A.P. report informed readers that the "All-Chinese baseball team" outlasted the University of Kansas nine, 8–5, in their second match-up. The game was reportedly close and exciting throughout. But "the crack team of Americanized Chinese from the Hawaiian Islands" triumphed due to their better "base running and stick work." A good crowd watched the game "and the greatest interest was taken by all in the admirable work of the visitors." Another A.P. article painted a glowing picture of the Hawaiians' performance in Ames, Iowa, where the local college team was put down, 3–0. The AP correspondent declared, "The game was the prettiest and closest of the season and drew out an enthusiastic crowd of fans who greatly admired the playing of the visitors."[26]

From Missouri, "the genial Sam Hop" wrote the *Star-Bulletin* that the tour was going very well. He reported that the Hawaiian ballplayers had arrived in St. Louis on April 25 and would soon leave for Rolla, Missouri, to take on the Missouri School of Mines. Hop boasted that the Travelers had won 18 games so far while suffering but five losses, all of which, Hop emphasized, were inflicted by "professional" teams and reinforced by bad weather. No college nine had conquered the Hawaiian ballplayers, Hop proudly proclaimed. The "boys are well," Hop maintained, "and enjoying the trip." Hop closed "with Aloha to all."[27]

Moving into the Great Lakes region, the Hawaiians moved Wisconsin's *Eau Claire Leader* to publish a photo of the "Chinese team" and advise readers that the visitors would appear in town to play the Eau Claire Continentals. The newspaper assured readers as well that every member of the visiting team was "a real Chinaman." It pointed out that Native American and African American ballplayers had performed in Eau Claire, but the town had never seen "Celestials" in baseball uniforms before. Moreover, the visitors were good; they knew something about the "American pastime."[28]

Outfielder Sing Hung Hoe dispatched several reports to the *Star-Bulletin* over the course of the 1913 trek. From Burlington, Iowa, on April 27, he declared that the Travelers were improving as they headed eastward and enjoyed better weather. "They have been on the road long enough now," he added, "to get used to constant traveling, and the long jumps between games are not spoiling the play as at first." Missouri's Westminster College was expected to give the Hawaiians a tough game. Hoe said that the college had "never" lost a game in football, soccer, or baseball. Furthermore, the college nine featured a "Cuban" pitcher who "would surely puzzle the Chinese." Still, the Hawaiians got 11 hits while cruising to a 9–5 victory.[29]

An injury to Kan Yen Chun changed things a bit. The catcher had to switch to first base after hurting his hand behind the plate. Identified as the

Notre Dame University inflicted the first loss on the Travelers by a college team in 1913 (courtesy of the Notre Dame University Archives).

"field" manager of the team, he was still able to help his team beat Rollins College in Missouri. The multi-talented Markham took over as catcher. The game was not easy, according to Sam Hop and Kan Yen Chun. The Rollins pitcher was good, Kan Yen Chun later lamented. His curve was working and the Hawaiians had a hard time staying patient as they anxiously hacked at low pitches. "But," Kan Yen Chun concluded, "we won the game and that's all that we came for."[30]

Soon, Honolulans discovered that the Los Angeles Angels of the Pacific Coast League were reportedly scouting Kan Yen Chun and Foster Robinson. The *Star-Bulletin* conceded that Robinson ought to lure interest from mainland pro teams, but it doubted that Kan Yen Chun would inspire much demand. The *Star-Bulletin* hailed Kan Yen Chun as a good catcher. However, it did not think he was physically strong enough to handle the heavy load of a PCL backstop. Several months later, the Angels were still attached to the idea of signing Robinson. A mainland newspaper described the Maui native as "part-Chinese" and the "Honolulu club's star pitcher with speed, control, and curves."[31]

The Hawaiians' first loss to a college nine occurred at South Bend, Indiana, where they ran into a fine Notre Dame nine. S.H. Hoe did not exactly blame the defeat on the weather, but he insisted in *Baseball Magazine* that the "game of snowballs" was played in South Bend. The experience was "distinctly new to us — as the grounds were covered with snow." Lathrop, the Notre Dame pitcher, also certainly had a hand in the Hawaiian defeat. Hoe recalled that a Notre Dame student told the visitors that Lathrop was the only reason "you China boys" lost.[32]

On May 17, the *Star-Bulletin* published a series of dispatches from S.H. Hoe on games played from mid–April to early May. On April 16, Manhattan College, now Kansas State, hosted the Hawaiians and generously offered them a victory, 7–3. Hoe remarked that En Sue, "Ah Lee" or Henry Kuali, and Luck Yee led the team. Hoe must have sent along clippings which informed Honolulu readers that one Kansas sportswriter considered the local team "a little out of the" visitors' class."[33]

Continuing their journeys in the Midwest, the Travelers easily handled a nine representing Knox College in Galesburg, Illinois, on April 28. The game ended 12–2 and could have been worse but was rushed because the visitors had to catch a train for Ames, Iowa. Hoe reported that Luck Yee struck out eight Knox College batters in "pretty cold 54 degrees" weather. While in Ames, Apau Kau shut out Iowa State and the Hawaiians won, 4–0. A nice crowd of 3,000 attended the game on April 29, according to Hoe, who also declared that Iowa State coach George Clark was slated to pitch against the Travelers. Clark had once hurled in the major leagues for the "New York

Americans." However, Iowa State's eligibility committee justly banned Clark from the mound.³⁴

While in Minnesota, Hoe informed hometown readers that the Travelers had mastered the University of Minnesota team, 15–5. Hoe assured the *Star-Bulletin* that his teammates were in "fine fettle" even though the team was crisscrossing the Midwest daily. He had no complaints about how the host colleges treated the Hawaiians, adding that En Sue Pung's play inspired "fans and fannettes" in the Midwest.³⁵

From Delaware, Ohio, Hoe told the *Star-Bulletin* in a correspondence published on May 31 that the college season on the mainland was drawing to a close. Hoe did not seem to shed tears over the matter as he conceded that contesting college teams was not earning the Hawaiians much money. He could recall only one game in Columbia, Missouri, that helped the Travelers meet expenses. At that game, a crowd of 1,226 watched the proceedings. The split on gate receipts for the Hawaiians was 50/50 according to Hoe. And, apparently, 50 percent of not much offered cold comfort to Hoe and his teammates.³⁶

Notwithstanding the monetary problems facing the Travelers, Hoe seemed gratified that the team had encountered several Honolulu acquaintances on their journey. For example, a Hawaiian named John McCandless threw a banquet for the Travelers after they beat Ohio Northwestern in Ada, Ohio. McCandless apparently went to Ohio Northwestern, but was not at all put out over his college's team loss to the Hawaiians. Hoe, moreover, reported that he and his teammates serenaded "the little college town" after the banquet.³⁷

Dipping southward, the Hawaiians took on the Kentucky State University nine on May 23. According to the *Lexington Herald*, "the little copper colored men" won, 7–1. The *Herald* praised the work of "Lucky" as pitcher, as well as "Captain Kanyin." Moreover, the visitors "ran wild on the bases" against the Kentuckians. Curiously, the *Herald* informed readers that the Hawaiians came from four colleges of the "University of Hawaii." The visiting ballplayers spoke three languages—English, Hawaiian, and Chinese. Several were "full-blooded Chinese," while most were "Chinese and Hawaiian." In any event, the *Herald* insisted, "They are a fine set of men and would be a credit to any American institution."³⁸

In the wake of the Travelers' victory in Kentucky, dissension surfaced among the Hawaiians. The talented shortstop Vernon Ayau was reportedly "sulking" and "benched for insubordination." Ayau's teammates were said to have referred sarcastically to Ayau's "fine spirit so far away from home." Indeed, he was almost shipped back to Honolulu. Kan Yen Chun took over for Ayau at shortstop, while Markham assumed the duties of catcher. Eventually, however, the breech in the ranks of the Travelers was ostensibly healed.³⁹

At the University of Illinois, the Hawaiians played a nine composed of students ineligible for the varsity baseball team because they had had played professionally or had poor grades. Previously, the school newspaper announced that the Travelers wanted to oppose the university nine on dates that conflicted with the latter's set schedule. The university's "Chinese students" especially wanted to see Travelers in action, leading the athletic director to allow the Hawaiians to play the "Ineligibles" if students truly wanted such a game. He also declared that since the game would not be "regular," the university would not honor season tickets and any proceeds would go to the university hospital. In any event, according to the *Urbana Daily Courier*, the "Chinamen Beat Varsity Orphans." The game started badly for the "Celestial Ball Team" as the Orphans pitcher "initiated the little fellows into a new brand of fan-tan." Then he lost his stuff and "the Chinese batting demons" had their way with "the white twirler."[40]

The Ohio town of Elyria greeted the Hawaiian ballplayers with interest and media hype. The May 13 edition of the *Elyria Evening Telegram* announced that the visitors would oppose the local Elyria Athletics. On May 15, readers discovered an advertisement promoting a coming game between "Chinese University of Hawaii" and the local Elyria town nine. The advertisement urged baseball fans to attend the "Special Attraction," as "this will be your only opportunity to see these wonderful little players from the Orient." In the daily's sports section, a featured article noted that the Hawaiians had just beaten Northern Ohio University, 8–2, and stressed that local fans had an opportunity to see a "real Chinese team in action" for the first time. It also quoted from another, unnamed newspaper to the effect that peace reigned among the tongs inhabiting an unspecified Chinatown. Instead of committing acts of violence,

> members of rival tongs gather nightly over the "black smoke" [and] tell of the prowess of Goo Sun, Kan Yen Chun and Lai Tin, who are not, as you might suspect, mighty warriors or lawmakers of some bygone dynasty, but members of the Chinese University of Hawaii baseball team, now touring the United States.

The *Telegram* informed readers that "Goo Sun, Lai Tin & Co" had shouldered a rigorous, game-a-day schedule, similar to that of the "big leagues." This schedule "goes to show that the Chinese athletes have evidently discovered the secret of getting into condition, hitting up a winning pace and holding it." The *Telegram* predicted that the Hawaiians would face stiffer competition from college teams in the East and that a "battle royal ... will follow" when the they face the Williams College nine, winners of the intercollegiate championship in 1912.[41]

On May 15, the Hawaiians defeated Oberlin College, and the next day the Elyria Athletics. Pitcher Foster Robinson, just called Foster in the *Telegram's* account of the Oberlin game, and catcher Markham or Mark formed an effective battery for the "Chinese University of Hawaii," while Ayau and "Ensue" made spectacular fielding plays at shortstop and center field respectively. After the defeat of the Elyria Athletics, the *Telegram* published a game description titled "Chinamen Show Big League Class and Continue Streak of Victories 8 to 5." The article praised the skill of the "Chinese University team," especially the battery of Apau and Mark, as well as the fielding of "Ensue." It also mentioned that the Hawaiians were able to fool an Elyria base runner with the hidden ball trick. But the *Evening Telegram*, like other mainland dailies, also used terms such as "Foreigners," "Chinamen" and "Chinks" to describe the Hawaiian ballplayers.[42]

On the East Coast, the Hawaiians played plenty of games and received plenty of publicity. A wire story from Pittsburgh late in May announced that "the Chink team has real class." In early June, the Travelers defeated Penn State, 4–1. The Hawaiian pitcher Apau Kau, according to the *Washington Post*, "proved an enigma" to the Pennsylvanians. Hoe maintained that the final score was actually 5–2 in the Hawaiians' favor. He declared that the game featured a tight pitching duel between Apau Kau and the Penn State hurler. It took an extra-inning squeeze bunt by Apau Kau to bring in Lai Tin and put the Hawaiians up for good. A wire story in the *Washington Post* called the contest with Penn State "the fastest game seen here this year." On June 21, the formidable Williams College nine edged the Hawaiians, 5–4, after the Travelers managed to tie the score during the top of the ninth.[43]

In July, the *Washington Post* ran an article occasioned by the Hawaiian ballplayers attending a game in New York City between the New York Giants and the Brooklyn Dodgers. The article began, "There's a real yellow peril in baseball now!" The Hawaiians had achieved baseball supremacy over mainland teams, according to the *Post*. That is, "the Chinese University of Hawaii" had won 64 of 65 games thus far on its 1913 tour over "strong college and professional nines." That the Hawaiians had done so well "is all the more remarkable when it is considered that they have been playing our diamond game in Hawaii for only a few years." Of course, this was wrong. Hawaiians had been playing baseball for almost as long as most mainlanders. The *Post* observed that while watching the Giants-Dodgers game, the Travelers showed a "surprising" knowledge of baseball and lack of adherence to the "laundryman" stereotype. "The Honolulu students speak English fluently. There's nothing of the collar and cuff about them. Each one, from big Kan Yan to little Ensue has followed the big leagues." They knew about the Giants and "most of the Dodger celebrities also were well known to their little yellow brothers." The *Post* observed that all of the Hawaiian ballplayers kept score but that probably the two most interested spectators among them were pitcher "Foster Robertson [*sic*] ... the Matty of the Far East" and "Kan Yen the Hans Wagner of the team." The *Post* declared incorrectly that the "Celestial" pitcher's real Chinese name was "Aheong."[44]

The *Post* then focused on manager Sam Hop and pitcher Foster Robinson. It remarked, "Sam Hop ... with just a slight tussle with the English language told why the Chinamen were so successful on the diamond and how the sport was introduced in Hawaii." Hop, according to the *Post*, erroneously claimed that baseball was transported to Hawai'i in 1898 when Albert Spalding brought his all-star team of major leaguers to the islands. But Hawaiian ballplayers, such as those he managed, had learned the game quickly and well. "We have studied your ways a lot. The boys know what you call inside stuff—that is, to play with their heads as well as their hands. They are good athletes. Five members ... are football players. Third Baseman Lai Tin is a fast sprinter." Indeed, the *Post* declared, "Manager Sam Hop delighted in telling how wonderful the men were on the bases. Because of their great speed the players never stop when once on the bases, and their daring running has caused many a catcher to feel like changing his laundry." Called the "PE director of the Chinese University of Hawaii " by the *Post*, Hop was quoted as saying that 15,000 fans regularly watched his team on the islands—a bit more than an exaggeration. Moreover, he told the *Post*, "The Chinamen are all fans. They root good and hard." The *Post* described Foster Robinson as an 18-year-old who had been playing baseball since he was a youngster. Robinson claimed that he had a good "in and out curve and a slow ball." He added, "Lately, I have perfected the spitter and can use it with fairly good control."[45]

New York City and its environs offered the Hawaiians many games and at least some recreation. "The Chinese players of the College of Hawaii" beat Long Island University, 8–2, in June. The *Washington Post* remarked that "Four thousand skeptical 'fans' went home fully convinced that the Orientals could play real American baseball." Within a week, the *Brooklyn Eagle* informed readers that "Chinese Students" beat the Cypress Hills nine, 8–7, at Dexter Park. "The Heathen Chinee," the *Eagle* purported, used a "sly trick" to deceive those in attendance into thinking that the home team was on its way to victory. Then the visitors grabbed the lead in the late innings and would not give it up. On June 21, the Ridgewood Club pulled out an extra-inning victory over the Hawaiians before 7,000–8,000 fans. The *Eagle* described the game as the best played on the Ridgewood Grounds that season, adding "the Chinamen are well versed in the American game and pulled off some smart plays." Kan Yen Chun managed to excite the crowd with a homer in the 11th inning. On July 6, the Hawaiians savaged the Danbury Athletic Club at Olympic Park, 13–0. *Boston Globe* readers learned that 7,000 watched

the "Chinamen" win and "Foster" pitch superbly for the "Mongolians." Subsequently, some controversy arose over the Danbury game. Organized baseball's National Commission investigated the charge that the host team misrepresented themselves as the Danbury affiliate of the New Jersey–New York minor league. In actuality, according to the accusation, the losing team was comprised of non-professional New York City boys.[46]

On July 4, Hoe wrote to the *Star-Bulletin* that the Hawaiians were resting in New York City—shopping, sight-seeing, and just enjoying their temporary freedom from "the grind of daily games." Hoe confessed that "this has been a strenuous trip, although a grand success from the standpoint of baseball and Hawaii publicity." Later in the month, Hoe reiterated that the team was enjoying itself immensely in New York City and experienced "no dissension" in the ranks. Still, he conceded that it was a long way from New York City to Honolulu and the team would welcome the journey home.[47]

Nat Strong, Hoe reported, escorted the visitors to Coney Island, where they had a great time among thousands of fun-seekers. The ballplayers took in a prizefight at St. Nicholas Athletic Club. They were introduced by the fight announcer and reportedly received a standing ovation. In addition, they witnessed several big league ball games, featuring teams such as the Chicago White Sox, Washington Senators, Cleveland Indians, Brooklyn Dodgers, Chicago Cubs, Philadelphia Athletics, and New York Yankees. Hoe added that the team had "been very fortunate in always being the guests of the management." When watching a New York Giants game at the Polo Grounds, the Travelers were accommodated to three boxes along the first base line. Furthermore, John McGraw, the Giants' famed manager, and Artie Shafer, a fine player for the upper Manhattan-based team, came over to visit with the Hawaiians for awhile.[48]

Charles Ebbets also invited "the Chinese baseball team from Hawaii" to Brooklyn's Ebbets Field. "The yellow men" were reportedly engrossed in watching Brooklyn's pitcher Earl Yingling because, as a piece in the *Syracuse Herald* maintained, they heard Yingling was a "fellow countryman." Although Yingling was European American, the Hawaiians expressed pleasure when he got a hit. They cheered, moreover, when catcher "Chief" Meyers took off his

Opposite: While in New York City, the Travelers spent a great deal of time at the Polo Grounds watching the New York Giants. Apparently, manager John McGraw considered the Hawaiians something of a good luck charm. In 1928, McGraw would give Lai Tin, then known as Buck Lai, a chance to make his famed team. In this 1913 photograph, McGraw is sitting eighth from the left in the front row. Seventh from the left is the great Christy Mathewson. Standing fourth from the right is the remarkable, versatile Native American athlete, Jim Thorpe (courtesy of Library of Congress, Prints & Photographs Division, LC-DIG-ggbain-13891).

mask. Then, *Herald* readers learned, they were told by an "interpreter" that Meyers was an Indian. These readers also learned that the Hawaiian ballplayers "appreciated the finer points of the game." It is possible that the Travelers did not know about Yingling's ethnic heritage, but given how much publicity Honolulu papers gave big league baseball and that many of the Travelers had been on the American mainland for several months, it is doubtful that they were ignorant of the well-known fact that "Chief" Meyers was a Native American.[49]

At least one of New York City's big league clubs was keeping a keen eye on En Sue Pung. According to Nat Strong, Hoe reported, the Brooklyn Dodgers sought the swift outfielder's services. Hoe maintained, moreover, that other Travelers such as Foster Robinson, Kan Yen Chun, and Vernon Ayau, who reportedly caught the attention of the Detroit Tigers in 1912, had attracted interest from mainland professional franchises.[50]

The *New York Evening World* acknowledged the Hawaiians' stay in the city with a cartoon reproduced in the *Star-Bulletin* of July 30. The cartoon showed "pigtail Chinese" trying to play baseball. These ballplayers represented Chinese laundry workers in the big city "on strike" from their usual occupation in order to take up baseball. The cartoon's caption read, "Chinese Team Has Ruined New York's Laundry Business." The *Star-Bulletin* could only surmise that "Chinese athletes of class were a novelty back east."[51]

New York's Chinese community honored the Hawaiians. The Chinese Association of New York treated the visiting ballplayers with a dinner at a local Chinese restaurant. Connie Mack, the noted manager of the Philadelphia Athletics, was a guest speaker who acknowledged the international reputation of the Hawaiian team. Also in attendance were "Chief" Bender, Mack's ace pitcher of Native American ancestry, and Liang Luen, the Chinese consul stationed in New York City, in addition to several managers of local semipro nines such as the Bronx Athletics and the Lincoln Giants. On a different occasion, the Chinese National Society of New York presented the team with "a beautiful silver cup" three feet high and bearing the inscribed names of each of the players.[52]

The team had struck a popular chord in New York City. Because their games drew well, Hoe maintained that he and his teammates were promoting Hawai'i effectively. The infamous East Coast heat had not wilted the team's spirits or health, as Hoe announced that the Travelers were all in "fine fettle" and "send their aloha" to the folks back home. Indeed, the Travelers won several games in and around New York City in late July, although the Ridgewood nine seemed to offer more than the Hawaiians could handle. On July 20, an overflow crowd watched the Travelers lose to Ridgewood in a game in the Bedford Stuyvesant area of Brooklyn. The *Brooklyn Eagle* described those in attendance as good-natured, especially "the many Chinamen ... who coached loudly in the Chinese language. As for the Travelers, the *Eagle* characterized the "Chinese students from the University of Hawaii" as "a ... manly and sportsmanlike lot of athletes." They played the "American game" well without resorting to unrefined obscenity. The crowd seemed divided in its loyalties, the *Eagle* conceded. They were especially solicitous of Kan Yen Chun when he hurt his ankle sliding into first. Lai Tin's work was admired along with that of Apau Kau and En Sue Pung.[53]

Fred Markham, according to the *Star-Bulletin*, wrote his father that since making New York its home base for six weeks, the team had started to earn a profit. The talented Hawaiian ballplayer asserted that the Travelers had made $11,200 thus far, clearing about $1,000 and hoping to make more. The Hawaiian ballplayers, Markham revealed, were playing relatively fewer games in the East than the West because they drew better on the East Coast. That is, they had to play seven games a week west of the Mississippi just to make expenses. Thus, he and his teammates not only hoped to break even financially but come home with a little extra. John Markham, a prominent haole politician, also learned that his son was enjoying some edifying fun. Apparently, Fred Markham and Foster Robinson had been sightseeing in America's biggest city. They had taken in "many points of interest" such as the Zoological Park and the Woolworth Building—"the highest building in the world." Markham reported that the team commonly watched big league games every Monday. McGraw's Giants and the Brooklyn Dodgers provided them with a free box. "By going to these games," Markham insisted, "we learn much about baseball." He also told his father that the team expected to head home by way of Philadelphia, Pittsburgh, Cincinnati, Chicago, Michigan, and even make a short jaunt to New Orleans. Then they would depart for San Francisco, from which they would board a boat home to Honolulu sometime in October. Finally, Markham assured his father, "I am O.K., in good health and so are the rest of the boys."[54]

Semipro nines in mid- and western Pennsylvania encountered the Hawaiians perhaps more often than they wished. Consequently, the *Star-Bulletin* proclaimed, "As a publicity proposition, the Chinese team is a sure winner and through it Hawaii has had much desired publicity." In York, Pennsylvania, according to a report in the *Philadelphia Inquirer*, "the Chinks" managed to "pile runs" against a local team of "all-stars." Even though York supposedly had a professional in the box, the Hawaiians won easily, 13–4. The "Chinese University [nine] ran wild on the bases and could not be stopped."[55]

Philadelphia and its environs hosted the Travelers for several games against local semipro contingents. On July 12, the Hawaiians took on the Stetson Athletic Club. The *Trenton Evening Times* informed readers that

"Foster, the Mathewson of the East" would lead the Hawaiians against the confident home team. Moreover, the *Times* pointed out that "baseball teams representing the oldest nation in the world and the youngest will clash." The game ended in a close, 4–3 victory for the visitors. The *Philadelphia Inquirer* headlined its story of the game: "Chinks Know How To Play Ball" and called the visitors the "Travelling Mongolians." The *Inquirer*, indeed, strove to compliment the Hawaiians. It asserted, "The Chinese were as agile as crickets on the bases and in the field they killed hits with an ease that was surprising. Stetson hit the ball hard but the fleet footed Mongolians were always in the way." A game account in the *Reading Eagle* linked the U.S. citizens from Hawai'i to China by proclaiming that if baseball ever developed in the "Mongolian Republic," American major leaguers would then face "a real yellow peril." On August 12, the *Star-Bulletin* boasted that a later game against the Stetsons "created a world of favorable comment for the Honolulu team." A crowd of 6,000 showed up to watch the visitors win, 9–4, on July 26. Reportedly, scalpers had a field day "so anxious were the Quaker City fans to see the wonders from Hawaii." As for the game, Apau Kau generally mastered the home team. His curve was working and he got four hits to boot. In addition, Lai Tin collected three hits, while En Sue Pung made another one of his spectacular catches in the outfield and subsequently "was forced to doff his cap" to the cheering spectators.[56]

Philadelphia area newspapers furnished an abundance of publicity for the Travelers. On July 19, the *Chester Times* warned readers to give "ample notice" to their local Chinese laundry operators as the daily expected a run on Chinese laundries when the ballplaying "Celestials" arrived in town. The Chester newspaper boosted the work of Apau Kau in the Stetson game, claiming that he had become "the idol of Philadelphia Celestials — the first Chinese baseball hero Philadelphia has seen." Moreover, in subduing the Stetson nine, the Travelers had not only changed the minds of those Philadelphians who lightly regarded their skills, but displayed "unsmiling oriental fatalism," although at least a couple of the Hawaiians apparently smiled. That is, refusing to surrender to pressure, the visitors saw "Foster," who pitched with a "fixed smile," give up the slab in the nine to the "smiling, brown faced" Apau Kau. Seemingly in jest, the *Chester Times* cautioned, major league baseball had best take up Chinese Exclusion. Otherwise, some big league manager would pick up a "rattle-free" team from "the new republic." The Travelers' calmness in the heat of battle could give big league stars "apoplectic fits." On August 9, the *Philadelphia Inquirer* informed readers that the "Chinese University team" would meet the Strawbridge and Clothier semipro nine that day on the latter's home field situated at 69th and Walnut. Interest in the game was high, the Philadelphia daily asserted, "as it is seldom that an opportunity is presented of seeing a team of Celestials perform" — a somewhat stunning assertion given that the Travelers had been competing on the East Coast for a couple of months.[57]

Philadelphia seemed enamored with the Hawaiians, according to the *Star-Bulletin*. The paper told readers that the August 10 edition of the *Philadelphia Inquirer* had reproduced a four column-wide photo of the "All-Chinese" accompanied by a column of type. The *Star-Bulletin* gathered, "Certainly, the local men are getting newspaper publicity, and the regularity in which they win is getting monotonous." In describing the defeat handed to the Strawbridge and Clothier semipro nine by the Hawaiians, the *Inquirer* declared, "The little band of yellow men, playing under the name of the Hawaii University team, once more invaded our fair city yesterday." The *Inquirer* averred that the Hawaiians had gained a reputation as weak hitters. However, "if this is true," the daily countered, "Ty Cobb isn't worth his salt and Frank Baker should quit before he gets to the gate." The "worst weaklings" were "Kanyen" and Ayau, who managed two singles, a double and three homers between them. Indeed, the "diminutive" Ayau slugged two round-trippers. Making matters worse for the befuddled Strawbridge and Clothier fielders was that "the Chinese ran wild on the bases." Luck Yee, described as "a young Mongolian," started but needed relief from "Foster," called the best pitcher on the "alien" nine. Robinson apparently was not as good as advertised but was good enough — especially when he had to be. En Sue Pung was credited for making a "pretty catch" in the outfield.[58]

In Atlantic City, the Hawaiians played a series of games against the local minor league nine in August. In the first game, the Atlantic City nine came out on top, 2–1. The headline of the game story in the *Philadelphia Inquirer* read, "Chinks Nosed Out," while the box score consisted of intriguing spellings such as "Unsire" in center field, "Sai" at third, and "Suck" in the box. On August 12, *Inquirer* readers learned that the "Chinese" came back against Atlantic City, taking a 3–1 victory. They also read that "remarkable fielding and base running brought victory for the Mongolians." Somebody by the name of "Tinki" cavorted in left field for the Travelers, according to the box score. This was probably En Sue Pung's brother, "Pinky" — more formally known as Ping Kong Pung. The Travelers encountered bad luck as well against Atlantic City. Lai Tin, designated by the *Star-Bulletin* as a "speed marvel on the bags," broke his ankle, while the versatile Fred Markham hurt his hand.[59]

Still, Henry Chillingsworth, well-known in Honolulu as a ballplayer, received a letter from one of the Travelers, perhaps either Lai Tin or Luck Yee — the *Star-Bulletin* did not clarify which. Chillingsworth had just returned to Honolulu with another barnstorming team of Hawaiians. Organized by

Guy Green, who had earlier assembled Native American traveling teams, this nine was originally intended to include nothing but Hawaiians of indigenous ancestry. Still, haoles such as Chillingsworth had also been asked to make the trip and a few Native Americans joined up once the team reached the mainland. While not nearly as successful as the Travelers, this team had won some games and supposedly stirred positive publicity for Hawai'i by giving Hawaiian music concerts.[60]

The Traveler correspondent congratulated Chillingsworth on the fine work the other Hawaiian team had done on the mainland. Then he boasted that the "All-Chinese" had become nearly as famous on the East Coast as major league teams. "Wherever we go we get the fans going with our neat playing and clean sportsmanship. We have never played dirty ball, yet, and would rather get beaten than break this rule."[61]

Semipro nines in New York City and Philadelphia, the Traveler maintained, were strong. However, he justifiably boasted that the Hawaiians beat nearly all of them except for one team in Brooklyn — probably the Ridgewood club that had edged the Travelers, 3–2. The Brooklyn nine had the Hawaiians' "number." Still, demand for their games was such on the East Coast that the Hawaiians had delayed their return home until at least Labor Day. The team would journey home by way of Cleveland, Buffalo, Detroit, and Chicago. The Traveler wrote that the Hawaiians were waiting for "the settler's rate," which would lower the cost of the usual fare from Chicago to the West Coast by half. This special fare would, however, not go into effect until September 25.[62]

The Hawaiians had, meanwhile, been outfitted with new, "very classy" uniforms by Nat Strong. The old gray uniforms with green stripes had been worn to pieces. They were replaced by white uniforms striped in navy blue. A large "C," presumably standing for Chinese, adorned the shirts, while an "H," presumably standing for Hawai'i, was placed inside a diamond on their left sleeves. The caps were likewise navy blue. Their coats, for some reason, were maroon with black stripes.[63]

Before journeying west, the Travelers continued to oppose semipro and professional nines on the East Coast in mid- and late August. On August 16, readers of the *Philadelphia Inquirer* discovered the following headline to a small story on the Hawaiian-Stetson game in Reading, Pennsylvania: "Chinks Do It Again." The game ended with the visitors coming out on top, 7–1, thanks to Robinson's three-hit pitching. Under the title, "Velly Nice Time For the Chinks," the *Inquirer* declared, "Celestials Make Chop Suey Out of Southmark." A fine crowd of 8,000 to 9,000 supposedly attended the game at Southmark Field in Philadelphia. There, they saw Lang Akana's hitting aid the Travelers in a 14–7 victory.[64]

Nat Strong outfitted the Travelers with a brand-new uniform in 1913. With a large C on the chest and an H on the sleeve, they appear to represent their Chinese and Hawaiian backgrounds. Seated first row right is En Sue Pung, a legendary Hawaiian track star turned just as legendary Hawaiian baseball star. It is hard to tell but the controversial baseball entrepreneur, Nat Strong, might well be straw-hatted gentleman sitting between Vernon Ayau and Fred Markham (author collection).

The Hawaiians seemed to be crisscrossing the Delaware River quite a bit. On August 23, the Travelers visited Camden, New Jersey, where they took an 11–6 game against the Camden semipro nine. According to a report in the *Inquirer*, the best crowd in years of Camden baseball witnessed the game. "The Chinks played wonderful ball in the field, especially Ayau," the story averred. The visitors, as the score would suggest, hit well too. The Camden nine was reputedly unnerved by the visitors' reputation. "The Chinks" got off to a big lead and never gave it up before an overflow crowd. Because "spectators surrounded the field," *Inquirer* readers learned that the typical ground rules were suspended. Thus, "the Chinamen hit six doubles into the crowd," while Camden batters managed seven. On August 26, the Travelers played what the *Brooklyn Eagle* called their last game in the region. Things did not go well as they lost to the Crescent Athletic Club, 11–1, at Bay Ridge Park in Brooklyn. A large crowd of 7,000 watched the game, inexplicably expecting a "burlesque." The Travelers were beaten badly, the *Eagle* admitted, but "the Chinese players from the University of Hawaii" evinced signs of brilliance. In the meantime, the *Trenton Evening Times* announced the "Chinks" would play in New Brunswick. Referring not to any superhuman capabilities, the *Evening Times* called the Hawaiians "ironmen," but reminded readers that the Hawaiians had downed some of the best semipro aggregations in the area. Playing a "lot [of] inside ball," the visitors could run, slide, and hit well. Accordingly, New Jersey baseball fans should catch "the almond-eyed ball tossers."[65]

Back in Philadelphia the next day, the "Mongolians" beat the Strawbridge and Clothier nine again despite suffering through a rash of injuries. Prior to the game, the locals expressed confidence they could avenge an earlier loss against the "foreigners." They thought they might have won then, but their regular battery was not in the game. Clearly, they underestimated the Hawaiians and Vernon Ayau, the "diminutive shortstop" who starred for the "Chinks." In the process, Ayau convinced the *Inquirer* that he combined the outstanding skills of top major league shortstops such as Honus Wagner, Jack Barry, and Mickey Doolin "and a few others thrown in for good measure."[66]

Toward the end of its tour, the Hawaiians opposed the Chicago American Giants, a powerful African American nine—an interesting event given the animosity which Giants manager and owner Rube Foster held for the often ruthless Nat Strong. In publicizing the game, the *Chicago Defender*, the leading African American newspaper at the time, informed readers that the American Giants were going to play a "crack Chinese team." The day after the game, a not very impressed *Defender* insisted that the "the Giants had easy pickings and played horse with the little men from the University of Hawaii and the best the brown men could do with the curves of Lindsay was to connect twice." To be fair to the Hawaiians, the game was close, 3–2.[67]

Despite the relative success of the 1912 team, one wire story appearing in the late summer reported that the Travelers had surprised mainland baseball fans in 1913. All of this pleased Sam Hop, who asserted that his team wanted to show mainlanders that Hawaiians were their equal. The team manager maintained that the Travelers represented a people "who have as much sporting blood" as anyone.[68]

Hearing about the publicity attached to the barnstormers, Hawaiian-based ball teams were, of course, anxious to test their mettle against the Travelers once they returned. This was no less true of the 25th regiment team, which was struggling to hold itself together so that it could send its best possible ballplayers up against the returning Hawaiians. Backers of the 25th confidently asserted that they would give the Hawaiian barnstormers "some game."[69]

Before leaving for the islands from San Francisco, the Travelers received one last mainland honor. Former Honolulan Wong Tuck had, according to the *Star-Bulletin*, become a prominent merchant in San Francisco's Chinatown. In San Francisco, he presented the Travelers with a silver cup, honoring them for defeating so many "American clubs." No less insistent than many of his European American counterparts upon recognizing the Travelers as representative of a global Chinese nation, Wong Tuck added, "I am proud that my fellow countrymen were able to gain such high honors ... all over the continent."[70]

On October 12, the Travelers were back in Honolulu. They had arrived with the All-Hawaiian team, but the "Chinese" with the non–Chinese Hawaiian Fred Markham on hand got more notice, because, according to the *Star-Bulletin*, they had "been away the longest and having something of an international reputation, being made much of by their fellow countrymen." The Chinese consul was at Honolulu Harbor to greet the Travelers, while members of the Chung Wah Merchants Association picked them up in automobiles and drove them around the city to a reception hosted at the Chinese Consulate.[71]

The *Star-Bulletin* praised the team and its manager, Sam Hop, hailed as a tremendous promoter of Hawai'i, even though he was not a trained, professional publicist. The daily noted Hop's "famous smile" and also how happy the players were to see Diamond Head even though they publicly expressed joy in their trek.[72]

The *Star-Bulletin* editorialized its pleasure with both the "All-Chinese" and "All-Hawaii" nines. Both contingents played well and cleanly, it declared. That is, "there has come from the mainland not one whisper of rowdyism or anything like it, nothing but praise for the lads and their conduct. And this record is much more worthwhile than a high percentage of games won." The Hawaiian ball teams' "splendid" advertisement of Hawai'i merited attention from the Promotions Committee, the daily insisted, urging that the committee use the touring ballplayers more expeditiously and even "pay part of the players' expenses. It will be money well spent."[73]

Upon returning home, Sam Hop confirmed that the team would make its third trek eastward in the spring of 1914 and that American mainland professional teams were interested in some of the Travelers. Overly optimistic, Hop expected that Yale and Harvard would add the Travelers to their schedules. Apparently, the two Ivy League giants had balked at playing the Hawaiians until they had earned a reputation for playing good ball. That, Hop believed, had been settled. Hop asserted to the Honolulu sportswriters that the team needed to head off to the mainland early in 1914 in order to make sure it would be ensconced in the East when top college teams were still playing.[74]

The journey to the mainland made money, Hop insisted. The *Star-Bul-*

letin advised its readers, however, that the Chinese Hawaiian entrepreneur did not bother to go into details. He did, however, boast that the Travelers had become a known commodity from one coast of the mainland to another. Had they played in larger parks, they would have sold more seats, Hop asserted. The Chinese Hawaiian claimed that he once saw one fan offer another a "five spot" for a ticket and was turned down.[75]

Hop claimed that some "Class B" minor league teams took a shine to at least a few of the players, while major league franchises were intrigued. The big league Brooklyn franchise, indeed, according to Hop, could see Foster Robinson in its pitching rotation. Nevertheless, the sought-after Hawaiians were not enticed, Hop guaranteed, because they wanted "to stick with their comrades" and return home to Hawai'i. Hop credited Robinson for much of the team's success as he substantially lifted the burden of pitching off the shoulders of Apau Kau and Luck Yee. Thus, the team ran up a good record, which, Hop argued, could have been better if injuries had not plagued the Travelers toward season's end.[76]

Of the mainland baseball figures encountered by the Travelers, Hop seemed most taken with John McGraw. The Hawaiian team had visited the Polo Grounds several times and elicited sound advice from the great manager. The superstitious McGraw enjoyed the Hawaiians' presence because he considered them a good luck charm. Every time they watched the Giants at home, Hop revealed, McGraw's team won.[77]

Some leaders of Honolulu's Chinese community feted the returning heroes at Sun Yin Wo Hall on Hotel Street. According to the *Star-Bulletin*, "The fine record of the team and the large part it can play in upbuilding [*sic*] clean sport and high ideals in the community was the subject of toasts and addresses by a number of those present." Chuck Hoy, described as a prominent Chinese Honolulan, served as toastmaster, while Chinese consul Chen Ching Ho attended and declared that all of China was proud of the team's achievements and that he personally hoped that the ball club would travel to his country and teach baseball to the Chinese. An influential haole, W.R. Farrington, also addressed the gathering. The President of Honolulu's Ad Club and future territorial governor, Farrington praised the team's ability to inspire positive advertisement for the islands. He furthermore "urged that the Chinese consider themselves as they are considered, a part of all Hawaii, not any one race community, and work for all Hawaii." Mr. Cottrell, identified by the *Star-Bulletin* as Collector of Internal Revenue on the islands, claimed he was a longtime fan of Honolulu baseball. He insisted that the Hawaiian ballplayers were able to "prove ... that high personal character and qualities of manhood are above any distinction of race and character." Cottrell declared that the Travelers represented a "new idea of Hawaii ... an idea ... where merit counts and where blood is no bar to advancement." Riley Allen of the *Star-Bulletin* chimed in that the "Chinese" ballplayers had become role models for "thousands of boys and youths, because they have done much to promote clean and hard playing." Sam Hop, however, reminded those in attendance that the Travelers were more than just symbols, but good ballplayers who won 105 games and lost but 40 in the 1913 tour. Lai Tin, described as team "captain" and "crack third baseman," thanked Honolulu's Chinese community for the banquet and all of Hawai'i for its support.[78]

After taking two games from an all-star Maui nine on the "garden island" in late October, the Travelers suffered their first defeat in a while to a local team. The Portuguese Athletic Club (PAC) handed them a close, 8–7 defeat. Outfielder Ping Kong was injured in the game, while Kan Yen Chun got thrown out for arguing a call. The wagering crowd lost its collective shirt as betting was heavy on the nine the Honolulu press called the All-Chinese.[79]

In early November, Honolulu baseball fans officially learned that the Travelers would make their third trek to the mainland. The team was scheduled to depart Honolulu on March 13 and would, according to Nat Strong, oppose several good college and semipro nines, all of whom "were anxious to take the Chinese on."[80]

Honolulu's Chinese community continued to demonstrate its support for the returning Travelers. On November 7, the Chinese Students Alliance at Honolulu's Mills Institute invited the Travelers to its "monthly entertainment." Outfielder Sing Hung or Solomon Hoe told the gathering that the trip was educational and that the Travelers had gained invaluable insights into American society. The next day, the team defeated a military nine. During the game, according to the *Star-Bulletin*, "The Chinese clubmen on the other side of the fence set off a cannon cracker for every inning up to the fourth, when they ran out of ammunition. Also there was Chinese music in profusion."[81]

Just as was the case a year earlier, accusations were flung about in Honolulu concerning the alleged greed of the Travelers nine. The *Advertiser* stated that the All-Chinese wanted too much money to play in an Inter-Island series—$1,500 to be exact. Such a demand outraged the *Advertiser*, which claimed that baseball had survived in Honolulu for months without the Travelers and would continue to do just fine without them in the future.[82]

The Travelers seemed beatable, however. The PAC handed them another defeat, 7–1. The ostensibly Portuguese nine won all the gate receipts while humiliating Robinson. According to the *Advertiser*, the loss was a blow to not only the Travelers but also their Chinese Hawaiian followers who had fiercely wagered on their favorites. Sam Hop was characterized as "jumpy" during the game. He apparently threw John Notley, a haole supporter of Honolulu baseball, off the bench and "signal[ed] for the setting off of fireworks over at the joss house, but it did no good." Vernon Ayau appeared to be the only highlight of the Travelers' game. Even though he repeatedly had to cope with hard smashes off of PAC bats, according to the *Advertiser*, the shortstop's "lightning pick-ups and throws across the diamond made them all look easy." Interestingly, the *Advertiser* claimed that Japanese spectators were rooting for the PAC nine. When one of the victors socked a home run, the Nikkei fans supposedly "made more noise than any hundred of the other fans."[83]

Aside from corresponding with the *Honolulu Star-Bulletin*, S.H. Hoe penned a piece about the 1913 tour which was published in the March 1914 edition of *Baseball Magazine*. Perhaps ironically titled "America Invaded by Oriental Foes," Hoe's article revealed that he and others "on the Chinese Baseball team" were taken aback by a newspaper article that displayed a headline, "America Invaded." They thought the story concerned some kind of "international crisis." Instead, it concerned them.[84]

Hoe claimed the Travelers had journeyed 25,000 miles in six months. They had played 144 games, approximately 24 a month and six a week. At the tour's outset, Hoe and his teammates believed they would be lucky to manage victories in 55 percent of the games they were scheduled to play. The difficulties of so much traveling and the fact that they always played "away games" seemingly made victories hard to come by. That is, they would appear on over "one hundred diamonds far from home, with no knowledge of the strength of our opponents or the peculiarities of the umpires and climatic conditions." In addition, the team would carry only three experienced pitchers on a relatively small roster of 14. Still the Hawaiians won 105 games. This was "going some," according to an "American organization, the Honolulu Ad Club," which gratified Hoe by inviting the team upon its return to a play at the Honolulu Opera House and provisioning them with comfortable box seats.[85]

The fact that the Hawaiians won 44 of 49 games against college competition inspired pride in Hoe. Apparently ashamed that they had not done better against mainland collegians in 1912, Hoe asserted that the Travelers wanted to "retrieve the reputation" of the 1912 outfit. That team, Hoe said, was inconsistent because "we had more managers and substitutes than players," as well as only two effective pitchers, one of whom "was a mere youngster with practically no experience."[86]

"Everywhere we went," Hoe wrote, "we were given the glad hand." The great Chinese Hawaiian athlete especially enjoyed the reception accorded the Travelers by "American college students and fans." He insisted that they consistently cheered good plays, whether made by "the invaders" or the home team. Even after games won by the Hawaiians, students and college authorities generally "celebrated" with them "as though our victories were theirs." Hoe added:

> The receptions, concerts, and banquets arranged for us were pleasant testimonials of genuine friendship between our Chinese people and the better classes of Americans. It made us almost ashamed to cop off all but five games against 49 different American college teams, but the strict rules of sportsmanship decreed that we must fight for all we were worth.

Hoe, intriguingly, praised one unnamed college president for announcing in the Travelers' presence, "The Yellow Peril! We have seen it to-day on the athletic field. We have seen it here this evening. That's the only kind of yellow peril that I know. Let Providence give us more of this kind."[87]

Unfortunately, Hoe conceded, "prominent" Eastern colleges, presumably Harvard, Yale, and other Ivy League institutions, did not schedule games against the Hawaiians. The rationale was that the Hawaiians had not convincingly built up a reputation and by the time they did in the Midwest, it was too late. "So if we are to have a crack at some of the Eastern colleges which have not been on our program during the two years," Hoe asserted, "we will have to make another trip next year, an undertaking which means the expenditure of a large sum of money."[88]

The games against semipros seemed to have aroused less nostalgia from Hoe. Recalling the aftermath of one game against the Stetson team in Philadelphia, Hoe explained that the Hawaiians had defeated the Philadelphians, 4–3, thanks, in part, to Apau Kau's achievement of picking off two baserunners with his "famous side throws." One angry fan confronted the Hawaiians, berating them as "queueless yellow men." He supposedly declared, "We've taught you the great game of baseball, but you've turned 'round and beat our sons in our back yards. Hm that's ingratitude." The almost unvaryingly sanguine Hoe wrote the fuming fan off as a "uniquely poor loser," maintaining that most mainland fans were gracious in defeat, "otherwise we would have been mobbed."[89]

In June, Hoe admitted, "staleness" caught up to the Travelers. From March 28 to June 14, the Hawaiians had won all but ten of their first 68 games. Then they hit the wall and won just four of their next nine. Hoe wrote, "The lack of sleep and the effects of the journeys from town to town began to tell on the boys. Mind you, there were no serious injuries up to that time. So this will bear out my statement that never in the history of baseball has there been recorded a trip so strenuous as this one." Thus, the team took a rest in late June and early July and then went to town against semipro nines, winning 16 of 19 games.[90]

In August, injuries and illness hampered the Travelers, although Hoe bragged that the team did well despite the disadvantages they encountered.

Hoe described En Sue Pung as "the speed demon around the bases and the man who surprised thousands of fans by beating out bunts and catchers' throws to second." Unfortunately, Pung lost two toenails sliding into third. Lai Tin, who apparently had taken over as manager, broke his ankle in Atlantic City. Luck Yee contracted such a bad case of typhoid in Philadelphia that physicians feared for his life. And Hoe's season was ended when he smashed his fingers on a hit-and-run play. Things got so bad that Sam Hop was forced to play. All he had to do, according to Hoe, was "let the other eight men bat in enough runs, and to chase after the sphere should it come in his direction, without letting out any secrets to the opponents."[91]

The versatility of the team kept it above water when injuries, illness, and fatigue piled on. Lang Akana helped take up some of the pitching slack. Apau Kau handled first when he was not in the box, while "Foster" took over at second when needed. Kan Yen handled third and other infield positions, while Henry Kuali, Ping Kong Pung, Clement Akina, and Sam Hop substituted in the outfield.[92]

The Hawaiian ballplayers, Hoe stressed, picked up the "finer points of the game" by playing well over 100 games on the mainland. But they also gained valuable lessons in the American National Pastime by watching big leaguers. Hoe elaborated, "We have seen a majority of the big league teams in action, for we have always been invited to be the guests of the different managers around the circuit."[93]

Hoe expressed delight in the acknowledgement of many that he and his teammates had become "the Apostles of the great American National game." However, he also articulated the team's strong connection to China when he wrote that the Hawaiian ballplayers' mission would not be achieved until baseball was as popular in China as in the United States. He insisted that the "worthy title" of "Apostles" should not be applied to the Travelers until they helped translate the rules of baseball into Chinese. The trek through the mainland, furthermore, revealed to Hoe "immense educational possibilities" among its colleges and universities. The outfielder hoped that "our contact with the American people has really brought the two friendly nations to a closer relationship — a fact which we all feel proud of."[94]

Despite their accomplishments, the Travelers, Hoe emphasized, were glad to return to the islands, which were, after all, their true home — not China. In the process, Hoe's cheerfulness abated somewhat. In Hawai'i, "we are safe and free — safe because we no longer have to jump on moving trains with our heavy suitcases and baseball paraphernalia in order not to disappoint our white cousins in the different cities." They would not have to hurry their meals as they did in their treks throughout the mainland. They would not have to deal with "the quick-order dinners at the crowded railroad stations and 'dog houses,' with many curious eyes staring at you." They could sleep soundly at home rather "than [on] the noisy night trains or on the twelfth or fifteenth story of some hotels."[95]

Hoe at the time could not predict whether the Hawaiian ballplayers would make another trip to the mainland in 1914. He proclaimed, "It is just a little too remote to make a definite decision." However, by the time mainlanders read his article in the spring of 1914, the Travelers were making their way eastward from San Francisco.[96]

Three

The Not So "All-Chinese," 1914

As the new year of 1914 began, Honolulu's baseball fans were excited about the Travelers opposing the All-Oahus, with Johnny Williams in the box. Because Hop's team had just suffered a loss to the PAC, many knew the Chinese Hawaiians were not invincible and that the Oahus, with a top-notch professional hurling for them, had a chance. Still, the Travelers were seen as so "classy" and "consistent" that plenty of "Chinese money" was wagered on them.[1]

The Chinese Hawaiians beat the Oahus, 4–2, in ten innings. The *Star-Bulletin's* Lawrence Reddington pointed out that at the game's outset about half of the 4,620 in attendance were rooting for the Chinese Hawaiians but that number bounced to 90 percent by the game's end. Reddington insisted that the Oahus' failure to play honestly lost whatever favor they had with the spectators.[2]

Reddington, the *Star-Bulletin's* sport editor, stood out as a big supporter of the "All-Chinese." A few days after the team beat the Oahus, he declared that Honolulu saw a better brand of baseball thanks to the Chinese Hawaiian team. Most Honolulu fans recognized the "Chinese team" and rewarded its ballplayers by coming out to watch them in strong numbers. Reddington wrote, "When a small-town team can draw more than $500 as its share of the gate at a single game, as did the Chinese on New Year's Day, the goose that lays the golden egg should be very carefully tended and fed the best in the market."[3]

In mid–January, the *Star-Bulletin* praised the All-Chinese nine as "royal hosts" to two mainland visitors, W.A. Bowen and S.T. Chan. Both had feted the Travelers during their 1913 trek. Bowen declared at the banquet thrown by the ballplayers that the Travelers were "admired" everywhere they journeyed on the mainland, while Chan said they represented "good, clean sport." Haole boosters such as W.R. Farrington attended and praised the ball team's ability to publicize the islands. Fred Markham's father, John, made it to the festivities, as did the president of the Chinese Students Alliance.[4]

The *Star-Bulletin* complimented "the Chinese" fashion-sense and baseball guile. It maintained, "You don't see the Chinese standing at bat with their breeches falling down to their ankles." If so, spectators could not notice it. What they did notice was that Lai Tin, Ayau, and company "tuck-em right around their knees where they belong, and don't have the lower ones called strikes in consequence."[5]

The daily also took time to commend individual players. Foster Robinson could hit and field as well as any of his teammates, while "being a crack slapster." When pitching, Apau Kau was all business. However, when playing first he was "the biggest kidder on the team." Because both Robinson and Apau were good "stickers," each had to stay in the lineup even when not in the box.[6]

Still, even well before the Travelers' return to the mainland, the *Los Angeles Times* advised readers of the Hawaiian ball club arriving on the West Coast on March 1. It mistakenly maintained that for the Hawaiian ballplayers, "The first sight of this country, taken collectively at least, will be on March 1." The Los Angeles daily plunged inaccurately ahead by pointing out that "the men will be accompanied by Matt C. Strong, an American who is said to have accomplished wonders with this squad" and that "Lai Pin captains the team." In February, a *Los Angeles Times* writer noted, "The next sporting event will be the game with the Chinese baseball team. Wonder if the players have their 'chock chee.'" On March 13, readers of Georgia's *Columbus Daily Enquirer* found out in a supposedly humorous short piece that the U.S. was to experience the "invasion" of a champion Chinese baseball team. This skilled nine should cause "American players to mind their P's, the Chinamen already have their queues."[7]

Meanwhile, the Honolulu sporting public had become aware that dissension had broken the ranks of the Travelers. Lai Tin, Lang Akana, and perhaps others just did not want to go to the mainland. On January 29, therefore, the *Advertiser* reported that "war" had erupted among the Travelers. Lai Tin's mother and En Sue Pung's wife wanted their loved ones home instead of traipsing around the mainland. Moreover, Kan Yen Chun refused to play with either Lang Akana or Vernon Ayau.[8]

A few days later, Sam Hop was forced to deny the *Advertiser*'s story that quarreling was tearing apart the Travelers. Whatever was bothering Lai Tin, Hop contended, could be easily fixed. Moreover, the team would emerge stronger than ever thanks to Albert Akana's desire to make the trip along with Alvin Robinson, Foster's brother. Kan Yen Chun showed up at the *Star-Bulletin* offices to refute the story of discord among the Travelers. Called the team

Albert Akana, who captained the 1912 and 1914 teams, was not only one of the better hitters for the Travelers but also played first base and pitched. In this photograph, c. 1914, he is standing with the captain of the Columbia University nine (courtesy of Library of Congress, Prints & Photographs Division, LC-DIG-ggbain-16146).

captain and "hustling little leader," Kan Yen Chun admitted that Lai Tin would not go to the mainland, but denied that dissension was a factor. The speedy third baseman, Kan Yen Chun conceded, would be missed.[9]

Early in February, Hop tried to smooth things over even though an organization called the Chinese Athletic Union was assembling a team to remain in Honolulu. This team would reportedly consist of Lai Tin, En Sue Pung, Kan Yen Chun, Vernon Ayau, and even hapa haole Fred Markham. Hop, nevertheless, insisted that all of the "All-Chinese" nine would head to the mainland. He admitted that due to personal reasons Lai Tin and En Sue Pung were thinking about hanging back. But Hop had met their objections and they would join the rest of the Travelers—"hence," the *Star-Bulletin* reported, "the smile on Hop's countenance." Hop also announced that Alvin Robinson would make the trip for the first time as would two others — pitcher Hoon Ki and someone named "Aki," who might have been Luther Kekoa, a versatile ballplayer who would play under the name of "Ako" on the mainland. In terms of the team's schedule, Hop told the press that the Travelers would leave on March 3 even though they had not yet gotten a complete schedule from Nat Strong. In any event, Hop was hopeful they would draw well. The Travelers had made money, Hop boasted, and would continue to make money.[10]

A week later, Hop reinforced his optimistic pronouncements by claiming that Kan Yen Chun, Lai Tin, En Sue Pung, and Markham would all make the trip, rumors to the contrary. What is more, they and their teammates would wear what Hop declared was a new, "very classy" uniform — dark blue with white stripes and the left sleeves adorned with crossing American and Chinese flags.[11]

The *Star-Bulletin* continued to drum up positive publicity for Hop's team as departure time drew closer. Since returning home, "the Chinese," according to the *Star-Bulletin*, "have been playing ... a class of ball that is far and away the best ever seen on the islands." Thus, the Honolulu Ad Club sponsored a benefit game for these "Chinese Americans who spread publicity with a baseball bat." The daily expected a joyful street parade and a big crowd for the game against the Oahus, who would go with Barney Joy on the slab.[12]

Some encouraging publicity headed in Hop's direction by way of the *Star-Bulletin*. He and his team hosted a contingent of ballplayers from Maui at Honolulu's Sun Yun Wo restaurant. The *Star-Bulletin* reporter expressed delight in the proceedings by proclaiming, "Manager Sam Hop and the Chinese deserve much credit for the fellowship they have fostered by these dinners, which are always pleasurable events and result in much good to the diamond sport." Apparently, "Charlie En Sue Pung" was asked at the dinner why he slid into bases head-first rather than legs-first. The veteran outfielder responded that his "legs are too short" to do otherwise. The *Star-Bulletin* informed readers that newcomer Luther Kekoa possessed Chinese ancestry even though many in the Chinese community believed he was a "full-blooded Hawaiian." Moreover, the Honolulu Ad Company feted the Travelers to a happy send-off, according to the *Star-Bulletin*. Each player was loaded down with leis and a band played them off to the East. Sadly, four "old timers" — Kan Yen Chun, Vernon Ayau, Lai Tin, and Lang Akana — stayed behind. The *Star-Bulletin* remained philosophical. No one should have expected the team to stay intact forever.[13]

On March 2, the *Star-Bulletin* announced that the team would ultimately wind up making the "big jump" from Hawai'i to Cuba in 1914. Ayau would journey with the Travelers after all. And Sam Hop assured the local press in an open letter that he would assiduously promote the islands on the mainland, while thanking the Ad Club for its support.[14]

Since players like Lai Tin and Akana did not make the trip, the *Advertiser* was worried that the Travelers were fatally weakened on the eve of the team's big trip. The barnstormers might fail to show the mainland "what the Chinese can do as players," hurting gate receipts across the Pacific. However, the *Advertiser* was just as glad that some very good ballplayers would stay around to furnish local fans with top-notch ball.[15]

In an article subtitled "Sam Hop and Thirteen Chinese and Near Chinese Left for Another Invasion of Mainland" the *Advertiser* analyzed the makeup of the 1914 traveling squad. It described Sam Hop as the team's "manager, trainer, hustler and all around factotum on Hawaii's premier ball club." It mentioned that one of the new team members was Kekoa, "a full-blooded Hawaiian," and another was William Apau, a recent graduate of the Chinese Junior League. Alex Desha, a ballplayer of part–Native Hawaiian ancestry, had been considered by Hop as a possible team member. However, he was left behind as were two other talented Hawaiian athletes — Alex Asam and Henry Kuali. To strengthen the team, Hop reached beyond one of the more robust ethnic divisions among Asian Hawaiians. Therefore, of all the new players only Japanese American standout Chinito Moriyama, according to the *Advertiser*, equaled those remaining on Oahu — players such as Lai Tin, "the crack third baseman," and Lang Akana, "the fastest leftfielder Hawaii has ever known barring none." Accordingly, the *Advertiser* could only say, "The team which left yesterday is far from being the formidable aggregation it was on the former two trips to the mainland, but good accounts are expected of it, however."[16]

Baseball fans in Honolulu's Chinese community voiced displeasure with the ethnic composition of the team heading to California. Pronouncing themselves tired of Hop's "methods," merchants from Honolulu's Chinatown backed a truly "All-Chinese" team composed of players entirely of the "Chinese race." This nine would play in the Oahu baseball league with other leading nines on the island. Several players who had formerly competed for the traveling team would, these Chinatown merchants hoped, appear on the new team — players such as Lai Tin, "Honolulu's premier third baseman," Lang Akana, and Sing Hung Hoe. These men had, the anti–Hop faction claimed, grown tired of Hop's "graft."[17]

A leading Chinatown sports enthusiast, Li Hong Kong, condemned Hop for failing to organize a truly "All-Chinese" nine:

> Not one half of the men wearing that uniform are Chinese. Denny Markham, Foster Robinson, Alvin Robinson, Kekoa and Chinito Moriyama are not sons of the New Republic and Hop knows it and every fan in Honolulu knows. Perhaps when the team first started for the mainland a couple of years ago it was a representative All-Chinese organization, but it is not now.

Kong declared that only three or four players on the traveling team actually possessed Chinese ancestry. The rest were Japanese Hawaiian and part–Native Hawaiian. He believed that Honolulu's Chinese community deserved representation in Oahu baseball circles by a truly "All-Chinese" team much as the Asahis represented the local Japanese community. Oahu League director Bert Lowery, who also edited the *Advertiser's* sports page, hoped that a Chinese Athletic Union team would be organized and gain acceptance in the league.[18]

W. Tin Chong, president of the Chinese Athletic Union, echoed Li Hong Kong. Chong wrote a letter to the *Advertiser* supporting a CAU team in the Oahu League. Chong argued that a CAU team, with players of Chinese ancestry, would lure fans — particularly fans from Honolulu's Chinese community. He said that many Chinese Honolulans had become not only baseball followers but baseball "bugs." However, they wanted to see a team that actually stood for them and fielded good players such as Lai Tin and Lang Akana. The *Advertiser* agreed, saying that the CAU "represents the sports-loving Chinese of Oahu, and they are loyal in their support of a baseball team, and a representative team as W. Tin Chong proposes putting in the field would be a great drawing card."[19]

There was some opposition to a CAU team joining the Oahu League, based upon the fear that too many teams in the league would divide the gate up in such a way that each club would get too little money. The *Advertiser* thought that a CAU nine would actually bring more paying customers to watch Oahu League ball and would make more money for everyone. It further argued that local fans had wearied of Sam Hop parading his nine, "made up of Hawaiian players, a Japanese and part Chinese players as a representative Chinese team." Once local fans forgot Hop's team as a "representative Chinese" aggregation, W. Tin Chong's CAU nine would receive all the support it deserved. Eventually, the CAU nine, with Lai Tin as captain, was allowed into the Oahu League. Pushing Oahu League "magnates" was the threat of a rival league to accommodate a CAU nine.[20]

Meanwhile, Hop's travelers turned up in a bit of a jam before playing their first mainland game. According to the *Advertiser,* the team was waylaid at Angels Island in San Francisco Bay — an island on which the U.S. government had installed an immigration center to detain and investigate Chinese immigrants it believed wanted to enter the country using false documents. Apparently, "the citizenship of Sammy Hop's artists was put in question." The Hawaiian ballplayers might have had to wait on the island for 24 hours. However, Albert Taylor, a former employee of the *Advertiser* and at that time the San Francisco representative of the Hawai'i Promotion Committee, made the necessary calls and the ballplayers were permitted on shore. At least that was the *Advertiser*'s story.[21]

In a wire story published around the mainland, a different account of how the Travelers got off Angels Island was made available to American sports fans. Readers of the *Fort Worth Star-Telegram*, for example, learned that immigration authorities had insisted upon interrogating the Hawaiians because they were "Mongolians." However, when authorities were informed that "En Suey" was "Ty Cobb the second," they proclaimed their love of the tempestuous "Georgia Peach" and let the Travelers onto the mainland.[22]

On March 12, 1914, a wire story in the *Washington Post* noted, under the headline "Chinese Nine in US," that "Fifteen Chinese baseball players and their manager, Hop Sing, arrived [in San Francisco] today from Honolulu" and that the visiting team reigned as champion of the Hawaiian Baseball League. The Hawaiians lost their first game against Cal. En Sue Pung wrote to his brother, a merchant in Honolulu, that the Travelers had the Berkeley nine beaten, but their errors allowed the game to slip away. En Sue Pung lamented that the game did not start until 4:15 P.M. and ended at 6 when the Bay Area had grown dark and cold.[23]

Although the *Oakland Tribune* had predicted back in January that the "Celestials" would play several games in the Bay Area, the Cal game seemed to be it. The Travelers headed southward to Bakersfield, where they enjoyed warmer weather than in the Bay Area. The Hawaiians beat the local, Cozy nine, 8–1, behind Apau Kau's pitching. En Sue Pung acknowledged that the Bakersfield Chinese found baseball to their liking, although only a few reportedly understood the game. That night, the team departed by train for Los Angeles, where they arrived at 9 A.M.[24]

Upon arrival in Los Angeles and before their game with Occidental College, the *Los Angeles Times* described the Hawaiian visitors as the "Yellow Peril" and published a cartoon displaying stereotyped Chinese males playing baseball. The article accompanying the cartoon was headlined "Chinese Ballplayers Meet Tigers Saturday" and promised readers that "international baseball will take place." Hailing the work of the Hawaiian ballplayers on the U.S. mainland in 1913, the *Times* added that they had assembled a record that would "bring pride to the fans across the sea." In the process, these U.S. citizens had "swept across Uncle Sam's acres, smothering our own college teams in a maze of wonderful baseball." The Hawaiians thrived on "sensational baserunning and perfect fielding." The Hawaiians' speed was their primary offensive weapon, according to the *Times*, which admitted that it was "almost impossible to check their uncanny system of getting around the bases." The Hawaiians were good contact hitters because they used short, choppy swings that consistently put the ball into play. "The steady fusillade of singles combined with daring base running proved too much for their opponents," the *Times* maintained of "the men from the land of chop suey and noodles."[25]

The Occidental student newspaper promised a fine game. The "Chinese," it asserted, were "good ballplayers." While inaccurately claiming that Lai Tin and Lang Akana were on board for the Travelers, *The Occidental* advised college baseball followers that they should feel fortunate because they would get to see the only game the Hawaiians were playing in the "southwest."[26]

The day of the Occidental game witnessed the *Times* warning: "every Chinese laundry and vegetable wagon in the city will be out of commission this afternoon." Above the article titled "Chinese To Make Oxy Step Some," the *Times* printed the phrase, "You, sabe"—an expression that "Pidgin English"-speaking Chinese were thought to use widely. The daily added that the Hawaiian ballplayers came to Southern California "from the land of the 'yellow peril.'" However, "the men from Hawai'i play as well as the best of them."[27]

When the Travelers won, 6–4, with Foster Robinson and Luther Kekoa pitching, the *Times* declared that "Nine little Chinamen" proved "that baseball follows the flag," as well as the possibility that "Kipling was ... mistaken and that the East and West had at last met." Indeed, the *Times* found it intriguing that the Hawaiian ballplayers ridiculed the umpire and opponents with as much fervor as mainland players. Countering the image of relatively compliant athletes offered by other mainland publications, the *Times* writer declared, "To hear the Chinese college students from Hawaii roasting the umpire with deadly sarcasm was almost as interesting as the ball game." One Hawaiian, angered by an umpire's call, was quoted as remarking, "Well, for the love of Mike, did you ever see anything to beat that guy? He ought to get a job blowing safes." After seeing the Occidental catcher attempting the hidden ball trick, En Sue Pung, called "the Ty Cobb of the South Seas" by the *Times*, did not hide his disgust. "I thought we were going to learn something about baseball by coming across the Pacific Ocean. I didn't expect to see any one try such a bush league trick at least a century old." As for En Sue's swiftness, the anti-union *Times* insisted, he "runs with the speed of an IWW who smells beer."[28]

Pioneering Los Angeles female journalist Adele Rogers wondered why the Hawaiian ballplayers eschewed what she considered appropriate "Pidgin English." Quoted extensively in the *Star-Bulletin*, Rogers wrote that the Hawaiians arrived "educated, occidentalized, and American-tailored." Not only were they "well-tailored" by Rogers' standards but the ballplayers "resembled a masculine fashion show." She had expected, instead, that they would arrive in Los Angeles wearing kimonos, queues, and feathers. Rogers claimed that in preparation for interviewing team members, she had learned "Pidgin English." She found, however, that the Hawaiian ballplayers could manage a conversation in conventional, American English quite admirably. Rogers confessed that she had complimented one player by saying, "You velly much fine Chinese ballplayers" and tried to interrogate others in "pidgin." However, one unnamed Traveler asked this apparently confused mainland reporter, "What can I do for you?" Rogers went on to describe another player, a "coffee-colored youth," as carrying a ukulele case and replying in "perfect English" to her "pidgin" inquiries.[29]

The "coffee-colored youth" Rogers "accosted" was "the most gorgeous exponent of an American fashion show." The ballplayer "wore a purple-blue suit, cut high over a silk-striped shirt. Over this hung a mackinaw in red and black." She asked the Hawaiian if the team's pitchers hurled "heap big spittee ballee?" The player responded in what Rogers labeled as a "slight Bostonese tone." He and his teammates had a hard time figuring out Rogers' purpose but they finally realized that she was asking them about their exploits as members of the "Chinese University of Hawaii" team. Accordingly, the mackinaw-wearing ballplayer said the team's pitchers did not resort to the spitter much. He supposedly said, "I greatly fear that use of saliva is injurious in that it breeds disease. I do not find it altogether expedient."[30]

The *Occidental*'s account of the game was headlined, "Chinatown Out in Force Last Saturday." The college publication explained that the Chinese Angelenos in attendance "yelled and cheered just like regular fans.... They crabbed the 'umps,' they tried to rattle pitcher, they 'kidded' our team." Moreover, they advised the visitors to "tly the sleze play." Angeleno's Chinatown did not ignore the Travelers' appearance even though several of them did not possess Chinese ancestry. According to En Sue Pung, around 200 "Chinamen" appeared for the game against Occidental. Los Angeles' Chinese merchants treated the Travelers to a "Chinese supper" at 12 midnight that night. Some four and a half hours earlier, the team ate a "haole dinner."[31]

En Sue Pung reported that the Travelers boarded a train from Los Angeles the next morning for Yuma, Arizona. After a "300 mile trip across the desert," they arrived at their destination at 4:15 P.M. Then they managed to get their uniforms on in seven and one-half minutes for a 4:30 game. The game lasted but four innings before it was called on account of darkness. By this time, the Hawaiians claimed a 9–3 lead with Kekoa on the rubber.[32]

The Travelers caught an 11 P.M. train out of Yuma for Tucson, arriving at 7:40 A.M. A few hours later, they victimized the University of Arizona, 10–1, with Apau Kau pitching. The university's newspaper, *Arizona Life*, commended the Travelers' performance: "The Hawaiians simply had the UA boys sewed up all the time." Of course, the Travelers could score but the *Arizona Life* writer was more impressed with their defense. "They play deep and can get in the road of most any kind of hit, and further progress of the pill is temporarily abandoned." Kekoa and Alvin Robinson hurled for the Travelers the next day. But it probably did not matter who pitched as the Travelers humiliated the home team, 21–8. Local fans had to fork over 50 cents apiece to watch these lopsided affairs. The *Arizona Life* said a nice crowd turned out for the second game. They witnessed the Travelers playing for fun once the game got out of reach. The university publication asserted, "The yellow-skinned boys were at all times very clean in their playing, depending at no time on shady decisions" for victory. The Arizona manager said the Hawaiians were "the cleanest bunch of players he had ever witnessed" and that he would gladly play them again. As for Hop, he complimented the University of Arizona for treating him and the Travelers generously.[33]

En Sue Pung expressed delight in the team's stay in Tucson. The ballplayer claimed that Tucson was home to about 500 Chinese, many of whom ran restaurants, chop suey shops, and grocery stores. The leaders of Tucson's Chinese community threw a dinner for the Hawaiian visitors "and even opened champagne to celebrate our victory over the haoles." The *Tucson Citizen* also noted the support of the town's Chinese community for the visitors. It claimed that Tucson's Chinese merchants were out in force to watch the Travelers. It insisted, moreover, that it was worth "the price of admission" to witness the Chinese spectators and hear them yell "kill the ump" in Chinese.[34]

Despite the criticisms it had leveled at Hop's team, the *Advertiser* professed satisfaction with the Travelers' early work on the U.S. mainland. On March 27, it published a photograph of team captain Kan Yen Chun, who made the trek after all, and "manager" Apau Kau as the ballplayers arrived in Los Angeles. *Advertiser* readers could note a headline to the photograph proclaiming that the two were "Boosting Hawaii on the Mainland." Nor did the *Advertiser* ignore the Hawaiian ballplayers' victories in Bakersfield and Yuma. Still, it also acknowledged that a planned trip to Japan of an "All-Hawaiian" baseball team was scrubbed partly because Hop took too many of the ballplayers who would have made that trek to Asia's baseball capital.[35]

Journeying eastward, Hop's aggregation won more often than it lost. A postcard from En Sue Pung maintained that the Travelers had arrived in El Paso at 11:30 A.M. In the border city, "a Chinese boy" from Honolulu owned a restaurant and invited the team to lunch before it played a game at 3:30 P.M. En Sue Pung claimed that a local El Paso fan "wanted references" as to what kind of team the Hawaiians were before the game. After the Travelers won, 12–4, En Sue could only say that he and his teammates gave "references" with their bats. Pung also wrote to his brother, Enfree Pung, from Tucson on March 17. "The Ty Cobb of the All-Chinese team" said the team was doing well, winning six of its first seven games. At the same time, the players had endured stiffness from extensive train treks and looked forward to shorter hops the next week.[36]

Beginning in late March, the Hawaiians encountered several Texas nines. Even before they arrived in the Lone Star State, the *Fort Worth Star-Telegram* informed readers that Daniel Brown, a tiny Presbyterian school in Brownwood, was ready for the "Chinks." Two days later, the Travelers beat Daniel Brown, 7–0, in a game the *Star-Telegram* described as "fast and classy." Apau and Mark formed the winning battery.[37]

A game with Texas Christian University in Fort Worth was cancelled over a week later. The TCU manager hoped to arrange another date but, according to the *Star-Telegram,* found that the "foreigners" had already departed for Dallas. Fans were disappointed because they were interested in seeing "the choppy style of play that has been credited to the Chinese." On April 1, the "Chinese University of Hawaii" beat the University of Dallas, 11–0. Presumably with tongue in cheek, the *Fort Worth Star-Telegram* declared that the Hawaiians had "administered a staggering blow to the tradition of Occidental superiority."[38]

In mid–April, the *Star-Bulletin* published a photograph of the "Chinese Ball Team" on the road. It asserted that the team was concluding its first journey through the American southwest and had done quite well. While generally happy with the reception accorded the Travelers in the American southwest, the *Star-Bulletin* seemed concerned about Sam Hop's "boosting" of a "mythical" University of Hawaii. Moreover, the daily understood that the players themselves had bought into the "myth."[39]

To be sure, the "myth" that the Travelers comprised a contingent of college students was circulating through the mainland. Readers of the *Waco Morning News* read a piece, reproduced in the *Star-Bulletin*, describing the Hawaiians as "typical college students." The writer queried, "Do they speak English?" The answer was, indeed, they spoke "English better than the average American." As to "how they act," the Hawaiian ballplayers acted "as a bunch of wealthy, well-bred young men from any of our colleges." Admittedly, "their faces ... show their race, but in dress they run largely to the newest fads in tight fitting clothes." In other words, "they are cosmopolites — each of these youngsters who have toured our land. They are able to fit anywhere."[40]

While in Waco, the team stayed at the New Katy Hotel. There they regaled the hotel owner and guests with their musicianship and singing. A quartet of Ayau, "Ako," "Foster," and "Alvin" particularly impressed the reporter. The shortstop sang lead. "Ako" or Luther Kekoa took up tenor, while Foster Robinson and Alvin Robinson sang baritone and bass, respectively. The latter also played piano. The hotel proprietor was so delighted he invited the quartet to his apartment for a more private concert. The Waco reporter especially liked Alvin Robinson's piano playing. The Maui resident "rags like a Vaudeville star," but could also handle "the classi-cal."[41]

The Waco reporter insisted that the team of Hawaiians was a product of "Uncle Sam's Old Tricks." The players demonstrated that Hawaiians were acquiring as good an education as Washington could give. The athletes also proved "that we haven't an uncivilized people under our control in the Pacific, but a people of mixed nationalities, if you will, but of a class in intelligence and training that take their places in every way as citizens of the republic." The hotel proprietor insisted, moreover, that he had never encountered "a more gentlemanly set in my place." The ballplayers had even made sure to take off their muddy shoes before entering his establishment after practicing in the rain.[42]

The *Star-Bulletin* complimented the Travelers for continuing to promote Hawai'i. "The boys" carried photographs of the islands to show off to mainlanders. They seemingly spent a lot of time explaining Hawaiian water sports to mainlanders as well. Apau Kau boasted that several of his teammates were expert "surf riders" — a sport which, he added, was not easy to master.[43]

Under the headline "Sam Hop's Outfit Having Many Troubles," the *Advertiser* of April 30 cited an anonymous source on the team for the intelligence that Albert Akana had inexplicably assumed the team's captaincy from Kan Yen Chun. Moreover, Moriyama, En Sue Pung, and Ping Kong were downed by injuries and illness. Still, the *Advertiser* assured local fans that the Travelers were playing effectively through the apparent personnel problems and physical ailments.[44]

A little over a week later, the *Advertiser* sang the praises of the Travelers, while acknowledging that Kan Yen Chun remained in charge of the team's on-field play. "Kan Yin and his merry ball team of Chinese Hawaiians and Japanese from Hawaii are showing the fans how the great game should be played." Clearly, the *Advertiser* still seemed intent on reminding readers that the Travelers were not a representative Chinese nine.[45]

Moving into Kansas and then Missouri, the Hawaiians continued to win more often than lose. Emporia, Kansas, was introduced to the Travelers by way of a promotional piece published in the local *Gazette*. Under the headline "Look Who's Here," the piece printed a list of Chinese names, some of which were recognizable as belonging to Travelers — "U. Ayan" — some of which, not, like "Kid Fan Lo." The author insisted that this list did not belong to members of a Chinese Laundrymen's Convention but that of a team of ballplayers from "the Chinese University of Hawaii." Although they were "Chinks," the Hawaiians looked like any other college team in the U.S. The young men were fashionably dressed, wearing "brightly colored hat bands of Chinese feathers." However, the reporter called them "prima donnas" because they demanded first class accommodations at a local hotel. They wanted and got rooms with "bat-h, bat'h."[46]

The *Emporia Gazette* also had something to say about the Travelers' victory over Kansas Normal, 4–0. Calling the visitors "chinks" and "laundrymen," it declared, "Nine Chinese showed how the good old American game of baseball is played." A large crowd observed "the clever work" of the visitors. The Hawaiians' fielding merited praise from the *Gazette*, which, in particular, lauded "Ayan" as "the niftiest fielder of the lot." The newspaper was less enamored with the Travelers' hitting, although En Sue Pung whacked a hard drive that the Kansas centerfielder misplayed into an inside-the-park home run.[47]

On April 15, the *Kansas City Star* informed readers that Captain "Ken Yin" would lead his "speedy" team against the "University of Kansas." The "laundrymen," the *Star* advised, had just lost a game to the Wichita minor league nine, but had then beaten a team out of Emporia. The visitors were expected to do well despite enduring key injuries. Kan Yen Chun promised the press a good game regardless of the flagging health of the Travelers.[48]

On April 17, the Hawaiians beat the Kansas nine in an error-filled game, 7–1. Foster Robinson pitched excellently, managing ten strikeouts. The *Advertiser* cited a Kansas sportswriter who referred to "the visiting Hawaiian Chinamen" and called the Travelers the University of Kansas' "slant-eyed opponents." The journalist added, "The whole team was full of inside baseball but one individual seemed steeped in the real American baseball atmosphere. Ayau at short proved nothing short of a sensation. His all-round work is seldom seen on any short field."[49]

As the team made its way into Kansas City, Hop became the butt of Missouri humor. According to the *Kansas City Star* of April 19, he "naively" denied to the press that he had a sister, "Belle." Still, the *Star* had some good, but inaccurate, things to say about the Travelers upon their arrival at the Hotel Kupper. The headline of its story on April 19 read "A Team of Dapper Youths Register at the Hotel Kupper." Wearing mackinaws and "fancy headbands," the contingent of "almond-eyed pastimers" looked at first glance like typical, fashionable American college men. But those peering under the hats would find a "new variety" of young fellows — Chinese and not just any Chinese but "students from the College of Hawaii who have been teaching American ballplayers 'a thing or two' about the game." As for Hop, the *Star* reported that he spoke English and asserted that Hawaiians liked baseball. The team manager with the "kangaroo name" predicted that baseball would grow internationally, observing that Japan and China enjoyed the game so why not the rest of the world. Hop perhaps said too much as he insisted that the College of Hawaii, which the *Star* claimed had 600 students of all nationalities, was the team's home base.[50]

The next day, the *Star* hailed the versatility of those who played for the "Chinese team from Hawaii." It purported that the players were originally inspired to take up baseball by an exhibition game staged by American sailors in Honolulu. One Traveler reportedly said that he and his teammates were so motivated that they read all they could on baseball and learned the game expertly. The *Star* asserted that the Hawaiians "play a clean brand of baseball." They demonstrated "sportsmanlike ways," because they "put up with bad umpire calls." Indeed, the Traveler informant told the press that no one on the team expected "a square deal" from umpires. Every Traveler spoke English, according to the *Star*, but some spoke English better than others.⁵¹

In late April, the Travelers were expected to play in Iowa against the Ottumwa nine of the Central Association. However, according to the *Cedar Rapids Evening Gazette*, "Sam Hop's gang of celestial ball players" failed to appear. Ned Egan, who managed the Ottumwa nine, was incensed. Fans had shown up anticipating a game and instead listlessly watched the local ball players warm up. Claiming he had lost $160, Egan reportedly complained to Nat Strong, who agreed that the Iowa baseball man was in the right. Egan then hunted down Hop, who was staying in Monmouth, Illinois. Egan wanted his money back, but Hop refused. Egan, according to the *Evening Gazette*, was willing to accept $100, but the Chinese Hawaiian remained adamant. The *Muscatine Journal* surmised that Hop did not take the matter seriously enough. If Egan followed through with his threat to bring the issue to the organized baseball's National Commission, the *Journal* speculated that the Travelers could lose opportunities to play several lucrative games. Since the Travelers continued to occasionally play minor league teams associated with organized baseball, the controversy must have simmered down.⁵²

On May 1, the Travelers were in Cedar Rapids, Iowa, playing a local nine seriously called the Bunnies. Two weeks earlier, the *Cedar Rapids Republican* had announced that a team of "Chinese Students" would arrive in town to oppose the Bunnies. The *Republican* promised fans that the visitors comprised "a wonderful attraction" and would draw many from the area. Apparently, the Bunnies' manager had been angling for a game with "the famous Chinese college team" for a long time. To doubters, the *Republican* insisted that the Travelers comprised a good team and not just a novelty. The Travelers' management had been offered a financial guarantee, but the *Republican* was not worried about anyone going broke over the game as long as the weather held up.⁵³

As for the game itself, the Bunnies proved tougher than their nickname as they won, 8–2 — a victory that was not assured, however, until the late innings. Nevertheless, "the Mongolians proved good hitters and heady on running around bases." The *Republican* observed, in an interesting twist of phrase, that "the Oriental mind takes to your American game of baseball." The visitors seemed to embrace baseball not only because of its physical enjoyment but also its "scientific" points. Their baserunning, furthermore, was "full of pepper." Alert and smart, they pulled off the double steal. The Hawaiians' fielding impressed the *Republican* as well. In right field, "Alvin" made a fine catch, while Kan Yen Chun showed a rifle arm from third. As for Apau Kau, his cleverness often fooled the home team batters. The *Republican* was therefore pleased to note that "the Chinks" were all they were advertised to be. That is, "everyone was a genuine Mongolian from the manager to the score keeper. One [Foster Robinson] had an English name, but this evidently was taken for linguistic advantages as he looked as much like a Chinaman as the others."[54]

On May 25, the *Star-Bulletin* published a letter from Fred Markham under the title "All-Chinese Successful." Writing as the team visited the Midwest in early May, the not very Chinese ballplayer reassured Honolulu fans. To those with dollar signs in their eyes, Markham reported that Albert Akana had been conscientiously distributing promotional literature on the islands. In terms of baseball performances, Markham gushed over the pitching of Foster Robinson, Apau Kau, and Luther Kekoa. Markham added, "We are receiving the glad hand in every city, and the welcome is getting stronger as we get further east. Aloha from all the boys."[55]

After two and a half seasons of barnstorming the mainland from the Hawaiian Islands, the Travelers were still treated as foreign invaders by the press. In early May, the *Fort Wayne Journal Gazette* maintained, "Indiana University's crack baseball nine successfully repelled the invasion of the fast Chinese players representing the University of Hawaii ... this afternoon, defeating the brown-skinned men, 9 to 5." The *Journal Gazette* added that "the orientals were fast at base running."[56]

A headline in the June 9 *Star-Bulletin* lamented, "Hard Sledding for the Traveling Chinese Team." The text worried that the 1914 edition of the team was not up to the standards set by the 1913 team. The *Star-Bulletin* conceded, "There are some strange names in the block score, and the old combination is more or less broken up." Still, the team was promoting Hawai'i effectively in that "the players are at all times loyal boosters for Hawaii, and the islands are reaping full benefits."[57]

On the East Coast, the *New York Times* announced that the "Chinese University of Hawaii" would play Columbia on the school's South Field on May 20. Originally, the date had been set aside for a game between the Keio University nine and Columbia. However, the Keio team had been called back to Japan and the Hawaiian contingent took its place. The *Times* observed incorrectly, "The appearance of the Chinese team at Columbia will be the first in the East and unusual interest in the contest is already being evidenced on the campus." A syndicated sportswriter called "Chum Bob" noted, "New Yorkers have seen all kinds of baseball players and all kinds of ball played by home talent, but the next week reserves for them the treat of seeing Chinamen from the University of Hawaii in action with the Columbia University team." On the day of the game, a *Times* headline informed readers that "Columbia Plays Chinese Today" and the text explained that the game would help celebrate the 50th anniversary of the Columbia School of Mines. Below a headline reading "Columbia Bows to Chinese Invaders," the *New York Tribune* blamed

Columbia's overconfidence and carelessness in the field on its defeat at the hands of the "Chinese University of Hawaii." The winners' aggressiveness kept the New Yorkers off balance, the *Tribune* maintained. "The Celestials" hit and fielded expertly. Indeed, "the Chinese players outshone their white opponents" in every way. Striking out nine, Apau Kau proved particularly impressive to the *Tribune*. Likening the Hawaiian to Christy Mathewson, nicknamed "Big Six" supposedly because he stood a relatively tall six feet, the *Tribune* depicted "Big Six Apau ... as a small edition in yellow binding of Christy Mathewson." Unfortunately, the game's umpire, according to the New York daily, gave little satisfaction to either side. The *Brooklyn Daily Eagle* added that "the Chinese furnished much amusement by their coaching on the bases as it was done in their native language."58

The *Advertiser* reported that the Columbia game's outcome was somehow stunning to New York fans. Apparently, "followers of baseball" expected to see "the Celestials" lose despite the Travelers' ability to win quite frequently in and around New York City in 1913. The Travelers, the *Advertiser* asserted, had put up a fine record even though it had played on many "strange grounds" at places where there was "hostility to the race." The Honolulu daily added that baseball scouts connected with the American Association league had ostensibly expressed interest in En Sue Pung, Foster Robinson, Albert Akana, and Kan Yen Chun.59

Brooklyn's Dexter Park was not kind to the Hawaiians on May 31 as they lost a game to the Cypress Hills nine, 8–2. The *Brooklyn Eagle* claimed that the "University of Hawaii Chinese baseball team" was surprised by the locals. Indeed, the usually reliable "Foster" was roughed up for 13 hits. Moreover, the Travelers were so upset with the umpire that he was replaced by someone who, according to the *Daily Eagle*, satisfied both teams.60

On June 2, according to Indiana, Pennsylvania's, *Gazette*, the "Chinese University baseball team" beat the Normal School nine, 11–2. The daily conceded, "The Chinks put up a fine article of ball from start to finish." Apau Kau was hit hard by the mainland college boys but he hung on to pitch the complete game. The *Gazette* wondered, however, if the large but apathetic crowd was at fault for dampening the spirits of the home team.61

A couple of days later, the Hawaiians departed Pennsylvania briefly for New Jersey. On June 6, they opposed the Camden Athletic Club nine. The *Philadelphia Inquirer's* headline above the game's account read, "Camden Easy for Chinamen." The story told readers that the locals were, indeed, no match for the "Hawaii boys" as over 6,000 witnessed "the famous Chinese team of the University of Hawaii" win, 9–1. The *Inquirer* maintained, "The clever Chinese team gave a wonderful exhibition of the national game and appeared much stronger than on their first visit to these parts." Foster Robinson pitched excellently and the spectators who "saw the speedy yellow boys at their best" stayed for the whole game even though Camden was far behind.[62]

In Morrisville, New Jersey, the Travelers faced a formidable semipro nine affiliated with the Delaware River League. Prior to the game in mid–June, the *Trenton Evening Times* promised that fans would see "the genuine Chinese university team which toured the country last year." The Morrisville manager had, according to the *Evening Times*, arranged with Nat C. Strong for the game the newspaper hailed as an "extraordinary attraction." The *Evening Times* recalled that the "Chinks" drew well in Philadelphia the previous summer even with Connie Mack's powerful Athletics playing a home stand. Thus, the New Jersey daily exuberantly claimed that the Hawaiians comprised the "greatest baseball attraction in this country today."[63]

The Sunday edition of the *Times* reassured fans that the "Celestials" would play excellently, that they "have mastered the great American game" as have no other "foreign" team. Since they were all attending the "University of Hawaii," the *Evening Times* guaranteed that the Hawaiians were "well educated." Moreover, the "colorful" visitors comprised the "highest price" independent team around. In other words, Trenton had better show up for the game. The *Evening Times* counseled readers to keep their eyes out for pitchers "Apau" and "Foster." They were both big league material. Kan Yen Chun, the daily advised, was also a good catcher. Thus, whoever was in the box, the "Celestial battery" matched up with any in the nation among independent teams. At the same time, the Travelers' "Celestial characteristics" had amused fans, according to the *Evening Times*. The team was full of "pep," the daily asserted, and its coaching in "pigeon English" entertained spectators. Still pumping up the fan base, the *Evening Times* the next day declared that the Hawaiians regularly played before 4,000 to 7,000 fans.[64]

The Travelers lost to the Morrisville nine, 4–2. Nevertheless, the *Evening Times* asserted that the "Chinese Played Remarkable Ball" in the headline of the game's story. One inning and a "rank" call by the umpire apparently did the visitors in. The "Celestials" surprised the 1,000 spectators with their skills, outplaying the home team even if the score suggested otherwise. Their strong arms especially impressed fans. Ayau's throws from shortstop were praised by the *Evening Times*. However, the Travelers' left fielder, called "Pring" by the local press, astonished local fans. "Pring's" throw from deep in left field caught a Morrisville base runner at home, the *Evening Times* declared, but the umpire outrageously gave the run to the home team. A few days after the game, an *Evening Times* columnist hailed "Pring's" throw from left as the best seen in ten years of baseball in Trenton. The columnist added that many local fans had expected that the "Chinks" constituted a "freak show," but were happily mistaken.[65]

A few days later, the Hawaiian ballplayers were in Amsterdam, New York. Earlier the *Amsterdam Evening Recorder and Daily Democrat* informed readers that a "Crack University team of Celestials" was coming to town to battle the Empires at Crescent Park. The daily maintained that the visitors comprised a good team that had "cleaned up" on college nines on the mainland. It added, "It will probably surprise a great many people that this team of Chinese ball tossers which represents the University of Hawaii, while composed of Chinese or Chinese-Kanakas are all American citizens." As for the game itself, it was not all that memorable. "The Chinese Students" won in the 11th inning, largely due to the home team's errors. The visitors did not play a "snappy game," but the Amsterdam newspaper was inclined toward forgiveness, declaring that the Travelers had spent much of the previous 24 hours traveling by rail from Williamstown, Massachusetts. Still, the Hawaiians evinced "flashes of speed at times" for the large crowd that attended the game.[66]

In mid- and late June, newspapers in Frederick, Maryland, publicized the impending arrival of the Travelers in their town. On June 17, the *Frederick Daily News* proclaimed that the "Orientals [are] Coming." The "Chinese University of Hawaii" had three dates to play in and around Frederick on June 30, July 1, and July 2. The daily added, "It is expected that they will prove a big attraction." On June 26, the *Daily News* published an advertisement for the game in Frederick—a game that would cost the public 25 cents admission. The advertisement also maintained that it was the "First time here for Chinamen." On June 29, the *Daily News* ran an article entitled "Blossoms Contest With Orientals" and subtitled, "Chinese Ball Players First Ever seen on Local Diamond." After just beating a team in Bridgeport, Connecticut, 9–4, the Hawaiians showed up in Frederick and "the appearance of the Orientals on the streets attracted considerable attention." The *Daily News* claimed as well that the "Chinese ... are a fast, husky looking bunch and a good game is promised."[67]

In the meantime, the *Frederick Post* informed readers that the "Chinks rolled into Philadelphia" and would board a morning train for Frederick. The very absent Lai Tin, according to the *Post*, was the team manager. The *Post* predicted a sizable attendance, because the "Chinese University of Hawaii" played only the best teams available and the "largest guarantee of the season was sent to the Hawaiian management." The *Post* cautioned that season tickets would not be honored for the game with "the boys from the Celestial Empire." It added, "Don't forget to see the Chinks today. It will perhaps be the chance of your life of seeing an Oriental crew in action."[68]

The Blossoms defeated the Hawaiians, 3–2, but the *Frederick Daily News* was impressed. The daily maintained, "Chinese University of Hawaii baseball team gave as fine an exhibition of the American national game as one could want to see." While they lost to the locals, the visitors "deserve great credit for the clean, fast, snappy game they put up." In addition, the "orientals ... are fast as lightning and jump on the ball the same as a cat on a mouse." The *News* reporter enthused that "love of the national game grows all the more after witnessing that contest yesterday." One of the reasons why the "Foreigners" lost was that they seem, according to the *Daily News*, bothered by the large crowd in attendance that zealously rooted for the home team. This seems hard to believe given the Travelers' past experiences playing in well-attended games. At any rate, Ayau hit a home run for the Hawaiians. The next day, the Travelers played in Hagerstown, where they lost easily, 10–2. The *Daily News* complained that they played "real Chinese ball"; that is, not well. It declared, "The Chinamen had several players in the line-up who were not in the game here and neither of their two pitchers twirled the fine game that their box artist (Apau Kau) did here on Monday." Indeed, "Alvin"—Alvin Robinson—pitched for the Hawaiians. While no doubt a talented ballplayer, he was hardly his brother's measure as a pitcher.[69]

On July 4, the Hawaiian contingent was scheduled to play a strong semi-pro nine in Philadelphia. The previous day the *Inquirer* announced that "the Chinese University of Pekin, China" would take on the Victrix Catholic Club at the latter's home field on 58th and Haverford Streets. The daily assured fans, as if they needed any assurances after the Hawaiians' previous visits in Philadelphia, that "the Oriental representatives" know baseball from "A to Z."[70]

On July 5, the Travelers were in Brooklyn to confront the Bushwicks at Wallace Park in the borough's Ridgewood section. The "invaders," as the *Brooklyn Eagle* called the Travelers, got off to a good start but could not hold off the home team and lost, 11–7. The *Eagle* lauded En Sue Pung's work in the outfield and Foster Robinson's fine throw from right field to cut down a runner at home. The daily even thought "Ako" did fine as a pitcher, despite the numerous runs the Bushwicks scored.[71]

The Allentown Tri-State minor league team found the Hawaiians easy pickings on July 6. The professionals, according to an *Inquirer* correspondent, "mowed down the Chinks at will." The fact that Alvin Robinson pitched was perhaps an important reason why the score ended 11–5 in the mainlanders' favor.[72]

On July 8, the Travelers appeared on the Philadelphia mainline, beating a nine in the town of Media. The *Chester Times* asserted, "The ballplayers of the Chinese University of Hawaii proved to be a real yellow peril to the Media team ... as they administered a Whitewash" to the locals. A good crowd watched the game—a crowd curious about seeing a team of players "associated with laundries and chop suey houses." Media fans had probably heard that the visitors were capable ballplayers but apparently did not believe it until they saw the Travelers in action. The *Times* subsequently claimed that Media's spectators were influenced by the "American idea that there is no nation that can beat us as at our own game." But they took the beating in stride, in large measure because "the Chinese turned the trick so politely, so smilingly and in such a clean sportsmanlike way." They were particularly taken with the pitching of "Kau Apau whose pleasant smile and rather awkward delivery are remembered by all who saw the game."[73]

On July 11, the Travelers beat the Strawbridge-Clothier contingent, 8–2, at Philadelphia's Sixty-Third and Walnut Street grounds. A reportedly overflow crowd of 2,500 saw the action. Indeed, fair balls hit into the spectators became ground rule doubles. Subtitled "Almond-Eyed Team" and "Christians Never Had a Chance to Win From Confucius' Lively Followers," an *Inquirer* account of the game asserted that the Hawaiian ball club appearing in Philadelphia was "not as strong as the Chinese representations visiting America last season." Still, the team's "speed on the bases and quickness on the field" proved more than enough for Strawbridge-Clothier to handle.[74]

Still in Pennsylvania, Sam Hop stirred controversy. In an article headlined, "Chinese Team Left Before Game," the *Gettysburg Star and Sentinel* reported that "Sam Hop and his yellow warriors" had arrived in Gettysburg after losing badly to a team in nearby Chambersburg. However, the "Chinks" left before the game was played because Sam Hop believed that inclement weather would drastically limit the gate receipts and lingering in Gettysburg until the sky cleared would not be profitable. The *Star and Sentinel* declared, "Argument to the contrary could not convince the little manager otherwise."[75]

Still, the "Traveling All-Chinese" were doing fine on the mainland, according to an unnamed correspondent to the *Star-Bulletin*. The correspondent conceded, much as Hoe did regarding the 1913 trek, that the 1914 mainland journey was long and hard for the Hawaiians. He wrote, "There are times when Hawaii and the life simple look a lot better than day coaches and strange diamonds."[76]

On July 30, the *Star-Bulletin* published a letter sent by En Sue Pung to his brother, En Fee. Writing in Philadelphia, the dynamic outfielder said the team was looking forward to a game against the Stetsons, although En Sue expected a hard-fought contest. In general, Pung declared, the team was having a great time and did not know when they would return. However, he insisted to his brother that "they were laying away a little *kala* for wintry days." That is, they were saving money.[77]

On August 14, the *Star-Bulletin* published extracts of a diary supposedly kept by one of the "Traveling Chinese" ballplayers. On July 3, the team was in Hanover, Pennsylvania, where it "visited the noted Hanover shoe factory." On Independence Day, the Travelers were appropriately ensconced in Philadelphia. In the "City of Brotherly Love," they saw President Wilson at Independence Hall. Otherwise, the Fourth was quiet for the Hawaiians. On July 6, the Travelers had a day off and wound up watching a Philadelphia Athletics-New York Yankees game. On July 11, the team had another day off in Philadelphia and "the boys went shopping." The next day they had a "party at Coney Island." On July 13, they spent a day watching a New York Yankees-Chicago White Sox doubleheader in New York. There they "met a few Hawaiian boys." On July 14, they visited the Bronx Zoo "and the magnificent aquarium." Six days later, the Travelers had time off again to see a doubleheader pitting the Yankees against the St. Louis Browns.[78]

In early August, the Travelers were in southeastern Pennsylvania. There they encountered a team in Rockdale — a team that beat the "traveling Celestials," 9–4. In the process, the Pennsylvanians roughed up Apau. The *Chester Times* declared that the game drew the largest crowd in some time to Rockdale's baseball field. The nearby mills had closed down in order to allow workers to get home and dressed up in their finest attire for the game. The *Chester Times* maintained that much of the region was represented at the game. It counted "two score automobiles" and many carriages, adding that fans left their "machines" behind to sit in the stands.[79]

Located in Pennsylvania's Delaware County, Upland, according to the *Chester Times*, eagerly awaited the arrival of the Travelers. Not only would Upland's baseball fans show up, the daily speculated, but fans from nearby Chester would flock to the game. Thus arrangements were made for "special cars" to transport spectators to Upland's ball park. In addition, the game was scheduled for 5 P.M. so that "business men" could attend.[80]

The *Star-Bulletin* praised the "Traveling All-Chinese" as their mainland tour wound down. Readers of the daily learned on August 15 that the Hawaiian ballplayers played admirably on the mainland despite their arduous travel schedule. The Travelers were drawing good crowds and making good money, the *Star-Bulletin* insisted. Apparently, "the previous tours have whetted the public's appetite for more." Still, the Honolulu daily confirmed, the ballplayers were anxious to return home.[81]

In mid– to late August, the Travelers were working hard for victories in New York City. On August 16, the barnstormers blasted the Cypress Hills nine, 10–3, at Dexter Park. The *Brooklyn Eagle* could only comment, "The visitors from the Far East put up a great game." On August 23, the *Eagle* maintained, "Fast Chinese Team Defeated Bushwicks." The Hawaiians had lost several games on the Wallace Grounds to the likes of the Bushwicks in 1914. However, in this game, "the Chinese outfielded, outbatted, and outgeneraled the Bushwicks." In so doing, they "surprised many" spectators.[82]

On September 5, the *Star-Bulletin* announced the upcoming return of the Travelers. The "Traveling All-Chinese" would head out of New York City on September 15. They would make their way to San Francisco by train, stopping at Buffalo, Niagara Falls, Detroit, and Chicago. The daily printed a letter written by En Sue Pung and dated August 24. The outfielder conceded that the 1914 team was not as good as the previous year's aggregation. Out of 137 games they had played, the Travelers had won 80 and lost 54 while three ended in ties. En Sue Pung hailed Philadelphia and New York City for turning out the best crowds for their games. He said that the team promoted the Islands "pretty well." Mainlanders were curious about Hawai'i, En Sue added. But, he conceded, they could ask "foolish questions," such as the businessman who asked if Hawai'i "was in the north of the U.S."[83]

In September, Hop's aggregation garnered positive publicity in the *Philadelphia Public Ledger, Indianapolis Star* and *Washington Post*. The *Public Ledger* evaluated the Travelers as a drawing card, but saved special praise for Apau Kau. The Philadelphia daily called the pitcher "one of the sensations in baseball this season ... without question the greatest hurler of his nationality." Under the headline "Chinese Baseball Players Who Have Made A Record," the *Star* asserted, "if you do not think the Chinese can play baseball you will be treated to the surprise of your life in seeing a performance of the doughty team of the University of Hawaii with its mighty pitcher, Apau Kau." The *Star* added, "These Mongolian youngsters have taken to the American national game as though it had been theirs for long generations, only they have orientalized it so that some of its outward signs are puzzling to the beholder used to strict convention." The *Star* proved less than clear, however, as to how the Hawaiians "orientalized" baseball.[84]

The *Washington Post* asserted that the 1914 journey had proven successful for the "Chinese baseball team of the University of Hawaii." Disputing En Sue Pung, the *Post* claimed in late September that the Hawaiians had won 125 out of 150 games, even though the last three months of their tour had confined them to playing independent nines in New York and Pennsylvania. Moreover, "the business men of Honolulu" who had financed their trip also considered the Hawaiian ballplayers triumphant in playing America's national game on mainland soil.[85]

Unhappily, the team had to abandon a proposed trip to Cuba and return home to the islands even though the Caribbean excursion would have been a good economic opportunity for the Hawaiians. According to a 1915 *Star-Bulletin* article, the Travelers' lack of pitching depth decided against the trek to Cuba, where they would have faced some of the best teams in the world.[86]

In Honolulu, the CAU team showed its mettle thanks in part to the play of Traveler veterans Lang Akana and especially Lai Tin. Chinese merchants in Honolulu were reportedly anxious to support a CAU nine in the Oahu

League. The *Advertiser* expected that unlike "Sammy Hop's aggregation," the CAU would field a team that could truly represent the "Chinese population."[87]

On April 19, the team that the *Advertiser* called the "All-Chinese" beat the Portuguese nine, 5–0. On the day of the game, the daily published a cartoon of two players digging into a box labeled "Real Players." One ballplayer represented the Chinese and the other the Portuguese. The Chinese figure wore a straw hat and striped suit. The cartoon's caption read, "Everyone of 'em is All Chinese Alright [*sic*]." More than suggesting a contrast to the Travelers, the *Advertiser* boasted that every member of the CAU nine possessed some kind of Chinese ancestry.[88]

In late April, the *Advertiser* promoted an upcoming game between the CAU nine and the Asahis. Honolulu baseball fans ought to get excited because the game would feature teams that "represent different Oriental races." The daily also displayed a photo of Lai Tin in a batting stance. The third baseman was described as the "leader of the All-Chinese." Tin Chong, who managed the CAU nine, was quoted in the *Star-Bulletin* as saying, "There can be no dispute over the fact that when China meets Japan on the baseball diamond a hard fought game is in sight." At the same time, Tin Chong professed his respect for the Asahis.[89]

In late June, Cal's baseball team arrived on the islands, encountering the CAU nine twice. Both games aroused considerable interest from the local press and the fans. For the first game, spectators were entertained by a Hawaiian band and a Chinese quintet. The "record crowd" was also entertained by an exciting game in which Lai Tin stood out. The *Star-Bulletin* gloated, "If every ball player would run out hits the way Lai Tin does there would be a lot more runs scored…. 'Tin' goes to first at full speed whether his chances are good or bad."[90]

According to the *Advertiser*, "Chinatown is talking nothing but baseball" after the first game between Cal and the CAU ballplayers. "The whole Celestial colony" was expected to appear for the second game, the *Advertiser* predicted. The "pride of Chinatown," Luck Yee, would pitch for the Chinese Hawaiian nine. The game proved just as exciting as fans hoped. The CAU contingent edged Cal in extra innings, 8–7, before another record crowd of 4,800.[91]

Because of the CAU's success against Cal, the possibility surfaced that the CAU nine would tour the mainland. This would mean, according to the *Advertiser*, that a "real All-Chinese team" would head east under the direction of W. Tin Chong. In the meantime, the CAU nine became a bigger deal than ever in Honolulu baseball. The *Star-Bulletin* reported that the Portland Beavers of the Pacific Coast League had sent a contract to outfielder Lang Akana as well as to another standout Honolulu athlete, haole Bill Inman. It was expected that Akana, at any rate, would sign with the Beavers. The Star-

Bulletin also speculated that members of Sam Hop's contingent would ultimately join the CAU — athletes such as Kan Yen, En Sue, Ping Kong, William Apau, and perhaps Apau Kau.[92]

However, the CAU's supremacy in Honolulu was challenged by the 25th Infantry. On August 9, the African American nine defeated Chong's squad in what the *Star-Bulletin* called a "see-saw battle." Consequently, the *Star-Bulletin* observed, "Pandemonium reigned in the 25th infantry stands and joy was unrestrained for the 25th had realized one of their fondest dreams, the defeat of the All-Chinese."[93]

Meanwhile, the Pacific Coast League baseball world was all aflutter over the fact that the Venice team was slated to head to the Hawaiian Islands at season's end. The *Advertiser's* Herbert Lowery supposedly would arrange the trip. Hawaiian teams, according to the *Oakland Tribune*, would challenge the PCL nine. In particular, *Tribune* readers learned, the Venice ballplayers would have to deal with the All-Chinese nine, "every member of which is a full-blooded Chinamen" At the same time, "every one of these men are fast on their feet, great throwers, and swell hitters." The fact that the Coast Leaguers intended to head to the islands during the winter prompted the *Advertiser* to wonder if Hop's aggregation would have a chance to play the Venice nine. The daily speculated that if Hop did not wish too much of the gate receipts, his team would be accommodated.[94]

Significantly, the Oahu League tried to attain some kind of affiliation with the mainland's organized baseball. However, the *Star-Bulletin* reported that organized baseball's adherence to the color line barred the Oahu League from even lower division, minor league ranking. Lowery was told by PCL President A.G. Baum that "no negroes or Orientals" were allowed in organized baseball. Yet, the *Star-Bulletin* contended, the Oahu League's very best players were "Japanese, Chinese, and colored" and would not consider raising "the bars of race" against them. The Honolulu daily also speculated that race may have kept En Sue Pung and Vernon Ayau out of organized baseball.[95]

On September 1, the *Star-Bulletin* reported that Lang Akana was leaving the CAU nine. The Hawaiis, an Oahu League team supposedly consisting of athletes of indigenous Hawaiian ancestry, had just played at Schofield with Akana in the lineup. The CAU nine, meanwhile, was simultaneously competing elsewhere. The *Star-Bulletin* ventured the opinion that Akana was bothered by rumors that the CAU would welcome players from "the traveling All-Chinese team."[96]

While they did not make the trek across the mainland in 1914, Lang Akana and Lai Tin as well as other Chinese Hawaiian ballplayers attracted the interest of mainland baseball followers. Significantly, the *New York Times* published an article about the Cal-CAU games in December 1914, several months after the fact. The CAU squad was "made up entirely of fullblooded Chinese," according to the *Times* piece. A photograph of the CAU nine accompanied the story although the player names listed in the caption fit another, European American, team. The *Times*, in any event, declared that the photo depicted "Hawaii's Crack Chinese Baseball Team." The *Times* maintained, "As an American possession it is natural that the Hawaiians should have taken most kindly of all the Antipodean countries to our national game — baseball. They seem to have taken it with their Americanism, play it cleverly, and have developed an army of 'fans' that would do any American possession credit." The *Times* purported that Honolulu fielded a dozen teams and that half of these nines played baseball as well as any amateur contingent on the mainland. However, "the true enthusiasts of the sport outside the American-born contingent are the Chinese. They are an athletic-loving lot and play the game with much skill and thorough understanding of its fine points."[97]

Times readers discovered that the CAU team edged the Californians, 6–5, before 5,500 Honolulu fans in the first game. Captain Lai Tin was called a "speed demon" by the *Times* correspondent, who also declared that "Lai Tin, leader of the Chinese team, who plays at shortstop, worked his players so well that they seemed the strongest in both attack and defense." The next game, witnessed by a reported 7,000 spectators, saw the CAU come from behind to top Cal, 8–7. According to the *Times*, the game went into extra innings. Cal jumped ahead by two runs in the top half of the tenth. "But the Celestials showed plenty of sand" and achieved victory in the bottom half of the tenth. The New York daily added, "The Chinese spectators came to the game prepared to see their fellow countrymen win," which meant "2000 firecrackers as well as the cheers and other characteristic demonstrations of a true baseball fan." The *Times* remained dazzled by Lai Tin as it praised his speed and flawless fielding.[98]

While all this publicity about Hawaiian and Chinese Hawaiian baseball was surfacing, Akana and Lai Tin reportedly signed contracts with prestigious organized baseball franchises — Akana with the Portland Beavers of the Pacific Coast League and Lai Tin with the major league Chicago White Sox. On December 5, 1914, the *Nevada State Journal* told readers that "a full-blooded Chinese player" had been signed by the White Sox, who had ordered "Lai Tin" to report to the team's training camp in Paso Robles, California, the next spring. A *Fort Worth Telegram* headline writer labeled Lai Tin as a "full-blooded Chink." Meanwhile, the *Washington Post* declared in a headline of an article on Lai Tin: "Chinese For White Sox." The accompanying article proclaimed, "Organized baseball is threatened with an invasion from China. Cubans, Indians, and Italians have been successful in America's national game but, up to the present, no Chinaman or Japanese has shown himself sufficiently proficient to be carried on the roster of a major league team." Calling the Hawaiian Chinese athlete "Capt. Lai-Tin of the Honolulu Chinese," the article averred that if the infielder made the White Sox, he would "enjoy the unique honor of being the first Celestial to play on a National or American League team." Negligent about geography, it added that Lai Tin was "one of the best shortstops in the Far East" and that he was a versatile athlete, a "clever fielder" and a "crack batter."[99]

Frank Menke, a notable syndicated sportswriter, urged readers in a December 12 column to "think of the complications that would come in case Mr. Tin horned into a regular job." A wire story expressed disappointment that Chief Bender had jumped to the outlaw Federal League. Had he remained with the Philadelphia Athletics, he would have pitched against Lai Tin, "the new Chinese infielder of the White Sox" ... [and] afforded a spectacle of race conflict not provided elsewhere." Writing in *Sporting Life*, Ren Mulford, Jr., joked along similar lines in the December 19 edition, "Now that the White Sox have corralled that Honolulu Chinaman — Lai Tin — every paragrapher in Balldom will be ringing the challenges on the

Lang Akana was a hard-hitting, speedy outfielder who reportedly signed a contract with the Portland Beavers of the Pacific Coast League in December 1914. However, racism seems to have denied Akana an opportunity to be the first Asian American to play organized baseball in the United States (courtesy of Library of Congress, Prints & Photographs Division, LC-DIG-ggbain-18237).

possibility that Tin will be canned." Another anonymous *Sporting Life* writer insisted, however, that "if all is said about Lai Tin is true there is no doubt he can make it."[100]

While he did not mention Lai Tin by name, "Sportsman" in the *Baltimore Afro-American* informed readers on December 12 that a "Chinese" had been signed by a major league baseball team. The columnist identified the ballplayer as coming from Honolulu and being signed "because of his superior ability and not because of a peculiar fascination with members of his race." "Sportsman" hoped that organized baseball might extend the same courtesy to African Americans.[101]

On the West Coast, the *Portland Oregonian* supported the Beavers' acquisition of Akana. Veteran *Oregonian* sportswriter Roscoe Fawcett told readers that Akana was a good outfielder, while observing that since he possessed both Hawaiian and Chinese ancestry, "No ballplayer blending half portions of poi and chop suey ever before has embellished a professional diamond." Meanwhile, Henry Carr of the *Los Angeles Times* complained that managers of the two Los Angeles PCL teams had made a mistake in not trying to sign Akana. Carr maintained that Akana had pitched well for the "University of Hawaii pigtail squad" when it took on Occidental earlier in the year. Carr had probably confused Lang Akana with his brother Albert. The former, we should remember, did not make the trip to the mainland in 1914. Indeed, Carr might have been even more confused since Albert infrequently pitched for the Hawaiians.[102]

Carr's apparent bewilderment pervaded the *Times* building. On December 15, 1914, the *Times* published an article by Donald O'Brien headlined "McCreadie's Chinese Pitcher Seen Here." McCreadie was the Portland Beavers owner and the story was largely based on O'Brien's interview with an athlete he identified as Lang Akana, when the Hawaiian traveling nine played Occidental several months earlier. Most likely referring to brother Albert, O'Brien echoed Carr in lamenting that "[I]f Akana, the half-caste Chinese pitcher ... turns out to be a star it will be another instance of the local baseball magnates being asleep at the wheel." To O'Brien, Akana had demonstrated great promise as a pitcher for the "University of Hawaii." If Akana made it with the Beavers, O'Brien advised PCL fans in Los Angeles not to "get ready to see a Chink come out in a pigtail and padded Chinese shoes ... or to hear him talking about, 'You catchum ball.'" Rather, Akana was a university student capable of speaking "better English than about nine-tenths of the American baseball players."[103]

According to O'Brien, Akana as a "Chinese boy, being a half caste, is rather large and strong." Akana spoke both Hawaiian and Chinese, the reporter declared. Indeed, O'Brien pointed out that the Traveling Hawaiians did much of their coaching in Chinese. Akana, O'Brien asserted, apparently was fast and could hit. He added, "I found, however, that none of the Chinese depended much on their hitting. They seemed to have no special desire to make extra-base hits. Their idea of baseball is to get on first base, then get around the rest of the way by speed and skill."[104]

Sportswriters to the east of the Rockies considered Akana's signing newsworthy. Thomas Richter in *Sporting Life* lamented that Portland had signed Akana and not the Phillies. It seems as though Richter confused Akana with either Ayau or perhaps Lai Tin. That is, he called Akana "a wonderful Chinese shortstop" who had performed well in the Philadelphia area. In any event, he expected Phillies manager Pat Moran to keep an eye out for Akana's progress. A few weeks later, Chandler D. Richter, in the same weekly, noted, under the headline "A New Yellow Peril," that a "Chinese has broken into professional baseball." Akana was just the beginning, Richter predicted. More, such as Lai Tin, would follow. Richter conceded that there had been a "little prejudice" against the Chinese in organized baseball. He doubted, moreover, that major league ball clubs such as the White Sox would have been interested in Lai Tin if they had not heard that McCreadie had "broken the ice" by signing Akana. Richter was convinced that Akana possessed major league potential and was a better prospect than Lai Tin. In any event, he asserted that Akana, Lai Tin, and a handful of other "Chinese" players had held together an otherwise mediocre traveling team.[105]

Chandler Richter went on to comment more about the Travelers and their key players. He averred that it was impossible to determine just how old these players were. However, he insisted that Akana was 18 and, just as important, had mastered the English language. In contrast, Richter deemed En Sue Pung a prospect, but, curiously, lacking in English proficiency. Foster Robinson had decidedly impressed Richter. The mainlander asserted that not only was Robinson expert at English, but was a notably versatile ballplayer who could not only pitch but do other things to help a ball club. Richter even likened Robinson's baserunning talents to Ty Cobb. He admitted, however, that all of the Travelers, regardless of position, loved to run. As for Lai Tin, Richter doubted he could stick with the White Sox, because speed was his only real talent. Still, if Lai Tin made the White Sox, Richer speculated, he would draw fans to White Sox games.[106]

By the end of the year, McCreadie's ardor had cooled for Akana. The PCL mogul was reportedly willing to ship his services down organized baseball's ladder to Spokane of the Northwest League. Roscoe Fawcett argued that it made little for sense for McCreadie to pay $175 in transportation costs for Akana to show up in Portland. After all, Akana was nothing but a "busher."[107]

As for the Travelers, Nat Strong was planning another mainland journey in 1915. Indeed, in October 1914, the *Tulsa World* reported that the ubiquitous promoter sought a game against Oklahoma's Kendall College in the early spring. It is doubtful Strong expected much of a pay day for the Hawaiians at Kendall.[108]

Four

Never the Home Team, 1915

As the New Year began, it became somewhat clearer why Walter McCreadie had backed off putting Lang Akana in a Portland Beavers uniform. On January 2, 1915, the *Pacific Commercial Advertiser* proudly announced that Akana and Lai Tin would become "the first Orientals to be given a tryout in organized baseball." Others on the mainland, however, opposed Akana wearing a Beavers uniform. Taking a cue from the anti–Asian trade union movement on the American west coast, white PCL players warned McCreadie that they would rather go on strike than let Akana join the Beavers. They claimed they were offended by Akana's skin color, which they maintained was darker than Jack Johnson's. McCreadie denounced the racism pervasive in organized baseball, but reportedly buckled under demands that he get rid of Akana. Writing for *The Sporting News*, Roscoe Fawcett declared that McCreadie had "exploded a bombshell" when he announced the signing of "a half Hawaiian, half Chinese outfielder." Fawcett also called Akana a "Chinese horticulturalist" and a "poi eating prodigy." Moreover, he pointed out that Akana's release "leaves the Chinese field clear to the Chicago White Sox. The Sox recently signed a full-blooded Chinese whose mission in life will be to combat Buck Weaver for the job of shortstop."[1]

On the West Coast, Jack McCarthy, a long-time PCL umpire, supported Akana. McCarthy told Fawcett that he could not understand why McCreadie would release the Hawaiian outfielder. McCarthy described Akana as "a big rangy fellow" who could make good in the PCL. He swung the bat too hard, but, McCarthy insisted, that could be remedied. He dismissed arguments that Akana was "black." Indeed, the umpire described him as "white."[2]

Keeping Portland readers abreast of Akana's tenuous position in organized baseball, the *Oregonian* reported on January 12 that the outfielder had helped a team of Honolulu "all-stars" defeat the Travelers, on which his brother Albert played. The account of the game asserted that Akana was fast and could the hit ball hard. However, he had a difficult time catching up to high and tight fast balls — a problem Akana had trouble explaining, although undoubtedly familiar to many left-handed batters down through the years.[3]

The idea of someone like Akana playing professionally on the mainland continued to incite the strained efforts of would-be humorists. A wire story published in the *Lima Daily News* was headlined, "Wait Until This Chink Bumps Into a Bold Ump." The writer depicted Akana as a good ballplayer, but wondered what would happen when an umpire called a strike against him. "Ow, wowee. Whatee malla you? You all time givee ploor Chinese worst from ittee; way outsidee, way outsidee!" A similar article was published later in the month regarding Lai Tin.[4]

In the January 18 issue of the *Portland Oregonian*, Roscoe Fawcett revealed the rather helpful comments made about Akana by Bill James, a major leaguer and former Beaver who had played against "the Chink." James maintained that Akana had the potential to do well in the PCL, but he was more impressed with the "Chinese shortstop." Either Ayau or Lai Tin, this shortstop had to field plenty of powerfully struck balls in his direction, but he "scooped everything up.... He made plays that would have baffled any major league shortstop." Unfortunately, this ballplayer was not a particularly good hitter. As for Akana, James somewhat denied the racial fears of PCL ballplayers. Akana was not all that dark-skinned, but he was "very brown." The Hawaiian was, in other words, "not black, like a negro." Moreover, his hair was straight. James, accordingly, believed that ballplayers could tolerate playing with and against Akana, but was not sure if hotels would welcome the outfielder. At the same time, Akana could "speak and write English" like a "penmanship teacher." Roscoe Fawcett, meanwhile, asserted that McCreadie was pulled in different directions on Akana. He wanted to bring Akana in for a tryout but was dubious about doing so due to the Hawaiian's "skin color."[5]

Justin Fitzgerald similarly backed Akana in a lukewarm fashion. A PCL ballplayer, he had, according to the *Oakland Tribune*, written McCreadie that Akana had talent. Describing Akana as 5'11" and 175 pounds, Fitzgerald admitted that the outfielder was "dark"— possessing a "strain of Chinese blood" but looking like a "Kanaka."[6]

The *Pacific Commercial Advertiser* supported Akana. It pointed out that the PCL players who refused to play with and against Akana were either racially bigoted or feared they would lose their jobs if organized baseball erased the color line. According to the *Advertiser*, a member of the Venice PCL team was the primary instigator of the proposed strike. In Hawai'i during the off season, he had played against Akana and was not enchanted with the Chinese Hawaiian's skills. The author of the *Advertiser* piece insisted, "Perhaps so, but the writer is of the opinion that the Coast League is simply enforcing an old standby rule not to let Orientals and colored men into the ranks."[7]

The *Star-Bulletin* chimed in as well. Hardly mincing its words, it asserted that Akana's treatment by the PCL "reeks of narrow-minded prejudice and fathomless ignorance." The issue went deeper than baseball. That is, "it is not unlikely that most of the ballplayers in the Coast League think of Chinamen as ... laundrymen and Hawaiians as surf-riding savages." The *Star-Bulletin* declared, "local fans are thoroughly disgusted over the whole affair." Likewise, they "will be pulling hard for Lai Tin to make good with the White Sox. If he develops into a star the Portland management may have a few regrets coming."[8]

If Akana could not latch onto a Beavers roster spot, the *Star-Bulletin* speculated, he might make it in Spokane. The Honolulu daily reported that Jack McCarthy considered Akana a "wonder in all branches of the game." McCarthy believed that the Hawaiian would help Spokane and quickly move up the minor league ladder. Apparently, Spokane's president was also convinced of Akana's effectiveness. The *Star-Bulletin* even shaped Akana's fate into poetry: "Everybody talks but Akana,/ He sits round all day,/With a contract in his pocket/ And nothing at all to say." The *Star-Bulletin* also asserted that West Coast newspapers were backing Akana and that McCreadie might reconsider.[9]

Akana's fate lingered into February. At this time, McCreadie stated that he was willing to give Akana a tryout. However, he declared that Akana would have to pay his own way to the mainland. As the *Oakland Tribune* put it, the further away Akana was from McCreadie "the darker the poor chink got," even though the Hawaiian could probably draw fans to the Beavers' games. Akana perhaps wisely decided not to waste his time and money and remained in Hawai'i, shunning even Spokane as an option.[10]

Possibly because anti–Asian politics were not as strong in the Midwest as on the West Coast, the White Sox's signing of Buck Lai Tin caused less open hostility. A syndicated sports columnist writing under the pseudonym of "Bob" speculated in early January that Lai Tin might escape the duress experienced by Akana because he had "lighter skin."[11]

The potential of Lai Tin playing big league ball did inspire sorry displays of wit. On January 2, 1915, the *Boston Journal* published a panel of cartoons. The major caption read:

> Comiskey's got a Chinee man — no cleannee shirt, no makee pan chop suey, neither yok. [Comiskey's] Oriental gent is here to earn an honest cent by givin' ball fans shock. That washboard presentation there should make those White Sox boosters stare. And if Lai Tin can't spank the ball or bag the screeching liner, still Lai Tin can washee suits.

When word got out that the Chicago White Sox wanted to give Lai Tin a tryout in 1915, the sporting press reacted in a variety of ways. This cartoon represents one of the more unfortunate reactions (reprinted in the *Boston Journal*, January 2, 1915).

One cartoon depicted a stereotypical Chinese man giving a washboard to a figure representing Lai Tin. While other Chinese figures stood in the background, Lai Tin's figure said, "Thanks, velly much." Another cartoon had Lai Tin doing laundry, the caption proclaiming, "No excuse for soiled uniforms with Lai on the job."[12]

Along the same lines, a wire story constructed an imaginary argument between Lai Tin and a big league umpire. Lai Tin is quoted as protesting, "Wattee Malla you? No can do! Lobber! You all time give ploor Chinee worst from itee! way outside! way outside!" Later in January, the *Oakland Tribune* and the *Fort Wayne Sentinel* published photo stories on "William Tin Lai." On January 17, the *Oakland Tribune's* story was headlined "Chink to Join White Sox." The text informed readers that Lai Tin would be the first "Mongolian" major leaguer. The *Tribune* vaguely pointed out that he had played "in different parts of the Eastern world" and incorrectly pointed out that he had played on the 1914 touring team. In any event, the *Tribune* depicted Lai Tin as talented and therefore expressed little surprise at his signing. The headline to the *Fort Wayne Sentinel* story misrepresented "William Tin Lai" as a pitcher and claimed that he "has earned the name of 'Yellow Peril'"[13]

The *Freeman*, an African American newspaper published in Indianapolis, advised readers that Chicago baseball fans were already joking about Lai Tin's signing. Calling the infielder "Willie," one wag speculated that Lai Tin had an advantage over other ballplayers in arguing balls and strikes because he could protest in hard-to-interpret Chinese rather than English.[14]

In the March 1915 issue of *Baseball Magazine*, William Phelon noted the signing of Lai Tin, "the Chinese wonder." He declared that Lai Tin's signing sent "ripples of merriment" throughout the major leagues. It also apparently caused Phelon to claim that Lai Tin was the nephew of "Pie Tin" and closely related to "Tin Horn." Phelon conceded that Lai Tin was "a great ballplayer:" "He is from the famous traveling team of Chinks — allee samee they are really half white and half Chinese — sons of rich Hawaiians — and can play a brilliant shortstop, besides batting heftily."[15]

Nevertheless, Lai Tin, like Akana, did not get a chance to wear an organized baseball uniform in 1915. Perhaps one reason was that the manager who recruited Lai Tin was replaced. Another was that the White Sox were well stocked with infielders, including a solid third baseman named Buck Weaver, who later figured in the Black Sox scandal of 1919. However, a wire story published in the *Wilkes-Barre Times* claimed "one element in the baseball melting pot will be missing next season." Apparently, "Lai Tin, the Chinese shortstop decided on his own to pass on the White Sox because he did not want to play on a team that did not carry any other of his 'fellow countrymen.'"[16]

At the same time, the mainland press floated rumors that Frank Bancroft, who ran the Cincinnati Reds, wanted Foster Robinson, while Apau Kau had also tempted mainland professional franchises. A wire story reported that Bancroft had seen "Foster" in action against the major leaguers who had visited the Islands over the winter and was duly impressed. Moreover, the *Brooklyn Eagle* maintained that Apau Kau had turned down a contract from a Western League team, because, like Lai Tin, he did not wish to play apart from his "native companions."[17]

In announcing the approaching departure of the Hawaiian ballplayers to the mainland, the *Advertiser* averred that "Sammy Hop, one time pilot for the team" would remain in Honolulu to sell soda water to the thirsty. After the Hawaiian ballplayers boarded the ship heading for the mainland, the *Advertiser* admitted, "Honolulu today is shy an even dozen perfectly good

From 1914 to 1916, ballplayers of Japanese descent joined the once All-Chinese team. Andy Yamashiro and Jimmy Moriyama stand between outfielder Yen Chin, to Yamashiro's left and Lai Tin, to Moriyama's right (courtesy of the Yamashiro Family).

players. When the Manoa pulled out yesterday afternoon she took along with her an aggregation of ball tossers who promised to eclipse the record made by the famous 'All-Chinese' teams which have previously toured the mainland." Once in San Francisco, the *Advertiser* continued, the team would get new uniforms with "All Chinese" printed on the breasts. Interestingly, the daily added, this "All-Chinese" team had but five Hawaiians of Chinese ancestry on the team — Lai Tin, Vernon Ayau, Apau Kau, Henry Kuali, and Al Yap. Three Japanese Hawaiians — Andy Yamashiro and the Moriyama brothers — also left Oahu on the *Manoa*, in addition to Hawaiians possessing indigenous ancestry — George Bush, Jimmy Aylett, Luther Kekoa, and Fred Markham. Foster Robinson stayed on Maui. The *Advertiser* speculated several months later that the team's leaders considered Robinson no longer effective.[18]

The *Honolulu Star-Bulletin* called the aggregation heading for the mainland the "Traveling Chinese." It reported that "Apau Kau, about the best the Chinese have in the pitching line, will act as manager, and Lai Tin will captain the team on the field." With Vernon "Shorty" Ayau at shortstop and Chinito Moriyama at second combined with Lai Tin at third, the *Star-Bulletin* expected the Travelers to have "a particularly fast infield." The *Star-Bulletin* added that "Nat C. Strong, the New York booking agent has been looking after the dates and has a good tour arranged, including a side trip to Cuba, which the players are looking forward to with great interest."[19]

Later in March 1915, the *San Francisco Examiner* informed readers of the arrival of the "Celestial Ball Tossers," who were "Chinamen born in the islands." Akana, "the Chink signed by McCreadie," ranked among the best of the Hawaiian ballplayers, according to the *Examiner*, which failed to recognize his absence. The *Daily Palo Alto* announced an upcoming game between Stanford and the Hawaiians, declaring that the visitors had just arrived "from the Orient." The daily called Lai Tin the team's leader and Kan Yen Chun its manager, even though the latter was also among the missing. It added, "The aggregation is composed of all-star players from all over the islands" and promised that a "unique baseball attraction will be the order of the day tomorrow when the Chinese University team of Honolulu, Hawaiia [*sic*]" would take on the Stanford varsity." Subsequently, the Hawaiians cavorted relatively freely on the base paths against Stanford, stealing seven bases and winning, 10–7.[20]

Before the Travelers' game against Cal, the *Oakland Tribune* declared, "The little men of the east are said to be exceptionally strong in the pitching line with a Manchurian of considerable height and bulk to call upon for the heavy work." The Cal game proved a bust for the "all-star Chinese-Hawaiian aggregation," as the *Tribune* called the Travelers. The visitors showed expertise as fielders but were "woefully weak" at bat as they lost to the Cal Bears, 6–0.[21]

We know about some of the details of the Hawaiian ballplayers' 1915 journey to and through the U.S. mainland thanks to the *Honolulu Star-Bulletin* receiving regular correspondence from one of the Travelers, Al Yap, who not only wrote about many of the games the Hawaiians played in the 1915 but about the excitement and boredom attached to traveling mostly by rail from one relatively little town on the mainland to another.

Yap reported that the team had arrived on the mainland at 11:30 A.M. on March 9 in San Francisco. He declared, "Every one is feeling fine and is ready for the battle royal" and added, "As we have no games on the 11th and 12th we have planned to take in the fair [the Pan-Pacific Exposition] and enjoy ourselves a little. The weather here is just right." In Palo Alto, according to Yap, the Hawaiians faced Stanford's best pitcher. But he proved no mystery to the visitors. In addition, Yap observed that "one brilliant play" evoked the applause of the Stanford crowd. Second baseman "Chin" or Chinito Moriyama stopped a hot liner heading toward center field and relayed the ball to shortstop Ayau, who quickly threw out a Stanford baserunner by several feet. The defeat at Berkeley occurred, Yap protested, substantially because of the weather, which was "foggy and chilly and only a few of the boys showed much pep at all."[22]

Lingering in the Bay Area, the Hawaiian ballplayers stopped in at San José to play the Salt Lake City PCL team. In advertising the game with Salt Lake City, the *San Jose Mercury* printed a publicity blurb that declared that the Hawaiian nine was "without doubt the greatest drawing card playing baseball in the United States." At the same time, the promotional piece published in the *Mercury* advised readers that even if the visitors from halfway across the Pacific were U.S. citizens they were colonial subjects and presumably non-white ones at that. Echoing almost word for word an earlier press release, the *Mercury* advised that the Hawaiian ballplayers had been somewhat de-exoticized by Uncle Sam's baseball. Readers discovered that they were well assimilated, "refined gentlemen of the highest type." The writer stated that the Hawaiians seemed like typical American "college boys" in that "they speak English, spend rainy afternoons around the piano, ragtime music and Hawaiian songs are popular with them. In fact," the writer went on, "the most interesting thing about these young fellows is that they are regular — not different, not unusual."[23]

Salt Lake City barely beat the Hawaiian barnstormers, 3–2, before a crowd that the *Mercury* announced was the largest ever to attend a baseball game at the local Luna Park. The *Mercury* reported that the Hawaiians were skilled and aggressive competitors. Even "skeptical fans" had been converted. The San José daily declared, "The Chinese baseballers played inside baseball all the way through. You might say that the team had a very good batting eye, the men were all fast and clever on the bases and they played with the ease of big leaguers, never at any time in the game getting the least bit fussed." For example, as would any big leaguer, Lai Tin knocked down the Salt Lake City second baseman while sliding into second in the hopes of break up a double play. Ordinarily, fans would have considered Lai Tin's contentious base running as typical of "inside baseball." However, a non-white exhibiting such bellicosity toward a white person apparently proved unsettling to some of those in attendance at Luna Park. Still, no major incident was reported.[24]

Lingering on the West Coast, the Travelers headed for Stockton. A *Stockton Evening Mail* journalist declared that the game between Stockton and the "Chinese University Club of Hawaii" had provoked quite a bit of comment from baseball followers in the Central Valley town. A few days later, the *Evening Mail* echoed the *San Jose Mercury* in calling the Hawaiians "university lads." After "the Celestials" were edged by a Stockton professional nine, 5–4, the *Evening Mail* recorded that the "Chinese lads" tried unsuccessfully to "kid" a Stockton batter into striking out at a key moment in the game. In any event, "The Chinese are a gentlemanly lot and certainly full of pep." The Stockton daily underscored the Hawaiians' forceful base running by pointing out that "the Celestials stole nine bases." Vernon Ayau stood out, accumulating three hits and stealing two bases. Ayau, the *Evening Mail* noted, had "some speed." "J. Chin" was another star, hitting a double and stealing four bases.[25]

The *Stockton Daily Record* headline referred to the Hawaiians as "Heathen." Still, the daily said they played a "fine ball game" that had drawn a surprisingly good, midweek crowd. Undoubtedly less exciting was the game played the next day against Stockton High School. The Hawaiians won, 9–1, and the *Daily Record* could only remark, "The Chinese had the local high men outclassed at every point."[26]

Yap informed *Star-Bulletin* readers that before its first game in Stockton the team had traveled on a "train for three and a half odd hours and this had a bad effect on many of the boys, besides a few have been slightly laid up from the game before." This and the fact that the "Chinese Travelers" stranded ten runners on base meant victory for the Stockton baseball team. Yap also revealed that since the Stockton Baseball team had beaten the Hawaiians, "the manager of the Stockton High School sought to have a game with us the next afternoon at Oak Park." Inexplicably, Yap insisted, the high school nine "was very confident of a victory." Apparently, their confidence plummeted by the end of the first inning. The game was highlighted, Yap asserted, by the Hawaiian hitting and the "many stunts pulled off just to amuse the Stockton High rooters."[27]

The Travelers played a forgettable game against the Portland Beavers in Fresno. The team for which Lang Akana would have tried out easily beat his former teammates, whom the *San Francisco Examiner* called the "China Boys," 20–4. The headline dispatched to the *Pacific Commercial Advertiser* referred to the "Traveling Chinese." However, the story alluded to "The Travelers of Honolulu, a mixed combination of Chinese, Japanese, and Hawaiians players," and claimed that the Beavers savaged the pitching of the Moriyama brothers. The *Portland Oregonian* disgustedly dismissed the game as a "farce." After the Beavers scored nine runs in the first inning, the *Oregonian* could only say that "the Chinese were in anything but form." Heading further south, the Hawaiians defeated a Redlands University nine, 2–1, convincing a *Los Angeles Times* writer that "the Chinese know something about the great American game of baseball." Calling the Hawaiians "Yellow Perils," this writer proceeded in depicting the Redlands game as filled with "brilliant plays and sharp rallies ... Kau, the Chinese pitcher" merited particular praise for his "mixture of spit balls, change ups, and slow balls."[28]

Meanwhile, the *Advertiser* received a letter from "William Lai Tin, who is piloting the Travelers on their journey through the mainland." The Chinese Hawaiian ballplayer reported, while still in the Bay Area, that the barnstormers were enjoying themselves. They "have played before good crowds, have seen some of the [Pan-Pacific] fair and hope to have a successful season." Lai Tin told the *Advertiser* he had hoped to arrange games in Southern California with Pacific Coast League teams such as Los Angeles and Venice as well as a minor league team from Indianapolis. These games did not take place, although it is interesting that youthful Lai Tin had shouldered some of Nat Strong's scheduling duties.[29]

Writing from Phoenix, Yap told the *Star-Bulletin* that the team felt "satisfaction" in winning a "great game from the Redlands, Cal., college team." The game had been knotted up after eight innings. However, Andy Yamashiro hit a homer to put the Hawaiians up by one run in the top of the ninth. In the last half of the ninth, Redlands loaded up the bases with no one out, but pitcher Luther Kekoa was able to retire the side. Yap declared, "The weather was warm and everybody played as if he was at home." The Hawaiians would have played errorless ball "but for one puzzling grounder to Third Baseman Lai Tin, who juggled the ball for a trifle too long."[30]

While the Travelers competed on the mainland's West Coast, the *Pacific Commercial Advertiser* condemned the way the team was advertised in California. It complained that "a ball team now on the coast masquerading as an All-Chinese combination evidently has a press agent in advance whose sole aim and idea is to fool the public." The *Advertiser*'s distress originated from the mainland press coverage which continued to insist that the Travelers were all Chinese Hawaiians and played for the fictitious Chinese University of Hawaii.[31]

Meanwhile, the *Advertiser* supported the efforts of the CAU to dispatch a truly "All-Chinese" nine to the Philippines, China, and Japan to play a series of games against local and U.S. military nines. On March 3, the *Advertiser* heralded the formation of the new All-Chinese team, managed by W. Tin Chong and Kim Tong Ho—a team already inspiring excitement among baseball fans in the "Far East." The *Advertiser* had heard that a great baseball venue had been constructed in Shanghai at Hongkew Park. Thousands were expected to fill the seats to watch the Chinese Hawaiians oppose Japanese university nines.[32]

Adding to the *Advertiser*'s support of the CAU team's trek westward was news that the Chinese Hawaiians would participate in the Far Eastern Games, held in Shanghai. The *Advertiser* declared, "It is a great compliment to Honolulans that a team from here should be asked to compete in the Far Eastern Athletic Association Olympiad which is an annual event in Shanghai, China, and in which crack athletes of Manila, China and Japan compete." The *Advertiser* reported, "The Far Eastern Athletic Association is for clean outdoor sports and many of the foremost men of China are sponsors for the organization.... The object of the Far Eastern Association is to introduce athletics among the Chinese and neither pains nor expense are spared to bring forth the benefits of outdoor sports."[33]

Early in April, the All-Chinese team headed for Asia. The *Pacific Commercial Advertiser* proclaimed their departure in an article headlined "All Chinese Ball Team Is Ready For Great Invasion Of Far East." Accompanying the article were photographs of each of the players and managers. The *Advertiser* perhaps stretched things a bit when it declared that the Hawaiian ball team's boarding of the steamer *Mongolia* "promises to be one of the greatest events in the annals of Honolulu." The daily described the team as "fourteen China boys," 12 players and two managers. It pointed out that "these boys are pure-blooded Chinese and each has a paper setting forth that he's a citizen of the United States." Each was educated on the islands, and co-manager Kim Tong Ho was an employee of the First National Bank of Hawaii and a graduate of the University of Wisconsin. As for co-manager William Tin Chong, he worked for Waterhouse Company. The 28-year-old had been managing the CAU team for two years.[34]

The *Advertiser* could not restrain its enthusiasm:

> Reviewing the proposed trip of this aggregation, it looms as one of the greatest, if not the greatest, ever taken by a baseball aggregation, and what makes this trip the more important is the fact that it is the first time in the history of the world that an All-Chinese baseball team embarked on a journey from an American port that will take them into foreign countries. In these foreign countries this aggregation of Honolulu boys will play the great national pastime, which can well be called an international pastime now against their own people, the Filipinos, the Japanese, and picked teams of American soldiers and college graduates who are located in the countries to be visited by the Honolulu All-Chinese baseball team.

The team was expected to play eight games in the Philippines, beginning April 25. On May 15, it would move on to Shanghai to compete in the Far Eastern games. Then the Chinese Hawaiians would head to Japan before returning to the islands. The *Advertiser* reckoned that the team would travel about 15,000 miles.[35]

The All-Chinese team, according to the *Advertiser*, was well taken care of financially. Honolulu's Chinese merchants had assisted, as did a Honolulu clergyman, William D. Westervet. Apparently, Westervet had not only aided the Chinese Hawaiian ballplayers with a donation but had helped convince the Far Eastern Athletic Association to field the "ball team of All-Chinese" at their games. Moreover, benefit games had supplied the Chong-Ho aggregation with about $300. Accordingly, "the team will be handsomely uniformed ... from the house of A.G. Spaulding [sic]."[36]

After a few days out to sea, a contingent of passengers on the *Mongolia* challenged the All-Chinese to an on-board baseball game. Unsurprisingly, the All-Chinese won the first game of their journey. The *Advertiser* speculated,

"Perhaps, the passengers did not know it but the majority of the All-Chinese play indoor baseball as well as outdoor baseball." While the All-Chinese were still en route to the Philippines, the *Advertiser* reported that Yuan Shi-Kai, President of the Chinese Republic, had donated $500 to aid the Chinese Hawaiian ball team so that it could help inspire the development of baseball in China. Curiously, however, the committee in charge of the Far Eastern Games had thought it was about to welcome the same team that had been barnstorming the U.S. mainland. Perhaps a little too insistent, the *Advertiser* declared that there was "no connection" between the two teams.[37]

On the mainland, the not so all-Chinese Hawaiian contingent left Southern California for Arizona, where they played six games in six days. On March 21, 1915, they beat the Class D Phoenix club, 4–2. Under the headline, "Orientals Add Politeness to National Game," the *Honolulu Star-Bulletin* reported that "The Traveling Chinese" were not only doing well against mainland opponents but were gaining admiration for their civility. To prove its point, the daily quoted extensively from an article written by Arizona journalist Sally Jacobs on the "Hawaiian-Chinese players."[38]

Jacobs called the first ball game of the Phoenix baseball season a "revelation" because of the "Chinese students'" victory. Jacobs maintained, "The introduction of the Celestials into the great national game will undoubtedly tend toward the moral uplift of the game." The reason was the politeness displayed by the visitors, which Jacobs insisted was "contagious." Accordingly, "there was not a single unpleasant[ry] directed at the players or even the umpire, for that matter." What fans could hear from the Hawaiians was "delivered in perfect English and their conversation proved so agreeable that the local pastimers rather regretted that the boys from the Hawaiian islands talked in their native tongue when in the field."[39]

Jacobs "rather regretted" that the Hawaiian ballplayers were not more Oriental. She wrote, "Although we are all under one flag, it does seem deplorable for the chaps to give up many of their distinctive styles and customs and to adopt our less attractive ones." She believed it more picturesque for the Hawaiians to appear "in mandarin coats" and sport queues. She lamented, "All that reminded one that the visitors were from the land of chop and noodles were the names in the line-up."[40]

Jacobs highlighted Lai Tin's performance. "Mr. Lai," Jacobs wrote, proved "a favorite with the grandstand for it was popularly neutral applauding the good work of the strangers with the same enthusiasm with which they cheered their own men." Lai apparently caught one Phoenix base runner "napping off third." Moreover, in the eighth inning, he performed "spectacular plays ... [that] won the unstinted admiration of the grandstand." Jacobs insisted, "He has the most marvelous way of doing things, getting a great deal out of nothing, you know." Lai's ability to stretch a single into a triple because "of a little home grown error" dazzled Jacobs as did his opportunistic theft of home.[41]

The *Star-Bulletin* printed another account of the same game by an anonymous sportswriter who claimed that "500 wildly excited fans" watched the "Chinese students from the Hawaiian Islands" in action. While the Phoenix nine and the Hawaiians seemed equally matched, the sportswriter admitted that the "impression gained circulation that the Orientals were laying low at times and sort of drawing the Phoenicians out." Nevertheless, the game was competitive even though "no special efforts were made to kill the umpire."[42]

Like Jacobs, the writer admired the visitors' skill and demeanor. The journalist called "the Chinese ... a clean fielding bunch" and declared that "several times the crowd was brought to its feet with the clever stunts pulled." At the same time, "they displayed the traditional Oriental calmness in the pinches, never batting an eyelash when things looked bad." Nevertheless, the *Republican* writer lamented that the multi-lingual facility displayed by the Hawaiians gave them an advantage over the Phoenix players. When one of the latter got on, "they would relapse into their native tongue or tongues, and the base runner never knew what was on their minds."[43]

Unable to escape the orientalist but flattering appraisals of presumably white sportswriters, the Hawaiians journeyed to Tucson, where they easily handled the University of Arizona, 10–5 and 10–2. Previously, the *Tucson Citizen* informed the locals that "the flowery boys" were coming into town to play "the biggest games of the year." Exaggerating just a bit, the newspaper claimed that "a goodly portion" of previous team members had gone on to the major leagues. Calling the Travelers the best team outside of the United States, the *Citizen* maintained "the Chinamen" showed that not only Americans played baseball well. Indeed, the *Citizen* compared the Hawaiian squad favorably to professional contingents. The *Tucson Citizen's* account of the second game applauded the alertness of the visitors, who seemed to be in the game every minute, while taking advantage of the home team's mistakes.[44]

The University of Arizona's yearbook furnished a summary of the "Chinese games." The yearbook praised the visitors as "fast" and referred to them as "semiprofessional." The Arizona team tried, the yearbook insisted, but was overmatched by a nine that could play "in major league style."[45]

In Douglas, Arizona, the Travelers beat a local team of soldiers twice in a row. The *Star-Bulletin* claimed that "it must have been like old times to the Chinese Travelers" to play against a service team and before a crowd largely comprised of military personnel. Indeed, Al Yap wrote home saying, "It seemed like home to see so many soldier fans. The attendance was good, averaging about 1250."[46]

From Arizona, the Hawaiian ballplayers headed to Texas, where they were scheduled to play ten games but wound playing nine because rain canceled their match-up against Texas Christian University in Fort Worth on April 7. On March 28 and 29, the Hawaiians were in San Antonio where they lost two games to a Texas League professional team, 3–2 and 11–4. Yap declared that "our team demonstrated that we could play baseball by holding the fast Texas team to a 3 to 2 score." He claimed that many of those in attendance "were quite interested in our knowledge of the game and whenever there was good play made we got hearty applause for it."[47]

Apau Kau was especially effective, holding "the husky sluggers of the Texas aggregation to 5 hits and 2 passes." Yap alluded to a "good write-up" of the Hawaiian pitcher in the *San Antonio Express*. Apparently, the daily praised Apau Kau's "wonderful spitter, control, and excellent headwork." Moreover, it even claimed that Apau Kau possessed "real big league stuff and that he ranked better than some of the major league pitchers." After the second game, the *San Antonio Light* declared that "the Celestials seemed befuddled" by the minor leaguers. In any event, the *Light* asserted, "Lai Tin, the Chinese Kid, was the base stealer par excellence for the amateurs, making an extra base upon three distinct occasions." Yap reported that "nearly a thousand curious Texas ball fans" appeared at the March 28 game.[48]

The Travelers moved on to Houston, where they won two games from Rice Institute, 5–2 and 4–1. In the second game, the *Galveston Daily News* reported that George Bush, otherwise known as "George Bo, a stocky Mongolian with a hooked curve," kept Rice bats at bay. On April 1, they got a day off from baseball before confronting the University of Texas nine, on April 2 and 3. The Travelers won the first game, 11–3, but lost the second, 9–8. In an article headlined, "Travelers Are Showing Texans National Game," the *Star-Bulletin* somewhat snidely declared as a consequence of the Rice series, "the Traveling Chinese are still cleaning up the *little fellows* in the Southwest and apparently are making a good impression along the way" [italics mine].[49]

Writing from Norman, Oklahoma, Yap lamented that Luther Kekoa's unusually ineffective pitching led to the University of Texas victory in the second game. Yap was not trying to demean the Longhorns. He declared that they played "good ball [and] fielded better and batted better than they did the day before." Nevertheless, "Ako" walked in the winning run in the ninth. Yap wrote, "The Longhorns' supporters flocked into the field and congratulated their team for their fine playing." The University of Texas players conceded to the Hawaiians later that they would have preferred to have won on a hit than a walk. A bit patronizing, Yap remembered, "When we told them that the best team had won, they became satisfied."[50]

Yap was obviously displeased with Kekoa. He told fans in Honolulu that

Four. Never the Home Team, 1915

The 1915 team managed to play several games in Texas, primarily against university nines. This team photograph was taken at Rice University in Houston, where the Travelers won both games. Lai Tin, second from the left in the bottom row, was missing from the 1914 squad but was back to field manage the team (courtesy of Ervin A. Kalb Scrapbook, 1913-1915, Alumni Scrapbooks, Woodson Research Center, Fondren Library, Rice University).

"Ako must have had too much of a good time at the reception the night before, and that probably accounts for his poor showing." Perhaps Yap's irritation was not misplaced as Kekoa's lack of control resulted in eight walks and two hit batters. "Luckily," Yap insisted, "his teammates played a good game, otherwise, the game would have been lost long before it was over." Yap pointed out that the second game against the University of Texas drew much better than the first. He speculated that this was because "it was rumored throughout the town that Texas was going to line up their best men and expected to win." Yap commended those fans who appeared. He wrote, "They applauded generously for all good plays."[51]

On April 5, the team that the *Advertiser* derided as the "so-called All-Chinese" was in Waco, Texas. There, according to the *Advertiser*, the "near All-Chinese" nine beat Baylor, 16–8, and became something of a big hit among the Texans who watched them. The Travelers then opposed Baylor in another game. This time Apau Kau pitched a no-hit, no-run game against the Texans. According to a newspaper clipping sent to *Baseball Magazine*, "the clever young American citizen of Chinese descent" struck out 20 batters and did not seem to know he had a no-hitter going until the seventh inning.

The *Star-Bulletin* was ecstatic with Apau Kau's performance against Baylor. The headline of Yap's account of the game declared, "Apau's No-Hit Game About the Best On Record," while the subheadline informed readers that the Hawaiian's pitching performance was indeed superb: "Chinese Pitcher Fanned 20 Men and Only Three Balls Went to Infield."[52]

Writing from Lindsborg, Kansas, Yap reported that in the first game against Baylor "our slugging easily gave us the game." Everyone hit well — so well that even the Travelers were surprised. Not only did it seem that "everyone on the team is having a good hitting streak now, [but] many have improved a lot in fielding since leaving home." Yap praised the weather conditions "so far" and maintained that "everyone seems to find himself at home all the time." As for the second game against Baylor, Yap recorded that "the pitching of Apau Kau, who always pitches good, and our stick work turned the trick." Apau Kau's "spitball was working fine" in pitching his no-hitter. Moreover, "his other offerings were too puzzling for the Baylor batsmen. All they did was to go up to the batter's box, take the count and slip back to the bench."[53]

An excited piece printed in the *Trenton Evening Times* averred that "Kau's" performance against Baylor was "unequalled in college annals." The anonymous journalist wrote, "It is undoubtedly one of the most marvelous feats ever performed in any class of ball," while incorrectly asserting that Apau Kau had previously beaten a PCL team. In any event, the "Chinese" were too strong for college teams in the West. However, "their invasion of the East [was] awaited with interest."[54]

The *Fort Worth Star-Telegram* announced the impending, but doomed by rain game between the Hawaiians and the Texas Christian University nine with the following headline: "T.C.U. Plays Chinks Here Wednesday." The *Telegram* pointed out that the "Chinese University of Hawaii" comprised "one of the fastest college teams in the world" and that the Travelers hit better than in previous years. The Fort Worth daily further reported that "Lai ... possesses a shotgun whip and a good head."[55]

The Travelers had plunged deep into the U.S. heartland. From Texas, they headed northward to Oklahoma and then Kansas. In Norman, Oklahoma, they were scheduled to play two games against the University of Oklahoma on April 9 and 10. Rain canceled the first game, however. The next day, the Hawaiians were shut out, 3–0. Yap prefaced his account of the April 10 game by informing the *Star-Bulletin* that "everyone is well and having a fine time. The weather has been good with a few exceptions. From now on, we will have shorter jumps and better railroad connections." As it turned out, Yap was overly optimistic regarding transportation. As for the game itself, Yap declared, "There was plenty of snap and pep on both sides and the 100 per cent fielding of each team kept the spectators very interested." However, the barnstormers simply could not hit. Yap complained, "Luck was either against us or the excellent pitching of some Southern Leaguer shut us out" He further wished that Apau Kau could have taken his turn in the box against Oklahoma. Yap was convinced "the story might have been different."[56]

The Hawaiians played six games in six days in Kansas. On April 11, the Travelers subdued the Newton Baseball Club, 19–5. Yap reported that the Hawaiians made a disappointing discovery in Newton. They had been told that the Newton nine would give them a "good game." However, "we found everything that was told to us was untrue. The men in the team really didn't show that they knew the game, and besides, they haven't got a strong enough battery to cope against our batters." Yap informed *Star-Bulletin* readers that "if we didn't stop to play foolish," the slaughter would have been worse. Moreover, while Apau Kau was going to pitch, "our estimation of the opposing team found that Yim (Yamashiro) was good enough." As it turned out, Yamashiro did fine, pitching five innings of no-hit ball. "The attendance was very good," according to Yap, "and it was composed of mostly baseball fans of Newton and its neighborhood." The fans were the most entertaining part of the game for the Hawaiians "for they frequently hollered out something to the players that would cause the whole grand stand to laugh. Asking the batter to hit the ball a mile was one of their favorite interrogations."[57]

The next day, the Travelers were in Lindsborg, Kansas, where they defeated the Bethany College nine, 9–4. Yap wrote that before the game, "the Chinese Travelers ... pulled off the shadow play which made a hit with the crowd." Moreover, while the Bethany College team was engaged in field practice, "five of our boys did the juggling game, which also won over the spectators," but one suspects not the Bethany College players. The correspondent added, "We could have run the score to the twenties if we wanted to, but for the sake of making the game interesting, we kept the score as low as possible." Still, Yap enjoyed the student support for the losing team. "Had it not been for their constant cheering and the frantic screams by the excited girls, the game would probably have been listless and uninteresting." On April 13, the Hawaiians beat St. Mary's College in St. Mary's, Kansas, 6–2, bunching five runs in the fifth inning. Yap mentioned that the Travelers played "a very snappy game" against St. Mary's. He credited live music for the inspiration; "As a rule, when there is a band playing the game is snappy and fast."[58]

The "Chinese travelers" headed to Manhattan, Kansas, where they took on Kansas State Agricultural College. They won easily, 18–0. From St. Louis on April 26, Yap dispatched the following to the *Star-Bulletin*: "Before the game started our boys were teased, told that we couldn't play but the teasing made the players red-hot and as a result they showed more pop and fighting spirit than they had displayed since leaving Honolulu." On April 15 and 16, the islanders were in Lawrence for a two-game series with the University of Kansas. The first game was a close, 4–3 victory for the Kansans. Yap complained, "It was unfortunate that the Chinese lost this game, as victory would have meant a clean sweep of the state of Kansas." The Travelers made several infield errors, according to Yap, grumbled, "The ground was all pebbles." The second game was won easily by the Hawaiians, 15–1.[59]

After leaving Kansas, the Travelers trekked to Missouri, where they bit off more than a week's worth of games. On April 17, the Hawaiians opposed the State Normal School in Warrensburg, winning 5–3. The *Kansas City Star* reported that this game lasted only seven innings. The *Star*'s correspondent maintained that the Warrensburg players were apparently nervous at confronting "unusual opponents." The correspondent also hailed the hurling of "Aupan, the fast Celestial." A few days later, the Travelers confronted the University of Missouri nine and tied the home team after six innings. However, rain halted this game as well. On April 22, the Hawaiians finally completed a nine-inning contest. According to Yap, they "easily defeated" the University of Missouri nine, 3–0. Apau Kau pitched the shutout.[60]

The *Star-Bulletin* published a more detailed report of the Travelers' games against the University of Missouri. The author was a University of Missouri student named H.L. Chung, who called the visitors the "Chinese Travelers of Hawaii." Chung observed that in the 3–0 Hawaiians victory, "one of the main features ... was the use of the Hawaiian and Chinese languages on the coaching line by the Travelers." This apparently puzzled the Missouri nine, which also had a hard time judging Apau Kau's "Chinese curves."[61]

The University of Missouri newspaper pointed out that Apau Kau struck out 11 batters in his shutout victory. The student publication seemed suspicious of the advertised identity of the opponents, referring to them as the "so called Honolulu baseball team." It also described the visitors as "The Yellow Peril — assuming that the Tigers' opponents were Chinese and not ordinary Hawaiians." The *University Missourian* pointed out as well that H.L. Chung was Lai Tin's former classmate.[62]

Still in Missouri, the Travelers opposed Westminster College in Fulton and the Concordia Seminary in St. Louis. The former did not give the Islanders much of a fight as the Westminster nine lost, 13–1. However, Yap commended the Concordia Seminary team. It took a "hard fight" to defeat Concordia, 5–2. Yap added, "Our men looked like pigmies alongside of those tall husky Concordia players, but nevertheless, we delivered them the goods. Who says that ministers can't play ball?"[63]

The Hawaiians saw a great deal of the Midwest. On April 26, the team took in the sights of St. Louis before heading to Ames, Iowa, where the Travelers played Iowa State on April 27. They had an "easy time" in the game, winning 6–2. Then they "made a rush to the 7:05 train for Vermillon S.D," where they defeated the University of South Dakota, 5–2, on April 28. According to Yap, "it took 10 thrilling innings to fight for this supremacy." A wire story printed in the *Aberdeen Daily American* declared that the "Celestials" were just too much for the South Dakota nine. On April 29, the barnstormers left Vermillon at 4 A.M. in order to return to Iowa. Nineteen hours later they arrived at Decorah, Iowa. Yap could only exclaim, "Some jump!" The next day, they beat Luther College, 7–1. Yap wrote, "The mayor of the town threw [out] the first ball. The attendance was very good and was chiefly made up of the town's ball fans." At 11:05 A.M. on May 1, the barnstormers departed Decorah for Prairie du Chien, Wisconsin.[64]

On the way to Prairie du Chien, the team "jumped off at North McGregor's Landing, and then took a gasoline launch across the Mississippi." The Travelers arrived at 3:15 P.M., May 1, for a game with Campion College. The game was supposed to have started at 2:45 P.M. While the Hawaiians "went into the game without any batting practice," the visitors still won, 12 to 3.[65]

After having a game postponed because of rain on May 2, the Hawaiians defeated Williams College at Aledo, Illinois. Rain threatened to postpone that game as well. Indeed, according to Yap, he and his teammates witnessed continuous lightning and thunder for about an hour. But the downpour halted and the game was finished in sunlight. On the way to Chicago, the Travelers stopped in at Kankakee, where they vanquished the "fast St. Victor's College team," 3–1. Yap observed that the St. Victor's nine "played very good ball" but could not hit.[66]

On May 5, the University of Chicago slipped past the Hawaiians, 1–0, as the visitors mustered only two hits at the game played on Stagg Field. Yap claimed that the cold weather in Chicago bothered the Travelers and that Wah Kai Chang, a Chinese Hawaiian athlete, played right field for the home team. However, the wire report of the game noted that "the spectacular fielding of the Chinese athletes who make up baseball teams from Hawaii" was the game's highlight.[67]

On May 10, Yap dispatched to Honolulu a report on a game in Kokomo, Indiana, between the Travelers and the Kokomo Red Sox. The headline read, "Travelers Get Good Support From Fans." Nearly 2,000 arrived to watch the Travelers beat "a strong Kokomo Red Sox team," 4–1. Half the crowd, Yap reported, supported the home team while the other half rooted for the Hawaiians. The fans were especially excited when the visitors scored their winning runs in the fifth and sixth innings. Luther Kekoa pitched well for the visitors, striking out 11. He was also supported excellently by a defense led by Ayau's heads-up play. The next day, the Travelers took the field in Greencastle, Indiana, to oppose De Pauw University. They won, 3–1. Yap claimed in a dispatch from Cincinnati that the game against De Pauw was a "hard fight." But the Hawaiians enjoyed themselves nonetheless. Yap wrote:

> The De Pauw students are very loyal to their team and cheers and yells from them could be heard almost continuously. They also cheered for us whenever we made a good play and their constant teasing of some of our players was very amusing. So throughout the game there was shown the most friendly feeling between the two teams, though the match was a real hot one.

Meanwhile, in a May 11 column, Hugh Fullerton, the famed sportswriter, wrote, "That Chinese University of Hawaii baseball team would be the most popular in the world — with copy readers and compositors and headline writers" with so many monosyllabic names like Lai, Chun, Yap, and Mark.[68]

On May 25, a Yap dispatch to the *Star-Bulletin* reported that the "Travelers" had performed effectively so far. Up to that point they had won 37 of 49 games. Achieving this record was no small feat, Yap boasted. The ballplayer asked readers to "note ... that the team has been playing almost every day, and making considerable jumps between games. For a road club, the percentage is remarkable."[69]

On June 10, 1915, the *Star-Bulletin* published a May 22 dispatch from Yap. In it, the first baseman described two games played in the Cincinnati Reds ballpark against a nine called the Shamrocks, which Yap called the best semipro outfit in the Ohio city. Only a few hundred people appeared, but Yap maintained that "we demonstrated to these fans that we know how to play ball." In the first game, the Shamrocks pitched a fellow named Smith, who Yap claimed once hurled for the Reds. Still, "our little [Grover Cleveland] Alexander, alias Ako, was the pitching star of the day" and the Hawaiians won. The second game was a 12–2 laugher for the Travelers. Kuali was the big hitter for the Hawaiians. However, Lai Tin, the team's "Duffy Lewis" in reference to the Boston Red Sox stalwart star, also hit well and Apau Kau pitched well.[70]

A wire story from Cincinnati in the *Lincoln News* further described the ventures of the Travelers in Ohio. The piece began with the assertion that baseball was "no longer an American game." That is, "full-blooded Indians" played the game as did the Japanese. Now, the *Enquirer* emphasized, "John Chinaman" proved to be a "proficient player." This intelligence came by way of the "Chinese college boys from Honolulu"—"Celestials" who had won more than their share of games against mainland opposition. Turning up at St. Xavier's College, "nine small-statured, full Americanized" ballplayers humbled the home team, 10–1. According to a wire story, a "large crowd" watched "the yellow skin athletes from the Chinese University of Hawaii."[71]

Apau Kau reportedly showed up at the offices of a Cincinnati newspaper to promote the Travelers. The pitcher had noticed the famous names of John

L. Sullivan, Eddie Foy, Christy Mathewson, George M. Cohan, and James Jeffries on the office's register. Since Apau Kau was "up on everything American," he said he had heard of all of them, which seemingly surprised his hosts. In terms of sports, Apau Kau said he followed boxing as well as baseball, and poignantly pledged that if the U.S. entered the war, "Chinamen in Hawaii would fight for the stars and stripes." Described as "pretty husky," Apau Kau purportedly claimed that he and his teammates came from the "Chinese University" and were "rank amateurs." That is, the players earned expenses but all other money went into a "university fund."[72]

A May 21 Yap dispatch from Buchanon, West Virginia, reported that the team had taken "a very long and tiresome ride from Cincinnati" to Lexington, Kentucky. Upon their arrival, the players were "more dead than alive." Still, they had three hours to recover, take on the University of Kentucky nine, and win, 6–4. "C. Chin, our spitball artist, was on the mound" and pitched competently. Yap was told that the Travelers had drawn the biggest crowd ever at the University of Kentucky's playing field. He added, "Many of the fans were from nearby towns and came solely to see what we could do with a bat and ball. They wondered how we could play such a brand of ball and win the game besides."[73]

Before the game against the University of Kentucky, the *Lexington Herald* announced that the Travelers had successfully handled most mainland opponents. Accordingly, the Hawaiians comprised "about as hard a proposition as the Wildcats have run up against this season." After the game, the *Herald* commended "the yellow men" on defense. Only Lai's muff of an easy grounder caused dismay. In addition, "the foreigners" entertained the crowd "with juggling and clever passing of the ball" before the game.[74]

Later in May, the Travelers were in Maryland. There, they encountered a nine from the all-black college of Wilberforce. Yap's dispatch from Emmitsburg, Maryland, told Hawaiian readers the Wilberforce team had overcome a 3–0 deficit in the ninth inning and won, 4–3. "George Bo" pitched consistently, but "the weather was fairly cold and this accounts for the poor hitting and slow fielding on our side." Yap added, "The attendance was quite large and many colored notables were present."[75]

A June 17 *Star-Bulletin* edition headlined a June 1 Yap correspondence, "Chinese Have No Chance to Get Corpulent." The subheadline informed readers that "crowded schedules keep them on the run." Yap pointed out that the Travelers had beaten a Marshall College nine in Huntington, West Virginia, 8–1. He wrote, "Our hitting was strong and came in bunches, while Chin pitched a steady game, allowing only eight scattered hits." After leaving Huntington, the Hawaiians journeyed to Ohio, where they edged Ohio University, 3–2. Returning to West Virginia, the Travelers had their first game with West Virginia Wesleyan in Buchanon cancelled because of rain. The Hawaiians rallied from behind to win the second game, 6–4. A few days later, the Hawaiians shut out a semipro nine in Packersburg, 4–0, with Apau dominating the West Virginians. Moving on to Pennsylvania, the team saw its game against the University of Pittsburgh scrapped due to rain. Yap commented, "When we arrived at midday Pittsburg [sic] was as dark as Honolulu at 8 o'clock." Yap expressed satisfaction with how the trip had gone. "A game every day and lots of railroad traveling in between doesn't give a ball team much time to get fat, and all the Travelers are doing fine. The hard work seems to agree with the boys, who are playing a better article of baseball all the time."[76]

On June 6, Yap sent a dispatch to Honolulu, claiming that the good shape of the team members had allowed the Travelers to mount a winning record in 63 games. The fact that the team had won 47 games, lost 15, and tied one, according to Yap, was remarkable. He understandably bragged, "This is some record for a road club that has played 63 games in a couple of months and covered the United States from coast to coast. In fact, it is the good condition of our players that has made our winning percentage possible. The team has played in luck so far as accidents go and hopes that the streak will keep up." Nevertheless, Yap reported, the Travelers had lost a close game to Pennsylvania's Indiana State Normal, 7–6. Yap observed, "The crowd was about the most enthusiastic we have seen for some time."[77]

After the Indiana State Normal game, the Indiana *Evening Gazette* reported, "the Chinese University of Hawaii" ballplayers were invited to the local Outing Club. There they entertained guests with some Hawaiian music. Seemingly, folks in Indiana, Pennsylvania, had heard "the weird" music on their phonographs but never in person.[78]

The Travelers remained tied to a hectic itinerary. After the Travelers defeated St. Mary's College in Emmitsburg, Maryland, they headed in late May for the local train station and took, according to Yap, the 4:45 P.M. express to Philadelphia, arriving nearly six hours later. On May 29, the Hawaiians opposed the Victrix club in Philadelphia and lost. "Chin" was wild early in the going, Yap claimed, and the hitting lacked punch. Yap noted, "I noticed that our hitting ability has dropped considerably, and the 'pep' of a month ago is not so strong and lasting. If we only had some of the old stuff we could have easily won most of our eastern college games." Yap seemed to think that the team had "started out too fast" when it hit the mainland and did not preserve its strength for the tough Eastern swing. Nevertheless, Yap claimed in a June 13 dispatch from Reading, Pennsylvania, that the attendance was good for the Victrix game and "the Philadelphia fans are all good baseball enthusiasts."[79]

On May 30, the Hawaiians journeyed into Brooklyn. There they contested the Brooklyn Bushwicks at the Wallace Grounds in Ridgewood. The day before the *Brooklyn Eagle* announced that Lai Tin, "the greatest Chinese baseball player in captivity," captained the "University of Hawaii." The daily also pointed out that the preliminary game had been scheduled at an earlier time to give the "Chinese" plenty of time "to show their wonderful practice exhibition." Yap claimed that 2,000 fans watched the game. Unfortunately, rain cancelled the contest. Yap, however, was impressed with the fans who took the news of the game's cancellation fairly stoically. Perhaps a bit naively, Yap wrote, "This goes to show that the followers of baseball are all good sports."[80]

Yap's next correspondence, sent from Orange, Massachusetts, on July 1, lingered on the theme of East Coast baseball supremacy. The Travelers continued to perform competently, "winning a fair percentage of games, but losing more frequently to the eastern college teams than to those of the west." The reason was simple. Easterners played better ball. However, according to Yap, making rail connections did not help the Hawaiian ball club's winning record. On the way to Lewiston, Maine, where they were scheduled to confront the nine from Bates College, the Travelers discovered that taking a train to Lewiston from Hanover, New Hampshire, was no easy matter. The team had to leave its hotel in Hanover at 3:30 A.M. to catch the train. Then the Hawaiians suffered through five transfers to arrive at Lewiston at 12:30 P.M. Yap understandably maintained, "Though we lost to Bates College it was fairly excusable." Indeed, Bates won 14–6, but Yap would not concede much: "We hit the ball almost as hard as they did, though we were fatigued. We had many chances to score through a number of consecutive hits, but our poor tired legs couldn't carry us any faster." Still in Maine, the Hawaiians traveled to Bangor to play the University of Maine nine. The Travelers won, 8–3, thanks to timely hitting. Yap reported, "The game was witnessed by a fairly large crowd, who applauded the different good plays throughout the entire game."[81]

The next morning, the Travelers arrived at Providence, Rhode Island, at 7 A.M. Consequently, Yap reported, the team had a chance to look over "the place," since the Travelers were scheduled to play Brown University at 3:30 P.M. The Hawaiians lost, 4–0. Apau Kau seemingly pitched adequately but the Brown hurler pitched better. Yap told Honolulu readers that "an immense crowd witnessed this game and fully enjoyed the afternoon there." Helping the crowd's mood was that Apau Kau, Henry Kuali, Lai Tin, and Chinito Moriyama "gave an exhibition of juggling the ball" while the Brown team took part in fielding practice. Yap wrote, "The boys ... did it so well that they won the applause of the crowd. Through the medium we won about 50 percent of the crowd to our support." Weak hitting, according to the *Pawtucket*

Times, doomed the visitors. The "Chinese invaders in the realm of Brown," did, however, perform well according to the *Times*.⁸²

The Hawaiians hit a physical and mental stone wall on their return to Pennsylvania, losing to Lehigh and Penn State. In a July 6, dispatch from Reading, Pennsylvania, Yap informed the *Star-Bulletin*'s readers that the Travelers lost by a wide, 11–3 margin to Lehigh. Yap maintained that it was not only "our poor playing" that contributed to the lopsided defeat but "the unfair deal by the umpire." Yap did not elaborate on why he blamed the umpire for the team's "downfall."⁸³

After the Lehigh game, the Hawaiians boarded a 7:30 P.M. train from South Bethlehem to Harrisburg, where they spent part of the night. They had to arise at 2:30 A.M. to board a 3 A.M. train to State College. Yap claimed, "The morning [in Harrisburg] was cold and it was a sight to see us hustle down to the depot. We made record time it was said." Yap reported that the ballplayers arrived at State College about eight o'clock in the morning and were driven to the State College Track House before 8:30 A.M. in "several machines." The barnstormers napped at the Track House until dinner. An alumni parade preceded and delayed the game until 3:30 P.M. According to Yap, the attendance was large, approximately 6,000, thanks to the parade and the fact that the game "between the Penn nine and the Chinese was extensively advertised." This was the third time "the Chinese team" had played Penn State on Alumni Day. The previous games had gone the Hawaiians' way. "So," Yap maintained, "[Penn State] had planned to stop this outrage by staging their best athletes in the lineup. They had also taken precautions in the way of reinforcements. There were many substitutes in the field practice, but there were more in the bleachers and grandstand ready at the cheer-leader's call for vocal emergency." Penn State finally defeated the Travelers, 5–4.⁸⁴

Moving down to Maryland, the Travelers opposed the Bellfonte Academy nine in a two-game series. Yap, writing from Pittsfield, Massachusetts, said the team had been "going along playing a hard schedule and winning a fair percentage of their games." The fact that Lai Tin was nursing a "charley horse" from the sidelines had not helped matters. Still, Yap conceded, Lai Tin "makes a good coach, though, and puts in lots of pep into the boys from the sidelines." The Hawaiians won the first game, 10–5. "Yim" pitched effectively, striking out eight and walking but three. The next day, the Hawaiians won again, 8–5. George Bush struck out 11 Bellfonte batters.⁸⁵

Back in Pennsylvania, the "Chinese University of Hawaii" beat Susquehanna University, 7–4. The visitors fell behind early, 4–1. Lai Tin came off the bench to help the team's comeback with his hitting and baserunning. Apau Kau's relief pitching helped, as well. Yap, however, felt compelled to point out:

The umpire was the worse one we ever ran across. He was so unfair that we had to argue with him. Every close play, especially in the pinches, was not given to us. Therefore, we had to fight with all that was in us. We were mighty glad that we had won. Every clean sportsman knew we were playing against 10 men.[86]

According to the *Philadelphia Inquirer*, the game against Bucknell took place on commencement day before a large crowd. The "Chinamen" played well for six innings and then reportedly collapsed, due, in part, to "Chinn's" three wild pitches. The next game was to occur in Pottsville, but rained cancelled it and, according to Yap, "we left for Reading that night to break up the jump." The Travelers met Lafayette College in Easton. The Travelers put the game away in the first inning thanks to a run-scoring triple by Ayau and Apau Kau's home run. Apau Kau, moreover, did a good job of pitching, especially in the early innings, while "Buck [Lai Tin] was a terror at bat, making four hits out of five chances." The attendance was "very large" and the weather "very warm."[87]

The Travelers returned to New York. There they lost to Rensselaer Polytechnic Institute of Troy, 5–4. Yap lamented that the Hawaiians simply could not effectively hit the off-speed pitching of Rensselaer's starter. The Chinese Hawaiian estimated that about 500 watched the Travelers play a local athletic club nine at Gloversville. The Travelers won, 4–1, and, according to Yap, "did not have to exert ourselves much." Due to a sprained ankle, Ayau could not play but a makeshift lineup of Lai Tin at short, Yap at third, and Kuali at first did the job. After "a long ride from Troy," the Hawaiians fell in Hamilton to Colgate University, 3–0. Yap complained that the team "lost our 'pep'" after the trip. "Bo" pitched competently, however, and "a very large commencement day crowd witnessed this game. Cheering and class yells were frequently heard at intervals. The weather was quite cold."[88]

The Travelers moved up to Williamstown, Massachusetts, where they confronted the Williams College nine before "a very large commencement crowd." The Williams College nine beat "the Chinese," 5–2. Yap explained that the "weather up here was cold and chilly, and so the boys did not display their usual form," although Apau Kau pitched "his usual steady game." However, he did not get offensive help from his teammates. The *North Adams Transcript* testified that the Williams pitcher had the "Orientals well in hand."[89]

Writing from New York City, a sunny Yap told readers that "the Traveling Chinese baseball team is setting a good record this summer in the latter part of June the team playing several hard games, winning the majority and losing a few by close scores." New York City had become "the boys from Hawaii's ... headquarters" and they were playing most of their games either in or near the city. On June 21, the team joined the "Chinese Sunday School" excursion to Bear Mountain in upstate New York. Yap said that the Hawaiians had "a very good time." They especially enjoyed rowing in the lake. The next four days saw the Travelers shopping and sightseeing, although they took in a game between the Philadelphia Phillies and the Giants at the Polo Grounds. On June 25, the team left New York City at 6 P.M. for Schenectady. The boat ride up the Hudson was, according to Yap, "beautiful." Moreover, "our boat's searchlight was in action and caught many couples spooning without any warning beforehand." The next day, the Hawaiians bobbled away an early lead to the General Electric nine and lost, 7–4. Yap noted, "A very good crowd attended the game, but would have been larger had it not rained at noon." On June 27, the Travelers were in Brooklyn to oppose the Bushwicks at Ridgewood Field. After six innings, the game was ended on account of rain. Unfortunately, the potent semipro team was ahead, 1–0, even though the Hawaiians outhit the Bushwicks, four to two. The *Brooklyn Eagle* called the game "well played" and well pitched.[90]

Curiously, Yap did not report on a controversial defeat and an exciting victory over the Bushwicks a few weeks later. On June 6, umpire Frank Wilson was forced to quit a close game between the Bushwicks and the Travelers. Wilson, considered a good umpire by the *Eagle*, called Yamashiro out at third because the third base coach took the Japanese Hawaiian by the arm. Wilson's call was legal, but perhaps not well advised as a crowd surged onto the field demanding the umpire's ouster. Wilson was replaced and the game became a "beauty," according to the *Eagle*. Although the visitors committed four errors, their fielding was commended by the Brooklyn daily as was "Ako's" pitching. Tied at one in the eighth inning a few weeks later, the Hawaiians burst out with four runs in the ninth, thanks in part to Yamishiro's triple. Apau Kau's pitching was masterful, while he, Yap, and Markham performed fielding gems.[91]

In early July, the Travelers headed for New Haven, where they would confront "the fast Colonials." While in New Haven, the Travelers visited Yale University, where, according to Yap, they were awed by the Yale Bowl, a 75,000-seat monument to college football. The sun appeared for the first time after a couple of days of rain on July 3, according to Yap. This "was very fortunate, because many people would have been disappointed had we been unable to play." Apparently, baseball fans in New Haven "hear so much of us that they just die to see what we can do with a ball and bat." They found out that the Hawaiians could play pretty well as they handed the Colonials, which included three Yale ballplayers, a 4–3 defeat. Yap wrote, "It was a great game, not just because we won, but because it was fast and well played on both sides, and featured by sensational fielding. Every seat in the big park was taken."[92]

On July 4, the Travelers were at Dexter Park in Brooklyn. There they beat the Cypress Hill semiprofessional nine, 9–6. Yap made an interesting observation about East Coast baseball fans. He noted, "The game was well attended and more than half the crowd was pulling for us. It seems a common thing in the East to knock the home team and root for the visitors in case they are winning."[93]

On July 5, the barnstormers celebrated Independence Day in Reading, Pennsylvania, where they played a doubleheader against the Reading Independents. In the morning game, the Travelers pounded the home team, 10–3. Attendance was small, according to Yap, because of the cold weather. "Bo" pitched solidly and "Lee" or Kuali hit his fourth homer of the tour. The afternoon game was tougher. The Independents had their ace in the box — a spitball artist named Kunkle. George Bush earned the title of "Iron Man" by pitching and winning this second game of the day, 6–3. That evening, the Hawaiians "set off hundreds of thousands of firecrackers" to honor both American independence and their victory. Yap reported that "hundreds of people were attracted by our celebration, and came to cheer us, standing packed on the sidewalks near our hotel. Then we went to all the places of interest in Reading, which are not many." Yap also told readers that the team rested the next day in Reading and that the ballplayers were "going in great shape and everyone is full of pep."[94]

On August 17, Yap dispatched an account of games played on July 7 and July 9 in Ephrate and Boyertown, Pennsylvania. On July 7, Yap reported, the team arrived in Ephrate at 2 P.M. after departing Reading "on two big machines." Yap observed, "It took us about an hour and a half to get there. The country roads were very good in most places and we sped along them at a pretty fast clip." The game against the Ephrate nine "was a very good exhibition with the Chinese at the bigger end of the score." The locals got sixteen hits off of "C. Chin," but due to "the good support both in the outfields and infields," the Hawaiians managed to eke out a 5–4 victory. The next day the Travelers "loafed at Reading." On July 9, they took on the Boyertown club and lost easily, 9–2. According to Yap, the barnstormers "were at sea" when it came to hitting Boyertown's "big southpaw."[95]

In mid–July, the *Trenton Evening Times* laid it on a bit thick in promoting the "Chinese University of Hawaii" nine as "the greatest baseball attraction in the country." On July 11, its Sunday edition announced in a headline, "Chinks Play Here Next Wednesday." The Travelers were scheduled to take on the Trenton club at American Bridge Field and the Trenton newspaper, as it did in 1914, obviously wanted to make sure a big crowd packed the stands. The "Celestials," the daily asserted, had been drawing "record breaking crowds" wherever they performed and they were essentially the same team that in 1914 had wowed Trenton fans with their "fast fielding." The *Times* misinformed readers that the players were members of the "varsity nine of the Chinese University of Honolulu" and were so successful in 1914 that Nat Strong sought to represent them in 1915. The *Times* admitted that a year earlier local fans did not attend the Hawaiians' game because they thought the visitors comprised a "freak organization" and not "the great baseball machine" that vanquished teams throughout the mainland. A couple of days later, the Trenton daily praised the Travelers' fielding, in particular, claiming their defensive work was the best that one could see outside of the major leagues. It informed readers that Trenton entrepreneurs, realizing "the Chinks drawing ability," had promised the Hawaiians a large guarantee. To boost attendance, the *Evening Times* promised that the Travelers would give an exhibition of "horse play" that had presumably thrilled Trenton baseball lovers in 1914.[96]

The game itself witnessed the Travelers winning, 7–5. The *Evening Times* admitted that the fielding was miserable on both sides. Still, the contest proved entertaining as the Travelers came from behind to take the victory. The visitors did not seem as talented as they were in 1914 to the *Evening Times*, but they were good enough — especially Lai Tin, Ayau, and "Yim." Moreover, "the Chinks" delighted fans by playing "shadow ball" before the game.[97]

During the first half of August, the Travelers beat a nine in Chester but lost to the Bushwicks. On August 11, the Hawaiians encountered former major leaguer George Mullin on the slab for Chester, but still won, 3–1. Before the game, the *Chester Times* observed, the visitors delighted southeastern Pennsylvania's baseball fans. "The first part of their program was a little song service while they were sitting on the bench. The next and final act was a juggling baseball game during batting practice. The Celestials demonstrated that they were from the race of the most clever people in the world." A former star for the Detroit Tigers, the devious Mullin succeeded in holding down the Hawaiians with his "emery ball"—an illegal pitch in which the ball was surreptitiously cut by an emery board. Markham, "the clever catcher of the Chinese team," discovered Mullin's ruse, according to a wire story. "Mark" then persuaded Apau Kau to get his own emery board out. The Hawaiian pitcher subsequently won the game. On August 15, the Travelers fell to the Bushwicks, 5–1. Yet the *Brooklyn Eagle* maintained that the game produced "high class baseball." Both nines demonstrated "big league stuff all the way," although the Hawaiians committed two key errors. Apau Kau generally kept Bushwicks batters in line, but Girard, the Brooklyn pitcher, did better. The *Eagle* claimed that great fielding plays by the Travelers highlighted the contest fought at Ridgewood Field.[98]

The Strawbridge and Clothier nine fell to the Hawaiians on August 21. According to the *Philadelphia Inquirer*, "John Chin" hit a tenth-inning home run to win the game for the "Chinks." Pitching for "the smiling sons of the Far East" was "Charley Chin." "Mark" was the team star according to the Philadelphia daily, while Al Yap added further punch to the offense. On August 30, the Travelers drew a good crowd to a game at Long Island's Clifton Park. Readers of the *Brooklyn Eagle* learned that the "Chinese Nine Wins" and, indeed, easily outclassed their flustered Sea Cliff nine opponents, 10–4. The newspaper estimated that about 5,000 fans showed up, while automobiles lined the roads to the park.[99]

On September 11, the *Honolulu Star-Bulletin* reported that the "Chinese Travelers" were still winning on the East Coast. The *Star-Bulletin* remained optimistic that "the Chinese team" would still make it to Cuba. At least, East Coast newspapers indicated they would. The Honolulu daily asserted, "The string of victories on the mainland should make them a good drawing card in Cuba, where they will meet teams of championship caliber."[100]

The Travelers' first baseman and *Star-Bulletin* correspondent, Alfred Yap, left the team in mid–September to enroll at Lehigh University. A South Bethlehem, Pennsylvania-datelined wire story published in the *Star-Bulletin* announced that the Lehigh baseball team "will receive a good recruit for next spring." It identified Yap as "a Chinese of Honolulu, Hawaii, a son of a bank official there" and advised readers that Yap was a "seasoned player, having performed at first and third base for the Chinese University team which is now touring the country." Below the wire story, the *Star-Bulletin* ran a brief account of its own of Yap's exploits, describing him as a "prominent figure in local athletics for years." Yap had graduated from the elite prep school of Punahou and studied for six months at the College of Hawai'i, today's University of Hawai'i's predecessor. Yap had informed his family of his desire to enroll at Lehigh with the intention of subsequently heading to law school. The *Star-Bulletin* declared, "Yap was one of the leading figures on the diamond with the Travelers and his place will be hard to fill."[101]

September marked the last full month the Travelers of 1915 spent on the mainland and witnessed New York fans watching the Hawaiians matched against the formidable Lincoln Giants. The September 2 edition of the African American *New York Age* announced the game with the headline, "Chinese To Play Lincoln Giants." The *Age* called the visitors the "Chinese University team" and reminded readers that the Hawaiians, thanks to "star pitcher" Apau Kau, had previously done well against the Giants. The *Age* remarked, "The Chinese players have a big following and a great crowd is expected to be on hand at Olympic Field to cheer and root for them." The first game between the Travelers and the Giants was not close. The *Age* headlined the game's story in the following manner: "Lincoln Giants Take Chinese Cues." The African American weekly reported that the contest drew 7,000 fans, the largest crowd to see a game at Olympic Field in months. While the game was not particularly close, the *Age* pointed out that the fans were entertained by the "Chinese [who] gave an exhibition of shadow ball that earned them rounds of applause."[102]

The *New York Times*, meanwhile, found the game between the Giants and the Travelers as scarcely worthy of respect. "Chinese Minus Pigtails Lose Game" headlined the *Times* account of the game. The *Times* correspondent maintained that since the visitors did not wear any "pigtails," they were helpless "before the darktown balltossers." The visitors' "funny names" did not seem to bother "the men who hibernate about the 135th Street section." Moreover, the *Times* insisted, "the Chinamen" took the "American pastime" too lightly. They were too prone to engage in "acrobatic stunts," performing "handsprings" while the African American nine won. When the visitors scored two runs, "the Orientals jabbered delightedly," the *Times* observed. Still, the "watermelon smile never faded from the dusky Lincoln players."[103]

The next week Apau Kau's pitching led the Hawaiians to a 5–0 victory. Once again, the *Age* reported that a large crowd arrived at Olympic Fields and "the Orientals played a flashy brand of ball that kept the 7,000 fans on edge from start to finish." The *Age* described Apau Kau as a "great pitcher," while claiming that "the wonderful fielding and hitting of the Chinese team held the big crowd spellbound." The *Baltimore Afro American* reported that the Giants were "furious" over getting shut out by the "Chinese University" nine. A "battle for blood" was expected for the rubber match which would pit Apau Kau against the magnificent Cyclone Joe Williams. Rain, sadly, scrubbed the rubber match between the two teams, because the Hawaiians were scheduled to quickly board a boat to Cuba.[104]

The Travelers, indeed, journeyed to Cuba. In early September, the *Advertiser* published extracts of a correspondence from Jimmy Aylett. Writing from Philadelphia, the outfielder of indigenous Hawaiian ancestry claimed there was a good chance the team was Cuba-bound. Bad weather had interrupted the East Coast trip and Cuba had made a good offer to the Hawaiians. Aylett expected that because of the Cuban trip, the Travelers would not return home until December. On October 2, the *Star-Bulletin* announced that the "Chinese Travelers" had set sail for Cuba on September 28. On October 22, the *Advertiser* informed readers that the Travelers would journey home soon. The Cuban trek had not worked out as well as hoped. "Cubans are a wee bit too fast for the Hawaiian representatives and the boys do not appreciate being on the short end of the score." On October 14, the team returned to New Orleans from Cuba. The ship's manifest listed them as follows: Luther Kekoa, 21, Hilo; Clement Moriyama, Keolia, Kanai, Hawai'i, 21; Vernon Ayan [*sic*], 26, Honolulu; James Moriyama, Keolia, Kanai, Hawai'i, 22; William Tin, 22, Honolulu; Henry Kuali, 22, Honolulu; James Aylett, 23, Honolulu; George

Bush, 20, Honolulu; Masayoshi Yamashiro, 24, Wailuku, Maui. All provided a U.S. address in New York City.[105]

Meanwhile, the "All-Chinese" team had returned from its journey to Asia. It won plenty of games and reportedly a great deal of respect in China, Japan, and the Philippines. Crucial to the team's success were former Travelers Luck Yee Lau and Kan Yen Chun. According to W. Tin Chong, Manila's Chinese merchants and business people "were tremendously interested in our team." They suggested that after the young men played in the Far Eastern games in Shanghai, the Chinese Hawaiians should return to the Philippines and establish a "Chinese team in the Manila League." The ballplayers were promised well-paid jobs if they relocated and Chong admitted that from a financial standpoint some of the Chinese Hawaiians were well advised to linger in Manila. However, Chong complained, "Manila is too hot. We were there during a hot spell of the hot season, and we were mighty glad to get away on that account. After cool Hawaii the Philippine climate doesn't stack up."[106]

Former Traveler Luck Yee's memories of the 1915 journey to Asia appeared during the next year in Hawai'i. The 1916 edition of *Ka Palapala*, published by the College of Hawai'i, printed a piece the pitcher wrote. Editors of the publication introduced Luck Yee Lau by saying that he belonged to the college's class of 1917 and had performed excellently on the teams that had barnstormed the mainland. They added, "We are proud to own him as a fellow student not only because he is a star player, but because on the field and off he is known for his gentlemanly conduct and sportsmanship."[107]

Luck Yee told readers that China needed a baseball team to represent it adequately at the Far Eastern games. Thus, sports-minded Chinese authorities went to Hawai'i for help because they knew that "a Chinese baseball team" had made several successful journeys to the American mainland. Furthermore, "Manila people" were anxious to see a Chinese Hawaiian team in action.[108]

The son of a Chinese immigrant father and a native-born Hawaiian mother, Luck Yee described the trip westward as pleasant. He said that he and his teammates would climb on deck to do some warming up. However, "It was a queer experience to get out there the first time, throwing the ball while the ship was dipping and rolling. All the boys, except one or two, held conferences with the sharks and other fishes for a day or more, and then were well, ate heartily and slept nicely."[109]

Luck Yee had generally kind things to say about Japan. After 11 days at sea, the Chinese Hawaiian ballplayers reached Yokohama. Upon arrival, the team roamed by foot the city's streets because they could not communicate with the "*jinrikisha* men." Eventually, they ate at a Chinese restaurant and spent the night at the Hotel De France. The team seemed to like "Tokio" more. There, they took an "enjoyable" ricksha trek around the city. "Wherever we stopped the people would gather around us wonderingly. We had a hard time trying to obtain information from the policemen. All we could get out of them was a shake of the head."[110]

Luck Yee expressed less warmth for China. Upon arrival in Hong Kong, the Hawaiians noted the *Sampras* harboring "poor women, carrying children on their backs and rowing the boats too. Some of them had clothes that were tattered and worn out — poor miserable things. They were hungry creatures." Before actually setting foot on Hong Kong the Hawaiians were accosted by a disagreeable Chinese customs official, according to Luck Yee. The pitcher claimed this bureaucrat "had the hauteur of an absolute ruler of the place." He searched the players' trunks for opium, firearms, and cartridges, and his arrogance, Luck Yee stressed, almost led "to blows."[111]

Still, Hong Kong merchants entertained the visitors. Luck Yee recalled that during one feast put on by local merchants, "beautifully dressed girls" sang for the players. However, the Hawaiians could not understand the lyrics of what the entertainers were singing until the young women sang Mendelssohn's "Spring Song" and the "famous Tipperary."[112]

A motorcade greeted the Chinese Hawaiian ballplayers upon their arrival in Manila. They were then driven to the local YMCA where they stayed. Unable to practice for the 26 days they were ship-bound, Luck Yee and his teammates tried to work out in Manila their first day. The Chinese Hawaiians drew a large crowd to their practice — a crowd that included several opposing players. However, the weather was so hot they decided to do something else with their time after 15 minutes of exercise.[113]

The Manila sporting press, Luck Yee complained, generally "knock[ed] us" before the Chinese Hawaiians took the field. Luck Yee conceded that there was one "contrarian" among the local sportswriters who praised the visitors. Luck Yee wrote, "It was fun to see them jeer at each other through the columns of their respective papers. The more they knocked the harder we played."[114]

Even though the team played effectively, the Manila sportswriters continued to scoff, maintaining that the Hawaiians were more lucky than good. Still, the visitors drew well — hefty crowds of as many as 10,000. Luck Yee reported proudly that the team tied the "much touted" Manila nine and then savaged another nine of hometown heroes, 10–0. The Manila press started to change its tune, while the city's Chinese community invited the Hawaiians to a dinner.[115]

Returning to China, the Hawaiians were feted by Chinese President Yuan Shi Kai. The ballplayers received "little mementoes." However, political trouble was brewing for the President and the Hawaiians were feeling sorry for Yuan Shi Kai. Luck Yee asserted, "Wonderful indeed must be that man who will eventually lead 500,000,000 countrymen."[116]

On November 11, the *Advertiser* announced that Travelers Lai Tin, Ayau,

Aylett, Kekoa, Chinito Moriyama, and Andy Yamashiro were all safely ensconced in Honolulu. The daily pointed out that the Travelers had done their job on the mainland, winning 102 games, while losing 53 and tying three. Apau Kau and Markham remained on the East Coast, while George Bush stayed in San Francisco. Al Yap, of course, was at Lehigh. "William Lai Tin" wanted to keep the Travelers squad together as much as possible in Honolulu. He sought to add a few players to the squad and oppose the 25th, the First Infantry, and Oahu League nines. Lai Tin suggested Saturday games so as not to conflict with the Oahu League competition on Sunday. However, the latter did not agree. If the Travelers could not compete as a team, the *Advertiser* did not worry. Eight highly skilled Hawaiian ballplayers scattered throughout the Oahu League would only strengthen that league and give Honolulu fans more enjoyment.[117]

Meanwhile, Honolulu's baseball world was hoping to see either the "All-Chinese" or "Lai Tin's Travelers" opposing the 25th Regiment nine. The *Advertiser* claimed that the rivalry between the Travelers and the 25th was bitter. It declared, "These two teams feel for each other as does [*sic*] a couple of strong bull dogs with a bone handy." A prior game between the "All-Chinese" and the 25th was called a "battle royal" by the *Advertiser*. On November 27, a team combining talent from the Travelers with the "All-Chinese" lost to the 25th, 3–2, in what the *Advertiser* described as "a hotly contested game." The fielding was "brilliant," as was the pitching. And both teams were more than ready for a return match. The next week, a nine the *Advertiser* called the Travelers beat the 25th, 6–2. Lang Akana, "Charley En Sue," and Kan Yen Chun were the game's big hitters, while En Sue, Lai Tin and "C. Moriyama" sparkled in the field. Luther Kekoa pitched competently and was provided with better support than his counterpart, who had to overcome several crucial errors by teammates. The 25th came back to edge the "Lai Tin Men," 4–3, the following week. Chinito Moriyama hit a home run, but it wasn't enough to help his brother get the victory as a pitcher.[118]

Just before the year ended, a story printed in the *Boston Journal* reported, "Chinese Baseball Team Coming Back Next Year." Lai Tin had corresponded with the mainland press, promising that the team that would emerge "faster than ever" in 1916. Apparently Ayau, "the acrobatic shortstop," would collaborate with Lai Tin in arranging for the 1916 trek. Lai Tin declared that "Mark, the rangy catcher and Bo, who ranked next to Apau on the pitching staff" were doing business on the Pacific Coast but would eventually join the team. Yap, "the hard hitting first baseman," was in college but might play with the Travelers, Lai Tin incorrectly predicted. The *Journal* piece asserted that the Hawaiian team was particularly popular in New England. The Travelers would, indeed, return to the mainland one last time.[119]

FIVE

One Last Time, 1916

Even more than in previous years, the last Travelers nine to tour the U.S. mainland included a culturally diverse mixture of ballplayers possessing Chinese, Japanese, indigenous Hawaiian, and haole ancestries. The team consisted of players such as haoles Bill Inman and Roy Doty, as well as non-white Hawaiians such as Buck Lai Tin, Yen Chin, Fred Markham, Apau Kau, Fred Swan, Luther Kekoa, Andy Yamashiro, Chinito Moriyama, and George Bush.[1]

Bill Inman was a great all-around athlete from Punahou Preparatory. Believed on the mainland to possess some indigenous ancestry, Inman pitched a bit for but was ultimately cut by the San Francisco Seals. However, Inman's appearance at the Seals' training camp caused something of a stir since Hawaiians of any racial background playing mainland ball enticed an exotic image. The *Star-Bulletin* expressed pride in Inman's ability to persuade the Seals he had potential. It noted that John Williams had been vital in getting Inman a tryout with the Seals and quoted Inman as saying that he would "do his best to boost Hawaii to a still higher position in athletics." The *Los Angeles Times* reported, moreover, that Inman was 22 years old, stood 6 feet tall and weighed more than 200 pounds.[2]

While readying in Oahu for the trip to the mainland, the Travelers nine played against local teams, including the formidable 25th Regiment nine, which stood out as a strong rival for supremacy in Honolulu baseball. It fielded great players such as Wilbur "Bullet" Rogan, who would eventually illuminate African American baseball on the mainland for many years. According to baseball historian Jerry Malloy, the 25th Regiment team took part in Honolulu baseball from 1913 to 1918, winning city and island championships. Indeed, the *Pacific Coast Advertiser* declared Rogan the best player on the islands in 1916. Kan Yen Chun and Hoon Ki of the All-Chinese were also mentioned among the most elite ballplayers in Hawai'i, but the *Advertiser* claimed neither was in Rogan's class.[3]

Five. One Last Time

Roy Doty (second from the left) was a haole who joined the 1916 Travelers squad. Here he stands between outfielder Yen Chin (far left) and Lai Tin (third from the left). Japanese Hawaiian outfielder Andy Yamashiro stands at the far right (courtesy of the Yamashiro Family).

On February 29, the *Star-Bulletin* announced an upcoming promotional game between the 25th Regiment and the Travelers. The daily expected a large attendance, hoping that many Honolulans would appear because only by playing such games could the Travelers raise enough money for their 1916 trek to the mainland. The *Star-Bulletin* expressed disappointment that Hawai'i's Promotions Committee had not helped the Travelers out financially for the upcoming journey. The team, after all, had always publicized the Hawai'i effectively, the *Star-Bulletin* fumed.[4]

The *Advertiser* also claimed excitement over the game early in March between the Travelers and the 25th Regiment. In publicizing the upcoming contest, the *Advertiser* called William Lai Tin the manager and leader of the "Travelers Baseball Team." The proceeds from the game were to help defray the Travelers' expenses on the mainland, the *Advertiser* reminded local baseball fans. Moreover, Luther Kekoa was scheduled to take the box for the Travelers.[5]

The *Advertiser* informed readers that "Lai Tin, Homerun Johnson, Vernon Ayau and the other stars of the swatting stick will be in uniform and the fans should witness an interesting game of baseball." Johnson, by the way, was the hitting star for the 25th Infantry. As it turned out, the Travelers beat the soldiers.[6]

An ostensibly amateur contingent from San Francisco had, meanwhile, arrived in Honolulu to stir up some baseball excitement. The "Chinese Travelers" announced in early January their intention of playing the Olympic Club nine, despite opposition from official league teams in Honolulu. The *Star-Bulletin* backed the Travelers' bid. It argued that the Travelers would assemble a "strong squad" and had advertised Honolulu more than any other aggregation of Hawaiian athletes. "On the mainland they know our athletics by the performances of Duke Kahanamoku and the Travelers. Each year the ball tossers from Hawaii play hundreds of games in every section of the country, and hundreds of thousands of people have watched them play." By seeing the Travelers in action, mainlanders gained a positive "impression" of the islands, the *Star-Bulletin* insisted. Moreover, the Travelers furnished "direct advertising of Hawaii" by distributing promotional literature wherever they went. The *Star-Bulletin*, emphasized that the Travelers were not just "boosters" but good ballplayers.[7]

As various Honolulu baseball clubs geared up to oppose the Olympic Club nine, Lang Akana proved something of a "bone of contention." The *Star-Bulletin* wondered whether the outfielder would wear the uniform of St. Louis, Punahou, or the "Chinese." Apparently, it had been anticipated that Akana would play for Punahou, but he was sending mixed signals.[8]

The Chinese team slated to meet the mainlanders was going to be tough with or without Akana, according to the *Star-Bulletin*. Kan Yen Chun would catch, while Hoon Ki and Luck Yee would pitch. As for "Lai Tin," he "will be the star of the infield." The Chinese nine was not as good as some of the past Travelers squads, according to the *Star-Bulletin*, but it "should be a mighty good drawing card."[9]

On the day before the Travelers would meet the Olympic Club, the *Star-Bulletin* emerged in full promotional mode. It predicted that Luck Yee would take the box for Lai Tin's team and show "the visitors a good class of heaving." Kan Yen Chun earned considerable praise from the daily. The *Star-Bulletin* called him "one of the niftiest catchers in the city." Moreover, he "is a hard worker and fans look upon him as one of the gamest backstops in Hawaii." In addition, "the peppery little catcher" possessed a good arm. Cheong at first and Kai Luke at second were deemed as competent. But the big stars of the infield were, of course, on the other side: "Lai Tin and Ayau are both good hitters, fast, and nice fielders." The outfielders, En Sue Pung, Lang Akana, and Yen Chin, were all fine batters. Suiting up with Lai Tin's nine, Akana could hit to all fields, while he and En Sue Pung were fleet defenders. The *Star-Bulletin* promised a good gate for the game between the Olympic Club and "the Chinese organization."[10]

The next day the *Star-Bulletin* published a photo of Luck Yee, "one of the star pitchers of the Chinese team." Luck Yee and his teammates had been practicing for the Olympic Club. Indeed, the San Franciscans watched the Travelers practice and were duly impressed. The *Star-Bulletin* also reported that day that Lang Akana would decidedly not compete for St. Louis despite the fact that he had graduated from the school. The team's board had mysteriously declared the outfielder ineligible. In any event, he was free to play for Lai Tin's nine.[11]

According to the *Star-Bulletin*, the Olympic Club players expected victory over the Chinese Hawaiians. After all, the San Franciscans had their ace in the box. However, the "Chinese played rings around the much-touted Winged O players and the fans of Honolulu cheered themselves hoarse as the contest ended at Athletic Park on Saturday with the score: Chinese 5, Olympic 2." Lai Tin, "the fast third baseman," rapped four hits for the locals. "Pegging like a shot," Kan Yen Chun did well at catcher, as did Luck Yee at pitcher. And Ayau made "six startling plays [that] had the Olympic players popping their eyes out." Yet the big reason why the locals won was that their speed caught the visitors by surprise. "The Celestials," the *Star-Bulletin* concluded, won so many games on so few hits mainly because of their baserunning skills.[12]

On the same sports page discussing the Olympic Club game, the *Star-Bulletin* printed a photograph of "Chinese star" Lai Tin. The swift infielder, according to the Honolulu daily, shared "star status" on the Chinese Travelers with Vernon Ayau. Here too, the *Star-Bulletin* stressed the Travelers' ability to win games and promote the islands as the newspaper announced the team's next trek to the mainland.[13]

The *Star-Bulletin* predicted one of the largest crowds ever at Athletic Park for the second game between the Chinese Hawaiians and the Olympic Club, with most of the local fans rooting for Lai Tin's team. The home team's infield, the *Star-Bulletin* forecast, would "outclass" that of the mainlanders, while its outfield, primarily because of Akana's hitting, would also perform excellently. While the Chinese Hawaiians lost to the Olympic Club, 4–1, the

Star-Bulletin extolled the locals. A nice crowd viewed the game, proving, the *Star-Bulletin* insisted, "that the Chinese are a great drawing card."[14]

On March 8, Hawai'i bid goodbye to the Travelers. The *Advertiser* insisted that this Travelers nine was as good as any Hawaiian club that had previously headed to the mainland. The daily did not have much information about the team's itinerary other than that manager Lai Tin hoped to arrange several games in the San Francisco Bay Area against St. Mary's, Stanford, Santa Clara, and the San Francisco Olympic Club.[15]

On March 9, the *Advertiser* announced, "Nine ball tossers representing several nationalities left for the mainland yesterday morning in the Matsonia, for a tour that is expected to embrace every large city of the States and to cover a period of at least seven months. The team [is] to be known as the Chinese University Team of Honolulu." Aside from Inman, another newcomer for the Travelers would, in a sense, be performing in "yellowface." That is, among the players ultimately taken was a European American surnamed Doty, who apparently played with the Portland Beavers of the Pacific Coast League. A Roy Doty, indeed, competed with an Atlantic City minor league team in 1913. He played in 116 games and batted a mediocre .252 as a 20-year-old. When it seemed that the Hawaiian team was going to bring Doty and another player called "Blondie" by the *Advertiser*, the daily wondered "how they intend to pass as Chinese or Hawaiian especially [Blondie] with that beautiful blonde hair of his." The *Advertiser* also mourned the impact the Travelers' departure would have on the local baseball scene. The All-Chinese nine, managed by Kim Luke, would lose Buck Lai Tin, Vernon Ayau, and Kan Yen Chun, who, it turned out, remained on Oahu. The St. Louis College team faced the departure of Chinito Moriyama, Fred Swan, and Bill Inman, while Doty had apparently played for Punahou.[16]

The S.S. *Matsonia*'s passengers disembarked in San Francisco on March 14, 1916. The ship's passenger manifest listed nine Travelers. A handwritten note designated outfielder and newcomer Yen Chin, V.L. Ayau, Lai Tin, M. Yamashiro, and C. Moriyama as "Hawaii born." The four other ballplayers— Fred Swan, W.L. Inman, L.W. Kekoa, and M. Doty—received no such designation. The difference presumably was that the former group of Hawaiians more manifestly bore the Asian "racial uniform."[17]

As usual the publicity for the Hawaiian ballplayers preceded them. In February, a small Texas town newspaper announced that local entrepreneurs were trying to lure the "Chinese baseball team" for a game on April 4. However, the Hawaiians wanted a $150 guarantee and it seemed unlikely that the sum could be raised. Nevertheless, the *Cleburne News* urged fans to consider that the visitors comprised a good team and they would get their money's worth. The *San Francisco Chronicle* announced in early March that the

"Chinese stars of Hawaii will invade California." The daily claimed, "The Orientals are wonderful fielders ... and faster than Mauser bullets on the paths." When the team arrived in San Francisco, its first game was in Palo Alto against Stanford.[18]

The *Daily Palo Alto Times* announced the upcoming contest in an article headlined "Chinese Tossers Here Tomorrow." It called the Hawaiians a "fast Chinese Team from the University of Hawaii" and promised readers that "the speedy En Sue will again cavort on the diamond" despite the fact that the veteran outfielder had chosen to remain on the islands. Moreover, the student newspaper warned readers that Stanford's "graduate manager finds it an impossibility to allow spectators admission to this contest on season tickets as a certain guarantee has to be met to obtain a game with the island team." The *Daily Palo Alto*, Stanford's newspaper, described the game as an "Oriental Contest" and noted that it was both "snappy" and "well played." The very un–Chinese Bill Inman hit what the paper called the longest home run of the season at Stanford, driving a ball into deep left field.[19]

The *San Jose Mercury* predicted that Stanford would play the "Chinamen" in a three-game series, but one game would have to suffice. Indeed, the Travelers' schedule in California proved fairly empty. The day after the Stanford game, the Hawaiians were in Stockton where they lost to local nine, 7–6. Then they moved south to Bakersfield, where they were on the winning end of a 5–3 game.[20]

After California, Arizona was the next stop for the Travelers. On March 15, the *Tucson Citizen* notified readers that the "Chinese players from the University of Hawaii" would encounter the University of Arizona nine on March 20 and 21. The "crack foreign aggregation" lost its first game to the University of Arizona, 5–4. But, according to the *Citizen*, the "Celestials" gained "revenge" on the Wildcats, 7–0. Lai Tin wrote to the *Star-Bulletin*, complimenting Fred Swan's pitching as well as the hitting of Yamashiro and Doty against the Arizona Wildcats.[21]

The Travelers did not linger much in the mainland's Far West. From Arizona, Lai Tin reported to the *Star-Bulletin*, the team headed to Stamford, Texas, a town in the central part of the state. Writing on March 24, Lai Tin boasted that his team handled the Stamford nine easily, 16–4. Clearly, the Hawaiians "scored at will." Lai Tin praised the "heavy hitting" of the team he interestingly called "the Chinese," despite haole teammates such as Inman and Doty. He was especially generous in his praise of the way "Chin" and "Yim" hit. Lai Tin said the game was played in a strong southerly wind that challenged fielders. He asserted that the Stamford match-up drew many fans evincing a great deal of generosity toward the Travelers. The next day, the Hawaiians edged Simmons College, 3–2, with Swan in the box. The *Abilene*

This photograph of the 1916 team was undoubtedly taken early in the season. Catcher Fred Markham is not in the photograph, although he would join his fellow Hawaiians later. Jimmy Moriyama, who was an excellent second baseman, sits in the front row, second from the right and next to Andy Yamashiro. Moriyama is wearing the catcher's shin guards since he did the bulk of the catching until Markham assumed his old position (courtesy of the Yamashiro Family).

Reporter pointed out in an article abstracted in a Commerce, Texas newspaper that "the Chinks are a team of mechanically perfect baseball players, with a thorough knowledge of the game and the ability to take advantage of the least break." They were the best fielding college team seen by the Abilene reporter. They were also swift on the bases and dangerous hitters.[22]

A wire story published in The *Fort Worth Star Telegram* on March 30 pointed out that "the Chinese baseball team" had just won two games from Howard Payne College in Brownsville, Texas. The Howard Payne nine was routed and the two games were hardly worth mentioning according to the correspondent. However, a clever play performed by the Hawaiians drew attention. With Ayau up and "Chin" on first, the shortstop dropped a bunt along the first base line. Howard Payne's first baseman fielded the bunt and noted that Ayau had stopped running to first. Hesitating, the first baseman then started to run Ayau down and "Chin" flew to third. The first baseman then threw the ball to one of his teammates covering first. The ball was dropped and everyone was safe.²³

The *Brownville Daily Bulletin* appeared somewhat impressed. It declared that the "Chinese baseball team from the University of Hawaii" showed that they knew how to play baseball and beat "an average college team." After the second game, the *Daily Bulletin* bore witness that the Howard Payne nine was "no match for the wily Chinks," who managed to steal an astonishing 18 bases. The Hawaiian ballplayers then supposedly regaled the press with stories about Hawai'i and the imaginary University of Hawaii. The university presumably featured all sorts of athletic endeavors such as baseball, basketball, football, and swimming. Lai Tin claimed that football was not easy for Hawaiians because of the warmth of the islands' fall and winter. In any event, Inman was designated as the university's football coach. The *Evening Bulletin* declared that he and "Dot," as Roy Doty was called in the press, were the only "Americans" on the team and lamented that neither game in Brownsville drew enough to make money.²⁴

Conceivably, the *Evening Bulletin* was making up what the Hawaiians were saying about the University of Hawaii. Just as conceivably, Lai Tin and his players were prepared to reinforce what had to have been by 1916 a laughable ruse to them. One can well imagine that deceiving the mainland press was an unnecessary burden to the Hawaiians. One can also well imagine the young men enjoying their tales about a non-existent university.

According to Lai Tin's correspondence to the *Star-Bulletin*, at least the first game with Howard Payne was fairly close. Swan was the big hitter in leading the Hawaiians to a 9–6 victory. Lai Tin also commended the pitching of Bill Inman and Andy Yamashiro. The second game, Lai Tin disclosed, was a 14–6 rout in the Travelers' favor. "Bo" did fine in the box as did Apau Kau in relief. Since Howard Payne was clearly overmatched, the Hawaiians decided to speed up the game in order to catch a train. Thus, after the sixth inning they did not bother to swing at pitches. The Travelers' next stop in Central Texas was apparently Georgetown, which housed Southwestern University. There they edged the home team, 3–2. Lai Tin said he and Yamashiro sparked the offense, while Doty starred in the field.²⁵

The Texas trek continued to inspire good play from the Hawaiians. On March 30, they journeyed to Austin, where they won the first of three games with the University of Texas nine, 7–2. The next day, the Travelers lost, 9–6, with Inman taking the defeat. After this game, the "Honolulu Chinamen" were tendered a reception at the local YMCA. The *Dallas Morning News* reported that several Texas students attended and were rewarded with the Hawaiians entertaining them with ukulele strumming and island songs. The *Morning News* informed readers on April 2 of "the prettiest game of the season" as the "Chinese" downed the University of Texas, 6–4. "Chin" and Lai Tin hit round-trippers for the visitors, while "Suan" did a fine job of relieving Apau Kau. The *Morning News* correspondent added, "The Chinese played a perfect fielding game."[26]

Moving into the northeast section of Texas, the Hawaiians and Inman beat Commerce's East Texas Normal College nine, 5–1, on April 12. The *Commerce Journal* testified that the largest crowd ever at the local ball park watched the "Chinese University of Honolulu" in action. All the businesses in Commerce were apparently shut down to boost attendance and the 900 spectators were not disappointed according to the *Journal*. They saw a rare treat — a baseball team from "Celestial Country." In addition, they witnessed a "clever bunch of athletes who put up a clean article of ball." On April 13, the Hawaiians could not overcome a three-run lead posted by Austin College. The *Dallas Morning News* asserted that "the Chinese University nine seemed to loaf" and that "Bo" was wild for the Chinamen." Lai Tin's correspondence to the *Star-Bulletin* reveals another perspective on the game. Lai Tin expressed disappointment that the Travelers had lost for the first time in three years against Austin College, but did not seem overwrought by his team's performance. "Bo" had started and was relieved by Ayau, who, according to Lai Tin, "did pretty well." The game drew a relatively small attendance, Lai Tin pointed out, because of the imminent threat of rain.[27]

Journeying out of Texas at last, the "the Chinese University" lost easily to Oklahoma A&M, 10–3, on April 18. The *Tulsa World's* headline read: "Aggies Crush the Yellow Peril." Pitcher Inman proved no "Yellow Peril" in more ways than one. At the same time, only "Mark" and "Dot" hit effectively for the visitors. Indeed, Markham, who had wintered on the mainland, rejoined the Travelers in Oklahoma. In the process, he took over the catching duties from Chinito Moriyama, who could then return to his customary spot at second base.[28]

After playing several games in Kansas and Missouri, the Travelers appeared in Indiana. On May 10, the Travelers opposed the Taylor ABCs, a strong African American team out of Indianapolis. Previously, the *Indianapolis Star* announced that the "foreigners" would make their first appearance in Indianapolis. The next day the *Star* predicted that ABCs ace Dizzy Dismukes would take the box against the Travelers. Actually, the ABCs were scheduled to play a doubleheader that day, the second game of which would pit the Indianapolis nine against the Kokomo Red Sox — the aggregation that had beaten the "Chinese" a week earlier. The *Star* promised readers two exciting games as the Red Sox and the Travelers were strong. Moreover, the *Star* expected the Hawaiians to put on an exhibition of shadow ball and juggling for the spectators. Although the Hawaiians lost, the *Chicago Defender* declared that "some of the Chinese act like real ballplayers and there is no doubt that they like the game. They were caught on the bases several times by snappy throws, but appeared to know many of the American tricks."[29]

In Ohio, the Travelers opposed a nine from Wilberforce University on May 15. A wire story published in the *Savannah Tribune* was headlined "Chinese University Defeats Wilberforce." Dispatched from the Wilberforce campus, the story said that the Hawaiians "outbatted" and "outslugged" the home team in "one of the most exciting and interesting games ever witnessed here." A good crowd watched the home team perform competently save apparently in baserunning. "Suan" did a good job of relieving Apau Kau as "the yellow men," including Inman and Doty, won, 8–6.[30]

Crossing the Mason-Dixon Line, the Hawaiians confronted the Mt. St. Mary's College nine in Maryland. Reporting on the game, the *Frederick Daily News* claimed that in a "sensational game" the "Chinese University of Hawaii" edged St. Mary's, 2–1. Moreover, "the contest was replete with brilliant fielding by both teams and a splendid pitchers' battle between Gleason and Inman." A few days later, the Travelers were in Indiana, Pennsylvania, where they beat the Normal School nine before what the *Indiana Weekly Messenger* called "the largest crowd of the season." An unnamed "Chink" apparently hit the longest home run seen in the area in recent years.[31]

The Hawaiians got busy on the East Coast in June. On June 2, 6,000 fans crowded into Jersey City's West Side Park to watch the Jersey City Cubans down the Travelers, 6–0. A band and choir surfaced to entertain the crowd more than ball game. In the next game, the Hawaiians outslugged the Nat Strong-owned Brooklyn Royal Giants, 11–8. Attended by 5,000 at Brooklyn's Ridgewood Field, this game was actually the second of a doubleheader the local African Americans were scheduled to play. Lai Tin shined as the hitting star for the victors, accumulating four hits, including a triple. "Suan," "Dot," "Yim," and "C. Chin" hit well too. Apau Kau pitched competently for five innings, and then took himself out thinking, the *Brooklyn Daily Eagle* surmised, that the game was "on ice." It was not as the Royal Giants battled back to make the game relatively close.[32]

After a brief sojourn into New York City, the Travelers trekked back into Pennsylvania. On June 5, Lehigh University downed the "Chinese University" nine, 3–2, in an extra-inning affair at Bethlehem, Pennsylvania. The Reading professional nine beat them the following day before a large crowd. The Hawaiians snapped back against Bucknell University on June 9, behind Inman's pitching. In Easton, Pennsylvania, the Travelers lost again. The story in the *Philadelphia Public Ledger* was headlined "Lafayette Repels Chinese Attack." Replete with military metaphors, the story itself informed readers that the Lafayette University team "was effective in repelling the foreign invasion."

Before a commencement crowd, the Pennsylvania students "drove the enemy from the field" as they beat the visitors, 6–1.[33]

Moving into New England, the Hawaiians visited Trinity University at Hartford, Connecticut. Putting a damper on Trinity's commencement day, the Travelers won, 5–1. Three days later, the Travelers returned to New York City, where they were shut out by the Bushwicks, 3–0. Prior to the game, the *Brooklyn Eagle* tried to pumped up attendance by asserting that many professional franchises were trying to lure Lai Tin into "the big show." The Brooklyn daily described the Chinese Hawaiian as "a fine fielder, a hard hitter, and a clever baserunner." Still, the Bushwick pitcher, Girard, flung a no-hitter at Lai Tin's team. The *Eagle* claimed the largest crowd of the Bushwick season had watched the game. It also admired the pitching of "the Chinese boxmen,"—"Apau" and "Ako." Then the Hawaiians headed north to Rhode Island where Kekoa subdued the Brown University nine, 3–0. On June 23, the Comstock Cheney Company's baseball team defeated "the Chinese University baseball team from Hawaii." A report from Ivorytown, Connecticut, enthused that the game was attended by the largest crowd in local history. That is, "People came from every part of the county to see the Chinese play"— about 500 in all. Inman pitched in the 3–1 defeat, while Yen Chin and "J. Chin" starred for the visitors. Then the Travelers vanquished nines in New Haven and Bridgeport.[34]

In July, reports filtered back to Honolulu that things were not going well on the mainland for the Travelers. The team lost too often compared to earlier years. Individual Travelers complained to folks back home, according to the *Star-Bulletin*, that the losses were caused by their inability to compete effectively as a team. More disturbing, it seemed that the "Chinese Travelers" had made their last trip to the mainland. Why things were falling apart was left unreported.[35]

Swan, Kekoa, Apau, and Bush had been doing most of the pitching, Honolulu was told. Apau Kau was not as efficient as in the past, but Swan and Kekoa had picked up the slack somewhat. Newcomer Yen Chin and Yamashiro emerged as the team's best hitters. Lai Tin, Chinito Moriyama, and Swan were fielding well. Curiously, Ayau had been shifted to the outfield. Doty was performing satisfactorily in the field, but his bat had not helped matters. Honolulu was also informed that Al Yap was doing a good job for Philadelphia's Strawbridge and Clothier nine. Indeed, on July 8, Yap's "fast fielding" helped S&C win a game.[36]

In July and August, the Travelers played several games in and around Philadelphia and New York City. On June 25, the *Philadelphia Public Ledger* announced that the "Chinese team from the University of Hawai'i" would play its first game in Philadelphia in 1916. The game was scheduled for July

1 and would pit the Hawaiians against the Stetson semipro nine on the home team's grounds at Fourth and Berke Streets. Stretching things a bit, the *Public Ledger* declared that since taking on Stanford a few months earlier, the Travelers' "record has been one of almost continual victories and the Mongolians have upheld their reputation of being the sensation of independent baseball."[37]

A headline to a *Philadelphia Inquirer* story of the Travelers game against the Stetsons on July 1 read, "Washee, Washee Men No Sabe Defeat." No less subtle, the subheadline proclaimed, "Almond eye visitors Made Heap Biggee Rush and Beat Stetson." The *Inquirer* also referred to the "Chinese team from the University of Hawaii" as "Chinks" and "Celestial Sluggers." In any event, "Suan" and "Ako" pitched while the Travelers batted their way to an 11–9 triumph. The *Public Ledger* claimed, however, that the "Chinks" were lucky to win the well-attended game, although their performance excited the crowd.[38]

On the field, the Hawaiians had their ups and downs in and around the Quaker City. On July 2, the Travelers lost what the *Public Ledger* described as a "weird game" in Roxborough. No elaboration was offered. On July 4, the Hawaiians opposed the Strawbridge and Clothier nine. The headline proclaimed, "Chinks Fall Victims to Young Merchants." The home team was led by the pitching of John Ogden, a student from nearby Swarthmore. Indeed, the future major leaguer shut out the Hawaiians as his nine triumphed, 7–0. Perhaps adding salt to the Travelers' wounds, Al Yap appeared in the Strawbridge and Clothier lineup. The Hawaiians played another game on July 4 against a nine representing the Disston Saw Company, winning easily, 15–7, with Swan in the box.[39]

In Norristown on July 6, the Roy Thomas All-Stars performed "a remarkable feat" in defeating the "Chinese." According to the *Public Ledger*, the game featured great defense by both nines. On July 9, Inman pitched the Hawaiians to a 6–1 victory over Newark. Within a week, the Travelers were back in New Jersey after playing two games on Long Island.[40]

On July 14, the Hawaiians faced the "S&C" nine again. The *Public Ledger's* Walter F. Dunn reported that a large crowd attended the game. Indeed, every seat was packed for "the little fellows from a far-off land." John Ogden hurled another shutout for the home team. Such was his command, according to Dunn, that "the traveling 'eukuleleans' were more desirous of reaching a plate of rice and chicken" than facing him. Moreover, Yap got a key hit, inspiring Dunn to write that he no doubt "wanted to show his former associates" what he could do. The next day, the Camden Athletic Club nine barely beat the Travelers before a capacity crowd. The home team won, 3–2, in what an *Inquirer* correspondent called a "thrilling game." Pitching for Camden was a fellow named Mahaffey who had just been released from a minor league team in Richmond. Meanwhile, fans in Southampton, Long Island, were expecting the Travelers to appear for a game. The *Brooklyn Daily Eagle* complained that a large crowd was disappointed by the Hawaiians' unexplained absence.[41]

About a week later, the "Chinese University of Hawaii" won a "narrow gauge" victory in York, Pennsylvania, over the Grantley Park nine. "Sunn" was in the box. A few days later, Atlantic City's Bacharach Giants, described as the "Colored All-Stars" in the *Star-Bulletin*, managed a slim 6–5 victory over the Travelers. Meanwhile, a game with Strawbridge and Clothier had been postponed, leading to some disappointment as the *Public Ledger* believed that "a great crowd was expected." Philadelphia fans were undoubtedly fired up by the promotional work of local dailies. In announcing an upcoming game against the Stetsons, the *Public Ledger's* story was headlined, "Chinese Will Invade Stetson Park," while affirming that "the Chinese" composed one of the best draws in "independent ranks."[42]

As in earlier journeys, the Travelers kept a heavy schedule in the urban centers of the mainland's mid-Atlantic region in August. Not far from Philadelphia, the Travelers lost a game in Rockdale, 6–1, on August 11. Lai Tin's throwing error did not much help, but the third baseman's double did bring in the Hawaiians' only run. Several of the local mills were closed down to boost attendance. However, other mills were too busy to give their workers a break. Thus, according to the *Chester Times*, the crowd was down a bit. On August 12, the Strawbridge and Clothier club again topped "the almond-eye boys" at Philadelphia's 63rd and Walnut Streets grounds. John Ogden once more pitched masterfully for the winners, while "Suan" too rarely fooled the home team. In the meantime, the *Brooklyn Daily Eagle* reported that "crack" pitcher, Apau Kau, had received offers from several minor league teams.[43]

In mid-August the Travelers journeyed to Poughkeepsie, New York, to oppose a black team called the Poughkeepsie Cubans. The *Poughkeepsie Eagle News* headlined its announcement of the game, "Chinese Team Plays Today." Local fans, the newspaper reported, considered the game between the "Cubans" and the "University of Hawaii" nine as the baseball event of the season, primarily because of the praise many had heaped on the "Chinese players." Despite his travails in 1916, Apau Kau sparked considerable interest from the *Eagle News*, which called him "the greatest Chinese pitcher in the United States." The newspaper also promised fans that the Travelers would give an exhibition of "Shadow Ball."[44]

To their credit, the Travelers took two games from the Strawbridge-Clothier nine. On August 26, "The Chinks Smother the Store Boys," according to a headline in the *Inquirer*. "The Chinese ball team from Honolulu" romped to 14–5 triumph, delivering, in the process, "the worst defeat" ever suffered by the locals. The "Chinese" rapped 20 hits, while "Suan" rendered the opposition helpless. "Jimmy Chinn," "Yim," and Ayau slugged home runs, while Al Yap hit a four-bagger for the home team. The game had been "exciting" until the Hawaiians broke loose in the seventh inning. Called "the wiley Celestials" and "the little yellow boys" by the *Philadelphia Inquirer*, the Hawaiians triumphed on September 2 in a 7–4 extra-inning affair before a reported crowd of 2,500 at the 63rd and Walnut grounds.[45]

As the 1916 tour wound down, the Hawaiians confronted tough African American nines. In mid–September, the Jersey City Cubans shut out the Hawaiians, 2–0. In October, the "Chinese Baseball Club of Hawaii" played a doubleheader in Indianapolis against the Taylor ABCs. The Travelers lost both games, 4–2 and 5–3. Starring for the team the *Indianapolis Star* called the "Chinks" was Lai Tin as a fielder and "Yim" and "J. Chin" as clever baserunners. The *Kokomo Tribune* acknowledged that the "Chinese baseball club of Hawaii" lost both ends of a doubleheader, but reported that the "orientals" almost won the first game thanks to "Ako's" pitching. It added that the great Dizzy Dismukes beat Apau Kau in the second game, which lasted only five innings. The *Chicago Defender's* correspondent described the "Orientals" as entertaining despite their doubleheader defeat. Aside from the great fielding of Lai Tin, Yamashiro, and Moriyama, the Hawaiians pulled off the double steal twice.[46]

While not as good as previous editions and decidedly not as well publicized, the 1916 Travelers won admiration from some of the mainland press. A syndicated sports column asserted in September that just as the great first baseman, George Sisler, had never been fined for arguing with an umpire, none of the Travelers had been ejected for taking issue with an umpire's call. The *Brooklyn Eagle*, furthermore, eulogized the Hawaiians as they made their "last stand" in "greater New York City." The occasion was the "Chinese Baseball Club from Hawaii's" defeat by the Bushwicks on September 24. The *Eagle* declared, "This week the Chinamen leave for San Francisco, where they will take leave for home and the most gentlemanly aggregation of ball tossers ever seen on the local semipro diamonds will have passed on, perhaps forever, as it is by no means certain that they will return to the States again."[47]

The former Travelers who stayed home, as well as other Chinese Hawaiian players, acquitted themselves exceptionally in Honolulu's baseball world. The Waseda University nine visited the city in April. There, they were treated rudely by a Chinese Hawaiian nine, thanks to the hitting of Lang Akana and the pitching of Luck Yee and Hoon Ki. In late May, Santa Clara College ballplayers were edged by the Chinese Hawaiians, 6–5. Still, the best team over the summer of 1916 in Honolulu was the 25th regiment aggregation. In early May, "Big Chief" Waterhouse threw a one-hitter at the Chinese Hawaiians. "Charley En Sue," broke up Waterhouse's no-hitter in the ninth, inspiring the *Star-Bulletin* to proclaim, "If Charley En Sue ever enters a popularity contest among the ball players in Hawaii, you can mark down right now one vote he won't receive. 'Big Chief' Waterhouse said many evil things of the Chinese centerfielder yesterday." In early October, the 25th beat the "Celestials" 6–0. Rogan had carried a no-hitter into the ninth, when he was touched for a couple of harmless hits.[48]

The 25th was so good that no one team seemed capable of conquering Rogan and his teammates. An All-Oahu team was chosen to take on the African American aggregation. Kan Yen Chun and Lang Akana performed for the Oahu nine, but they were overpowered by Rogan, who not only hurled a shutout but struck out 15 in the process.[49]

By late October, most of the Travelers had returned. Lai Tin, Markham, Apau, and Yamashiro were, however, among those who remained on the mainland. While the *Advertiser* barely noted the Travelers' return, the *Star-Bulletin* greeted the ballplayers warmly. It published a photo of the "Chinese Travelers," minus Apau and Inman who were reportedly on the East Coast at the time the picture was taken. It boasted, moreover, that the team had played before over 230,000 fans, averaging 1,500 to 2,000 a game.[50]

In the same edition, the *Star-Bulletin* ran a story based on an interview with Bill Inman. The haole ballplayer, who somehow passed, along with Doty, Yamashiro, Swan and others as Chinese for thousands of mainland baseball fans, asserted that thanks to the Hawaiian barnstormers, "Honolulu received the biggest boost in history this year." The daily also made quite a fuss over Inman's meeting with one of baseball's greatest stars—Ty Cobb. Inman claimed that the feisty, white supremacist outfielder had asked him about En Sue and Lai Tin. He admitted that he was stumped by the question because he could not believe that Cobb had ever heard of Hawai'i's "swift outfielder" or the veteran third sacker. While Cobb's anti-social tendencies have become legendary, Inman said the Georgian seemed gracious and modest. Cobb even presented Inman with a ball autographed by the "Georgia Peach" and each of his Detroit Tigers teammates.[51]

Inman further articulated dismay that Honolulu's "promotion men" did not see fit to send along literature boosting Hawai'i with the Travelers. Inman declared that the Travelers consistently "talked up" Hawai'i while on the mainland and the musicians among the Travelers were particularly effective in advertising the islands as they fed into mainlanders' growing infatuation with Hawaiian music—an infatuation which led them to consistently ask the Travelers about the "Paradise of the Pacific."[52]

Meanwhile, Inman praised the Hawaiian musicians journeying throughout the mainland. They, too, advertised the islands effectively in the continental U.S. However, Inman added, they could not reach as many people as the Travelers, who performed before thousands. Even small towns, the ballplayer maintained, turned out for the Hawaiians. Stores were closed and schools went on holiday so baseball fans could see the Travelers in action. On the more urbanized East Coast, notable crowds showed up. East Coast fans, Inman bragged, consistently rooted for the "Chinese."[53]

The Travelers ran into old friends and acquaintances during the 1916 trek, Inman recalled. Many military officers formerly stationed on the islands greeted them. The Travelers, Inman conceded, may not have won as many games as in prior years, but that was because the team took on tougher opposition — an argument that Travelers veterans Lai Tin and Ayau could well have respected but probably considered wrong.[54]

The Travelers who did come back were expected to play the 25th nine and other teams. On October 26, the *Star-Bulletin* announced that at least some of the returning Travelers would take the field soon — playing for an all-star team scheduled to oppose the 25th. Fred Swan, in particular, was expected to show local fans that he had, as Inman claimed, improved 100 percent since

As did earlier editions of the Travelers, the 1916 team played plenty of games on the U.S. East Coast. This is a photograph of the squad as they are either arriving at or departing from Wildwood, New Jersey. Bill Inman, a versatile haole athlete from Honolulu, stands third from the left. In 1915 Inman was given a tryout by the San Francisco Seals. He failed to make the PCL team but showed promise (courtesy of the Yamashiro Family).

leaving Honolulu. The *Star-Bulletin* looked forward to seeing Ayau in action as well. Ayau would play shortstop for the all-stars "in such a way as to make fans think about real baseball." Chinito Moriyama, moreover, would guarantee that second was "well taken care of." As for Lai Tin's old position at third, Honolulu fans could expect to see Kan Yen Chun or Henry Kuali in the former track star's place. In the outfield, Bill Inman, En Sue Pung, and Lang Akana would roam. The trio, the *Star-Bulletin* insisted, was as good as any the 25th could muster.[55]

On November 11, the *Advertiser* promoted a game that day between the 25th and the "Traveling Chinese." Both teams were preparing for the visit of a contingent of mainland professionals called the All-Americans. In any event, the *Advertiser* promised fans that the "Traveling Chinese" would assemble a strong lineup, adding "it will be remembered that the Chinese have given the infantrymen a hard tussle." On November 12, the 25th lost its first game in Hawai'i since April to the "Traveling Chinese," which actually combined the skills of the islands' best available Chinese Hawaiian players. Led by Hoon Ki's pitching and En Sue Pung's fielding, the winners scored five runs to the losers' two. The 25th did not put Rogan in the box, however. He was held back so that he could face the All-Americans. Playing for the winners were En Sue in center field, Chinito Moriyama at second, Lang Akana in left, Fred Swan at third, Kuali on first, Kan Yen Chun at catcher, and Yen Chin at shortstop. On November 19, the "Traveling Chinese" lost to the "All-Americans" and Dutch Ruether's pitching, 6–3. The *Star-Bulletin* claimed that the "Chinese Travelers" played well against the All-Americans despite the loss. At shortstop, Ayau made heads turn with two great plays—"marked real big league stuff without any mistake." Hoon Ki did a good job relieving Luck Yee in the box for the "nomads." The daily also praised Kan Yen Chun, Lang Akana, Yen Chin, and En Sue Pung. The latter was charged for an error on a ball the *Star-Bulletin* contended few could have gotten to in the first place. The next weekend, the "Traveling Chinese" lost to the All-Americans in extra innings. "Chief" Johnson's pitching helped out the winners. Still, Vernon Ayau managed a home run off the veteran Native American professional.[56]

A "Picked Nine" of the islands' best ballplayers prepared to oppose the All-Americans. The team seemed to consist mostly of African American players from the 25th and Chinese Hawaiian standouts. Rogan would pitch to Kan Yen Chun—"a battery worth watching," the *Advertiser* exclaimed. As for centerfielder En Sue Pung, he "has no peer in the Islands." When the all-star team lost to the All-Americans, Kan Yen Chun stood out as he impressively threw out a mainlander on second. Competing for the "Picked Nine" were not only Kan Yen Chun and En Sue Pung, but Henry Kuali, Yen Chin, Vernon Ayau, and Fred Swan, who shared the pitching chores with Rogan.[57]

The 1916 version of the Travelers proved to be the last. In this photograph are several of the Hawaiian ballplayers posing with an unnamed youngster (courtesy of the Yamashiro Family).

Though far from home, Masayoshi (otherwise known as Andy) Yamashiro captured some national attention while attending school in Philadelphia. The *Philadelphia Public Ledger* headlined its story on Yamashiro's gridiron exploits with "Yim, Oriental Football Player, Temple Regular." The *Public Ledger* insisted that Yamashiro was the first "Chinese football player" to earn a regular spot. The daily conceded that "Yim" was not the athlete's real name but "Yamashire," adding that it was just as well he was known as Yim because rooting sections would find his real name harder to pronounce.[58]

"M. Yamashiro," according to a wire story printed in the *Star-Bulletin*, had been playing right guard for Temple Prep School's football team. Identified as possessing Japanese ancestry, the article pointed out that Masayoshi Yamashiro was called "Yim" by his teammates, inspiring the Hawaiian to say he would have preferred "a less familiar name." This nickname encouraged people to identify Yamashiro as Chinese — a belief buttressed, the article maintained, by his touring with the Travelers. Studying dentistry at Temple, Yamashiro was described as the only player of Japanese descent on a football team in the Philadelphia area. He told the press that he enjoyed playing football, but preferred baseball. Yamashiro reportedly said, "You can use your hands in baseball but not in football. I don't quite get the idea." In any event, the five-foot-five-inch Yamashiro put a great deal of effort into mastering the sport and was learning the "intricate" plays and formations. He played defense particularly well, but "is longing for the baseball season to grasp a trusty willow and bat the old sphere."[59]

A few of the Travelers looked like they might break into organized baseball in 1917, maybe even at a very high level. Sam Hop said he had received a letter claiming that Markham had been signed by the Philadelphia Athletics. The Athletics were persuaded, apparently, that if Markham improved he could make it to the big leagues.[60]

While Markham's situation seemed more rumored than real, the big news emerging out of the winter of 1916 was Vernon Ayau's signing of an organized baseball contract with the Seattle Giants of the Pacific Northwest League. On December 12, readers of the *Chicago Tribune* learned that Ayau was "said to be the first Chinese baseball player to enter organized ball circles." Many fans in Honolulu, according to the *Star-Bulletin*, were convinced that Ayau would star in the Pacific Northwest circuit. The shortstop's stellar performances against the All-Americans enhanced his growing reputation.[61]

A piece in the *Washington Post* also announced Ayau's signing by Seattle boss William Leard. At the time, Leard was heading up the All Americans' tour of the islands. The report wired from Honolulu described Ayau as the "shortstop on the local Chinese team which visits the mainland annually." The report asserted as well that Ayau was going "to be the first Chinese player to enter organized baseball circles" and that he had been a "sensation" in Hawaiian baseball for "several years."[62]

A *Philadelphia Public Ledger* sportswriter cheered Ayau's signing. The journalist revealed that a year earlier Spokane of the Pacific Northwest League had signed the shortstop but asked him not to report because of an "unwritten law banning Mongolians" from organized baseball. The sportswriter testified that he had seen Ayau in action and could verify that he was the best shortstop he had seen outside of the big leagues, although the Hawaiian would need some finishing touches to match the likes of Dave Bancroft.[63]

Meanwhile, the *Brooklyn Eagle* reported that Lai Tin, "the Chinese player," had not returned to the islands with his mates from "the Chinese Institute." Instead, he had gotten some kind of position with "a commercial house in Manhattan" and had seen snow for the first time. Ayau and Lai Tin would see plenty of action on mainland baseball diamonds in 1917.[64]

Six

Further Travels

The year 1916 marked the last excursion eastward by the "Chinese University of Hawaii" nine. There are a number of possible explanations. One was that World War I seemed to have put a damper on baseball barnstorming on the mainland for awhile. Another reason may have been that key players such as Buck Lai Tin, Andy Yamashiro, Fred Markham, and Apau Kau decided to remain on the mainland, while Vernon Ayau would eventually join them. A third was that Honolulu's business interests seem to have lost enthusiasm in supporting the Travelers despite promptings from the *Star-Bulletin*. Moreover, Honolulu's Chinese community had apparently abandoned its commitment to sustaining a team that had become not only increasingly non–Chinese but was employing whites such as Inman and Doty. Incredibly, the mainland press seemed more bound and determined to identify the Travelers as Chinese or students of a Chinese University of Hawai'i in 1916 than in earlier years. A final factor may have been that the 1916 excursion did not come off all that joyfully. The Travelers did not win as often as they used to, while dissension hampered their play.

Before heading off to the mainland in 1917, Vernon Ayau and other former Travelers, showed their considerable talents to mainland professionals. The Portland Beavers had decided to train in Honolulu. In the process, they opposed various local nines, which included several onetime Travelers. Lou Kennedy, a Portland sportswriter accompanying the Beavers to the islands, provided a glowing report to *The Sporting News* on Ayau and Kan Yen Chun, "two Chinese players from Hawaii." After watching Ayau hit a game-winning homer against Portland, Kennedy exclaimed, "If there is no Frank Merriwell for Chinese dime novel enthusiasts to marvel about, we nominate Vernon Ayau," who had rapped three hits for the "Celestials" as they beat the PCL nine, 9–7. Kennedy lauded Ayau's glove and arm, arguing that he knew of only one PCL shortstop who could throw better. Kennedy predicted Ayau would do well for Seattle if he got the opportunity and if he did not lose his nerve. As for Kan Yen, Kennedy maintained he had a "rifle arm." The Chinese Hawaiian catcher had easily gunned down a Beaver baserunner on third while bluffing a throw to second on a "31 play." Although only 130 pounds, Kan Yen could also hit. Indeed, Walter McCreadie had reportedly signed Kan Yen but wanted to send him down to the Pacific Northwest League.[1]

Chinito Moriyama, who played second base for the "Celestials," also caught Kennedy's eye. The Portland sportswriter described a double play involving Ayau and Moriyama as a stunner. "A Japanese boy [playing] for the orientals," Moriyama ranged far to his right to stop a hard grounder up the middle hit by the Beavers' Babe Pinelli. Then he acrobatically flipped the ball to Ayau, who pivoted and threw out the speedy Pinelli at first. The consequence was a play that astonished the Beavers and their boss, Walter McCreadie. They all claimed they had never seen anything like it. An account published in the *Oakland Tribune* asserted, under the headline "Jap Infielder Surprises Beavers," that "the play required the absolute perfect handling of the ball by both players." According to the *Tribune's* piece, Moriyama's "brainy work" deserved particular commendation.[2]

While not indifferent in general to the ability of Hawaiian ballplayers, Kennedy was most taken with the play of the "Chinese boys." They could cause one "to sit up and rub's one eye in amazement." Their coolness could be explained, Kennedy concluded, by their experiences on the mainland. Ayau and Kan Yen in particular appeared unflappable. Assuming the guise of a social scientist, Kennedy pointed out that the "Celestial" ballplayers were not "full-blooded." Rather they reflected the fact that Cupid was "cosmopolitan" in Hawai'i. The Portland sportswriter insisted that both Ayau and Kan Yen had "Native Hawaiian" ancestry.[3]

While Ayau and Kan Yen commanded the admiration of the mainland professionals and sportswriters, Lang Akana was not so fortunate. McCreadie was seemingly interested in taking another shot at Akana. However, the "China boy" did not look good to the Portland mogul. Described as a sturdy 181-pounder, Akana's lack of success was ascribed to rustiness.[4]

The Portland Beavers, assaulted by criticism back home for the inability to beat Hawaiian teams, managed to eke out a 4–3 victory over the "All-Chinese" in their last exhibition game on the islands. Nevertheless, McCreadie reputedly thought long and hard about recruiting Kan Yen for the PCL nine, but the "classy" catcher was just too light a hitter to suit the Beavers boss. Instead, McCreadie recommended the "Chinese Hawaiian" to Spokane of the Pacific Northwest League, but that franchise decided that Ayau was about all the league could handle when it came to players of Chinese ancestry. Readers of the *Salt Lake Telegram* had learned that McCreadie had signed a "no tickee, no washee" catcher in Kan Yen. The story continued, "It had been thought that Seattle had cornered the market of classy oriental material" when it recruited Ayau, but McCreadie could not resist Kan Yen's skills. As late as March 29, the *Portland Oregonian* had inaccurately predicted that Kan Yen was ticketed to Spokane, in part because he was good but also because his ethnicity would draw fans. Chinito Moriyama was also recommended to McCreadie, but he deemed the "Japanese player" a "fast fielder" but not a good enough hitter.[5]

In the spring of 1917, Vernon Ayau became the first Chinese American to play organized baseball. The mainland press was not uniformly pleased with the possibility. Apparently, the *Portland Telegraph* expressed pessimism as to whether Ayau ought to play in the Pacific Northwest League. The *Telegraph* complained that the Great Falls, Idaho, franchise would not welcome competing against a team with Ayau on its roster. Years earlier, the story went, a Chinese immigrant by name of Wong Quo had been murdered in Great Falls during a strike by white workers, and Chinese had been unwelcome in the vicinity since. In any case, the *Telegraph* insisted that Ayau would not make the Seattle team and, if he did, he would get a cool reception if he "ventures into forbidden land." The *Star-Bulletin* responded that Ayau would change the Portland newspaper's attitude. The Honolulu daily declared, "Ayau is a player of good habits and should become a popular star with the Seattle team."[6]

Generally, the mainland press treated Ayau more as a curiosity than an enemy to civilization. Still, readers of one small-town newspaper discovered the following headline in early January: "Yellow Peril Has Invaded Professional Baseball." Described as a "real Mongolian," Ayau's Hawaiian origins were also emphasized. The article quoted William Leard, who insisted that Ayau was "the greatest player in the land of the ukulele." More than that, however, Leard was convinced that Ayau could play shortstop in organized baseball and perhaps even at its major league level.[7]

Sports pages on the mainland tried more than occasionally to give Ayau something of a break. Early in 1917, the *Oakland Tribune* cited the views of Rowdy Eliot, who had caught for the PCL's Oakland Oaks, on Ayau. Eliot had been in Hawai'i with Leard and wished the Oaks had furnished him with a contract as he wanted to sign the Chinese Hawaiian shortstop after seeing Ayau in action. Eliot declared that Ayau was three-quarters white and was too good for the Pacific Northwest League. Roscoe Fawcett in the *Portland Oregonian* hailed Ayau's signing as proof of baseball's growing "cosmopolitanism." *The Sporting Life* reported that Leard's signing of Ayau had inspired some "tittering" among mainland baseball people. But *Sporting Life* added that folks who had seen Ayau play were persuaded he could make it in organized baseball, that he was "a wonderful little performer." When the "Hawaiian-Chinese" signed with Seattle, according to a press account in the *Fort Wayne News*, the sports pages in the Pacific Northwest treated Ayau's recruitment as a joke. However, the "snappy little shortstop" had changed minds. Ayau, moreover, "is about the fastest thing ever seen on a baseball diamond." The article quoted Riley Allen, a Honolulu journalist, who declared that Ayau "is a clean little gentleman." Referring to PCL standout Dave Bancroft, who would star for such major league teams as the Phillies and the Giants, Allen added that Ayau "can do stunts on the ball field just as flashy as those that made Bancroft the best fielding shortstop on the coast." A wire story printed in a small-town newspaper in Pennsylvania noted that Ayau's supporters believed that the shortstop could make it to the big leagues after a year in Seattle. In March 1917, the *Oakland Tribune* reaffirmed Ayau's talent, but reported the troubling information that Leard had grown a little disillusioned. Leard had hoped that Ayau's "orientalism" would draw fans to Seattle Giants games. However, Ayau, he had heard, was not sufficiently "oriental" and could not even speak Chinese.[8]

Seattle, according to the *Seattle Times*, expressed "a lot of interest" in Ayau before the baseball season began. As for the *Seattle Post-Intelligencer*, it inspired and indulged the curiosity many Seattle fans might have entertained regarding Ayau. In the weeks before the Seattle Giants began training camp, the *Post-Intelligencer's* Royal Brougham wanted to know how well Ayau had done against the Portland Beavers. Apparently, William Leard had asked Roscoe Fawcett about Ayau and the Portland sportswriter told him that Ayau did fine and, indeed, batted over .300 against the Beavers.[9]

Brougham also reported that Leard complained about Harry Wolverton's opposition to Ayau playing organized baseball. Wolverton, a long-time major leaguer who managed the San Francisco Seals at the time, declared that organized baseball might as well employ African Americans as allow a "Chinaman" to play for the Seattle Giants. Leard's response did not exactly exemplify democracy at its finest. The Giants manager said, "Think of it. Ayau is an American-born, half-Chinese-half-Hawaiian, has attended American schools and speaks English almost as well as I do. And Wolverton has on his San Francisco club Jacinto Calvo, a Cuban who butchers the American lingo."[10]

Previewing the Seattle Giants for the coming year, the *Post-Intelligencer* said that at shortstop "Leard has to offer Mr. Vernon Ayau of Honolulu, the only Chinese player in baseball." The reporter conceded that Ayau was an "uncertainty," but he had been a "wonder" wherever he has performed in the past. Ayau, if given a fair chance, seemed capable of making good.[11]

On April 3, the Giants started training camp and the *Post-Intelligencer* predicted all eyes would be on "the work of the Chinese star, Vernon Ayau."

The Seattle daily conceded that Ayau was "handicapped" in making good with the Giants, but it averred that Seattle fans and Leard would afford him every opportunity to succeed. And "if he does land the shortstop position, he will be the only Chinese player in organized baseball today." The next day, the *Post-Intelligencer* admitted that Ayau was small, but "has all the earmarks of a ball player."[12]

During the pre-season Ayau performed "more than satisfactorily," according to the *Post-Intelligencer*. Ayau's first pre-season game was a success. He batted 2-for-3 and played shortstop and centerfield. In a pre-season game against the University of Washington, Ayau struck onlookers positively with his fielding. According to the *Post-Intelligencer's* account of the game, "Vernon Ayau turned another neat play at short. The little Chinese star sprinted far back of second base, scooped a hot roller and tossed the runner out. It was a class bit of work." After another pre-season contest, Brougham wrote "Our little Chinese ballplayer Vernon Ayau tickled everybody by grabbing a double and a single."[13]

Brougham generally praised Ayau. The Hawaiian's fielding, unsurprisingly, was good, while his hitting progressed, according to the Seattle sportswriter. Brougham also reported that much of Seattle's Chinese community came out to watch Ayau's workouts with the Giants. Indeed, "whenever the little Chinese handles the ball well or pokes out a safe one, their faces are all smiles." Ayau, meanwhile, had been a guest of honor at a Chinese consulate banquet.[14]

Several days later, Brougham appeared to have tempered his enthusiasm for Ayau. Still he declared that "the only Chinese player in organized baseball" performed adequately. The "little phenom" had not gotten used to Seattle's cooler climate, but had shown ability in practice games.[15]

A few days later, readers of the *Washington Post* learned more about Ayau and Class B Pacific Northwest League baseball. The *Post* informed them that the shortstop was "the first Chinese ball player to make his debut in organized baseball" and that the Hawaiian was "a bright looking and English speaking Chinese." The former St. Louis College prep student had apparently asserted to the press that there were several Chinese Hawaiians capable of playing organized baseball in America. He added, "All play the game and are making progress." Japanese Hawaiians were also good ballplayers, according to Ayau. They could field and run the bases well. They could perhaps join the Chinese Hawaiians in organized baseball if they would only hit better.[16]

In May, readers of the *Fort Wayne Sentinel* learned that Vernon Ayau, a "full-blooded Chinese from Honolulu," was to play for Seattle, despite talk of a boycott conducted by rival teams in the Pacific Northwest League. However, managers of the Great Falls and Butte franchises seemingly backed off their advocacy of a boycott. Indeed, the Great Falls franchise had been concerned because a town law banned "a Chinaman within its limits." "The young Chinese," according to the press account, "is a hard hitter and clever infielder and is certain of making good in organized baseball."[17]

As the season dawned, Ayau's fielding sparkled substantially more than his hitting. Unfortunately, on May 21, the *Post-Intelligencer* announced that Ayau "the speedy Chinese" had been released. Leard and the team president regretted the move, but claimed Ayau just did not hit competently. Seattle's *Sporting News* correspondent concurred that Ayau could "field like a flash," but was sadly weak at bat. The *Salt Lake Telegram* was less kind, claiming the "Hawaiian-Chinese ... failed miserably."[18]

Ayau moved to Portland, where he registered for the draft on May 29. His registration card describes him as racially a Mongolian and working as a clerk. He was not done with baseball as he competed for semipro teams in both the Portland and Seattle areas. According to the *Portland Oregonian*, former teammate Roy Doty had persuaded Ayau to head to Oregon's largest city to join him on the Northwest Steel Company nine. The Oregonian described Ayau as "the only Chinese shortstop in captivity."[19]

Ayau was back in organized baseball in July. Tacoma of the Pacific Northwest League signed him and the Hawaiian proved something of a "success." On June 21, the *Anaconda Standard* reported that "Vernon Ayau of Honolulu" had not only joined Tacoma but did well in his debut against Spokane. When Tacoma beat Butte, the *Standard* reported that "as a novelty," the manager of the victorious nine produced a Chinaman for an infielder. He is Ayau ... and the grinning celestial plays the game a whole lot better than some of the white men" tried earlier by Tacoma. Ayau "knocked down most of the hot ones" and got two hits.[20]

In a few days, however, Tacoma released Ayau, due, the *Standard* asserted, to Great Falls' "aversion" to the "Chinaman." Indeed, the *Seattle Times* reported that Ayau's Tacoma teammates "kidded" him about winding up in the river when the team visited Great Falls. Ayau, consequently, decided to remain in Tacoma, "where the worst that will come to him is being taken for a ukulele artist." Calling Ayau "the yellow third sacker," the *Standard* lamented, seemingly in earnest, "Thus endeth the diamond career of a smiling Chinaman who 'saveys' the white man's sport pretty well."[21]

Still, Ayau managed to play a bit more in the Pacific Northwest League with Vancouver. However, he was soon headed eastward to play semipro baseball. On July 22, the *Oregonian* announced that Ayau was set to play in Wildwood, New Jersey, described by the Portland paper as "a large beach resort, where baseball was much in demand." "Lee Tin," Ayau's former teammate, was reportedly playing with Wildwood as well. The next day the *Oregonian* declared that Ayau had to choose between returning home to Hawai'i or staying on the mainland. But Ayau's "desire for a dish of the good old poi was not strong as his desire to play baseball." Getting Lai Tin's name right this time, the *Oregonian* informed readers that the Hawaiian infielder had invited Ayau eastward.[22]

By the end of the summer, then, Ayau was on the East Coast playing baseball with some familiar faces. There were plenty of opportunities for a skillful ballplayer to find a job shagging flies or scooping grounders for a vast assortment of semipro clubs in the urban mid–Atlantic region. While Ayau may have played in Wildwood, in August of 1917 the *Brooklyn Eagle* announced that "Vernon Ayau, formerly of the Chinese Club of Hawaii," made his debut with the Bushwicks. Playing with Lai and Mark, he got no hits against Nat Strong's all-African American Brooklyn Royal Giants but did a "brilliant" job at shortstop. Ayau competed in more games for the Bushwicks, but in mid-September, a photo-article in the *Philadelphia Inquirer* focused on the Upland, Pennsylvania, nine which competed in the Delaware Valley League. While semiprofessional, this league recruited many fine ballplayers. Upland even tried to lure into its ranks Boston pitching ace Babe Ruth. The team photograph shows Ayau standing in the back row next to Lai Tin, who by then was known as Buck or Bill Lai, while "Marks" or Fred Markham knelt in the front row. Both Lai and Markham were praised in the article, but no mention was made of the clever shortstop.[23]

The East Coast experiences of Yamashiro, Markham, and Lai will be explored in future pages. For now, we should note that Ayau continued to compete on the East Coast at least over the next few years, often with and against elite white and black ballplayers. In April and May, 1918, Ayau played shortstop and third base with the Chester Shipbuilding Company in the Philadelphia area. Markham, by the way, was the team catcher. Ayau was hailed by the *Chester Times* as a "celestial star." In May 1918, Ayau batted second and played shortstop for the Brooklyn Bushwicks against the Royal Giants. On the slab for the latter was Dick Redding, one of the best pitchers of his time. Redding, as it turned out, shut out the Bushwicks, who also fielded "Yim." As will be discussed more, Ayau then served in the military.[24]

After fighting in France, Ayau's ballplaying services were sought by a variety of semipro nines on the East Coast. A newspaper in Bridgeton, New Jersey, reported that the management of the Millville semipro team was trying to recruit "the speedy lad from Honolulu." Negotiations, the *Bridgton News* speculated, with the "dusky youth" looked promising. Perhaps so, but in late summer of 1919 "Ayua" was at shortstop and got a hit for Logan Square as it defeated the Philadelphia Athletics in an exhibition game in Atlantic City. An estimated crowd of 5,000 also saw Yamashiro and Markham play for the

Philadelphia-based semipro nine. About the same time, Ayau played shortstop for a nine called Frank Poth's All Stars. In a game in Wildwood, Ayau batted leadoff, collected three hits, and scored two runs as his team beat the locals, 6–2. He also competed with an aggregation playing out of Vineland, New Jersey. Ayau batted second and played second base for Vineland when it opposed the West End nine. Andy Yamashiro was in the lineup as well; Ayau was horse-collared at bat but still managed to score twice.[25]

Ayau remained active in relatively high level semipro circles into at least the early 1920s. In 1951, the *Chester Times* recalled that when the local Upland nine defeated the Ruthless New York Yankees in an exhibition game in 1920, "Bucky" Ayau was one of the hitting stars along with Frank "Home Run" Baker, a future Hall of Fame third baseman who was playing with Upland at the time. While playing for Upland and Chester, Ayau faced formidable African American nines such as the Bacharach Giants and Chicago American Giants. In 1921, Ayau was at shortstop when Chester edged the Chicago American Giants, 3–2. In October 1921, 5,000 fans watched Hilldale, a fine black nine, defeat Chester. Ayau batted second, got no hits, and handled shortstop. Opposing the South Phillies and his old teammate, Buck Lai, Ayau got one hit as Chester easily came out on top, 7–1. This may or may not have been the game in which Ayau was sent to the hospital due to a riot incited, according to the *Chester Times*, by a controversial umpire call. Reportedly, Ayau had grabbed a grounder and touched second base to get a force and then chucked the ball to first to complete a double play. However, the umpire called both runners safe, thus threatening his safety. Several years later, the *Chester Times* curiously remembered Ayau as "the crack Jap shortstop" for Upland. In 1937, the *Times* insisted that Ayau's nickname was "Wickie" when he played for Chester in the early 1920s. Indeed, in the mid–1950s the daily declared that "Wicky Ayau ... had no peer as an inner gardener." After World

Vernon Ayau was the first Chinese American to play organized baseball, after playing six seasons with the Travelers. A small and acrobatic shortstop, Ayau's professional career was short-circuited because of race and a light bat. After serving in World War I, he found a home on the East Coast of the U.S., playing semipro baseball and living and dying in New Jersey (courtesy of Debbie Davis).

War II started, Vernon Limalao Ayau registered for the draft in Penns Grove. The draft card describes Ayau as 48 and a wholesale confectioner. According to the Social Security Death Index, Ayau died in Penns Grove in 1976.[26]

Andy Yamashiro joined Ayau as the first Asian Pacific Americans to play organized baseball in the United States. Yamashiro competed for the Class D Blue Ridge League franchise in Gettysburg, Pennsylvania, using the last name of Yim perhaps because of the anti–Japanese fervor that was bubbling throughout the U.S. and perhaps because that had become his "stage name." According to an account in a 1938 edition of the *Gettysburg Times*, Buck Lai was responsible for persuading Yamashiro to remain on the East Coast. Indeed, like Lai, Markham, and Apau Kau, Yamashiro lived in the Philadelphia area, where, as mentioned earlier, he had attended Temple. While the 1917 season saw Lai and Yamashiro playing in different places, they would become teammates shortly.[27]

Before heading to Gettysburg, Yamashiro dabbled a bit in semipro ball in Philadelphia, playing center field and leading off for Roxborough in its game against Midvale in late April. In early May, the *Gettysburg Times* told readers that the local professional club was assembling its upcoming roster. Among those expected to suit up for the Blue Ridge League team would be Yim, who, the newspaper proclaimed, had been a member of the "Chinese University" team. The *Times* maintained that the outfielder was best known for his speed.[28]

The Hawaiian outfielder got off to a fast start with his new team. The *Gettysburg Times* pronounced "Mr. Andy Yim" as the "hero" of one early game. Yamashiro not only performed admirably in center field, according to the *Times*, but he socked a double and an inside-the-park home run. Yamashiro sprinted around the bases so rapidly that one opposition player reportedly said to another, "Just watch the Chink go." After a game with Hanover, the *Gettysburg Star and Sentinel* seemed more than a little taken with "Yim ... the little Chinaman." Its reporter declared, "Yim got a hand every time he came to the plate and responded each time the bases were populated. He drove in three runs and scored two times himself. And he can run. Nuf'Sed."[29]

The Japanese Hawaiian was not done. Yamashiro made a "wonder play" in center field — a great running catch which sewed the game up for Gettysburg. "Ten minutes later," recounted the *Times*, "the popular fielder was in his room strumming his ukulele [which] he can play almost as well as he can play baseball." The next day, "the popular little Hawaiian" scored the winning run with a finely executed slide.[30]

Yamashiro's ethnic background needed clarification, according to the *Gettysburg Times*. It informed its "exchanges" that "Yim" had never seen China nor could he speak a word of Chinese. He was, that is, "a native of Hawaii." Yamashiro, according to a report in the *Gettysburg Times*, ran into racial hostility. It cited a somewhat gracious denunciation of that antagonism published in Maryland's *Frederick Post*. "Yim" acted like a "little gentleman," the *Post* testified, and should be treated as such. Instead, fans in Hanover had proven especially abusive toward "the little Chinaman."[31]

A piece in a 1945 edition of the *Gettysburg Compiler* recalled that Yamashiro was something of a source of derision and dismay while playing in the Blue Ridge League. Former Blue Ridge League player and journalist Frank Colley, who insisted that Yamashiro was "Chinese," maintained, "Sure there was plenty of talk about him. How fast he was, how he could run the bases, and throw. He was a left hander and that is as far as he went." However, when Yamashiro was told to get ready for a road trip for the first time, he packed as though he was going on an excursion of the U.S. His teammates laughed at his ignorance of life as a minor leaguer on the American mainland. And when Yamashiro committed two key errors in a game against Martinsville, his teammates, Colley recalled, were angry. Colley claimed that while "Yim" never made the big leagues, he made "big league copy."[32]

According to Colley, Yamashiro's inept work in the outfield inspired future major league stalwart Jimmy Dykes to stroll over to where the Hawaiian was standing after he dropped a fly ball. The infielder promptly took out a pen knife and cut the pocket out of Yamashiro's glove. Why Dykes had a pen knife has gone unanswered.[33]

It is possible that the two harbored a grudge toward one another. Either before or after the pen knife incident, the Gettysburg nine got into a fight with their Martinsburg opponents. Colley wrote that "Andy Yim, a Chinese outfielder" climbed onto the top of one of the dugouts, took off his cleats, and threatened oncoming brawlers with a sound spiking. Dykes apparently jumped up on the dugout to calm his riled teammate down. Instead, the startled Hawaiian scarred Dykes with his cleats.[34]

Like a lot of minor leagues in the summer of 1917, the Blue Ridge League faced difficult times as America geared up for World War I. Claiming itself financially strapped, the Gettysburg franchise failed to keep up payments to its ballplayers. In early July, the team went on strike in order to attain back pay. The league did go under early with the Gettysburg team ending in third place. However, *Spalding's Baseball Guide* pointed out that the league seemed to do better than other minor league circuits. Indeed, Gettysburg wound up playing 94 games. A correspondent in *The Sporting News* observed that the nine, in any event, possessed "clean-minded" ballplayers, including "Yim the Hawaiian."[35]

Both before and after Yamashiro's 1918 minor league stint in Bridgeport,

Jimmy Dykes was a veteran major league infielder. Before that, however, he played with Andy Yamashiro on the Gettysburg, Blue Ridge League team in 1917. Dykes was seemingly not a big fan of the Japanese Hawaiian (courtesy of Library of Congress, Prints & Photographs Division, LC-DIG-ggbain-36110).

he played semiprofessional ball in and around Philadelphia and New York City. In the spring of 1918, Yim led off and played center field for the Bushwicks when they opposed the Brooklyn Royal Giants. In early August, he got a hit and played right field for the Wildwood nine against Wissimoning. In late September, he played for the Media, Pennsylvania, nine which normally competed in the Delaware Valley League. Media lost both games of a doubleheader against the Bacharach Giants, but Yamashiro got a hit in each game.[36]

Several years later, sportswriter John Flynn declared that Yamashiro and Buck Lai were "Chinese players" who helped make the old Eastern League colorful. He could say that because Yamashiro moved up the minor league ladder and played with Buck Lai on the class B Bridgeport, Connecticut, team. Managed by Paul Krichell, who would later serve ably as a scout for the New York Yankees, the Bridgeport nine expected that the left-handed-hitting Yim would supply the team with speed and some hitting punch. The *Bridgeport Telegram* introduced the outfielder to readers as a resident of Philadelphia but Hawaiian born and raised. The Bridgeport daily described "Andy Yim, the Chinese outfielder" as a "stolid type," unlike the more outgoing, "peppery" Lai.[37]

Both Hawaiians got off to exciting starts. Against Springfield on May 26, the *Telegram* reported, the "Chinese players ... shine[d]." That is, "Bill Lai, the Chinese third baseman and Andy Yim, the Oriental right fielder for the locals were the leading lights." The *Telegram* enthused that the "the Chinamen are leading players" for the Bridgeport Americans. The daily added, "Without the Chinamen who are playing for Bridgeport the locals would not be in the running and the evidence needs no corroboration. The men with the almond eyes and the yellow skin are very near the entire works for Bridgeport's team in 1918." In the game against Springfield, Yamashiro's speed and daring amazed onlookers who noted that when he scored on a sacrifice bunt, the Hawaiian was nearly home when the bunt was laid down. Yamashiro's hitting most delighted the *Telegram*, which gleefully tossed around ethnic stereotypes while admiring the outfielder's speed but considered Lai, "his fellow wielder of the iron," swifter. Against Providence, "the Chinese players of the locals, Bill Lai at third and Andy Yim in right, had another field day each." Yamashiro slugged a homer and went 3-for-4, while Lai rapped a double and triple. When Paul Krichell resigned, the *Telegram*'s T.F. Magner maintained that one of his accomplishments was recruiting Lai and Yim, "the only two Chinese playing in professional baseball."[38]

Yamashiro's outfielding remained spotty. He made a key error which allowed New London to beat Bridgeport in an extra-inning affair. His ukulele playing, however, apparently won esteem among teammates. While the team was en route to Hartford, "the Chinese right fielder" took out his ukulele and entertained his fellow ballplayers. After the game, he continued to divert teammates in his Hartford hotel room, with Lai singing along.[39]

According to a report in the *Telegram*, antagonism toward the Americans' suiting up Lai and Yamashiro came to a head in early June. The Eastern League franchises of New Haven and Providence particularly protested. League directors had to determine whether New Haven and Providence had a case. From the standpoint of the *Telegram*, the matter of the "Orientals" was very "much mooted." The Bridgeport franchise not only needed these players but was actively seeking a "Chinese pitcher"— the identity of whom was left unclear. At the same time, the *Telegram* maintained, many African American ballplayers in the Northeast were understandably wondering why the color bar was lowered for Lai and Yamashiro and not for them. Readers of the *Syracuse Herald*, meanwhile, learned that it seemed like a joke had been played on the American baseball world when it was reported that Eastern League moguls were aroused over Bridgeport's two Chinese players who immensely aided the team's success.[40]

By July, Yamashiro and Lai were no longer quite the novelty items they were earlier in the season. But they continued to play well. Magner hailed a victory over New Haven as a manifestation of "Andy Yim Day": "The slant-eyed Celestial registered two triples" in the game. Lai also performed well, but the day belonged to his Hawaiian teammate, "the slant-eyed ukulele stretcher."[41]

In mid–July, a "work or fight" order coming out of Washington, D.C. seemed to spell doom for the Eastern League. However, the circuit's director vowed to continue the season. World War I also compelled Yamashiro to register for the draft in September. In Philadelphia after the season ended somewhat prematurely, he registered under his real name of Masayoshi Yamashiro. He reported that he lived on Hamilton Street in the Quaker City, while working as a ship fitter for the American Shipping Company in a region of Philadelphia known as Hog Island, where today the Philadelphia Airport is located. Yamashiro's registration card declared that he was racially "Oriental" and, intriguingly, a subject of Japan.[42]

With the war done and the Eastern League's 1919 season about ready to begin, the *Telegram* reported that Yamashiro who was "formerly of Hawaii" insisted that he would have a better season in Bridgeport because he had learned the lessons of a veteran. Still, Yamashiro was soon playing the outfield for Hartford rather than for Bridgeport. Indeed, early in the season the Hawaiian outfielder smashed an impressive triple against Lai and his other old teammates. Yamashiro wound up playing only 19 games for Hartford of the Eastern League, however. Later in 1919, he competed for a semiprofessional nine in

Philadelphia called Logan Square. When this team encountered the Philadelphia Athletics in an extra-inning exhibition game in Atlantic City, Yamashiro scored the winning run on a passed ball. In 1919, as well, Yamashiro joined Ayau on the Vineland, New Jersey, nine. In the game against West End, "Yim" led off, patrolled center field, got a hit, and scored a run.[43]

The 1920 manuscript census reveals that M. Yamashiro lived in Penns Grove, New Jersey, Ayau's future home town. He was living as a lodger while working as an office clerk. Eventually, however, Yamashiro returned to the islands. In the 1930 U.S. Census, he shows up as a 36-year-old hotel clerk, living with his Issei parents as well as his wife and children in Honolulu. Yamashiro's father owned the hotel in which he worked — a father, by the way, who came to the islands to work on a plantation and remained sympathetic to Japanese Hawaiian community building and labor militancy. In 1937, according to the Honolulu City Directory, the former outfielder managed the hotel, which for years had been an important meeting place for Japanese Honolulans. The former ballplayer was, moreover, a politician. In 1930, he was elected to the territorial legislature, marking him as one of the first Nikkei elected to territorial-wide office. His son recalled that he would cultivate multiethnic, multiracial voters at Aala Park by singing Hawaiian songs, accompanying himself on the ukulele. Moreover, according to historian David Stannard, Yamashiro's election shocked many haoles and Native Hawaiians. Distressed haoles, consequently, called for ballots for whites only.[44]

In 1932, Yamashiro went to the Democratic Party national convention that nominated Franklin D. Roosevelt for president. En route to the convention, he was interviewed in San Francisco. Described as a "Japanese-American delegate to the National Democratic Convention" in Chicago, Yamashiro proclaimed that Hawai'i's delegates were pledged to FDR but he could not say to whom they would go next if the convention deadlocked. He did assert that the Hawaiian delegation stood for repeal of the 18th Amendment. Yamashiro subsequently traveled on the S.S. *Mariposa* to Los Angeles. Upon his arrival, the ship's manifest described "Andrew M. Yamashiro as a "Jap citizen" 36 years of age. Indeed, historian Ellen Tamura writes that Yamashiro was one of the many prominent Hawaiian Nisei who did not surrender their dual American and Japanese citizenship readily. Yamashiro did not do so until 1932.[45]

The ability of Japanese Hawaiians to achieve at least of modicum of prosperity and influence on the islands worried American officials as World War II grew closer. General George Patton, who served as Assistant Chief of Staff for the Hawaiian G2, gathered a list of Japanese Hawaiians to be seized in case of war with Japan. Described as a businessman, Andy Yamashiro was on that list. He would die, however, before Pearl Harbor was attacked.[46]

While reportedly signed by the Philadelphia Athletics, Fred Markham never played for Connie Mack's team. Instead, he showed up playing with Buck Lai on the Upland nine as well as a host of other semipro outfits in the mid–Atlantic region. In April, 1917, the *Philadelphia Inquirer* informed readers that Upland had signed "Mark, the big Chinese University catcher." After the Delaware Valley League season got underway, Mark was batting .324 and prompting the *Inquirer* to report that the "the big Chinese catcher ... is the best catcher in the league." "Mark" also played catcher and first base for the Bushwicks. Meanwhile, Fred Markham registered for the draft in Philadelphia. His draft card described him as born on Kauai, an unemployed accountant, and racially "Malay."[47]

After World War I, Markham roamed around the world of East Coast semipro baseball. In January, the *Philadelphia Inquirer* reported that "Fred Marks, the Chinese catcher" was sought by the Upland nine. Later in 1919, "Marks" was catching for the New York Shipping Company nine when it played a game in Camden. In August, he hit a double and single for Logan Square when it beat the Athletics. Late in the summer of 1920, he was playing for at least two semipro nines. On August 19, "Marks" batted eighth and caught for the Aberfoyle nine of the Delaware Valley League. A few days later he caught and got one hit for a team called the Mowrey Reserves when they beat "Home Run" Baker's Upland nine, 6–1. Called "Freddy Mark" or just plain "Marks," he played along with Lai on the South Phillies, Pennsylvania Railroad and Chester nines in the early 1920s. In early May of 1922, the *Inquirer* let it be known that the South Phillies were looking for the best players possible. Accordingly, it made an "attractive offer" to "Marks, the well-known Chinese player." After playing with the South Phillies, he caught for a Paulsboro, New Jersey, team in a loss to none other than Lai and the South Phillies. In March, 1923, the *Chester Times* observed that the local nine had signed "Fred Mark ... the Chinese University Player." The *Times* noted that he was well known in the area because he had previously competed in the South Jersey League and for the Aberfoyle Manufacturing Company, located in Chester. The Chester team's management hoped that the Hawaiian would back up a former major leaguer at the backstop position. In any event, "Mark" caught for Chester in a game against the Bacharach Giants in July 1923.[48]

In 1924, "Fred Marks" joined Buck Lai on the independent Trenton nine. The *Trenton Evening Times* described him as a "capable catcher." After competing for Trenton for several weeks, the *Evening Times* announced that "Fred Marks, the Chinese relief catcher," was discharged by the Trenton club. "Marks," it was claimed, handled the defensive side of catching competently, but was not that good with the bat. The *Evening Times* added that Markham had been attending the University of Pennsylvania rather than returning to "native ball" in Hawai'i. In an event, the daily considered the Hawaiian a "brainy ball player" who should find a position with some independent nine.⁴⁹

By 1930, nevertheless, Markham was back in Honolulu. Described in the census manuscript schedules as a "Caucasian Hawaiian," he was working as a chief clerk in the territorial government. The 1937–1938 Honolulu City Directory listed the former ballplayer as an accountant for the Employees Retirement System.⁵⁰

In 1918, baseball took a back seat to World War I for Apau Kau. He, too, had remained in the Philadelphia area in 1917. In Philadelphia, Apau Kau had registered for the draft in June 1917. His registration card tells us he lived on Arch Street and worked as a salesman for Lit Brothers Department Store. The pitcher told the military that he was a natural born citizen who had previously served in the Hawaiian National Guard. Interestingly, he was racially categorized as "Malay," after "Mongolian" was crossed out.⁵¹

Perhaps not so surprisingly, Apau Kau pitched for the Lit Brothers nine as well as working for the department store. Early in July, the Lit Brothers contingent played the opening game on its home grounds at 44th and Parkside in Philadelphia. There, Apau Kau shut out the Ketterlinus Baseball Club, 16–0. The *Inquirer* correspondent enthused that "Appau was in great form." Apau Kau did all sorts of pitching for Lit Brothers. An August 28 advertisement printed in the *Inquirer* offered a sale on ukuleles and promised that "Appau Kau, our native instructor, will teach you to play for free."⁵²

As the war heated up for Americans such as Apau Kau, the pitcher was drafted into the U.S. military and rose to the rank of sergeant. In September 1917, the *Philadelphia Public Ledger* announced that "Sam Apau, the brilliant Chinese pitcher for Lit Brother," was "tendered a farewell dinner for donning khaki" at Philadelphia's Hanover Hotel. Apparently, Apau's co-workers and managers were responsible for the honor. The next month, the pitcher, then training at Camp Meade, was invited to a benefit dinner sponsored by Philadelphia's Ardsley Club. According to the *Public Ledger*, "Apau Kau, noted Chinese pitcher, will be in attendance to greet his many friends."⁵³

Early in 1918, the "twirler for the champion Chinese team" enrolled in an officers' training camp at Camp Meade. Significantly, the *Washington Post* reported in April 1918, that "Apau Kau, the Hawaiian baseball player," had resigned from officers' school and returned to his regiment. Had he decided to graduate from officers' school, he would have served a year at an officers' training camp at Camp Meade. However, in August 1918, a press report proclaimed that Fred Markham had heard from his former teammates, Vernon Ayau, Al Yap, and Apau Kau, all of whom were serving in France and "delighted" with their military experiences."⁵⁴

Apau Kau stands to the far left of this group photograph of the Travelers, c. 1915. Apau Kau pitched in all the Travelers' tours. Possessing a deceptive delivery and an even more deceptive pickoff move, he was usually a tough customer for opponents. He settled in the Philadelphia area after the 1916 tour. He entered the U.S. military during World War I and died in combat in 1918 (courtesy of the Yamashiro Family).

Sadly, the December 7, 1918, edition of the *Washington Post* announced that the pitcher who had taken the box for "the Chinese Club of Hawaii" had been killed in action. According to a wire story published in the *Kansas City Star*, Apau Kau had been previously promoted to sergeant because of his battlefield bravery. He had "caught a hun bullet" while leading a charge. The story's author felt compelled to point out that since Apau Kau was born in Hawai'i, he was a citizen. Another wire story printed in the *New Castle News* referred to "Andy Yim" as the source of information about Apau Kau's death in Europe.[55]

Like Lai, Yamashiro, Ayau, Markham, and Apau Kau, Al Yap stayed on the East Coast after his experiences with the Travelers ended. As mentioned earlier, Al Yap competed for the Strawbridge and Clothier nine in the summer of 1916. In January 1917, the *Philadelphia Inquirer* observed that "Yap of the Chinese University and Lehigh" was signed by the Chester team for the infield. A wire story reported that he suited up for a semiprofessional team sponsored by Bethlehem Steel Company later in 1917. On August 27, 1917, the *Philadelphia Inquirer* noted that he played third base for a team called the Lehigh Stars. After serving in the military, Yap returned to baseball. In September 1919, Yap was at first base for the Wildwood, New Jersey, nine against the famous Bacharach Giants. In 1920, the U.S. Census manuscript schedules reveal that Alfred Yap was living in Nazareth, Pennsylvania, where he worked as a physical educator for the YMCA. Curiously, given the prevailing "ethical" qualms about college athletes playing semipro baseball, Yap was in Lehigh's lineup when the university nine took on Swarthmore in April 1920. Yap apparently did well for Lehigh. After he left the school, a *Philadelphia Inquirer* correspondent complained that Yap was a hard man for Lehigh to replace at first base.[56]

Yap's peripatetic mid–Atlantic baseball career continued into the early 1920s. In June 1921, Yap joined the J&J Dodson nine in the Philadelphia area. Late in July, Yap was playing for the North Phillies. Yap even seems to have entered organized baseball. In 1922, a player surnamed Yap appeared at third base for Maryland's Crisfield Crabbers of the Class D Eastern Shore League.[57]

In the early 1920s, the *Washington Post* reported that Al Yap was planning on bringing to the U.S. mainland an "all-Chinese baseball team from Honolulu." The *Post* observed that Yap, who played on the "Chinese team which toured the United States," had graduated from Lehigh University. Yap's plans, however, must have fallen through because no trek of the U.S. by a new "All-Chinese" eventuated.[58]

Kan Yen Chun continued to highlight Chinese Hawaiian baseball into the 1920s. During World War I, he served as a Yeoman Third Class in the U.S. Navy. According to the Hawaiian military records, he was stationed at Pearl Harbor from March to November, 1918. Curiously, "Kanky Chun" shows up in a 1924 article in the *Brooklyn Eagle*. The Hawaiian was apparently a student at Delaware University, where he was doing some catching. He attracted press attention because he wore glasses, making him "the only spectacled catcher" in the U.S. For whatever reason, *Eagle* reporter Joe Devir shaved several years off of Chun's age, adding that the "yellow skin boy" was only 15 when he toured the Orient with a Hawaiian team in 1915, while failing to make the age limit for any of the earlier treks of the mainland. The 1930 U.S. Census Manuscripts tell us that Kan Yen Chun was married and worked as a sales clerk for a packing company in Honolulu.[59]

Pitcher Luther Kekoa journeyed throughout the mainland after his Traveler days were over but not as a ballplayer. He registered for the World War I draft in Canton, Ohio in May 1917. Apparently, he was a performer for a traveling Hawaiian musical troupe. Kekoa claimed that previously he had been a lieutenant in the National Guard. He claimed as well that his next

In this photograph, c. 1916, Vernon Ayau, Luther Kekoa, Lai Tin, and Jimmy Aylett pose for the camera. Kekoa was an outfielder and pitcher who often played as "Ako." He later became a professional musician, specializing in Hawaiian music. Jimmy Aylett, who was called Ah Let or Let in the press, was a utility outfielder (courtesy of the Yamashiro Family).

address would be the Palace Theater in New York City. With a little detective work online, one can find recordings of Luther Kekoa and Ben Hokea on a music website. Recorded in 1920 and 1921, the songs are *My Isles of Golden Dream, Missouri Waltz,* and *Pua Mohala.*[60]

Most of the other Travelers lived on in Hawai'i, working in lower level white collar jobs and minding their families. Among those that stayed were two athletes who came tantalizingly close to becoming the first athletes of Chinese ancestry to play organized baseball in the United States — Lang Akana and En Sue Pung.

Lang Akana remained in Hawaiian baseball but engaged in public service in a variety of capacities. Late in October 1917, he enlisted in the Hawaiian National Guard and served for several months before receiving an honorable discharge. Akana was described in Hawai'i's military documents as racially Hawaiian. He later worked for the California Feed Company, as well as serving as a preacher and as Honolulu's Assistant Coroner and Deputy Sheriff while Duke Kahanamoku supervised him as Sheriff. Akana also found time to tour Australia as part of a Hawaiian choral group. For several years, the versatile Akana managed the Hawaiians in the Hawai'i Baseball League — a team ostensibly consisting of Native Hawaiians. In 1946, *Honolulu Advertiser* columnist Bill Pacheco hailed Akana as one of the city's "Stars of Yesteryear." Pacheco reported that Akana had been involved in Honolulu baseball for 42 years beginning in 1904 when he played in the Boys' Brigade League along with En Sue Pung and Vernon Ayau. For 20 more years Akana would play baseball and then for 22 more years manage the Hawaiis, becoming, in the process, the only charter member of the Hawaii Baseball League still active with the same club as of 1946. Akana told Pacheco that the older he got, the more he loved baseball. "During my 42 years with the National Pastime, I have been tremendously benefited by the good fortune of meeting lifelong friends made possible by the fusion of good fellowship on the baseball diamond." Akana persisted in his belief in baseball. When the Hawaiian Islanders entered the PCL in the early 1960s, Akana owned a small share until he died in 1961.[61]

Probably as talented as any on the Travelers, if not more, En Sue Pung never dipped his toes in mainland organized baseball. In 1917, he registered for the draft in Honolulu. At the time, he was living in the Punchbowl area of Honolulu and gave his birth year as 1888. A private in the Hawaiian National Guard, Pung claimed he was a clerk for the hardware store E.O. Hall and Son in Honolulu. He was racially identified as "Mongolian."[62]

En Sue Pung played ball in Hawai'i into the 1920s. The U.S. census manuscript schedules in 1920 reported that he was working for the telephone company in Honolulu. The 31-year-old, second-generation Chinese American lived with a Hawaiian wife and several children, all of whom were designated as Asian Hawaiians by the census taker. Two of the children, Charles and Barney, would become notable Hawaiian swimmers. One child was called Tyrus Cobb Pung. That same year, the *San Jose Mercury* published a wire story featuring En Sue Pung and Chinese Hawaiian baseball. The headline read "Chinese Baseball Star Father of 12," while the story informed readers that En Sue Pung had been a standout in Hawaiian baseball for several years, as well as a busy parent. In 1922, Frank Menke authored a syndicated piece featuring Hawaiian baseball. Advancing the Hawaiian's age a decade or so, he referred to "En Sue" as the 46-year-old "Ty Cobb of Honolulu." Menke described the outfielder as possessing plenty of Cobb-like "dash and daring," with batting power as well as baserunning speed. In 1923, "Charley Ensue" was called a 45-year-old by an A.P. story published in the *Reno Evening Gazette*. Whatever his actual age, he reportedly led the "Chinese-Hawaiians" to a 6–3 victory over the visiting University of California nine in Honolulu. Pung hit a home run and "the Chinese outclassed the Bruins in all departments of the game." Meanwhile, "Charlie Ensue" had entered the political arena, running for a seat in the territorial house as a Democrat. He did not win even though a wire story in the *Portland Oregonian* asserted that he was aided by his reputation as a ballplayer and a "good citizen." In 1927, the *Newark Advocate* published a wire story about the "swimming Pungs." This piece claimed that Father Pung and his wife along with their ten children challenged any family of like size in a swimming contest. At a recent meet, a 14-year-old daughter had won a special event. Readers were told that Pung was Chinese, while his wife was Hawaiian. In 1930, the U.S. Census manuscript schedules tell us that En Sue Pung had returned to the hardware store business as a salesman.[63]

In a recently published biography of Jackie Liwai Pung, a magnificent hapa haole golfer and wife of Barney Pung, Betty Dunn writes that the Pungs lived for a long time on the crowded Honolulu waterfront. She also maintains that when Jacki started to see Barney, she learned about the pernicious side of race in Hawai'i. She had been welcomed to golf at the prestigious Waialae Country Club, but once it became known that Barney Pung was a permanent fixture in her life, the Country Club signaled that the future LPGA champion was no longer welcome.[64]

As for the two men who managed the Travelers in their earlier journeys, Robert Yap seems to have lived an interesting life on the mainland. Yap, who helped organize the first trip, was living in New York City in 1920 with a wife. Curiously categorized as white, he was a musician. Ten years later, Yap was still in New York City, only as a single lodger. He gave his occupation as a music teacher, and the census listed Yap as racially Chinese. Moreover, Yap gained a certain fame and even a little infamy as a musician and music teacher on the American mainland. On Christmas Eve of 1924, WEAF in New York broadcast "Robert Yap's Hawaiian Ensemble." Later in the decade Yap figured in a messy, well-publicized divorce case. A socialite wife was accused of having a sexual affair with Yap, while she insisted that she was just innocently taking music lessons from him. In 1935, the *Indiana Weekly Messenger* printed an advertisement promoting the ability of Robert Yap's Guitar Studios to help out Hawaiian guitar players around the country. All they would have to do was send money and a self-addressed, stamped envelope to his studios on West 71st Street in New York City. A few years later, the *Syracuse Herald* printed a brief story, headlined "Entertains Chinese Visitors." Reportedly, Esther McCoy, a well-known concert singer, invited Robert Yap, as well as his niece Ruth Yap, who taught at the University of Hawai'i, and his nephew Jerry Yap, to her home in Oswego, New York.

Staying on the islands, Sam Hop was 46 in 1930. He lived in Honolulu with his wife and two daughters. Describing himself as racially Chinese, Hop managed a chop suey shop, while one of his daughters clerked for a gas company.[65]

There remains, of course, one Traveler missing from this chapter. Indeed, as Buck, Bill, or William Lai, Lai Tin became the most famous American ballplayer of Chinese ancestry while making a permanent home on the American East Coast. In the process, he would test the permeability of racial and ethnic borders in twentieth century America.

SEVEN

Buck Lai's Journeys

Buck Lai's ethnic origins have been a source of some disagreement. Claims have been made that he possessed indigenous and even considerable English ancestry. Census data does not effectively clarify matters. A 16-year-old with the apparent name of Lai Tin can be found in the 1910 census manuscript schedules of Honolulu. Racially categorized as Chinese, he was living with his mother and siblings. Both parents were described as Hawaiian born. His maternal grandparents were also Hawaiian born. On the other hand, his sister, Jessie Lai Young, a long-time Honolulu educator, claimed in the 1930 U.S. census manuscripts that both her parents were born in China.[1]

Lai Tin decided to remain on the East Coast after the 1916 journey, largely because he met a European American woman named Isabel Reynolds from Brooklyn, New York, at a church service in what was called then the "city of steeples." While this might have caused something of a stir in California where such matches were illegal, the two appeared able eventually to settle down quietly in Audubon, New Jersey.[2]

Lai also apparently did his bit for Uncle Sam after departing the Travelers. In June 1917, a then-unmarried Lai registered for the draft. The registration card reveals that he gave his name as William Tin Lai and his address as 1421 Arch Street in Philadelphia. Interestingly, he was described as a "naturalized citizen" and a "Mongolian" who clerked for the Pennsylvania Railroad.[3]

According to a July 1917, wire story published in New York's *Middletown Press*, a "Chinese Ball Player Helps in Recruiting." The story depicted "William T. Lai" as a third baseman who lived in Philadelphia but commuted to Brooklyn on Sunday to play ball. The story continued that Lai had been assigned to recruit for the Ninth Regiment of Engineers, based in Philadelphia. Lai was described as a 22-year-old who worked full-time in the West Philadelphia car shop office of the Pennsylvania Railroad, while living in a local YMCA. The story noted that Lai had been signed by Charles Comiskey for the 1915 season but had chosen on his own to linger in Hawai'i. It added that while sojourning with the "Chinese team of the University of Hawaii" Lai had decided to remain on the American mainland when the nine played in Brooklyn. Love, the story failed to mention, was primarily Lai's inspiration. Apparently inaccurately, a similar account published in the *Brooklyn Eagle* predicted Lai would join the regiment after the baseball season ended.[4]

Southeastern Pennsylvania's Upland baseball team was considered a strong entry in the highly respected Delaware Valley League in 1917, due in part to the fact that it suited up "Mark, who caught for the famous Chinese team" and Lai, "another Chinese." An article in the *Philadelphia Inquirer* was a little bit more flattering toward Lai, calling him "the great Chinese player." A photo article of the Upland team printed in the *Inquirer* tried to praise the infielder as a "classy Chinese." Lai, as well as other former Travelers, aided Upland's drive for the league championship. Lai led the league in stolen bases, pilfering ten in 19 games, prompting the *Inquirer* to enthuse, "Lai, the classy third sacker of Upland, called the Ty Cobb of the Delaware County Leagues, holds the base running honors." While excelling with Upland, Lai began his long association with the Bushwicks. In an April 20 opening day game against Cypress Hill, Lai and Markham were both in the Bushwick lineup. Third sacker Lai, however, did nothing at bat.[5]

In the spring of 1918, Lai had a shot at making the Philadelphia Phillies. The *Washington Post* announced Lai's signing in an article entitled, "Chinese Player Gets Trial With Phillies." The *Post* pointed out that "Third Baseman Billy Lai, the Chinese lad" was in St. Petersburg, Florida, trying out with the Phillies. The *Post* added that Lai had played with the "famous Chinese baseball team from Hawaii." A *Philadelphia Public Ledger* columnist took the occasion to educate his readers on Chinese culture: "Tin is the Chinese-Hawaiian, and as Chinese always work backward, Tin Lai properly Chinesed into American is Lai Tin. A swell name, in any event!" According to the *Brooklyn Eagle*, Phillies manager Pat Moran may have been willing to give Lai a chance because several key ballplayers were holding out for higher salaries. At the same time, Moran considered Lai capable of making good in the National League.[6]

Indeed, the *Philadelphia Inquirer* reported that among those Phillies boarding a steam ship from New York City to St. Petersburg was "third baseman Lai, a Chinese who played with Upland, PA last year." The *Inquirer's* "Jim Nasium" maintained that in "picking 'Billy' Lai, the Chinese third baseman, the Phillies have added a cracker jack ukulele tickler." Pat Moran worked Lai at shortstop. According to a report to the *Inquirer*, "Billy Lai, the Chinese player" was a "speedy little infielder," but not yet ready for a steady job at short. Seemingly, he was a "little shaky" on grounders — if so, a decidedly fatal flaw for any infielder. *The Sporting News* observed that with the "Chinaman Lai Tin and the Indian Tincup" on the squad, the Phillies were assembling an "all-nations" team, especially since the National League team had so many German and Irish players in uniform. Readers of the *Lima Daily News* in Ohio could note on March 28 that "'Billy' Lai, the Chinese third baseman from Honolulu, who is getting a trial with the Phils, is a crack ukulele tinkler."[7]

The Phillies, to their credit, seemed to want to give Lai an opportunity to make the team. In an exhibition against an army nine from Fort Dade, Lai started at third base, batted 2-for-5 and initiated a double play. In Miami, he started three exhibition games at third against the Boston Braves. The results were not good. He batted 2-for-11 and committed two errors, but stole one base. Still, he had seemingly shown improvement through the three games. Lai went hitless in four at-bats in the first game, in which he committed an error. In the second, he got a hit in four at-bats, while in the final game he went 1-for-3. Moreover, the *Inquirer* continued to call Lai "a promising recruit"—an assertion agreed upon by the noted syndicated sports columnist Joe Vila, who referred to the third baseman as "Lai Tin, the Chinaman." On April 6, the *Inquirer* noted that Lai made an error in an intrasquad game. Still, Lai headed north with the Phillies squad and apparently made the team's opening day roster.[8]

Wire stories about Lai appeared in various newspapers around the country in April. Headlined "Hail the Chink," an April 7 wire story featuring the Hawaiian infielder surfaced in the *Des Moines Daily News*. The story suggested that Pat Moran's business acumen might have motivated Lai's recruitment. "The Chinese third baseman" would draw fans anxious to see an "Oriental" play baseball. Former boxer turned sportswriter James Corbett described "Lai Tin" as a "crack infielder" but weak at bat. He predicted that Lai would stay with the Phillies at least until May. In any event, Corbett echoed the notion that the "Celestial" might attract curious fans. On April 20, the *Salt Lake Telegram* published a wire story on Lai's stay with the Phillies. The story's headline read, "Phils Have Chinese Trying for Berth." Lai was described as "the only Chinese ever signed by a big league club." Lai, Utah readers could have noted, worked as a stenographer for the Pennsylvania Railroad, spoke "perfect English," and had a wife and child. Pat Moran was reportedly pleased with Lai's fielding ability and asserted that he could "run like a deer." However, Moran was less pleased with Lai's hitting—a factor that could inspire him to send the Hawaiian down to the minors for more experience.[9]

Indeed, a report in the *Utica Observer* of April 24, 1918, suggested that Lai's fate had already been sealed—the Bethlehem Steel League of Pennsylvania had offered contracts to both Lai and Fred Markham. On May 23 *The Sporting News* announced that "Billy Tin Lai, the Chinese infielder," had been released by the Phillies to the Bridgeport franchise in the Eastern League. The Eastern League was expected to play out a schedule of games from May 22 to Labor Day. *The Sporting News* speculated it would be especially strong in 1918 since the International League, a top-of-the-line minor league based on the East Coast, had folded for the year due to the financial pressures brought on in large measure by the war.[10]

The *Bridgeport Telegram* furnished readers with a positive introduction to Lai before the season officially started. About a week before the Bridgeport Americans' season opener, the *Telegram* observed that "Willie Lai, the Chinese player," would take over either third base or shortstop for the home team. The same edition praised Lai's performance in an exhibition game against a team of sailors. The headline read "Bill Lai, Chinese infielder, looks like a Real Find." In the game story, the *Telegram* enthused, "Billy Lai, the new Chinese infielder, was the attraction of the afternoon. He showed up well both in the field and at bat and looks like a really good man."[11]

The next day the *Telegram* said that it was decided that "Willie Lai, the Chinese infielder," would hold down third until he played himself out of a starting role. An exhibition game against the Philadelphia Red Caps, an African American nine, provided the Hawaiian with another opportunity to win compliments from the *Telegram*. "Lai, the Chinese addition," did well according to the daily. He not only got two hits, but "the Chinaman" impressed with his ability to "scamper" from first to third on a base hit. The *Telegram* observed, "The chink displayed plenty of pepper and he didn't talk in Hong Kong either." If he could hit, the *Telegram* predicted, Lai would help out the Americans. On opening day, the *Telegram* described the right-handed "Bill Lai, the third baseman," as a fast base runner, good fielder, and fair hitter who came from Hawaii but lived in New York City.[12]

By June, Lai and teammate Yim had proven integral to the Americans' success. The *Telegram* indicated that Lai seemed to enjoy the game and was enjoyable to watch. Lai was "full of pepper and is always in action." His fielding could be steadier, the Bridgeport daily surmised, but he was capable of making spectacular plays in the field. Lai had demonstrated that he was "a quick thinker," good hitter and very good base runner. Catchers simply could not gun down "the Chink" when he decided to steal a base. May 28 was an auspiciously hot day for the Bridgeport nine. Waterbury was the opponent and while players and fans wilted in the heat, according to the *Telegram*, "the Chinese players" seemed to thrive along with the "pop bottle man." Lai, "the Celestial third sacker," participated in a double steal along with player-manager Paul Krichell. A few days later, the *Telegram* hailed "Bill Lai" as the "prize pepper box of the Eastern League" who was always "chattering and moving in some direction."[13]

In July, T.F. Magner worried about Lai's immediate future with the Americans. On July 18, the *Telegram* reported that the Philadelphia draft board had ordered "Billy Tin Lai, the Chinese third baseman of the Bridgeport" team to quit baseball and work on behalf of the war effort. The daily maintained that Lai had been in the U.S. for four years and was now married. As opposed to a year earlier, Lai was presented in the press as befuddled by the process. He reputedly said that he was quite willing to help the American war effort but wondered what a "Chinaman" could really do. T.F. Magner feared that "Billy Lai" would be lost to Bridgeport. The sportswriter asserted that the Americans could not readily dispense with Lai's services since he was "easily the best third sacker in the league." However, Magner was eventually relieved to discover that Lai would continue to play for Bridgeport.[14]

By late July, Eastern League had prematurely ended because of financial reasons and the restraints of war. This gave the Americans a chance to play the major league Pittsburgh Pirates, edging the National Leaguers, 2–1. Pirates manager Hugo Bezdek came away impressed with both Lai and Yamashiro. He was particularly taken with "Bill Lai, the Celestial shortstop." Bezdek said he saw no reason why Lai could not make it into the big leagues. The Pirates manager maintained that Lai was faster than most major leaguers and too fast for the Eastern League. Yim got a key hit for the Americans, while T.F. Manager called "Lai's triple to the fence in center ... a pretty blow, [which] gave the fans a chance to see how fast the Hawaiian youngster can round the paths when he wants to." In the meantime, the *Bridgeport Telegram* lamented that with the Americans' season ending, local fans would "certainly miss Billy Lai and Andy Yim the two Hawaiian players." Fans, the daily maintained, had liked the two from opening day. "They were perfect gentlemen, well educated in the American way of things, and always in the game until the last out." A week after the Pirates game, Lai and two other Americans reportedly headed to Chester, Pennsylvania. There they would work in a ship yard. In September, the *Inquirer* reported that "Billy Tin Lai, the sensational Chinese player," competed for a baseball team out of Hog Island. Meanwhile, the *Brooklyn Eagle* announced that the Bushwicks had recruited Lai for the remainder of their 1918 schedule.[15]

With the war finished, Bridgeport was ready for a fuller season in 1919. While Yamashiro did not suit up for the team, Lai certainly did. In April, the *Bridgeport Telegram* expressed relief that "Bill Lai, the best Chinese ballplayer in the Eastern League last season, and one of the star third basemen of the circuit," had signed on for another season with the Americans. Just before the season began, the *Telegram* called Lai "the celebrated Hawaiian-Chinese (or do you say it, Chinese Hawaiian?)." Early in the season, manager Ray Grimes tried "Billy Lai" at shortstop. But the experiment did not seem to work out and the Bridgeport manager was criticized for not using the "Chinese athlete" more at third base where he had "some class." On offense, Lai came up with some big hits for the Americans. In June, the "the Chinese Hawaiian" rapped a triple that helped Bridgeport beat Worchester. The team management must have respected Lai's baseball judgment. Early in July, he was too hurt to play, but "Chinese Bill" was sent to Philadelphia on a scouting trip. There he was expected to interview a prospective pitcher.[16]

Some months after the 1919 season ended, readers of the *Duluth News Tribune* could run across a wire story about Lai. The writer maintained that Lai was "the only Chink in the [Eastern] League," adding that other Chinese wanted to take up baseball because playing the game was easier "than bending over a tub on a hot day." It was also pointed out that Lai, a natural-born U.S. citizen, "has an American girl for a wife and she lives in Philadelphia." The journalist then told what many might have thought of as an amusing tale about a contingent of "Bridgeport Chinese" coming to the Americans' ballpark to watch Lai play. Reportedly, these spectators were angered by an umpire who they believed mistakenly called the infielder out on the base paths. These Chinese Americans then dispatched a delegation to a local newspaper. Supposedly, this was what one of them said: "Stop the pless. I have some blig news for paper. Lotten umpire out to ball park today.... Man run to baseum, Lai touch, but he say safe, big stiff. You put him in paper, say Chinese boys don't want to be robbed by rotten umpire. You savey. We watch paper in the mornin' to give umpire a big roast."[17]

Lai's third season in Bridgeport did not seem all that happy, although the *Telegram* appeared happy that Lai was going to spend his third year in organized baseball in Bridgeport, dryly calling him "the best Chinese-Hawaiian of base-hitting." Early season cartoons of the Bridgeport team included one of "Third sacker Lai — our good old Chinaman standby." His new manager, future Hall of Fame pitcher Ed Walsh, might have been a major reason why things did not go well. In June, the Americans' infield was beset by injuries. Walsh decided to switch Lai to shortstop, where he once again appeared out of place and dangerous to the team's success. A wrist injury also forced him out of the lineup. Still, the Hawaiian remained popular in Bridgeport baseball circles as he received a nice ovation from fans when he assumed base coaching duties while recovering. Lai managed to not only return to the lineup but revved up his game by the end of the season. On August 17, Bridgeport swept a doubleheader from Albany, with Lai getting a key hit in the first game, while his great fielding brought the home crowd to its feet. The *Telegram* declared, "Buck Lai was on the job every minute of both games." The *Telegram* enthused about Lai "playing the same brilliant ball that caused the fans to sing so loudly his praises a year ago." The *Telegram* also reported that Walsh

Known as Lai Tin when he started his remarkable baseball playing career in Honolulu, Buck Lai was an exciting third baseman and baserunner, who could occasionally wield an effective bat. He was the most famous Chinese American baseball player of his time (courtesy of the Library of Congress, Prints & Photographs Division, LC-B2-3343-5).

had tried to drive Lai out of the league. Whether the reasons were racial or because the former pitcher did not seem to get along with any of his ballplayers are unclear. Nevertheless, Walsh claimed that he never tried to end Lai's Eastern League career, insisting that the infielder had announced his intention of retiring from the Americans before the season began. In any event, Walsh apparently turned the heat down on the Hawaiian, making Lai's life easier and paving the way for him to return for one more year in Bridgeport. Meanwhile, the U.S. Census manuscript schedules reveal that Lai, his wife, and son, William, lived in Philadelphia on North 21st Street and Brandywine. His occupation was listed as lead riveter for a ship building company on Hog Island.[18]

Lai's fourth season in Bridgeport proved his last. During the offseason, it appeared that Lai might not return after all. *The Sporting News* reported that "Buck Lai, the Chinese second baseman" would not report to the Americans. He had a good job in Philadelphia. His wife just had a baby. The "Baseball Bible's" correspondent said Lai wanted to stay home and watch "the little Celestial grow." Nevertheless, Lai managed to aid the Americans with his bat, legs, and glove somewhat in 1921. In April, the *Telegram* claimed the Hawaiian ran faster than nearly any big leaguer. In early May, he got a hit down the third base line, which helped Bridgeport beat Springfield. Lai also found himself playing the outfield for the Americans. But the *Telegram* observed he did not do well in the outfield and was moved back to third where he prospered, impressing the daily with an unassisted double play at his old position. Still, Lai's batting eye weakened in 1921 so much that the *Telegram* expressed surprise when he rapped a bases-loaded triple against New Haven in August. On September 19, the *Telegram* reported that Lai was through for the season and the Americans gave him permission to report to his full-time job with the Pennsylvania Railroad, where he would continue to play baseball for the company nine. Lai reportedly suffered a hand injury which put him out of action for several games and hurt his batting. Thus, he was not much use to the Bridgeport club.[19]

With Bridgeport behind him, Lai continued to compete in semipro ball in the Philadelphia area. In October 1921, he was batting cleanup and playing third for the Pennsylvania Terminal nine, which had won the Eastern Division championship of the Pennsylvania Railroad League. Lai got a double and a single, helping the Pennsylvania Terminal team to win the league championship before 12,000 fans at Shibe Park, the home of Mack's Athletics.[20]

In the spring and summer of 1922, we can find Lai playing for the South Phillies. Taking on the Fleisher nine in April, Lai's team opened up their new grounds, Shetzline Park, on Broad and Bigler Streets, before 12,000 fans. On July 4, a reported 18,000 packed Shetzline Park to watch the South Phillies compete in a doubleheader — first against the South Philadelphia Hebrew Association (SPHAS) nine and then the Cressona Tigers. The South Phillies won both games and Lai contributed with a run against the SPHAS and a hit, a stolen base, and two runs against the Tigers. That same month, the *Trenton Evening Times* lauded the South Phillies as one of the strongest semipro nines around. It insisted that several members of the South Phillies roster had accumulated professional experience — including Buck Lai, the "Chinese third baseman." However, Lai also suited up for the Bushwicks. On April 23, he played shortstop when the Brooklyn nine lost easily to the Philadelphia-based Bridesberg team, 13–2. Meanwhile, an *Inquirer* sportswriter, Gordon Mackay, reported that "Tin Lai, the Chinese player, says he's all washed up with baseball at present." A wire story in the *Lethbridge* (Alberta) *Herald* declared that "Tin Lai" had retired after four years in Bridgeport. It went on to ask if Lai was going to open up a chop suey restaurant or a chain of laundries instead.[21]

To be sure, Lai was hardly through with baseball. In the early 1960s, a teammate recalled that several of those who played for the Philadelphia Terminal nine also competed for a semipro outfit in Chester in 1923 and 1924. In 1923, the man described by the *Chester Times* as the "flashy Hawaiian" played for the Chester nine, which competed in the Philadelphia Baseball Association. Before the season began, the *Chester Times* announced the former Traveler's inclusion on the Chester roster. It maintained, "Buck Lai, the Chinese streak of lightning, who has delighted fans since coming here from Hawaii will knock 'em down at third." In late July, he got two hits in a game against the Bacharach Giants. A reporter for the *Chester Times* observed that the Hawaiian possessed an unusual batting stance in that he placed both his feet on the edge of the batter's box. Across the Delaware River and beyond, Lai put in some time with the Bushwicks. While Lai cavorted on semipro fields in and around Philadelphia for much of the week, he still found time to play for the Bushwicks in 1923. In April, the *Brooklyn Eagle* proclaimed, "Lai Tin, the Bushwicks' Chinese third baseman," got three hits against Harrisburg of the Central Penn League and was awarded with a bat by a grateful Bushwicks rooter.[22]

In 1924, Lai starred for both the Bushwicks and the Trenton entry in the Penn-Jersey League. The *Trenton Evening Times* described Lai as an infielder with "few peers" in independent baseball, while before an early-season game against the talented Lincoln Giants, the daily maintained that "Buck Lai, the greatest Chinese ball player in the country should make a wonderful impression." Playing in a doubleheader for Trenton on May 30 against a black team derisively described by a local sportswriter as the "Royal Blue Giants of Havana, New York City, or somewhere in between," Lai seemed to dominate. Especially contemptuous of the "dusky" performers in the first game, Henry

Coady Lindop of the *Evening Times* observed, "Buck Lai was the featured performer in the morning circus. The fleet fotted [*sic*] Chinaman always enjoys games in which he can run wild on the 'bases' without fear of consequences and in the morning he had the darkies all crossed up." Using his speed as his prime weapon, Lai beat out several infield hits and stole two bases.[23]

Lai's best day at bat in 1924 came on July 20, when Trenton tied Hilldale, 5–5. Lai drove two inside-the-park home runs into deep left-center. Claiming that Lai's feat was hitherto unmatched at the South Trenton baseball grounds, Lindop enthused, "Standing out heads and shoulders above his fellow men was Buck Lai, the fleet-footed Trenton third sacker, who first saw the light of day in the far away Hawaiian Islands." On the first round tripper, Lai almost caught up to the baserunner ahead of him.[24]

After the major league season ended by early October, it was typical for various major league stars to organize or be organized into various barnstorming teams. We have already encountered such teams that made their way to the Hawaiian Islands in the 1910s. One contingent of barnstormers was headed by Ed Rommel, a successful pitcher for Connie Mack's Philadelphia Athletics. In October 1924, Rommel's "Barnstorming Athletics" took on a team called the Norristown Pros in that town, some 20 miles west of Philadelphia. Rommel's nine edged the hometowners, 2–1. However, Buck Lai whacked one of the losers' few hits and scored their only run.[25]

After 1924 and for several years thereafter, Lai primarily suited up for the Bushwicks. In the fall of 1927, the Bushwicks met a barnstorming team headed by Babe Ruth and Lou Gehrig at Dexter Park. Approximately 20,000 spectators packed Dexter Park to see the "Bustin' Babes" win, 3–1. Lai led off for the Bushwicks and managed to go 1-for-3. However, he committed an error that allowed Lou Gehrig to score a key run.[26]

In 1928, Lai got one last shot at the big leagues when he was brought into the New York Giants spring training camp. Late in 1927, the *Chester Times* reported that Lai and another, unnamed, semipro standout had been a given a tryout at the Polo Grounds by John McGraw. The famed manager was impressed with Lai and offered him a contract. In January 1928, the *New York Times* averred that since the Giants had "exhausted all the resources of the United States" they had to sign a "Chinese infielder, William T. Lai by name." The *Times* said Lai's work with the Bushwicks had attracted McGraw, while conceding that the infielder might turn into a valuable utility player for the denizens of the Polo Grounds. Presumably because the "Chinese-Hawaiian" had "voluntarily retired" from Bridgeport, Lai had to apply to the head honchos of organized baseball for "reinstatement." A Universal Service wire story published in a small town newspaper was headlined "John McGraw Signs Chinese Third Baseman." Readers discovered that the famous manager was willing to sign players of all "races"; he already had two Jewish ballplayers on the Giants roster. "William W. Lai," the story went on inaccurately, had caught on at one time with the Phillies but was sent down to New Haven. Lai was supposedly not a "steady performer" but had been quite the slugger for the Bushwicks. When readers of the *Hagerstown Daily Mail* read the news of Buck Lai joining the Giants, they not only saw a photograph of the Hawaiian, but a cartoon of a queued ballplayer, bearing stereotypical Asian features, fielding a ground ball. A wire story in the *Seattle Times* was accompanied by a photograph of Lai in a Bushwicks uniform. The story described the infielder's invitation to the Giants training camp as a "novelty" and the ballplayer as part–Hawaiian and part–Chinese. Since the Giants were considering Jewish-American infielder Andy Cohen as a possibility, the story continued that if Lai and Cohen both made John McGraw's team, they would comprise "the most unusual infield in baseball." Readers of the *Lethbridge Herald* received mixed signals regarding Lai's opportunity to play big league ball. The wire story was accompanied by both a nice photograph of the Hawaiian and a cartoon displaying a queue wearing ballplayer. In announcing Lai's try out with the Giants, the *Gettysburg Times* insisted, "he is claimed by some to be Chinese and by others to be a native of the Hawaiian Islands." An anonymous *Los Angeles Times* writer responded, "Buck Lai, signed by the Giants, is the first Chinese player in major league baseball. Now give us a Chinese golf pro and we'd rate China among world powers."[27]

Lank Leonard, a famed reporter/cartoonist, responded to Lai's tryout with the Giants both visually and verbally in a piece published in February 1928, in the *Trenton Evening Times*. Above the article's text, a reader could linger over Leonard's skills as an illustrator and cartoonist. Leonard rendered a respectful and realistic drawing of the Chinese Hawaiian ballplayer. However, three not so respectful cartoons revolved around the drawing of Lai as he readied himself in fielding position. One showed a supposedly Chinese baseball fan yelling from the stands. The caption read, "There'll be plenty of laundry neglected around New York next spring." A second depicted an umpire whacked in the head with what appears to be an axe — presumably a tong axe. The caption explained, "It may be a tough year for umpires if 'Buck' makes good." Finally, a small group of standing ballplayers were shown singing, while a seated Asian-appearing ballplayer strummed a ukulele. According to the caption, "The Giants should be a happy team now that Lai's ukulele is on the job."[28]

Leonard's text mirrored the ambivalent character of his art work. He advised good humoredly that white New Yorkers should not expect their laundry done in time, since Chinese New Yorkers would most likely head to Polo Grounds, "making oriental wisecracks" at the New York Giants' opponents. They would cheer McGraw's aggregation, because "'Buck' Lai, the old Eastern League Chinaman," might appear in a Giants uniform, although Leonard warned that the Hawaiian's task of sticking with the Giants was daunting due to the team's large number of talented, veteran infielders.[29]

Leonard introduced "the colorful individual" involved as "Bill 'Buck' Lai," but added that the ballplayer's real name was Lai Tin. He then reminisced about that "all-Chinese" team on which Lai came to the mainland the previous decade. The Travelers, Leonard recalled, became a hit on the mainland. They, Leonard maintained, were "full of pep and took delight in giving crowds a laugh by yelling advice in their native tongue." Still, according to the journalist/cartoonist, they were all well educated and had mastered English, "but they appreciated the part they were playing and made the most of it."[30]

Leonard alleged that he had seen the Travelers in person at Port Chester, New York. He recalled that they put on an enjoyable show, performing their shadow ball routine and other pre-game antics. Leonard insisted, "Those Chinks were natural entertainers and 'Buck' Lai was one of the best." Yet although the Hawaiians liked to clown, Leonard insisted, they played well too.[31]

Unpacking a bagful of Chinese stereotypes, sportswriter Bill Ritt was clearly unimpressed with Lai's prospects after the Hawaiian arrived at the Giants' camp. He wrote, "New York's only Chinese ballplayer, Lai Tin, has been weighed and found wanting in base hits." Ritt added, "This naturalized laundryman holds his bat like an ironing board and swings like a ringer.... If the Giant celestial makes good ... and gets into the World Series all soap and suds shops will probably close and a national holiday declared in the best washtub circles." However, if he failed, Lai could "hurry back to China" and take in the latest revolution. Not satisfied to stick to sportswriting, Ritt proclaimed, "We understand the boys [in China] have some brand new civil wars and a few uprisings, slightly used."[32]

Ritt, in any event, was right about Lai's prospects with the Giants. According to one press account, Lai, "the Chinese infielder," was McGraw's first cut, and the famed manager wanted to dispatch the over-30-year-old Hawaiian with several years of relatively high level baseball playing to a Little Rock, Arkansas, team for more experience. A wire story, consequently, reported that Little Rock of the Southern Association had purchased Lai's contract from the New York Giants. The *New York Times*' Richards Vidmer wrote, "Buck Lai, the Chinaman, who never had a Chinaman's chance, had been sent to Little Rock." A title to one story printed in a small-town newspaper crudely read, "No More Chink."[33]

An Associated Press report said the Hawaiian did not want to head south to Little Rock. It maintained, "Buck Lai, the Chinaman with the New York

Giants, will open up a laundry in preference to joining Little Rock. Manager McGraw sent Lai to Little Rock the other day but he is still in camp here. 'I'll go in the laundry business first,' Buck declared in refusing to quit the Giants." Vidmer observed, "Buck Lai, the Chinaman, hasn't been sold to Little Rock at all. McGraw only thought he had sent him to that club."[34]

As opening day neared, the Giants were still wondering what to do with Lai. Mickey Lake of the *Trenton Evening Times* wrote that the "chink ball player" even got into a Giants exhibition game against Jersey City, connecting for two hits in the process. In so doing, Lai must have opened up some Jersey City eyes. On April 12, Frank Donnelly, secretary of the Jersey City franchise, announced that his International League team had acquired the services of Buck Lai from the Giants. Jersey City, Donnelly maintained, planned on using the "Chinese infielder" as a utility player. Lai's debut with Jersey City was something of a hit, albeit in an exhibition game against New Haven of the Eastern League. According to one account of the game, "Buck Lai, the Chinese player ... filled in cleverly at shortstop." Lai sparked the offense too as his bat directly and indirectly led to three runs. As the regular season began, Lai did show up in Jersey City's lineup, playing shortstop, against Newark and other International League teams. In all, he suited up in four official International League games. Yet Lai's stay in Jersey City was brief. As far as the *Trenton Evening Times* was concerned, Lai was headed back to the Bushwicks "after some heavy publicity as the only Chinese ball player in the majors." Indeed, the *Brooklyn Eagle* announced his return to the Brooklyn nine against Camden in early May.[35]

After seeing the end of his chances of making it to the big leagues, Lai surfaced in a footnote in a study conducted by University of Southern California professor William Carlson Smith. Exploring the different social relations between racial and ethnic groups on Hawai'i as opposed to the mainland, Smith examined the relative tolerance of interracial marriage on the islands as well as the Hawaiian enthusiasm for sports. The latter, Smith argued, "has made it possible for several Hawaiian athletes of oriental ancestry to marry white girls." In the footnote, Smith informed readers, ""A Chinese who was signed by the New York Giants' baseball team of the National League in the spring of 1928 married a white girl."[36]

After his flirtation with big league ball, Lai returned without bitterness to East Coast semiprofessional circles, according to his daughter-in-law, Mary Lai. Buck Lai could earn more money in semipro ball, while keeping a full-time job and staying close to his family, she remembered. In July 1928, Lai was at shortstop for a Philadelphia team called the Corley Catholic Club, based in the city's Southmark district. A few weeks later, Lai was in a Bushwicks uniform when the Brooklyn nine played two games against separate opponents. The Bushwicks beat the Harrowgate nine in the first game and the famed House of David team in the nightcap. Lai went 2-for-4 against Harrowgate and 3-for-5 against the bearded contingent. In the fall of 1928, Lai was in a Bushwicks uniform, as the Brooklyn nine took on a barnstorming team headed by Ruth and Gehrig. The Bushwicks actually won, 10–8, before 22,000 fans at Dexter Park. Lai went 1-for-5, but his one hit was a double.[37]

In the 1930 season opener against Trenton, Lai got no hits as 2,000 "Flatbush" fans saw former Athletics pitcher Stan Baumgartner hurl a 1–0 shutout. In late June, the Bushwicks lost a doubleheader against the "Stars of Cuba," led by the great Martin Dihigo. Lai slugged a triple and went 3-for-8 during the two games. At a game heralded by the *New York Times* as the first held under the lights, Lai went for 0-for-3 as the Bushwicks lost to the Springfield nine of Long Island at Dexter Park in July, 1930. About the same time, Lai showed up in Trenton as a member of Philadelphia's Mayfair nine. The *Trenton Evening Times* announced to fans that the "famed Buck Lai" would return to play his old Trenton teammates at a local high school on July 4.[38]

In July 1931, Lai's bat led the Bushwicks to a doubleheader sweep against the Brooklyn Royal Giants. Called a "Chinese boy" and a "China boy" by the *Eagle*, the 37-year-old Lai batted 3-for-5 in both games, including some hits off Dick Redding, one of the greatest Negro League pitchers of all time. Interestingly and inaccurately, the *Eagle* also took the opportunity to remind readers that Lai had nearly made the Giants. The daily declared that Lai had issued an ultimatum to McGraw— keep him on the Giants roster or let him return to the Bushwicks. Jersey City, in other words, would not work out because, according to the *Eagle*, he was pursuing a legal career in New York City.[39]

As Lai edged toward 40, he could still compete. In late September 1932, the New York Giants defeated the Bushwicks under the lights, 5–2. A nice crowd of 20,000 saw Lai go 2-for-5. But in the summer of 1933, we could find Lai playing in Middletown, New York, for a team called the State Hospital Grays against the Black Yankees. Lai went for 1-for-5 in the game won by the African American outfit. Two months later, Lai rapped a key hit and scored a key run that helped the Bushwicks beat the Cuban Stars before 8,000 at Dexter Park.[40]

Clearly, performing regularly for the Bushwicks was no small deal in the 1930s. When Max Rosner, who, along with Nat Strong, ran the Bushwicks, died in 1952, a *Sporting News* correspondent claimed that the Bushwicks comprised a "national legend." For years frustrated Brooklyn fans had regularly cracked that the Dodgers could not beat the team that played out of Dexter Park. Indeed, the team often outdrew the Dodgers. When the Bushwicks began in the 1910s, their home field was the Ridgefield Oval until the stands burned down in 1917. Then Dexter Park became the team's home. Lai was acknowledged as one of the Bushwicks' best players, but the nine fielded several future and former big leaguers such as Dazzy Vance and Lefty Gomez. Often, African American teams furnished the Bushwicks with their keenest competition until the Negro Leagues began to die out after World War II. The Bushwicks lasted until 1950 and Dexter Park stood until 1953.[41]

In January 1934, *The Sporting News* reminded readers of Lai's ill-fated attempt at a major league career. It did so by way of a cartoon accompanying Dan Daniel's article on Hawaiian Henry Oana's struggle to make it into the big leagues. The cartoon tried to depict baseball's effort to include ballplayers of different racial and ethnic backgrounds. It respectfully portrayed Oana, Cuban Dolph Luque, and Native Americans Chief Bender and Chief Meyers, as well as Japanese Hawaiian Kenso Nushida who briefly pitched in the PCL in 1932. It acknowledged "Lai Tin," however, as a queue-wearing third baseman in the act of committing an error and compounding his mistake by supposedly swearing in Chinese. The caption derided him as "a Chinaman who failed to make the grade with Giants."[42]

At 40 Lai continued to excel in East Coast semipro circles. In October 1934, the Black Yankees blanked the Bushwicks, 6–0, before a crowd of 15,000. The fact that a few stars from the World Champion St. Louis Cardinals appeared undoubtedly boosted attendance. The great Dizzy Dean, for example, threw three innings for the Bushwicks, while his brother Paul played in right field and Joe "Ducky" Medwick was in left. Lai went 1-for-3 and stole a base.[43]

Meanwhile, Lai gained some publicity not as a baseball player but as a professional basketball entrepreneur, coach and player. On December 19, 1921, Lai played for the "All-Chinese Collegians of Shanghai" against the Original Celtics. The Hawaiian apparently played the best of all of his teammates, holding his own against Celtics standout Jake Haggerty and even outscoring him. In early January 1922, the five-foot-nine-inch Lai played center for the All-Chinese quintet, scoring two baskets against the Delco Company quintet for a team the *Philadelphia Inquirer* called the "Celestials" and the "Mongolians."[44]

Ten years later, the *Gettysburg Times* promoted an upcoming game between the local Fleet Wings and "The Famous Aloha Hawaiian Stars," "a novelty quintet" coached by Buck Lai. The *Times* promised, "Buck Lai, the great Hawaiian baseball and basketball star, will bring the fastest basketball club in America" to the Hotel Gettysburg Annex. The daily also promised readers that Hawaiian musicians and dancers had accompanied Lai's team and would entertain spectators during halftime. According to the *Times*, the "Aloha Stars" had accumulated a record of 33 wins and eight losses, "compiled against the best teams in this section of the country." Depicted as a former major leaguer with the New York Giants, Lai apparently did not play much basketball "but directs his speedy dribblers from the bench." Only two players possessed Asian Pacific Islander names — Lai and a reserve named Akuna. All of the "Aloha Stars" wore hula skirts and leis during the first half of the games they played.[45]

In Maryland, the *Frederick Daily News* told readers in February 1932, they could expect "high class basketball, excellent string music, some nifty hula hula dancing and a free handout of chocolate cakes as the menu to be dished out to local court fans at the State armory." Escorting the text was a photo supposedly of Buck Lai wearing a hula skirt and a basketball jersey. Actually, the photo was clearly not of the veteran Hawaiian athlete. In any event, Lai was called accurately "one of the best all around Hawaiian athletes every produced." The next month, the *Rochester Democrat and Chronicle* announced the arrival of Lai's quintet. It mistakenly identified Lai as the only "native Hawaiian" to play big league ball. Several months later, the *Trenton Evening Times* welcomed Lai's team to its city. The daily remembered Lai as he had cavorted for the local nine nearly a decade earlier and described him as "the only Jap ball player who ever made the big leagues" when he "scintillated" for McGraw's Giants. The *Evening Times* also listed Lai as the starting forward and insisted that the team carried "Hawaiians, Filipinos, Japanese, and various other Orientals." Sometime in 1933, the players who composed the Hawaiian All-Stars apparently competed under the name of Philadelphia Passons, named after Philadelphia sports entrepreneur Harry Passon, and Lai seems to have disappeared for a while from team leadership.[46]

Nevertheless, in January 1934, a team called the Aloha Hawaiians appeared in Washington, D.C., to play a local professional five called the Heurichs. The *Washington Post* identified Lai as both coach and a former New York Giants player. The team still performed with hula skirts and leis. And spectators were still promised "a genuine hula dance" during a break in the action.[47]

In the mid–1930s, Buck Lai returned to Hawai'i to manage a baseball team of barnstorming Hawaiians. Like the team he played on 20 years earlier, Lai's squad toured the U.S. mainland, while adding Canada to its itinerary. It consisted of players of Japanese, Chinese, and Hawaiian ancestries.

Prior to Lai's journey home early in 1935, the *Brooklyn Eagle* published an intriguing story, which purported that before his death in 1934 Nat Strong encouraged the veteran Bushwick third sacker's venture. Apparently, African American nines had threatened to boycott the Bushwicks and Dexter Park, managed by Strong and Max Rosner. These franchises wanted a portion of the gate receipts at Dexter Park, in addition to a financial guarantee — a demand the two entrepreneurs thought presumptuous and exorbitant. Rosner, after Strong's death, also backed a mainland trek of a Hawaiian team because even white semipro clubs balked at his leadership since his partner's demise.[48]

By playing at least some games at Dexter Park, a Buck Lai-managed Hawaiian team would, Strong and Rosner hoped, offset the threats to their kingdom by black and white independent teams. James Murphy, the story's author, wrote that Lai had originally wanted to bring an all-Chinese Hawaiian squad to the mainland, but had learned that there was not enough "Celestial" talent available in Hawai'i. Thus he would have to recruit players from other ethnic groups. The famed Philadelphia-based sports entrepreneur, Eddie Gottlieb, would purportedly handle bookings for Lai's team. Murphy added that Lai was called "Buck" because he rode bucking broncos in Hawai'i, while declaring that "Papa Lai has been an interesting character in baseball in this country for 19 years."[49]

Lai arrived in Honolulu early in 1935. According to Murphy, "the popular Mandarin infielder" had a rough voyage, losing ten pounds on the Pacific. Still, he was greeted as a "conquering hero"—with a special tug and 50 leis. Old friends such as En Sue Pung, Henry Kuali, Luck Yee, Kan Yen Chun, Hoon Ki, Al Yap, and Henry Chillingsworth welcomed Lai, as did his mother, who had not seen Buck Lai in 18 years. Moreover, Lai acknowledged the existence of a Buck Lai Tin Baseball League conducted at Lanakila Field.[50]

It was an interesting time for Honolulu. Just a few years earlier, racial and class tensions ran high on Oahu over the alleged rape of a white wife of a U.S. Naval officer by youths of Asian Pacific Islander ancestry. A trial led to no convictions, inspiring calls among some important haole civilians and white mainlanders for a military takeover of the Hawaiian Islands. Things took a dramatic turn when the "victim's" wealthy mother, husband, and two confederates murdered one of the accused, inspiring an even more well-publicized trial featuring Clarence Darrow as the defense attorney.[51]

Soon after Lai's arrival, there was talk of organizing an exhibition game that would raise money for a bus that could transport Lai's team around the mainland. William Peet, a *Honolulu Advertiser* sportswriter, urged local baseball fans to support Lai's venture. He wrote, "Buck is a hustler and knows what he is doing all the time." This game would also serve as an audition for Hawaiian ballplayers wishing to head eastward with Lai. An "Old Timers" game was also bandied about. "Charley Ensue," as the *Honolulu Advertiser* called En Sue Pung, said such a game was possible. He hoped that Johnny Williams and his brother, Jimmy, would compete as well as Barney Joy. However, former Travelers such as "Kanky Yen," the Akana brothers, the Moriyama brothers, Andy Yamashiro, and Fred Markham were also viewed as possible competitors. To support his contention that these warriors of Honolulu baseball battles a generation earlier would show up, En Sue Pung insisted, "A man who has played baseball loves the sport, no matter what his age, and those old timers, I am sure, will go to this game like nobody's business." Moreover, the *Advertiser* promised that Lai would make every effort to assemble a ball club that would do Hawai'i proud. He would scour the talent on other islands aside from Oahu. Moreover, Lai would also scout the commercial and Japanese leagues. To the *Advertiser,* Lai was "shrewd and a good judge of baseball."[52]

By March 22, Lai's team was shaping up. He was considering such candidates as En Sue Pung's sons, Hans and Afro, as well as Tommy Kaulukukui, a magnificent all-around athlete of Hawaiian-Chinese descent. Ted Nobriega, a Hawaiian of indigenous and Portuguese descent, was also receiving consideration since he had previously pitched in the St. Louis Cardinals organization.[53]

The Honolulu press promoted the fundraiser for Lai's team, scheduled for March 31. Sportswriter Red McQueen noted the speech by a prominent Chinese Honolulan on Lai's behalf, yet managed to ridicule the speaker's command of English. On March, 30, the *Advertiser* printed a respectful cartoon of Buck Lai, while informing fans that Lai would manage one team in the "all-star" contest while "hapa haole" Earl Vida managed the other. The next day, a photo of "Lai Tin" appeared in the *Advertiser.* The veteran third baseman wore the team uniform, emblazoned with "Hawaii, U.S.A." on the front. Red McQueen worried that not enough fans would show up to raise the needed $3,000, even though Lai's team would promote Hawai'i to the mainland. As for the game itself, 2,000 watched Earl Vida's nine "humiliate" the team managed by Lai.[54]

The culturally diverse barnstorming team chosen by Lai included pitchers Earl Vida, William Vickery, Al Nalua, and Eddie Tam along with catcher Albert Holt. The infielders were Wallace Arakawa, Richard Yamada, Walter Rodriques, and Buck Lai. Hans Pung, Francis Goo, and Shipp Lo were the outfielders. Before shipping out of Honolulu Harbor, Lai's nine managed to beat a military nine, 11–3. Yet as the team departed, some Hawaiian baseball fans felt a better squad could have been dispatched to the mainland.[55]

Francis Goo remembered the 1935 trek for Rod Ohira of the *Honolulu Advertiser.* A bus must have been purchased for the team. Gray in color with "All-Hawaii Baseball Team" painted on the side, it transported the Hawaiian ballplayers from coast to coast. Goo remembered the team playing in San Francisco, Salt Lake City, Denver, Omaha, Chicago, St. Louis, Kansas City, Philadelphia, New York and Montreal. "It was my first time away from Hawai'i," Goo said. "We played mostly every day and stayed in first-class hotels. Buck gave us $1 a day for meals, and in those days you could eat good for 30 cents." The former ballplayer recalled, "A lot of people never heard of Hawai'i or only knew Hawai'i for hula skirts and coconut trees.... When they saw us on the bus, they were surprised we played baseball and could speak English." Things had not really changed all that much in 20 years.[56]

Lai's squad was often advertised as the "Chinese-All-Stars" in 1935. That year and the two other years it toured the American mainland, the Hawaiian nine played most of its games east of the Rockies. However, before the Hawaiians crossed into the great prairies, the *Brooklyn Eagle* informed readers that in Denver Lai earned the Hawaiian equivalent of the "hors de combat" after getting plunked in the head by a pitched ball. Meanwhile, the team stopped its bus when the ballplayers espied snow for the first time on the mainland. The *Eagle* reported that the Hawaiians frolicked in the white stuff for an hour. On May 20, Kansas's *Emporia Gazette* declared that local fans were excited about an impending game between the formidable Kansas City Monarchs and the "Chinese All-Stars." While familiar with the Monarchs, they were hoping for something unique when the famed African American nine took on the visitors. Later in May, a newspaper in Moberly, Kansas, reported that the "Chinese All-Stars of Honolulu" were coming to town. It revealed that the team's only loss so far had been imposed by the Monarchs. As it turned out, the Moberly Merchants beat the "Chinese All-Stars" in extra innings. One thousand fans watched what the *Moberly Monitor-Index* called an exciting game that witnessed the Hawaiians trying the old hidden-ball trick unsuccessfully. A Jefferson City, Missouri, newspaper advertised the arrival of the "Chinese All-Stars" to oppose a local team known as the Senators. The publicity blurb published a photo of Buck Lai wearing the "Hawaii, U.S.A." uniform. Lai was described, moreover, as the greatest of all Chinese athletes. On June 1, the *Chicago Tribune* announced that "Oriental baseball fans in Chicago will stage a celebration" when the "Chinese All-Star team takes on" the Mills nine in a doubleheader on June 2. The city's Chinese Consul was expected to throw out the first ball. Reading very much like an exaggerated promotional piece for Lai's team, the *Tribune*'s story claimed that Lai's all-star team of Chinese Hawaiians had played a Babe Ruth-headed American League all-star contingent in Honolulu the previous winter. Ruth apparently was so impressed with Lai's team that he advised the long-time semipro standout to take it to the mainland. Supposedly inspired by Ruth, Lai assembled a squad of players "famous in their homeland" for their skill.[57]

Later in the 1935 trek, Lai's nine competed in places like Syracuse and Oswego in New York and Helena, Montana. In August, Lai's team comprised of "Chinese, Japanese, and Hawaiians from Honolulu" came to Syracuse to oppose the African American Detroit Clowns in a doubleheader at the city's Municipal Stadium. Lai was scheduled to send Bill Vickery and the versatile John Kerr, a Hawaiian of Chinese and indigenous descent, to the mound. The *Syracuse Daily Herald* noted that the Hawaiians had lost 80 percent of their games up to that time. Thus, it kindly claimed that Lai had not passed up any hard opponents. In Oswego, Lai's nine lost to the Netherlands, 5–4 in extra innings. A local newspaper boasted that the game drew one of the best night-time crowds of the summer.[58]

In Helena, Lai's team was scheduled to confront the Higgins nine in September. Trying to pump up interest in the game, the *Helena Independent* told readers that the Hawaiian squad consisted of all-stars from the islands. The *Independent* focused attention on John Kerr, whom it described as a "pure Hawaiian" and "the greatest distance hitter ever developed in Hawaiian baseball." It pointed out that Kerr, while playing against the Negro League Philadelphia Royal Giants, was the first to hit a home run out of Honolulu Stadium — a blow estimated at 451 feet. John Kerr was later signed by the Phillies, but instead tried out unsuccessfully for the San Francisco Seals.[59]

Lai's team played a few games in his old Delaware County stomping grounds. In June, the *Chester Times* reported that local fans were anxious to see Lai and his "Hawaiian All-Stars" in action. Indeed, at least some of them planned a Buck Lai Day. The newspaper reminded readers that Lai was a standout semiprofessional a decade or so earlier in the area. It also warned that Lai would not play but insisted that fans would still enjoy watching the Hawaiians perform. It paid particular attention to infielder Lawrence Kunihisa, a fast "dwarf," and outfielder Francis Goo, who, the *Times* piece claimed, had the most talent of any of Lai's ballplayers. The *Times* advised, "If you hear the rumble of the rumba down at Sixth and Yarnell Streets this evening go into your dance and hie your carcass to that vicinity to get a load of the most colorful attraction in semipro baseball — the Hawaiians." On June 22, the *Times* good naturedly complained that after getting honored by Chester fans, Lai sent his team out to beat the local nine. John Kerr pitched the Hawaiians to a 2–1 victory over Chester in what the *Times* called the "fastest and best played ball game of the year." The Hawaiian ballplayers spent July 4 in Chester, losing to the local nine, 6–3. The *Chester Times* maintained that "sensational plays and lively maneuvers kept the game interesting." On August 25, "Buck Lai's Hawaiians" beat Chester before a small crowd of 800. The team from "wicky wacky," as the *Times* put it, was led by the pitching of Al Nalua and Dick Yamada, "the astonishing second sacker."[60]

Upon his return to the islands in 1936, the *Honolulu Star-Bulletin* tracked Lai's efforts to construct a nine that would successfully represent Hawai'i on the mainland. Readers were told that the "veteran Chinese athlete" arrived on the *Monterey* and planned on taking another "All Hawaii baseball team to invade the mainland this summer." Described as "the Chinese baseball figure," Lai had reportedly signed a number of players that had made the trek in 1935 but was hopeful of assembling a stronger team to represent Hawai'i. *Star-Bulletin* columnist Don Watson declared that Lai intended to lead his team on a trek through the U.S., Canada, Mexico, and perhaps Cuba. Watson maintained, "Last year's trip was very successful as far as getting publicity for the islands is concerned, although we would not go so far as to give the baseball tour as the reason for Honolulu hotels being crowded this tourist season." Nobody got rich off the 1935 tour, Watson insisted, but no money was lost. The proof of the tour's success was that many of the towns hosting Lai's team in 1935 wanted a return engagement in 1936.[61]

Yet the *Star-Bulletin* expressed disappointment with the team Lai led to the mainland in 1936. It declared, "Three of the boys Buck Lai had figured on going got into one jam or another and cheated themselves of the four and a half months' trip.... Buck isn't worried one bit. He'll play third himself if he fails to get representative players from the Pacific Coast." The team that departed for the mainland in May 1936, was, indeed, multiracial and multi-ethnic. It included catcher Kenichi Enomoto, Al Nalua, and Shipp Lo. The notable Japanese American player, Lawrence Kunihisa, was invited to head east but he was hurt and would have to join the team later.[62]

On May 24, 1936, the *Helena Independent* proclaimed that "Buck Lai's Hawaiian All-Stars" would meet the East Helena nine. The *Independent* asserted in the headlines that the visitors comprised a "Great Oriental Traveling Squad" that was "One of Game's Greatest Attractions." The *Independent* stated that in assembling his team Lai had not "confined himself to any particular nationality." Rather, "his team consists of a number of Chinese and Japanese, who will supply the fielding and running thrills expected of them by baseball fans." Japanese and Chinese players were "noted for their deceptive speed and agility" but were "not considered heavy hitters due to their short stature." To make up for this deficiency Lai had recruited six-foot Hawaiians, who could do the heavy hitting. All in all Lai had done a good job, the *Independent* insisted. Accordingly, "record crowds are expected wherever" Buck Lai's team went. Consequently, the daily urged readers to "come out and see baseball played with plenty of zip, dash, speed and color by Buck Lai's Hawaiian All-Stars direct from Honolulu, Hawaii."[63]

A few days later, the *Independent* published a publicity blurb on Lai's team. While it exaggerated, the fact was, as Helena baseball fans would find out, that Lai's team possessed some skill. In this promotional piece Lai was misleadingly described as a former "major leaguer." Perhaps less deceivingly, it claimed, "Like the chain of paradise isles, this outfit has everything—color, ability, and class. In a word, the all-Hawaii squad is simply the 'tops' in Hawaiian baseball and the player indeed is not worth mentioning who is not on it." Moreover, "the fates have been kind to the Chinese athlete who boasts of a career in the national pastime that few could equal" and that the 42-year-old native of Hawaii played like someone 15 years younger. The next day the *Independent* reported that "Buck Lai's Hawaiian All-Stars" handily won a game against East Helena, 13–2. In the process, "The Islanders played a snappy and interesting game." The "listless" East Helena nine simply could not handle "the little brown boys." The *Independent* added, "Buck Lai's boys were all they were advertised to be and possibly more. They were snappy, active little fellows and their actions showed they thoroughly understand this American game of baseball and could play it pretty well."[64]

Lai's team then trekked to the Midwest. In June 1936, Ohio's *Elyria Chronicle Telegram* announced an upcoming game between "Buck Lai's Hawaiians" and the Lorain Loyon Tailors. The paper declared that the contest would mark the first night game in Lorain's history. It told potential spectators they would not waste their time at the ball park, because "The Hawaiians ... boast what Honolulu sports writers agree is the most powerful team that has ever represented the Hawaiian Islands." Unfortunately, the game between Lai's nine and the Lorain Tailors was cancelled because Lai's truck carrying the lights got into an accident.[65]

As Buck Lai brought his team to Hartford, the *Hartford Courant* hailed the memory of the old Eastern League luminary. The Hawaiians were in town for a doubleheader against the Savitt Gems. The *Courant* maintained that a number of local fans recalled Buck as the slim, spry and graceful third baseman of the Bridgeport Eastern League club.[66]

In 1937, Lai and his ballplayers found themselves in a variety of smaller cities and towns on the American mainland. In an effort to drum up business, Tom Baird, described in the Texas *Big Spring Daily Herald* as business manager for Buck Lai's Hawaiian All-Stars, wrote small town newspapers around the mainland that the team consisted of "Hawaiians, Chinese, and Japs." Baird, a European American who also owned a chunk of the illustrious Kansas City Monarchs, claimed that the Hawaiian aggregation was financed by the territorial government and that Lai had played a year in the Southern Association and another for the New York Giants, while also managing the New York [sic] Bushwicks. Probably more accurately, Baird boasted that the team had traveled 4,000 miles in a bus purchased by the Hawaiian government. He advised that the players were willing to play at least part of the game in grass skirts and perform the hula.[67]

Oklahoma's *Ada Evening News* announced the coming of Lai's team, with a photograph of the veteran ballplayer and two of his players wearing hula skirts. The caption read, "They're baseball players — and hula dancers." A story published a few days later in the *Evening News* insisted that the Hawaiian ballplayers preferred cavorting around the ball field in hula skirts. The *Evening*

News admitted that for Ada's baseball fans the only problem with the Hawaiian ballplayers was that their names were hard to pronounce.[68]

In Ohio, the *Newark Advocate and American Tribune* publicized an upcoming game between Lai's team and the Richmer Oilers. The daily stated:

> Lai's team has achieved quite a record appearing against the country's leading professional and semipro clubs.... All are native Hawaiians and many, like Lai himself, are of Chinese ancestry. Their type of play reflects the Hawaiian trait of speed afoot, cleverness and a sense of showmanship to make up a colorful and interesting baseball attraction.

According to the *Advocate and Daily Tribune*, Lai's team had appeared in every state in the union and "everywhere they have been responsible for record turnouts and have managed to please fans with their clever baseball playing."[69]

At the end of June, "Buck Lai's Famous Hawaiians" were in Clearfield, Pennsylvania. A publicity blurb announced that Jackie Mitchell, a famed female ballplayer, would accompany Lai's contingent. It insisted that the team had been playing well — winning 75 percent of their games — and that Lai was "probably the best athlete to come out of the Pacific Islands." Not only were the Hawaiians talented ballplayers, but readers of the *Clearfield Progress* learned that they "made a big hit" wherever they went.[70]

In August 1937, the *Hammond Times* publicized a game at the Indiana city's Graselli Park between the East Chicago Giants and the Hawaiians. It pronounced the visitors the best team ever to journey from the Hawaiian Islands and Buck Lai a former major leaguer. And it made the astonishing claim that Lai's ballplayers were more comfortable performing in grass skirts than in regulation uniforms. "Feminine fans," indeed, would get new ideas about skirts by watching the Hawaiian ballplayers not only hit, run, and throw but perform the hula. As for the manager of the visiting team, the *Times* maintained that Buck Lai looked half his age and was faster than anyone on the team except for his son, Buck Lai, Jr., recruited for the 1937 trek.[71]

Lai's "Hawaiian All-Stars" did, in fact, perform at Dexter Park, although they did not make the Queens diamond their home away from home as Strong and Rosner had originally hoped. Moreover, while the Hawaiian barnstormers may have promoted the islands effectively on the mainland, there seemed to have been some stumbles along the way. In mid–May 1936, "Buck Lai's Hawaiian All-Stars" were scheduled to meet the Fresno Japanese Baseball Club at the latter's home grounds. This would have been an interesting game. The home team was managed by Kenichi Zenimura, who became a legend in Japanese California baseball after arriving in the Golden State from Hawai'i in the early 1920s. The nine he assembled was arguably one of the strongest in the Fresno area and would have given Lai's nine possibly more than it could handle. However, the Hawaiian contingent's arrival in California had been delayed and the game was unfortunately cancelled. The next year the failure of Lai's nine to show up in Douglas, Arizona, Carlsbad, New Mexico, and Lubbock, Texas, inspired anger and a threatened law suit.[72]

After the 1937 tour, Lai settled down to work and live on the East Coast, while keeping close to baseball. In 1939, Lai umpired in the Delaware County area, while reportedly serving as a scout for both the New York Yankees and the New York Giants and informing the local press that he counted baseball immortals Ty Cobb, Babe Ruth, Bill Terry, Tris Speaker and Connie Mack among his personal friends. In 1941, a *Chester Times* columnist interviewed Stan Jackson, one of Chester's foremost "Negro sportsmen." Jackson said that only two ballplayers had ever hit a home run out of Chester's local ball park. One was Negro League future Hall of Famer Judy Johnson. The other was Buck Lai. Nearing 50, Lai registered for the World War II draft. Lai's registration card informs us that he was living in Camden, New Jersey, in 1941. The 47-year-old Hawaiian was working at the time for the Cramp Ship Corporation in Philadelphia. He also managed a Camden-based semipro nine that trekked to Dexter Park to play the Bushwicks in August 1941.[73]

In January 1945, Washington Senators owner Clark Griffith signed Cuban infielder Manuel Hidalgo to a contract. This, in itself, was not unusual. Griffith had been interested in Latin American ballplayers for years as long as, of course, they appeared white. However, what made Hidalgo interesting was that he possessed Chinese ancestry. Thus, the press declared that he was the first ballplayer of Chinese ancestry to sign an organized baseball contract. A headline to an AP article published in the *Reno Evening Gazette* claimed, however, "The Giants Fielded First Chinaman." The article asserted that the New York Giants used "a Chinese utility infielder Buck Lai" for a few games about 20 years earlier. The *Gettysburg Compiler* also expressed some dissent on the matter. An article entitled "Chinese Star Once Played For Local 9" briefly explored the East Coast careers of Buck Lai and his teammate, Andy Yamashiro. Hagerstown sportswriter Frank Colley was quoted as pleading, "Give me a break" and insisting the Buck Lai had played a few games with the New York Giants. Culley, nevertheless, could not quite remember whether Lai was Chinese or Hawaiian but did remember that Lai had brought a basketball team of "Hawaiians" to Hagerstown. Furthermore, *The Sporting News* even claimed that Lai got into a couple of games for McGraw's nine.[74]

The signing of Hidalgo inspired the *Brooklyn Eagle*'s Harold C. Burr to devote an entire column to Buck Lai. Burr asserted that Pearl Buck should have written the column since she knew about a million Chinese, while he knew but his laundryman and Buck Lai, "a son of a dragon." Like Charlie Chan, Burr pointed out, Lai was a native of Honolulu, and just as Chan referred to his oldest son as "number one son," the title to Burr's piece referred to Lai as "No. 1 Boy." Recalling Lai's story with some accuracy, Burr wrote that the ballplayer went to Honolulu's McKinley High School, excelled in several sports, and arrived on the mainland with the "University of Hawaii" baseball team. This team, Burr maintained, was not only good but smart. While playing the University of Texas in one of its journeys to Lone Star State, they learned that the Texans had hired a Chinese person to sit on their bench and interpret the visitors' spoken signals to one another. However, the Travelers crossed the locals up by coaching in Hawaiian.[75]

While a member of the Travelers, the infielder was known as "Tin Lai," but changed his name to Bill when he settled down with an "Irish girl," Burr confided. Once ensconced on the mainland, Lai played for Bridgeport, where he supposedly groused to teammates, "I am more American than half you guys"— a complaint which Burr believed carried weight since the Americans had on their roster a "Mexican, an Italian, a Cuban, and an Irishman." Burr remembered that "Buck Lai could do almost as many things with a baseball as Ching Ling Foo with a bowl of goldfish." Likening Lai to the famous Chinese magician of the late nineteenth and early twentieth centuries, Burr maintained that the Chinese Hawaiian was "a magician in his own right in a pepper game and a big league fielder." But, Burr complained, there was little magic in Lai's bat. Perhaps his relative lack of heft was the problem. Lai was, according to Burr, only 158 pounds at most. Thus, major league teams like the Phillies and the Giants gave up on him. As for the White Sox, Burr insisted that Lai preferred not to give the South Side franchise a try. Still, Lai was "a good semipro and a good gate attraction."[76]

Buck Lai's son became a star college athlete at Long Island University, although he began his college life at Ursinus, where his athletic versatility stood out in baseball, basketball, and football. Aside from playing for his father's barnstorming team, Lai Jr. also played semipro ball in the Philadelphia area for the Lloyd Athletic Club nine, a team which often opposed top flight African American clubs. At Long Island University, according to a *Berkshire Evening Eagle* reporter, Buck Lai, Jr., starred as an outfielder and first baseman, in addition to playing forward in basketball.[77]

After serving as a Navy pilot in World War II, Lai Jr. distinguished himself as an educator, coach and athletic director at LIU. During LIU's great years as a basketball powerhouse in the late 1940s, Lai Jr. was an assistant coach to Clair Bee, one of the most notable basketball coaches of the time. LIU's basketball program faced permanent extinction after the point-shaving scandals of 1951. In 1952, Lai Jr. was named as athletic director to succeed Bee. Subsequently, Lai Jr. nurtured the basketball program back to life in the mid–1950s, while also coaching baseball. In 2000, Lai Jr. was recognized for his contributions to LIU when he was named to the university's Hall of Fame.

He also worked with the Brooklyn Dodgers organization as scout and coach, in addition to writing two much-read instructional books on baseball and basketball.[78]

After World War II, the *Brooklyn Eagle* announced Buck Lai's Jr.'s return to his alma mater as a freshman basketball coach and baseball coach. In so doing, it recalled his father, "the lithe and nimble third baseman" who played for the Bushwicks. Described as a "likeable chap" and "sturdier and stockier" than his father, Buck Lai, Jr., had excelled in baseball while competing for the Pensacola Naval Air Station nine. He not only batted .406 but attracted the interest of the New York Yankees. Meanwhile, he married Brooklyn native Mary Maneri, who had begun her long and honored stint as LIU's bursar.[79]

The LIU coach did not shield himself from his ethnic background. In 1950, the *Eagle*'s Jimmy Murphy wrote approvingly of a Chinese American youth baseball team competing in Brooklyn. The journalist proclaimed that Buck Lai, Jr., would throw out the ball at the first game this team would play in May. Murphy described the LIU coach as an "oriental whose dad ... originally came here as a member of the Hawaiian University nine."[80]

Ten years after Harold Burr wrote about his father, he devoted a column to Buck Lai, Jr., Burr asserted that the LIU graduate had wanted to follow his father into professional baseball, but World War II got in his way. According to the *Eagle* columnist, Lai, Sr. had played for not only the New York Giants but the Cincinnati Redlegs. This was not only thing the column had wrong as it asserted as well that Buck Lai, Jr., was born on the Hawaiian Islands, but had journeyed to the East Coast as a child. Since then "he has been thoroughly Americanized and bears the good old baptismal name of Bill."[81]

Meanwhile, Buck Lai, Sr. was not totally forgotten. In 1952, the *Berkshire Evening Eagle* showed a photo of Lai Jr. with a team called the "Brooklyn Stars of Tomorrow"—-a team of young New York City ballplayers scheduled to take on a nine from Berkshire. Interestingly, the *Evening Eagle*'s John Flynn displayed some confusion as to which Buck Lai was coming to town with the young Dodgers. Flynn had told readers that the Dodgers coach and scout was the Buck Lai who had played in the Eastern League and that "he was one of the few Hawaiians to ever play in organized ball." Buck Lai, Jr., straightened Kelly out, explaining to the sports columnist that his father suited up for Bridgeport and was presently coaching a semiprofessional team in Audubon, New Jersey.[82]

In 1956, sportswriter Roger O'Gara sighted Buck Lai, Sr. at the World Series, pitting the Brooklyn Dodgers against the New York Yankees. He wrote, "William T. (Buck) Lai, the Chinese-American third baseman whose fielding exploits thrilled Eastern League fans in 1919 and 1920 is attending the Series."

To O'Gara, Lai looked younger than his 50 years. Actually over 60, Lai told O'Gara that he worked for a shipbuilding business in Audubon and also served as a part-time scout for the Dodgers. Delaware County baseball fans with a long memory recalled Lai as a great semiprofessional ballplayer in the area. The small city of Chester honored him with membership in its Sports Hall of Fame.[83]

After his death in 1976, Lai's identity and career were still subject to confusion. A *Sporting News* obituary claimed he was the first person of Chinese ancestry to play major league baseball. More recently an on-line biography maintained that he was descended from "mostly European ancestry." More importantly, however, his daughter-in-law remembered him as a kind and gentle man.[84]

Epilogue

The respected anthropologist, Clifford Geertz, asserted that culture is a story people tell themselves about themselves and then, one assumes, to anthropologists. In that spirit, Hawaiian local culture has been constructed significantly by the "talk stories" locals tell one another. To a hard and fast social scientist such stories are distressingly subjective. Yet assembled together, they capture something important about the people who produce them.[1]

Since the Travelers left relatively little in the way of how they perceived their experiences, this book has counted on the impressions of others — mostly newspaper accounts written by and for European American mainlanders. Still, the Hawaiians' on-field performances tell all sorts of interesting stories. For one thing, they were very good baseball players — not generally on the level of major league nines or elite black teams but very good. After all, from 1912 to 1916 they averaged well over 100 games a season on the American mainland. Never the home team, they were always on the road, often bustling from one small town in the middle of Pennsylvania or Ohio to the next. Yet they won most of the time, defeating top-notch college and semipro nines. They were even capable of beating strong African American nines such as the Lincoln Giants.

Without the constant tutelage of baseball geniuses such as John McGraw, Connie Mack or Rube Foster, the Travelers learned to master what experts of the National Pastime at the time called "inside baseball." Considered the best way to score runs in pre–Ruthian times, "inside ball" concentrated on getting runners on base through well-placed hits, bunts, or bases on balls. Then the utilization of tactics such as the sacrifice bunt and aggressive baserunning would score runs. Trying to slug home runs 90 years ago typically proved futile. Rarely discarded by umpires, the balls were "dead"— often loaded up with dirt and saliva, while emery boards, human nails and prior contact with assorted bats defaced them. Moreover, it was the rare elite ballplayer who possessed the weight and muscle to even conceivably whack balls over the outfielders' heads. Generally smaller than their mainland counterparts, but not as small as they were often described in the press, the Travelers were smart enough to emphasize speed and wit to tally scores.

The Hawaiians were usually good at keeping the other team from scoring. It began, as it usually does in baseball, with exceptional pitching. Apau Kau and Foster Robinson, in particular, pitched well, sometimes dominantly. However, Luck Yee, Hoon Ki, Luther Kekoa, Fred Swan, and George Bush more often than not held their own. Exceptional pitching, however, usually means fine defense. And the Travelers were credited as excellent and even spectacular fielders. Kan Yen Chun and Fred Markham seemed to have been first-rate catchers. Vernon Ayau and Chinito Moriyama forged a dynamic double-play combination. Moreover, Ayau's work at shortstop often inspired awe from observers. Lai, it seems, may not have been the most consistent of fielders, but possessed athleticism capable of making stunning plays at the perilous position of third base. In the outfield, the Travelers could usually call on the services of swift outfielders such as En Sue Pung and Lang Akana.

The interest mainland organized and independent teams had in individual Travelers speaks to the genuine skills the team displayed. While no Traveler played in any official major league games, at least Buck Lai came tantalizingly close. Still Lai played for several years on the mainland, with and against some of the finest big league and African American ballplayers of the interwar era. Former teammates such as Andy Yamashiro, Fred Markham, and Vernon Ayau also competed with talented mainland professionals, only for a shorter length of time. Moreover, mainland professional franchises sought or considered seeking skilled ballplayers such as Lang Akana, Kan Yen Chun, En Sue Pung and Foster Robinson. Race and ethnicity posed a bar to their advancement up organized baseball's ladder, but how sturdy a bar is debatable. It seems apparent that none of the Travelers could have achieved major league stardom even if racism were somehow erased from the picture. One could imagine Buck Lai or Vernon Ayau as useful utility infielders for some big league club, but probably little more. Thus, while organized baseball was clearly more open to employing former Travelers than African American ballplayers, one cannot help but wonder why Lai's and Ayau's names never appeared in an official major league baseball box score.

Yet the fact that no Traveler has been enshrined in the National Baseball Hall of Fame should not detract from the commanding way in which the Hawaiian ballplayers asserted their agency on hundreds of baseball diamonds. The Hawaiian ballplayers apparently understood very well how people of Asian Pacific ancestry were perceived by mainlanders in the 1910s. Either out of generosity or naiveté, the Travelers seemingly regarded mainlanders as more

It seemed important to many of the Travelers that they be seen as not really all that different from young, middle-class American men. Duded up and ready for a drive are Luther Kekoa at the driver's seat, and in the back, from left to right, Vernon Ayau, Lai Tin, and Jimmy Aylett (courtesy of the Yamashiro Family).

influenced by ignorance than nastiness. Yet the Travelers were comparatively well-educated young men, possessing secondary and post-secondary school education. They knew, for one thing, that in the U.S., anti–Asian national, state, and local laws were largely supported by American voters. They knew, for another, that U.S. immigration and naturalization systematically worked against Asian immigrants. They knew, that is, that the only thing allowing them to step foot on the U.S. mainland was their Hawaiian birth — that their parents, if born in China or Japan, would be turned away if they could not document their ownership of private productive property or professional status. They knew that if their parents possessed Chinese or Japanese nativity, their social class would make no difference when it came to citizenship. In other words, Chinese and Japanese born people were regarded by the U.S. legal system as "aliens ineligible for citizenship." As such, they were denied the ability to farm land in states like California after 1913. Furthermore, states like California had prominently enacted anti-miscegenation laws directly aimed at preventing young men and women such as Buck Lai and the white woman he loved, Isabelle Reynolds, from getting married.

The Travelers read the local press around the mainland. They read the publicity blurbs, probably often originating from their own promoters. They knew that they were often presented as typical American young men, chanting team cheers, complaining occasionally about umpires, riding the opposition, and playing ragtime music. Understanding that team promoters and the mainland press were complicit in the matter, they read they were Chinese even though none of them were born in China and many, especially after 1913, possessed no Chinese ancestry. They also read accounts which insisted upon their foreignness, seemingly more bemused than disturbed by headlines referring to their "invasion" of America. They read of the surprise of mainlanders who did not expect the Travelers to play so well. It was not always clear why these spectators were surprised. Was it because the Travelers were colonial subjects? Was it because they were considered non-white? Was it because they were considered foreigners? Was it because they were considered Chinese? In any event, the Travelers could be forgiven for thinking that many mainlanders believed that baseball, like the U.S. itself, belonged to white Americans. They could be more than forgiven but lauded for entertaining, as did En Sue Pung, a desire to show up the mainland haoles — to convince them that baseball's ownership was in doubt. In the process, the Travelers perhaps chipped away at white America's confidence in its power over the United States and its empire.

While seemingly reconciled to their imposed Chinese identity, the Travelers and their promoters sought to remind mainlanders of their Hawaiian origins. Press accounts published in the *San Jose Mercury* and elsewhere may have originated in the creative minds of the Travelers' promoters. These accounts emphasized that the Hawaiian ballplayers were "Uncle Sam's" children, learning the game from American military personnel and helpful American mentors such as John McGraw. Thus, mainlanders were comforted that there was no shame in their teams losing to the Travelers since the Hawaiians owed their command of baseball to benevolent American tutelage.

Hawaiian commercial interests also expected the Travelers to "boost" Hawai'i to mainlanders with enough discretionary income to spend money on the islands as investors or tourists. In doing so, the Travelers lugged around promotional literature and entertained mainlanders with Hawaiian music. Like Duke Kahanamoku and the Hawaiian musicians that traveled the mainland in the 1910s and 1920s, they were supposed to offer a friendly face to mainlanders —-assure mainland haoles that if they came to the islands they could expect a warm greeting from dark-skinned people who would not try to cook them for supper or lure them into opium dens. There is little evidence that the Travelers resented their promotional work, although it is likely that En Sue Pung was not alone in his irritation with mainlanders' ignorance of their homeland. They knew very well that they were more than just athletic competitors but entertainers who, as it turned out, bridged the relatively parochial economic needs of the Hawaiian Islands and the broader requirements of American consumer capitalism.

The Travelers represented an ambiguous relationship to China and the Chinese diaspora, a relationship made murkier by the fact that only the 1912 team was "all-Chinese." Honolulu's Chinese community was hopeful that at least in 1912 and 1913 the Travelers would bring prestige to not only the Hawaiian Chinese but at least non-laboring class Chinese throughout the American Empire. As vibrant, living symbols of the Chinese diaspora, they were often as well bound to the turmoil enveloping China in the early part of the twentieth century. Many saw the Travelers and at least some of the Travelers saw themselves as hopeful signifiers of China's struggling new republic. Yet the Travelers, even Chinese Hawaiian Travelers, represented themselves as Hawaiians — as "locals" who were also, by the way, seemingly unabashed U.S. citizens.

The relevance of C.L.R. James' *Beyond a Boundary* is contestable but noteworthy. A canonical work in Sport Studies, *Beyond a Boundary* disputed the notion that black West Indians embraced cricket out of general deference toward their white Anglo colonizers. Rather, they saw in cricket an opportunity to express their agency by demonstrating their equality and even superiority to white players. While there is no evidence that the Travelers were distressed by American rule over the Hawaiian Islands, one catches glimpses of them enjoying victory not just because they won but because they defeated the kind of haoles that had colonized and ruled the islands.[2]

Accordingly, it seems difficult to apply uncritical notions of globalization to the genesis of Hawaiian baseball in general and the experiences of the Travelers in particular. Influenced by theorist Roland Robertson, historian Andrew D. Morris expresses a preference for the freshly minted, scholarly term, "glocalization" to describe what Robertson called both the "universalizing and particularizing tendencies" within the global movement of culture. Focusing on the development of baseball in Taiwan and admitting that "glocalization" does not exactly "roll off the tongue," Morris writes, "This dual nature of globalization often escapes analyses that can tend to focus on one-sided models of cultural contact, like the famed notion of 'Cocacolonization,' which describes a simple imprint of American ways on vulnerable Others." In other words, the Travelers may have symbolized the global reach of America's National Pastime in the early twentieth century, but, if so, they did so clearly on their own terms.[3]

Significantly, the Travelers were relatively privileged young men on the islands. While their economic backgrounds were generally hardly elite, their families were well enough off to allow them to attend secondary and post-secondary schools. Rather than help their families out extensively in the shop or on the plantation, they found time not only to become excellent baseball players but to compete in other organized sports such as American football, soccer, and track and field for secondary and post-secondary schools such as

McKinley High School, Punahou, St. Louis, and the College of Hawai'i. By and large, their post–Traveler careers saw these men in white collar jobs and, as in the case of Andy Yamashiro and Lang Akana, positions of some political influence.

While not exactly working class heroes, the Travelers disclosed an ambivalent tale about their own responses to racial relations on the island and the mainland. Beginning as a team comprised in its entirety of young men possessing Chinese ancestry, the Travelers developed into a lively multiethnic, multiracial character. We know that the Travelers did not always get along with one another. However, tensions did not seem to break down along racial/ethnic divisions. Significantly, the Travelers who remained on the East Coast into the 1920s, lived in relative close proximity to one another and often played on the same team were not only Chinese Hawaiians such as Buck Lai, Vernon Ayau, and Apau Kau but also Nisei Andrew Yamashiro and hapa haole Fred Markham.

Still, before we start to celebrate the Travelers as forming a vanguard of racial harmony, we should observe their edgy relations with African American ballplayers. The rivalry between Chinese Hawaiian ballplayers such as Albert Akana and the 25th regiment nine was marked by tension, perhaps comprehensible given the fact that the African American ball club invariably tangled with the Chinese Hawaiians for baseball supremacy on Oahu. We should also note that they continued to play against one another and that after the Chinese Hawaiians refused to take on the Lincoln Giants in 1912, they were willing to schedule black nines in subsequent years. A cynic might reasonably argue that gate money spurred the Travelers into sharing a baseball diamond with African Americans rather than interracial camaraderie. To be fair, however, virulent racism has often easily overlooked the lure of profit. Thus, the Travelers perhaps deserve some kind of credit for their willingness to take on African American opponents.

The Travelers perhaps also merit attention as cultural carriers and perhaps even creators. Interdisciplinary academic and non-academic scholars in recent years have written extensively about the portability of culture and how places such as baseball fields and dance halls can emerge as global, cultural encounter zones where people possessing varied cultural backgrounds interact. For example, during the early decades of the twentieth century, Hawaiian musicians, dancers, and athletes made their way to the mainland. They shaped and were shaped by their encounters. Mainland popular music, for example, was transformed by the adoption of the Hawaiian steel guitar. Traveling Hawaiian athletes such as the hapa haole George Freeth and Duke Kahanamoku introduced surfing to the mainland, while altering the way mainland aqua athletes played water polo and swam competitively.[4]

The Travelers carried with them to the mainland not only their love of baseball but also their musical prowess. In 1915 Hawaiian musicians and dancers at the Pan-Pacific Exposition in San Francisco helped make Hawaiian music a fad on the mainland. Hawaiian musicians had appeared on the mainland before. As a young man, the great African American entertainer Bert Williams performed in a Hawaiian musical group in San Francisco in the early 1890s. Indeed, the Travelers entertained mainlanders with Hawaiian music on the mainland in 1912 and afterwards. Moreover, the team's first manager, Robert Yap, in addition to pitchers Apau Kau and especially Luther Kekoa, made money performing Hawaiian music on the mainland. Thus it seems reasonable to credit the Travelers with some responsibility for altering popular musical trends on the mainland by way of instruments such as the ukulele and steel guitar as well as traditionally based singing styles.[5]

In the realm of what took place on the countless baseball fields on which the Travelers cavorted over the years, there surfaces something interesting out of the interaction between the Travelers and various African American nines. Through shadow ball or pantomiming the game of baseball, African American ballplayers entertained millions of black and white baseball fans between the world wars. However, the Travelers performed shadow ball on mainland baseball diamonds before World War I. Perhaps they picked up the baseball pantomime from African American ballplayers. Perhaps their engaging antics inspired African American teams to take up shadow ball. In any event, the Travelers' passion for shadow ball seems to blur the hard and fast racial categories that many of us today assume existed 90 years ago.

The subject of shadow ball, that is, should stress the futility of thinking about the globalization of sports such as baseball in anything but a complicated way. The baseball played by the Travelers was a product of the global movement of the sport throughout much of the Pacific Rim in the late nineteenth century. But how the Travelers performed "America's National Game" could well have influenced the way it was played by mainlanders.

Moreover, the Travelers' tales evoke the possibility that for all of its problems, baseball 90 years or so ago might have been more fun than it is today. The experiences of the Travelers and barnstorming black teams should remind us that baseball in contradictory, ragtime America could stand out as gut-wrenchingly vicious. But it also harbored democratic features that today's structured, hierarchical game lacks.

When Major League Baseball suffered through a players' strike in the 1990s, pundits seriously predicted the end of baseball if labor and management did not bargain more seriously. Were MLB's cultural roots so weakly democratic that baseball would cease in America if Barry Bonds and George Steinbrenner could not make millions upon millions of dollars out of the game?

If Fenway Park stood silent would Americans toss away their baseball gloves and balls? Perhaps so, since so many of us then and now look at sports as an elitist enterprise — that what legitimizes a sport is its ability to showcase highly paid athletes who can do things the vast majority of us cannot do.

In 1913, baseball was different. Very clearly, it abetted the very undemocratic rise of hierarchies throughout early twentieth century American empire. Just as relevant, through baseball Americans could justify and augment racial formation; so-called Orientals were inherently distinct from so-called Occidentals. However, baseball in 1913 might surprise in its ability to push people across treacherous cultural borderlands. Generally getting along, people of divergent cultural backgrounds played with one another on the Travelers. At other times and on other teams, individual Travelers played with and against African Americans and European Americans on the islands and the mainland. Moreover, the vast assortment of teams the Travelers opposed on the mainland reveal that Americans did not need Ty Cobb or the young Babe Ruth around to enjoy baseball as a participatory and spectator sport. In Pennsylvania, for example, every town seemed to have at least one baseball team. In Philadelphia, neighborhoods, religious organizations, stores, and industries formed baseball teams with stunning prodigality. Would anyone seriously have predicted then that the game would end if Joe Jackson or Tris Speaker laid down their bats and went on strike?[6]

In the end, it is hard to say if the existence and on-field effectiveness of the Travelers changed all that much. In fact, one of the most interesting and paradoxical revelations to come out of their experiences is how few stereotypes about Asian Pacific people were effectively weakened. To be sure, there might have been days when what scholar Elaine Kim has called "racism's traveling eye" might not have been able to catch up to the swift Travelers as they stole bases and raced to catch hot liners. But the Travelers, however, were not really fleet enough. The pernicious anti–Asian laws remained on the books for years after their last tour ended in 1916. For decades, moreover, Hawai'i was considered too non-white to attain statehood, although the Travelers, in a small way, helped to turn it into a profitable mecca for haole tourists. Meanwhile, Americans of Asian Pacific ancestry, regardless of generation and place of residence, would find themselves too often treated by often well-intentioned, non–Asian Pacific Americans and American institutions, as unnecessary, unwelcome travelers to American shores.[7]

Notes

Preface

1. Dorothy Seymour Mills and Harold Seymour, *Baseball: The People's Game* (New York: Oxford University Press, 1991).

Introduction

1. *Bennington Evening Banner*, 26 July 1912.
2. *Ibid.*
3. *Ibid.*
4. *Ibid.*
5. *Ibid.*
6. *Ibid.*
7. *Ibid.*
8. *Ibid.*
9. *Ibid.*
10. *The Chinese Students' Monthly*, 10 June 1913.
11. *Ibid.*
12. *Ibid.*
13. *Ibid.*
14. *Ibid.*
15. *Ibid.*
16. *Ibid.*
17. *Ibid.*
18. Ronald Takaki, *Strangers from a Different Shore: A History of Asian Americans* (Boston: Little, Brown, 1989); Gary Y. Okihiro, *Island World: A History of Hawai'i and the United States* (Berkeley: University of California Press, 2008); Sally Engle Merry, *Colonizing Hawai'i: The Cultural Power of Law* (Princeton, NJ: Princeton University Press, 2000); Elizabeth Buck, *Paradise Remade: Politics of Culture and History in Hawai'i* (Philadelphia: Temple University Press, 1993).
19. *Honolulu Advertiser*, 4 April 1964.
20. Michael Omi and Howard Winant, *Racial Formation in the United States: From the 1960s to the 1990s*, 2d ed. (New York: Routledge, 1994), 55–56.
21. Benedict Anderson, *Invented Communities: Reflections on the Origins and Spread of Nationalism* (London: Verso, 1983).
22. Takaki, *Strangers*, Chapter Four.
23. *Ibid.*
24. *Ibid.*; Gary Okihiro, *Island World*; *Pineapple Culture: A History of the Tropical and Temperate Zones* (Berkeley: University of California Press, 2009), 93–109.
25. Takaki, *Strangers*, Chapter Four.
26. *Ibid.*
27. Warren Sussman, *Culture as History* (New York: Pantheon Books, 1984).
28. Alan Trachtenberg, *The Incorporation of America: Culture and Society in the Gilded Age* (New York: Hill and Wang, 1982); Roy Rosenzweig, *Eight Hours for What We Will: Workers and Leisure in an Industrial City, 1870–1920* (Cambridge: Cambridge University Press, 1983); Kathy Peiss, *Cheap Amusements: Working Women and Leisure in Turn-of-the-Century New York* (Philadelphia: Temple University Press, 1986); Lizabeth Cohen, *Making a New Deal: Industrial Workers in Chicago* (Cambridge: Cambridge University Press, 1990).
29. Michael Oriard, *Reading Football: How the Popular Press Created an American Spectacle* (Chapel Hill: University of North Carolina Press, 1998).
30. Harold Seymour, *Baseball: The Early Years* (New York: Oxford University Press, 1960); David Voigt, *American Baseball. Vol. 1: From Gentlemen's Sport to the Commissioner System* (University Park: Penn State University Press, 1979).
31. Okihiro, *Pineapple Culture*.
32. Joel S. Franks, *Hawaiian Sports in the Twentieth Century* (Lewiston, ME: Edwin Mellen Press, 2003), 40–44.
33. Michael Rogin, *Black Face, White Noise: Jewish Immigrants in the Hollywood Melting Pot* (Berkeley: University of California Press, 1996); Camille F. Forbes, *Introducing Bert Williams: Burnt Cork, Broadway, and the Story of America's*

First Black Star (New York: Basic Civitas Books, 2008).
34. Peter Levine, *From Ellis Island to Ebbets Field: Sport and the American Jewish Experience* (New York: Oxford University Press, 1992), 144.
35. Edward Said, *Orientalism* (New York: Vintage Press, 1979).
36. John Kuo Wei Tchen, *New York Before Chinatown: Orientalism and the Shaping of American Culture, 1776–1882* (Baltimore: Johns Hopkins University Press, 1999), 142–145.
37. Robert G. Lee, *Orientals: Asian Americans in Popular Culture* (Philadelphia: Temple University Press, 1999); Darrell Y. Hamamoto, *Monitored Peril: Asian Americans and the Politics of TV Representation* (Minneapolis: University of Minnesota Press, 1994).
38. Takaki, *Strangers*; Alexander Saxton, *The Indispensable Enemy: Labor and the Anti-Chinese Movement in California* (Berkeley: University of California Press, 1971); Tomás Almaguer, *Racial Fault Lines: The Historical Supremacy of White Supremacy in California* (Berkeley: University of California Press, 1994).
39. *Ibid.*; Lee, *Orientalism*; Sucheng Chan, *This Bittersweet Soil: The Chinese in California Agriculture* (Berkeley: University of California Press, 1986).
40. Takaki, *Strangers*, Chapter Three; Charles McClain, *In Search of Equality: The Chinese Struggle against Discrimination in Nineteenth-Century America* (Berkeley: University of California Press, 1996); Ian Haney Lopez, *White By Law: The Legal Construction of Race* (New York: New York University Press, 1996); Andrew Gyorgy, *Race, Politics, and the Chinese Exclusion Act* (Chapel Hill: University of North Carolina Press, 1998); Jean Pfaelzer, *Driven Out: The Forgotten War Against Chinese Americans* (New York: Random House, 2007).
41. *Ibid.*
42. Takaki, *Strangers*, Chapter Five.
43. Elizabeth Buck, *Paradise Remade*; Sperry, *Colonizing Hawai'i*; Jon Kamakawiwo'ole Osorio, *Dismembering Lahui: A History of the Hawaiian Nation to 1887* (Honolulu: University of Hawai'i Press, 2002); Christopher Benfrey, "Herman Melville and John Manjiro: Toward a Wave-Theory of the Pacific," *Common-Place* V (January 2005), www.common-place.org.; Noenoe Silva, *Aloha Betrayed: Native Hawaiian Resistance to American Colonialism* (Durham, NC: Duke University Press, 2004); Gary Okihiro, *Island World*.
44. Osorio, *Dismembering*.
45. *Ibid.*
46. *Ibid.*
47. Silva, *Aloha Betrayed*.
48. *Ibid.*
49. Okihiro, *Island World*.
50. Okihiro, *Island World*, 185–186; Robert Rydell, *All the World's a Fair: Visions of Empire at American International Expositions, 1876–1916* (Chicago: University of Chicago Press, 1987); Eric Hobsbawm, *The Age of Empire* (New York: Vintage, 1989).
51. Sally Jenkins, *The Real All-Americans: The Team That Changed a Game, a People, a Nation* (New York: Doubleday, 2007).
52. Randy Roberts, *Papa Jack: Jack Johnson and The Era of White Hopes* (New York: Free Press, 1985).

Chapter One

1. Chan, *Asian Americans*, 56–57.
2. *Ibid.*
3. Joseph Reaves, *Taking in a Game: A History of Baseball in Asia* (Lincoln: University of Nebraska Press), 38–40; www.hml.org, accessed March 31, 2003.
4. *Honolulu Independent*, 5 September 5, 1905; *Pacific Commercial Advertiser*, 6 May 1906, 8 May 1906, 14 May 1906, 18 May 1906, 19 May 1906; *Honolulu Star-Bulletin*, 15 April 1916.
5. *Pacific Commercial Advertiser*, 26 September 1906.
6. *New York Tribune*, 25 February 1906; *Sporting Life*, 27 July 1907; *Decatur Review*, 8 June 1907, 19 September 1910, p. 4; *Washington Post*, 12 October 1907; *Reno Evening Gazette*, 21 October 1907.
7. *San José Mercury*, 4 August 1908, 13 August 1908; *Philadelphia Inquirer*, 19 February 1908; *Washington Post*, 17 March 1908; *Los Angeles Times*, 22 March 1908; *San Francisco Call*, 17 February 1909.
8. *Washington Post*, 27 July 1911.
9. Cited in *Portsmouth Herald*, 28 September 1911; *Washington Post*, 22 December 1911; *Los Angeles Times*, 22 December 1911.
10. *Baseball Magazine*, January 1914, 17; Mark Dyreson, *Making the American Team: Sport, Culture and the Olympic Experience* (Urbana: University of Illinois Press, 1998), 54.
11. *San Francisco Call*, 19 October 1906; *Washington Post*, 27 December 1906; United States Census Bureau, Manuscript Census Schedules of the City and County of Honolulu, 1930.
12. *Sporting Life*, 29 August 1907; *Washington Post*, 4 September 1907, 8 September 1907.
13. *Sporting Life*, 11 November 1911; Joel S. Franks, *Asian Pacific Americans and Baseball: A History* (Jefferson, NC: McFarland, 2008).
14. Herbert Lowery, "The Honolulu Trip," *Sporting Life*, 15 February 1908.
15. *Atlanta Constitution*, 19 March 1908.
16. *Portland Oregonian*, 15 March 1908.
17. U.S. Census Bureau, Manuscript Census Schedules of the City and County of Honolulu, 1930; John E. Spalding, *Sacramento Senators and*

Solons (Manhattan, KS: Ag Press, 1995), 25; *Sacramento Bee*, 1 April 1912, 10; 4 April 1912, 12.
  18. *San Francisco Chronicle*, 1 July 1915; *Pacific Commercial Advertiser*, 26 March 1914, 8.
  19. *Fort Wayne News*, 30 May 1914.
  20. Franks, *Asian Pacific Americans*, 30–31.
  21. *Washington Post*, 29 October 1905; Mills and Seymour, *People*, 169.
  22. Spalding, *America's National Game*, 396; Joel S. Franks, *Whose Baseball: The National Pastime and Cultural Diversity in California, 1859–1941* (Lanham, MD: Scarecrow Books, 2001); Mills and Seymour, *People*, 169.
  23. *Daily Palo Alto*, 19 April 1911.
  24. *Hawaiian Star*, 19 March 1912.
  25. *Pacific Commercial Advertiser*, 12 June 1911.
  26. *Ibid.*, 3 July 1911.
  27. *Ibid.*, 12 June 1911, 3 July 1911, 12 July 1911.
  28. *Ibid.*, 13 July 1911, 18 July 1911.
  29. *Ibid.*, 20 July 1911.
  30. *Ibid.*, 21 July 1911, 23 July 1911.
  31. *Ibid.*, 10 August 1911.
  32. *Ibid.*, 15 January 1912, 27 January 1912.
  33. *Ibid.*, 14 February 1912.
  34. *Ibid.*, 16 February 1912.
  35. *Ibid.*, 14 February 1912, 29 February 1912; United States Census Bureau, Manuscript Schedules, County of Cook and City of Chicago, 1910.
  36. *Hawaiian Star*, 4 March 1912, 5 March 1912, 13 March 1912, 19 March 1912.
  37. *Ibid.*, 5 March 1912.
  38. *Ibid.*, 13 March 1912.
  39. *Pacific Commercial Advertiser*, 15 March 1912.
  40. *Ibid.*, 19 March 1912.
  41. *Ibid.*
  42. *Hawaiian Star*, 20 March 1912.
  43. *Boston Daily Globe*, 4 March 1912.
  44. *Baseball Magazine*, April 1912.
  45. *Hawaiian Star*, 2 April 1912.
  46. *Sporting Life*, 16 March 1912, 6 April 1912; *South Carolina State*, 16 March 1912.
  47. *Sporting Life*, 13 April 1912.
  48. *San Francisco Call*, 28 March 1912.
  49. *Ibid.*, 29 March 1912, 1 April 1912.
  50. *Sacramento Bee*, 5 April 1912, 6 April 1912.
  51. *San Francisco Examiner*, 2 April 1912; *San Francisco Chronicle*, 2 April 1912.
  52. *San Francisco Call*, 2 April 1912.
  53. *Los Angeles Times*, 9 April 1912; *Oakland Tribune*, 2 April 1912; *San Francisco Chronicle*, 7 April 1912.
  54. *Pacific Commercial Advertiser*, 16 April 1912.
  55. *Ibid.*, 11 April 1912.
  56. *Ibid.*, 15 April 1912.
  57. *Ibid.*, 16 April 1912; 18 April 1912.
  58. *Salt Lake Herald Republican*, 11 April 1912, 13 April 1912.

  59. *Salt Lake Evening Telegram*, 12 April 12 1912.
  60. *Salt Lake Herald Republican*, 14 April 1912; *Pacific Commercial Advertiser*, 24 April 1912.
  61. *Pacific Commercial Advertiser*, 2 May 1912.
  62. *Sporting Life*, 27 April 1912, 11 May 1912.
  63. *Chicago Tribune*, 24 April 1912, 25 April 1912.
  64. *Daily Commonwealth*, 3 May 1912; *Sporting Life*, 4 May 1912; *Washington Post*, 25 April 1912; *Pacific Commercial Advertiser*, 14 May 1912.
  65. *Pacific Commercial Advertiser*, 15 May 1912.
  66. *Ibid.*, 17 May 1912.
  67. *Washington Post*, 3 May 1912, 13 May 1912, 14 May 1912.
  68. *Ibid.*, 14 May 1912.
  69. *Ibid.*, 15 May 1912.
  70. *Pacific Commercial Advertiser*, 30 May 1912.
  71. *New York Times*, 17 May 1912, 22 May 1912.
  72. *Sporting Life*, 1 June 1912; *New York Times*, 23 May 1912.
  73. *New York Times*, 23 May 1912.
  74. *New York Sun*, 22 May 1912.
  75. *Ibid.*, 27 May 1912; *Brooklyn Eagle*, 27 May 1912.
  76. *New York Sun*, 25 May 1912, *Pacific Commercial Advertiser*, 8 June 1912.
  77. *Newark News*, 23 May 1912.
  78. Newspaper Clippings, Special Collections, Seton Hall University.
  79. *Newark News*, 25 May 1912.
  80. *Ibid.*
  81. *Ibid.*
  82. *Syracuse Daily Journal*, 28 May 1912; *Syracuse Herald*, 30 May 1912.
  83. *Pacific Commercial Advertiser*, 8 June 1912.
  84. *Idaho Daily Statesman*, 2 June 1912.
  85. *Lexington Herald*, 6 June 1912.
  86. *Auburn Citizen*, 6 June 1912, 14 June 1912.
  87. *Ibid.*, 14 June 1912.
  88. *Ibid.*
  89. *Middletown Daily-Times Press*, 22 June 1912, 25 June 1912.
  90. *New London Day*, 21 June 1912; *Sheboygan Press*, 9 July 1912.
  91. *Honolulu Star-Bulletin*, 13 July 1912.
  92. *Ibid.*, 22 July 1912.
  93. *Amsterdam Evening Recorder*, 25 July 1912, 29 July 1912.
  94. *Honolulu Star-Bulletin*, 7 August 1912.
  95. *Sporting Life*, 3 August 1912.
  96. *The Decatur Review*, 29 July 1912, 5; Neil Lanctot, *Fair Dealing and Clean Playing: The Hilldale Club and the Development of Black Professional Baseball, 1910–1932* (Syracuse: Syracuse University Press, 2007), 39–42.
  97. *Sporting Life*, 24 August 1912.
  98. *Cleveland Plain-Dealer*, 19 August 1912.
  99. *Ibid.*

100. *Ibid.*
101. *Ibid.*
102. *Elyria Evening Telegram*, 17 August 1912, 19 August 1912.
103. *Fort Wayne News*, 23 August 1912; *Kalamazoo News*, 23 August 1912.
104. *Marshall Evening Chronicle*, 7 September 1912.
105. *Pacific Commercial Advertiser*, 3 October 1912; *Colorado Springs Gazette*, 20 September 1912.
106. *Pacific Commercial Advertiser*, 19 September 1912.
107. *Ibid.*, 16 April 1912; *Honolulu Advertiser*, 4 April 1964.
108. Jules Tygiel, *Past Time* (New York: Oxford University Press, 2000), 132; Lanctot, *Fair Dealing*.
109. *Ibid.*
110. *Honolulu Star-Bulletin*, 1 October 1912, 10 November 1912.
111. *Ibid.*, 14 October 1912.
112. *Ibid.*, 11 October 1912, 14 October 1912.
113. *Ibid.*, 14 October 1912, 15 October 1912.
114. *Pacific Commercial Advertiser*, 20 October 1912.
115. *Ibid.*, 2 November 1912, 3; United States Census Bureau, Manuscript Schedules, Maui, 1900.
116. *Pacific Commercial Advertiser*, 23 November 1912.
117. *Ibid.*, 7 November 1912, 9 November 1912.
118. *Ibid.*, 28 November 1912.
119. *Ibid.*, 3 December 1912.
120. *Ibid.*, 9 December 1912.
121. *Ibid.*, 23 November 1912.
122. *Ibid.*, 13 November 1912, 30 November 1912.
123. *Ibid.*, 18 November 1912.
124. "Tour of Chinese College Team," *Spalding's Official College Baseball Annual, 1913*, ed. Edward B. Moss (New York: Sports Publishing, 1913), 40.
125. *Ibid.*, 40–41.

Chapter Two

1. *Honolulu Star-Bulletin*, 1 January 1913, 8 January 1913.
2. *Ibid.*, 22 January 1913.
3. *Ibid.*, 27 January 1913.
4. *Ibid.*, 21 January 1913, 22 January 1913, 4 February 1913, 6 February 1913.
5. *Ibid.*, 25 February 1913, 28 February 1913.
6. *Pacific Commercial Advertiser*, 11 March 1913.
7. *Honolulu Star-Bulletin*, 10 March 1913.
8. *Ibid.*
9. *Ibid.*
10. *Ibid.*, 12 March 1913, 13 March 1913, 27 March 1913.
11. *Ibid.*, 18 March 1913.
12. *Ibid.*, 15 March 1913.
13. *Pacific Commercial Advertiser*, 18 March 1913.
14. *Honolulu Star-Bulletin*, 18 March 1913.
15. *Pacific Commercial Advertiser*, 20 March 1913; *Honolulu Advertiser*, 14 April 1964; Mills and Seymour, *People*, 173.
16. *Paradise of the Pacific*, April 1913, 8.
17. *Sporting Life*, 8 February 1913, 8 March 1913.
18. *San Francisco Chronicle*, 23 March 1913, 30 March 1913; Pacific Mail Steamship Company, Oath to Inward Passenger List, www.ancestry.com, accessed July 30, 2009.
19. *Oakland Enquirer*, 25 March 1913, 28 March 1913; *Oakland Tribune*, 25 March 1913.
20. *San Francisco Call*, 25 March 1913.
21. *San Francisco Chronicle*, 1 April 1913; *Daily Palo Alto*, 5 April 1913; *Honolulu Star-Bulletin*, 29 March 1913; *Racine Journal-News*, 2 April 1913; S.H. Hoe, "America Invaded by Oriental Foes," *Baseball Magazine*, March 1914, 68.
22. *Oakland Tribune*, 28 March 1913; *San Francisco Call*, 29 March 1913.
23. *San Francisco Call*, 29 March 1913, 8.
24. *Ibid.*; Hoe, "America Invaded," 68
25. Hoe, "America Invaded," 68; *Colorado Springs Gazette*, 8 April 1913, 9 April 1913.
26. *Pacific Commercial Advertiser*, 17 April 1913, 19 April 1913, 22 April 1913, 30 April 30, 1913; *Ogden Examiner*, 2 April 1913.
27. *Honolulu Star-Bulletin*, 8 May 1913.
28. *Eau Claire Leader*, 4 May 1913.
29. *Honolulu Star-Bulletin*, 10 May 1913.
30. *Ibid.*
31. *Ibid.*, 13 May 1913; *Oelwein Daily Register*, 5 September 1913.
32. *Honolulu Star-Bulletin*, 14 May 1913, 5 June 1913; Hoe, "America Invaded," 69–70.
33. *Honolulu Star-Bulletin*, 17 May 1913.
34. *Ibid.*
35. *Ibid.*
36. *Ibid.*, 31 May 1913.
37. *Ibid.*
38. *Lexington Herald*, 24 May 1913.
39. *Ibid.*; *Honolulu Star-Bulletin*, 5 June 1913.
40. *Urbana Daily Courier*, 28 April 1913, 12 May 1913; *Daily Commonwealth*, 5 May 1913, 10 May 1913; Mills and Seymour, *People*, 173.
41. *Elyria Evening Telegram*, 13 May 1913, 15 May 1913.
42. *Ibid.*, 16 May 1913.
43. *Lincoln News*, 28 May 1913, *Honolulu Star-Bulletin*, 24 June 1913; *Washington Post*, 11 June 1913; *New York Times*, 22 June 1913.
44. *Washington Post*, 13 July 1913.
45. *Ibid.*

46. *Ibid.*, 9 June 1913; *Brooklyn Eagle*, 13 June 1913, 23 June 1913; *Boston Globe*, 7 July 1913; *Sporting Life*, 12 July 1913.
47. *Honolulu Star-Bulletin*, 15 July 1913, 25 July 1913.
48. *Honolulu Star-Bulletin*, 25 July 1913; *Syracuse Herald*, 3 July 1913.
49. *Syracuse Herald*, 10 July 1913.
50. *Honolulu Star-Bulletin*, 25 July 1913.
51. *Ibid.*, 30 July 1913.
52. *Ibid.*; 12 September 1913.
53. *Ibid.*, 30 July 1913; *Brooklyn Eagle*, 21 July 1913, 28 July 1913.
54. *Honolulu Star-Bulletin*, 7 August 1913.
55. *Ibid.*, 22 July 1913; *Philadelphia Inquirer*, 8 August 1913.
56. *Trenton Evening Times*, 9 July 1913, 12 July 1913; *Philadelphia Inquirer*, 13 July 1913; *Honolulu Star-Bulletin*, 25 July 1913, 12 August 1913; *Reading Eagle*, 13 July 1913.
57. *Chester Times*, 13 July 1913; *Philadelphia Inquirer*, 9 August 1913.
58. *Ibid.*, 10 August 1913, 12 August 1913; *Honolulu Star-Bulletin*, 22 August 1913.
59. *Philadelphia Inquirer*, 12 August 1913, 13 August 1913; *Honolulu Star-Bulletin*, 12 September 1913.
60. Franks, *Asian Pacific Americans*, 30–31.
61. *Honolulu Star-Bulletin*, 12 September 1913.
62. *Ibid.*
63. *Ibid.*
64. *Philadelphia Inquirer*, 16 August 1913, 17 August 1913.
65. *Ibid.*, 24 August 1913; *Brooklyn Eagle*, 13 August 1913; *Trenton Evening Times*, 27 August 1913, 29 August 1913.
66. *Philadelphia Inquirer*, 29 August 1913, 31 August 1913.
67. *Chicago Defender*, 27 September 1913, 4 October 1913; Lanctot, *Fair Dealing*.
68. *Olean Times*, 25 July 1913.
69. *Honolulu Star-Bulletin*, 16 August 1913.
70. *Ibid.*, 13 October 1913.
71. *Ibid.*, 13 October 1912.
72. *Ibid.*
73. *Ibid.*
74. *Ibid.*
75. *Ibid.*
76. *Ibid.*
77. *Ibid.*, 14 October 1913.
78. *Ibid.*, 20 October 1913.
79. *Ibid.*, 25 October 1913, 27 October 1913.
80. *Ibid.*, 6 November 1913.
81. *Ibid.*, 8 November 1913, 9 November 1913.
82. *Pacific Commercial Advertiser*, 18 November 1913.
83. *Ibid.*, 29 December 1913.
84. S.H. Hoe, "America Invaded," 67.
85. *Ibid.*, 68.
86. *Ibid.*, 69
87. *Ibid.*, 68–69.
88. *Ibid.*, 70
89. *Ibid.*, 69.
90. *Ibid.*, 70–71.
91. *Ibid.*, 71.
92. *Ibid.*, 71–72.
93. *Ibid.*
94. *Ibid.*
95. *Ibid.*, 68
96. *Ibid.*, 72

Chapter Three

1. *Honolulu Star-Bulletin*, 1 January 1914.
2. *Ibid.*, 2 January 1914.
3. *Ibid.*, 6 January 1914.
4. *Ibid.*, 19 January 1914.
5. *Ibid.*, 26 January 1914.
6. *Ibid.*, 12 January 1914, 26 January 1914, 31 January 1914.
7. *Los Angeles Times*, 10 January 1914, part 3, 19 February 1914; *Columbus Daily Enquirer*, 13 March 1914.
8. *Pacific Commercial Advertiser*, 29 January 1914.
9. *Honolulu Star-Bulletin*, 31 January 1914.
10. *Ibid.*, 5 February 1914; *Pacific Commercial Advertiser*, 2 February 1914.
11. *Honolulu Star-Bulletin*, 12 February 1914.
12. *Ibid.*, 28 February 1914.
13. *Ibid.*, 21 February 1914, 25 February 1914, 4 March 1914.
14. *Ibid.*, 2 March 1914.
15. *Pacific Commercial Advertiser*, 2 March 1914, 3 March 1914.
16. *Ibid.*, 4 March 1914, 5 March 1914.
17. *Ibid.*, 9 March 1914.
18. *Ibid.*, 11 March 1914.
19. *Ibid.*, 16 March 1914.
20. *Ibid.*, 17 March 1914, 19 March 1914, 21 March 1914, 24 March 1914.
21. *Ibid.*, 18 March 1914.
22. *Fort Worth Star-Telegram*, 12 March 1914.
23. *Honolulu Star-Bulletin*, 31 March 1914.
24. *Ibid.*; *Oakland Tribune*, 19 January 1914.
25. *Los Angeles Times*, 10 March 1914.
26. *The Occidental*, 11 March 1914.
27. *Los Angeles Times* 14 March 1914.
28. *Ibid.*, 15 March 1914.
29. *Honolulu Star-Bulletin*, 26 March 1914, 9.
30. *Ibid.*
31. *Ibid.*, 31 March 1914; *The Occidental*, 18 March 1914.
32. *Honolulu Star-Bulletin*, 31 March 1914.
33. *Ibid.*; *Arizona Life*, 19 March 1914.
34. *Honolulu Star-Bulletin*, 31 March 1914; *Tucson Citizen*, 16 March 1914.
35. *Pacific Coast Advertiser*, 25 March 1914, 27 March 1914, 29 March 1914.

36. *Honolulu Star-Bulletin*, 31 March 1914.
37. *Fort Worth Star-Telegram*, 19 March 1914, 21 March 1914.
38. *Ibid.*, 31 March 1914, 2 April 1914.
39. *Honolulu Star-Bulletin*, 23 April 1914, 9; 28 April 1914, 9.
40. *Ibid.*, 28 April 1914.
41. *Ibid.*
42. *Ibid.*
43. *Ibid.*
44. *Pacific Commercial Advertiser*, 30 April 1914.
45. *Ibid.*, 8 May 1914.
46. *Emporia Gazette*, 13 April 1914.
47. *Ibid.*, 14 April 1914.
48. *Kansas City Star*, 15 April 1914.
49. *Pacific Commercial Advertiser*, 8 May 1914.
50. *Kansas City Star*, 19 April 1914.
51. *Ibid.*, 20 April 1914.
52. *Cedar Rapids Evening Gazette*, 29 April 1914; *Muscatine Journal*, 28 April 1914.
53. *Cedar Rapids Republican*, 14 April 1914.
54. *Ibid.*, 2 May 1914.
55. *Honolulu Star-Bulletin*, 25 May 1914.
56. *Fort Wayne Journal Gazette*, 5 May 1914.
57. *Honolulu Star-Bulletin*, 9 June 1914.
58. *New York Times*, 15 May 1914, 20 May 1914; *Miami Herald*, 25 May 1914; *New York Tribune*, 31 May 1914; *Brooklyn Eagle*, 31 May 1914.
59. *Pacific Commercial Advertiser*, 15 June 1914.
60. *Brooklyn Eagle*, 1 June 1914.
61. *Indiana Gazette*, 3 June 1914.
62. *Philadelphia Inquirer*, 7 June 1914.
63. *Trenton Evening Times*, 13 June 1914.
64. *Ibid.*, 14 June 1914, 15 June 1914, 16 June 1914.
65. *Ibid.*, 18 June 1914, 21 June 1914.
66. *Amsterdam Evening Recorder and Daily Democrat*, 17 June 1914, 21 June 1914.
67. *Frederick Daily News*, 17 June 1914, 26 June 1914, 29 June 1914.
68. *Frederick Post*, 29 June 1914.
69. *Frederick Daily News*, 30 June 1914, 1 July 1914; *Honolulu Star-Bulletin*, 29 July 1914.
70. *Philadelphia Inquirer*, 3 July 1914.
71. *Brooklyn Eagle*, 6 July 1914.
72. *Philadelphia Inquirer*, 7 July 1914.
73. *Chester Times*, 9 July 1914, 21 July 1914.
74. *Philadelphia Inquirer*, 12 July 1914.
75. *Gettysburg Star and Sentinel*, 6 August 1914.
76. *Honolulu Star-Bulletin*, 23 June 1914.
77. *Ibid.*, 30 July 1914.
78. *Ibid.*, 14 August 1914.
79. *Chester Times*, 5 August 1914.
80. *Ibid.*
81. *Honolulu Star-Bulletin*, 15 August 1914.
82. *Brooklyn Eagle*, 17 August 1914, 24 August 1914.
83. *Honolulu Star-Bulletin*, 5 September 1914.

84. *Philadelphia Public Ledger*, 7 September 1914; *Indianapolis Star*, 13 September 1914.
85. *Washington Post*, 28 September 1914.
86. *Honolulu Star-Bulletin*, 2 October 1915.
87. *Pacific Commercial Advertiser*, 2 April 1914, 6 April 1914.
88. *Ibid.*, 19 April 1914, 20 April 1914.
89. *Ibid.*, 28 April 1914; *Honolulu Star-Bulletin*, 30 April 1914.
90. *Honolulu Star-Bulletin*, 22 June 1914.
91. *Ibid.*, 29 June 1914; *Pacific Commercial Advertiser*, 27 June 1914.
92. *Pacific Commercial Advertiser*, 3 July 1914; *Honolulu Star-Bulletin*, 4 August 1914, 8 August 1914.
93. *Honolulu Star-Bulletin*, 10 August 1914.
94. *Oakland Tribune*, 3 July 1914; *Pacific Commercial Advertiser*, 8 August 1914.
95. *Honolulu Star-Bulletin*, 14 July 1914.
96. *Ibid.*, 1 September 1914.
97. *New York Times*, 6 December 1914.
98. *Ibid.*
99. *Pacific Commercial Advertiser*, 2 January 1915; Steven Riess, *Touching Base: Professional Baseball and American Culture in the Progressive Era* (Westport, CT: Greenwood Press, 1980), 193–194; *Nevada State Journal*, 5 December 1914; *Washington Post*, 3 December 1914; *Fort Worth Telegram*, 5 December 1914.
100. *Chicago Defender*, 16 January 1915; www.diamondangle.com, accessed January 7, 1998; *San Francisco Chronicle*, 10 December 1914; *Portland Oregonian*, 21 December 1914; *Miami Herald*, 12 December 1914; *Albany Evening Journal*, 17 December 1914; *Sporting Life*, 19 December 1914.
101. *Baltimore Afro-American*, 12 December 1914.
102. *Portland Oregonian*, 21 December 1914; *Los Angeles Times*, 15 December 1914.
103. *Los Angeles Times*, 15 December 1914.
104. *Ibid.*
105. *Sporting Life*, 5 December 1914; 19 December 1914.
106. *Ibid.*, 19 December 1914.
107. *Portland Oregonian*, 31 December 1914.
108. *Tulsa World*, 13 October 1914.

Chapter Four

1. *Pacific Commercial Advertiser*, 2 January 1915; Riess, *Touching*; *Chicago Defender*, 16 January 1915; *The Sporting News*, 7 January 1915.
2. *Portland Oregonian*, 1 January 1915; *Oakland Tribune*, 12 January 1915.
3. *Portland Oregonian*, 12 January 1915.
4. *Lima Daily News*, 2 January 1915; *Duluth News-Tribune*, 10 January 1915.
5. *Portland Oregonian*, 18 January 1915.
6. *Oakland Tribune*, 19 January 1915.

7. *Pacific Commercial Advertiser*, 6 January 1915, 7 January 1915.
8. *Honolulu Star-Bulletin*, 6 January 1915.
9. *Ibid.*, 6 January 1915, 23 January 1915.
10. *Oakland Tribune*, 25 January 1915; *Portland Oregonian*, 7 February 1915.
11. *Syracuse Daily Herald*, 8 January 1915.
12. *Boston Journal*, 2 January 1915.
13. *Duluth News-Tribune*, 10 January 1915; *Oakland Tribune*, 17 January 1915; *Fort Wayne Sentinel*, 28 January 1915.
14. *Freeman*, 23 January 1915.
15. *Baseball Magazine*, March 1915, 19.
16. *San Francisco Examiner*, 21 February 1915; www.diamondangle.com, accessed February 17, 1999; *Wilkes-Barre Times*, 26 January 1915.
17. *Brooklyn Eagle*, 26 January 1915; *Binghamton Press*, 9 February 1915.
18. *Honolulu Advertiser*, 14 April 1964; *Pacific Commercial Advertiser*, 19 January 1915, 1 March 1915, 2 March 1915, 3 March 1915, 10 October 1915; Ship's Manifest of Alien Passengers from U.S. Insular Possessions, For United States Immigration Officer at the Continental Port of Arrival, Manoa, Sailing from Honolulu, March 2, arriving in San Francisco, March 9, 1915. www.ancestry.com, accessed March 9, 2005.
19. *Honolulu Star-Bulletin*, 2 March 1915.
20. *San Francisco Examiner*, 9 March 1915; *San Francisco Chronicle*, 11 March 1915; *Daily Palo Alto*, 9 March 1915, 10 March 1915.
21. *Oakland Tribune*, 10 March 1915, 14 March 1915.
22. *Honolulu Star-Bulletin*, 23 March 1915.
23. *San Jose Mercury*, 12 March 1915, 14 March 1915, 15 March 1915.
24. *Ibid.*, 15 March 1915, 17 March 1915.
25. *San Francisco Examiner*, 19 March 1915, *Stockton Evening Mail*, 13 March 1915, 16 March 1915, 17 March 1915.
26. *Stockton Daily Record*, 17 March 1915, 18 March 1915.
27. *Honolulu Star-Bulletin*, 27 March 1915.
28. *Ibid.*, 30 March 1915, 15 May 1915; *Pacific Commercial Advertiser*, 18 March 1915, 20 March 1915, 21 March 1915; *Los Angeles Times*, 14 March 1915, 20 March 1915; *Portland Oregonian*, 19 March 1915.
29. *Pacific Commercial Advertiser*, 23 March 1915.
30. *Honolulu Star-Bulletin*, 30 March 1915.
31. *Pacific Commercial Advertiser*, 21 March 1915.
32. *Ibid.*, 3 March 1915, 11 March 1915.
33. *Pacific Commercial Advertiser*, 25 March 1915.
34. *Ibid.*, 2 April 1915.
35. *Ibid.*
36. *Ibid.*
37. *Ibid.*, 3 April 1915, 6 April 1915, 13 April 1915; *Honolulu Star-Bulletin*, 8 April 1915, 19 April 1915.
38. *Honolulu Star-Bulletin*, 5 April 1915.
39. *Ibid.*
40. *Ibid.*
41. *Ibid.*
42. *Ibid.*
43. *Ibid.*
44. *Tucson Citizen*, 10 March 1915, 13 March 1915, 24 March 1915.
45. University of Arizona Desert Yearbook, 1914–1915, Special Collections, University of Arizona.
46. *Honolulu Star-Bulletin*, 25 May 1915, 10 April 1915.
47. *Ibid.*, 25 May 1915, 14 April 1915.
48. *Ibid.*, 14 April 1915, *San Antonio Light*, 30 March 1915.
49. *Honolulu Star-Bulletin*, 17 April 1915, 25 May 1915; *Galveston Daily News*, 1 April 1915.
50. *Honolulu Star-Bulletin*, 21 April 1915.
51. *Ibid.*
52. *Ibid.*, 25 May 1915, 23 April 1915; *Pacific Commercial Advertiser*, 15 April 1915, 20 April 1915; "Our Letter Box," *Baseball Magazine*, July 1915, 91.
53. *Honolulu Star-Bulletin*, 23 April 1915.
54. *Trenton Evening News*, 27 April 1915.
55. *Fort Worth Star-Telegram*, 6 April 1915.
56. *Honolulu Star-Bulletin*, 28 April 1915.
57. *Ibid.*, 30 April 1915.
58. *Ibid.*, 4 May 1915, 25 May 1915, *Kansas City Star*, 14 April 1915.
59. *Honolulu Star-Bulletin*, 8 May 1915, 25 May 1915.
60. *Ibid.*, 19 May 1915, 25 May 1915; *Kansas City Star*, 18 April 1915.
61. *Honolulu Star-Bulletin*, 10 May 1915.
62. *University Missourian*, 23 April 1915.
63. *Honolulu Star-Bulletin*, 19 May 1915.
64. *Ibid.*; *Aberdeen Daily American*, 30 April 1915.
65. *Honolulu Star-Bulletin*, 19 May 1915.
66. *Ibid.*
67. *Ibid.*; *Nevada State Journal*, 6 May 1915; www.diamondangle.com, accessed May 7, 2002.
68. *Honolulu Star Bulletin*, 7 May 1915, 22 May 1915, 25 May 1915; *Indianapolis Star*, 10 May 1915; *Reno Evening Gazette*, 11 May 1915.
69. *Honolulu Star-Bulletin*, 25 May 1915.
70. *Ibid.*, 10 June 1915.
71. *Lincoln News*, 17 May 1915.
72. *Ibid.*
72. *Honolulu Star-Bulletin*, 9 June 1915.
73. *Lexington Herald*, 13 May 1915, 15 May 1915.
74. *Honolulu Star-Bulletin*, 16 June 1915.
75. *Ibid.*, 17 June 1915.
76. *Ibid.*, 22 June 1915.
77. *Indiana Evening Express*, 27 May 1915.

78. *Ibid.*, 26 June 1915.
79. *Ibid.*; *Brooklyn Eagle*, 29 May 1915.
80. *Honolulu Star-Bulletin*, 19 July 1915.
81. *Ibid.*; *Pawtucket Times*, 7 June 1915.
82. *Honolulu Star-Bulletin*, 21 July 1915.
83. *Ibid.*; *Philadelphia Inquirer*, 9 June 1915.
84. *Honolulu Star-Bulletin*, 21 July 1915.
85. *Ibid.*, 27 July 1915.
86. *Ibid.*, 3 August 1915; *Philadelphia Inquirer*, 13 June 1915.
87. *Honolulu Star-Bulletin*, 3 August 1915.
88. *Ibid.*; *Washington Post*, 12 June 1915; *North Adams Transcript*, 19 June 1915.
89. *Honolulu Star-Bulletin*, 17 August 1915; *Brooklyn Eagle*, 28 May 1915.
90. *Brooklyn Eagle*, 7 June 1915, 21 June 1915.
91. *Honolulu Star-Bulletin*, 26 August 1915.
92. *Ibid.*
93. *Ibid.*
94. *Ibid.*, 31 August 1915.
95. *Trenton Evening Times*, 11 July 1915, 13 July 1915.
96. *Ibid.*, 15 July 1915.
97. *Chester Times*, 12 August 1915; *Brooklyn Eagle*, 16 August 1915, *Portsmouth Daily Times*, 24 August 1915.
98. *Philadelphia Inquirer*, 22 August 1915; *Brooklyn Eagle*, 1 September 1915.
99. *Honolulu Star-Bulletin*, 11 September 1915.
100. *Ibid.*, 17 September 1915; *Syracuse Herald*, 15 September 1915.
101. *New York Age*, 2 September 1915, 9 September 1915.
102. *New York Times*, 6 September 1915.
103. *New York Age*, 16 September 1915, 30 September 1915; *Baltimore Afro-American*, 18 September 1915.
104. *Pacific Commercial Advertiser*, 9 September 1915, 22 October 1915; *Honolulu Star-Bulletin*, 2 October 1915; United States Census Bureau. Census Manuscripts, City and County of Honolulu, 1910; List of New Orleans Passengers, October, 1915, www.ancestry.com, accessed December 18, 2008.
105. *Ibid.*, 23 June 1915.
106. Luck Yee Lau, "A Baseball Trip to the Far East," *Ka Palapala*, College Hawaii, May 1916, 15.
107. *Ibid.*
108. *Ibid.*, 16; United States Census Bureau. Manuscript Census Schedules, City and County of Honolulu, 1930.
109. Luck Yee Lau, "A Baseball Trip," 15–16.
110. *Ibid.*, 16–17.
111. *Ibid.*, 17
112. *Ibid.*
113. *Ibid.*, 18.
114. *Ibid.*
115. *Ibid.*
116. *Pacific Commercial Advertiser*, 11 November 1915.

117. *Ibid.*, 17 November 1915, 21 November 1915, 26 November 1915, 27 November 1915, 5 December 1915, 12 December 1915.
118. *Boston Journal*, 9 December 1915.

Chapter Five

1. *Honolulu Advertiser*, 4 April 1964.
2. *Honolulu Star-Bulletin*, 16 February 1915, 5 May 1915; United States Census Bureau, Manuscript Census Schedules, City and County of Honolulu, 1930; *Los Angeles Times*, 14 March 1915; *San Francisco Chronicle*, 24 March 1915; *Pacific Commercial Advertiser*, 1 February 1916; http://www.baseball-reference.com/minors/player.cgi?id=inman-002wil, accessed April 6, 2009.
3. *Pacific Commercial Advertiser*, 2 March 1916; Jerry Malloy, "The 25th Infantry Takes the Field," *The National Pastime* 15 (1995).
4. *Honolulu Star-Bulletin*, 29 February 1916.
5. *Pacific Commercial Advertiser*, 4 March 1916.
6. *Ibid.*
7. *Honolulu Star-Bulletin*, 8 January 1916.
8. *Ibid.*, 25 January 1916.
9. *Ibid.*
10. *Ibid.*, 4 February 1916.
11. *Ibid.*, 5 February 1916.
12. *Ibid.*, 7 February 1916.
13. *Ibid.*
14. *Ibid.*, 11 February 1916, 14 February 1916.
15. *Pacific Commercial Advertiser*, 2 March 1916, 6 March 1916.
16. *Ibid.*, 9 March 1916; United States Census Bureau, Manuscript Census Schedules, City and County of Honolulu, 1930; Passenger Manifest, SS. Matsonia, Honolulu, 14 March 1916, www.ancestry.com, accessed March 18, 2007; http://www.baseball-reference.com/minors/team.cgi?id=11187, accessed April 6, 2009.
17. Passenger Manifest, S.S. Matsonia, 14 March 1916, www.ancestry.com, accessed March 18, 2007.
18. *Cleburne Morning News*, 25 February 1916; *San Francisco Chronicle*, 3 March 1916.
19. *Daily Palo Alto Times*, 15 March 1916, 17 March 1916.
20. *San Jose Mercury*, 8 February 1916; *Honolulu Star-Bulletin*, 26 October 1916.
21. *Tucson Citizen*, 15 March 1916, 21 March 1916, 22 March 1916; *Honolulu Star-Bulletin*, 13 April 1916.
22. *Honolulu Star-Bulletin*, 13 April 1916, 26 October 1916; *Commerce Journal*, 7 April 1916.
23. *Fort Worth Star-Telegram*, 30 March 1916.
24. *Brownsville Daily Bulletin*, 29 March 1916.
25. *Honolulu Star-Bulletin*, 13 April 1916.
26. *Ibid.*, 26 October 1916; *Dallas Morning*

News, 1 April 1916, 2 April 1916; *Salt Lake Telegram*, 31 March 1916.
27. *Honolulu Star-Bulletin*, 27 April 1916; *Commerce Journal*, 14 April 1916; *Dallas Morning News*, 14 April 1916.
28. *Honolulu Star-Bulletin*, 26 October 1916, 6; *Tulsa World*, 19 April 1916, sports section, 5.
29. *Indianapolis Star*, 10 May 1916, 11 May 1916, 12 May 1916, 13 May 1916; *Loganport Daily Tribune*, 10 May 1916; *Chicago Defender*, 20 May 1916; *New York Times*, 4 May 1916; *Honolulu Star-Bulletin*, 6 May 1916, 26 October 1916.
30. *Savannah Tribune*, 20 May 1916.
31. *Frederick Daily News*, 27 May 1916, *Indiana Weekly Messenger*, 31 May 1916.
32. *Chicago Defender*, 3 June 1916, 17 June 1916; *Brooklyn Eagle*, 31 May 1916.
33. *Philadelphia Public Ledger*, 6 June 1916, 11 June 1916; *Philadelphia Inquirer*, 7 June 1916, 11 June 1916; *Honolulu Star-Bulletin*, 26 October 1916; Lanctot, *Fair Dealing*, 30.
34. *New York Times*, 17 June 1916; *Brooklyn Eagle*, 17 June 1916, 19 June 1916; *Hartford Courant*, 24 June 1916; *Honolulu Star-Bulletin*, 26 October 1916.
35. *Honolulu Star-Bulletin*, 25 July 1916.
36. *Ibid.*; *Philadelphia Public Ledger*, 18 June 1916, 9 July 1916.
37. *Philadelphia Public Ledger*, 25 June 1916.
38. *Philadelphia Inquirer*, 2 July 1916; *Philadelphia Public Ledger*, 2 July 1916.
39. *Honolulu Star-Bulletin*, 26 October 1916; *Philadelphia Inquirer* 3 July 1916, 5 July 1916; *Philadelphia Public Ledger*, 5 July 1916.
40. *Honolulu Star-Bulletin*, 26 October 1916; *Philadelphia Public Ledger*, 7 July 1916.
41. *Philadelphia Public Ledger*, 15 July 1916; *Philadelphia Inquirer*, 16 July 1916; *Brooklyn Eagle*, 16 July 1916.
42. *Philadelphia Inquirer*, 22 July 1916, 25 July 1916, 19 August 1916, 6; *Philadelphia Public Ledger*, 3 July 1916, 7 July 1916, 15 July 1916, 23 July 1916, 27 July 1916; *Chester Times*, 12 August 1916; *Honolulu Star-Bulletin*, 26 October 1916.
43. *Philadelphia Inquirer*, 9 August 1916, 10 August 1916, 13 August 1916; *Brooklyn Eagle*, 12 August 1916.
44. *Poughkeepsie Eagle News*, 15 August 1916.
45. *Philadelphia Inquirer*, 27 August 1916, 3 September 1916.
46. *New York Age*, 14 September 1916; *Indianapolis Star*, 2 October 1916; *Kokomo Tribune*, 2 October 1916; *Chicago Defender*, 7 October 1916.
47. *Charlotte Observer*, 8 September 1916; *Brooklyn Eagle*, 25 September 1916.
48. *Honolulu Star-Bulletin.*, 10 April 1916, 8 May 1916, 26 May 1916, 27 June 1916; *Pacific Commercial Advertiser*, 9 October 1916.
49. *Honolulu Star-Bulletin*, 11 September 1916.
50. *Ibid.*, 24 October 1916.

51. *Ibid.*
52. *Ibid.*
53. *Ibid.*
54. *Ibid.*
55. *Ibid.*, 26 October 1916.
56. *Ibid.*, 20 November 1916; *Pacific Commercial Advertiser*, 27 October 1916, 11 November 1916, 13 November 1916, 20 November 1916, 26 November 1916.
57. *Pacific Commercial Advertiser*, 2 December 1916, 3 December 1916; *Honolulu Star-Bulletin*, 4 December 1916.
58. *Philadelphia Public Ledger*, 26 October 1916.
59. *Honolulu Star-Bulletin*, 21 November 1916.
60. *Pacific Commercial Advertiser*, 14 September 1916.
61. *Chicago Tribune*, 12 December 1916; *Honolulu Star-Bulletin*, 12 December 1916.
62. *Washington Post*, 12 December 1916.
63. *Philadelphia Public Ledger*, 19 December 1916.
64. *Brooklyn Eagle*, 16 December 1916.

Chapter Six

1. *The Sporting News*, 22 March 1917.
2. *Ibid.*; *Oakland Tribune*, 18 March 1917.
3. *The Sporting News*, 22 March 1917.
4. *Ibid.*
5. *Ibid.*, 29 March 1917, 5 April 1917; *Portland Oregonian*, 29 March 1917; *Salt Lake Telegram*, 9 March 1917.
6. *Honolulu Star-Bulletin*, 1 January 1917; *Sporting Life*, 20 January 1917.
7. *Connelsville Daily Courier*, 7 January 1917.
8. *Oakland Tribune*, 7 January 1917, 24 March 1917; *Portland Oregonian*, 31 January 1917; *Daily Northwestern*, 1 March 1917; *Fort Wayne News*, 17 April 1917; *Sporting Life*, 31 March 1917; *Warren Evening Mirror*, 24 March 1917.
9. *Seattle Post-Intelligencer*, 27 March 1917.
10. *Ibid.*
11. *Ibid.*, 1 April 1917
12. *Ibid.*, 3 April 1917, 4 April 1917.
13. *Ibid.*, 7 April 1917, 8 April 1917, 13 April 1917, 14 April 1917.
14. *Ibid.*, 15 April 1917.
15. *Ibid.*, 24 April 1917.
16. *Washington Post*, 22 April 1917.
17. *Fort Wayne Sentinel*, 18 May 1917.
18. *Seattle Post-Intelligencer*, 21 May 1917; *Salt Lake Telegram*, 24 May 1917; *The Sporting News*, 31 May 1917.
19. U.S. Draft Registration Cards, World War I, www.ancestry.com, accessed October 21, 2007; *Portland Oregonian*, 25 May 1917, 1 June 1917, 19 June 1917.
20. *Anaconda Standard*, 21 June 1917.

21. *Ibid.*, 5 July 1917, 9 July 1917; *The Sporting News*, 5 July 1917, 26 July 1917, *Seattle Times*, 11 July 1917
22. *Seattle Times*, 12 July 1917; *Portland Oregonian*, 22 July 1917, 23 July 1917.
23. *Philadelphia Inquirer*, 18 July 1917, 16 September 1917; *Brooklyn Eagle*, 27 August 1917, 3 September 1917, 10 September 1917.
24. *Philadelphia Inquirer*, 28 April 1918, 4 August 1919; *Chicago Defender*, 4 May 1918; *Chester Times*, 24 May 1918; *Pittsburgh Press*, 6 August 1918.
25. *Bridgton Evening News*, 9 May 1919; *Philadelphia Inquirer*, 11 August 1919, 9 September 1919.
26. *Philadelphia Inquirer*, 21 June 1920, 2 October 1921, 23 October 1921, 18 June 1922, 5 July 1922, 13 July 1922, 21 July 1922, 8 July 1922, 30 July 1922; *Chicago Defender*, 4 May 1918; *Chester Times*, 15 March 1923, 17 January 1934, 30 June 1937, 10 July 1937, 9 August 1937, 7 September 1951, 28 June 1952, 30 August 1952, 3 November 1955; United States World War II Draft Registration Cards, World War II, www. ancestry.com, accessed October 21, 2007; Social Security Death Index, www. ancestry.com, accessed October 16, 2007.
27. *Gettysburg Times*, 27 September 1938; *Bridgeport Telegram*, 22 May 1918.
28. *Gettysburg Times*, 8 May 1917; *Philadelphia Inquirer*, 22 April 1917.
29. *Gettysburg Times*, 12 May 1917; *Gettysburg Star and Sentinel*, 14 May 1917.
30. *Gettysburg Times*, 15 May 1917, 17 May 1917, 18 May 1917, 21 May 1917; *Gettysburg Star and Sentinel*, 22 June 1917.
31. *Gettysburg Times*, 23 May 1917, 5 June 1917.
32. *Gettysburg Compiler*, 20 January 1945; Mark C. Zeigler, "James Vincent Jamison, Jr.: Blue Ridge League President, 1916–1918, 1920–1930," *The National Pastime* (2009), 35.
33. *Hagerstown Morning Herald*, 5 November 1953.
34. *Ibid.*, 3 February 1951.
35. *Gettysburg Times*, 10 July 1917; *Spalding's Baseball Guide 1918*, ed. John Foster (New York: American Sports Publishing), 174; *The Sporting News*, 13 September 1917.
36. *Philadelphia Inquirer*, 3 August 1917, 26 September 1917; *Chicago Defender*, 4 May 1917.
37. *Berkshire Evening Eagle*, 11 July 1945; *Bridgeport Telegram*, 22 May 1918, 1 June 1918.
38. *Bridgeport Telegram*, 27 May 1918, 28 May 1918, 3 June 1918, 28 June 1918.
39. *Ibid.*, 13 June 1918, 27 June 1918.
40. *Ibid.*, 4 June 1918; *Syracuse Herald*, 30 June 1918.
41. *Bridgeport Telegram*, 12 July 1918.
42. *Ibid.*, 16 July 1918; United States World War I Draft Registration Cards, www.ancestry.com, accessed March 21, 2008.

43. *Bridgeport Telegram*, 6 May 1918, 27 May 1919; *The Sporting News*, 5 June 1918; *Philadelphia Inquirer*, 4 August 1919, 9 September 1919; *Gettysburg Times*, 4 August 1919.
44. United States Census Bureau. Manuscript Census Schedules, Penns Grove, Salem County, New Jersey, 1920; City and County of Honolulu, 1930; Honolulu City Directory, 1937–1938, www. ancestry.com., accessed 25 April 2009; *Edwardsville Intelligencer*, 28 October 1940; *Honolulu Star Bulletin*, 4 November 1949, 18 April 1961; Bob Kraus, *Johnny Wilson: The First Hawaiian Democrat* (Honolulu: University of Hawai'i Press, 1994), 209; Takaki, *Pau Hana*, 155; David Stannard, *Honor Killing: Race, Rape, and Clarance Darrow's Spectacular Last Case* (New York; Penguin Books, 2005) 78; Steve Fugita, "Frederick Kinzaburo Makina," in *Distinguished Asian Americans*, ed. Hyung-chan Kim (Westport, CT: Greenwood Publishing, 1999), 222; Telephone Conversation with Andrew Yamashiro, Jr., April 11, 2009; Interview with Andrew Yamashiro, Jr., June 22, 2009, San José, California.
45. *New York Times*, 24 June 1932; Eileen H Tamura, *Americanization, Acculturation, and Ethnic Identify: The Nisei Generation in Hawaii* (Champagne: University of Illinois Press, 1994), 88.
46. Dorothy Dee Buckingham, "General Patton's Hawaiian 'Internment List,'" www.hawaii reporter.com, 23 February 2002.
47. *Pacific Commercial Advertiser*, 14 September 1916; *Fort Wayne News*, 28 July 1917; *Trenton Evening News*, 23 August 1917; *Philadelphia Inquirer*, 8 April 1917, 26 August 1917, 16 September 1917; *Brooklyn Eagle*, 23 April 1917, 19 July 1917, 23 July 1917, 27 August 1917, 3 September 1917; United States. Draft Registration Cards, World War I. www.ancestry.com, accessed August 7, 2007.
48. *Philadelphia Inquirer*, 21 January 1919, 13 July 1919, 4 August 1919, 19 August 1920, 23 August 1920, 5 May 1922, 10 May 1922, 22 May 1922, 12 September 1922; *Chicago Defender*, 25 May 1918, 15 June 1918; *Delaware County Daily Times*, 17 July 1962; *Chester Times*, 5 March 1923, 20 April 1923, 28 July 1923.
49. *Trenton Evening Times*, 28 April 1924, 9 May 1924, 24 May 1924, 31 May 1924, 3 June 1924.
50. United States Census Bureau. Census Manuscript Schedules, City and County of Honolulu, 1930; Honolulu City Directory, 1937–1938.
51. *Fort Wayne News*, 11 August 1917; United States Draft Registration Cards, World War I, www.ancestry.com, accessed September 28, 2004.
52. *Philadelphia Inquirer*, 8 July 1917, 29 July 1917, 28 August 1917.
53. *Philadelphia Public Ledger*, 9 September 1917, 26 October 1917.

54. *Washington Post*, 13 January 1918; *Pittsburgh Press*, 6 August 1918.
55. *Washington Post*, 7 December 1918; *New Castle News*, 6 December 1918; *Kansas City Star*, 17 December 1918.
56. *Philadelphia Inquirer*, 28 January 1917, 27 August 1917, 4 April 1920, 19 February 1922; *Fort Wayne News*, 11 August 1917, 8 September 1919; United States Census Bureau, Manuscript Census Schedules, Nazareth, Pennsylvania, Northampton County, 1920.
57. *Philadelphia Inquirer*, 19 June 1921, 17 July 1921, 31 July 1921, 19 August 1921, 30 August 1921; http://www.baseball-reference.com/minors/team.cgi?id=15996, accessed April 4, 2009.
58. *Washington Post*, 15 July 1923.
59. United States Census Bureau, Manuscript Census Schedules, City and County of Honolulu, 1930; http://archives1.dags.Hawai'i.gov/gsdl/collect/worldwa2/index/assoc/HASH75ba/fe3261f7.dir/Chun%20Kan%20Yen.jpg, accessed November 13, 2008; Joe Devir, "Kanky Chun is Only Spectacled Catcher," *Brooklyn Eagle*, 31 December 1924.
60. United States Draft Registration Cards, World War I, www.ancestry.com, accessed October 13, 2005; http://www.last.fm/music/Ben%2520Hokea%2520%2526%2520Luther%2520Kekoa, accessed September 29, 2008; United States Census Bureau, Manuscript Census Schedules, City and County of Honolulu, 1930.
61. *Hawaii Herald*, 10 February 1951; *Honolulu Advertiser*, 14 March 1944, 28 April 1946, 4 April 1964; *Honolulu Star Bulletin*, April 22, 1940, 10; November 4, 1949, 15; April 18, 1961, 3; http://archives1.dags.Hawai'i.gov/gsdl/collect/worldwa2/index/assoc/HASH01ca/b6847a33.dir/Akana%20F%20Lang.jpg; http://archives1.dags.Hawai'i.gov/gsdl/collect/worldwa2/index/assoc/HASH01ca/b6847a33.dir/Akana%20F%20Lang.jpg, accessed November 13, 2009.
62. United States Draft Registration Cards, World War I, www.ancestry, com, accessed October 13, 2005.
63. United States Census Bureau, Manuscript Census Schedules, City and County of Honolulu, 1920, 1930; *San Jose Mercury*, 15 April 1920, section ii, 12; Frank Menke, "Honolulu Turns Out Semi-pro Baseball Nines; En Sue, 46-year Old Chinese, is Ty Cobb of Islands," *The Idaho Daily Statesmen*, 20 August 1922; *Portland Oregonian*, 19 November 1922; *Reno Evening Gazette*, 23 July 1923; *Newark Advocate*, 25 January 1927.
64. Betty Dunn, *Jackie Pung: Women's Golf Lefend: The Thrills and Heartbreak of an LPGA Professional* (Lincoln, NE: iuniversity, 2005), 4.
65. United States Census Bureau, Manuscript Census Schedules, New York City, 1920; City and County of Honolulu, 1930; *Washington Post*, 24 December 1924; *Reno Evening Gazette*, 5 April 1929; *Indiana Weekly Messenger*, 18 April 1935; *Syracuse Herald*, 7 August 1937.

Chapter Seven

1. United States Census Bureau, Manuscript Census Schedules, City and County of Honolulu, 1910 and 1930.
2. Telephone Conversation, Mary Lai, March 7, 2008; *Washington Post*, 24 March 1918, 21.
3. United States Draft Registration Cards, World War I, www. ancestry.com, accessed February 17, 2007.
4. *Middletown Press*, 21 July 1917; *Brooklyn Eagle*, 3 June 1917.
5. *Trenton Evening Times*, 23 August 1917, 14 October 1917, 22 October 1917; *Philadelphia Inquirer*, 5 August 1917, 19 August 1917, 26 August 1917; *Brooklyn Eagle*, 23 April 1917, 11 June 1917, 25 June 1917, 29 July 1917, 23 July 1917, 13 August 1917, 30 August 1917, 27 August 1917, 3 September 1917, 10 September 1917.
6. *Washington Post*, 24 March 1918; *Brooklyn Eagle*, 18 March 1918; *Philadelphia Public Ledger*, 22 March 1918.
7. *Philadelphia Inquirer*, 16 March 1918, 18 March 1918, 26 March 1918; *The Sporting News*, 28 March 1918; *Lima Daily News*, 28 March 1918.
8. *Philadelphia Inquirer*, 25 March 1918, 29 March 1918, 30 March 1918, 31 March 1918, 3 April 1918, 6 April 1918, 8 April 1918; *The Sporting News*, 4 April 1918, 11 April 1918.
9. *Des Moines Daily News*, 7 April 1918; *Macon Telegraph*, 11 April 1918; *Salt Lake Telegram*, 20 April 1918.
10. *Utica Observer*, 24 April 1918; *The Sporting News*, 4 April 1918, 23 May 1918.
11. *Bridgeport Telegram*, 16 May 1918.
12. *Ibid*., 17 May 1918, 20 May 1918, 22 May 1918.
13. *Ibid*., 28 May 1918, 29 May 1918, 1 June 1918.
14. *Ibid*., 12 July 1918, 18 July 1918.
15. *Ibid*., 23 July 1918, 29 July 1918, 7 August 1918; *Philadelphia Inquirer*, 7 September 1918; *Brooklyn Eagle*, 26 July 1918; http://www.baseball-reference.com/minors/player.cgi?id=lai---002wil, accessed April 24, 2009.
16. *Bridgeport Telegram*, 14 April 1919, 19 May 1919, 29 May 1919, 24 June 1919, 3 July 1919.
17. *Duluth News Tribune*, 14 March 1920.
18. *Bridgeport Telegram*, 30 April 1920, 27 May 1920, 9 June 1920, 21 June 1920, 23 June 1920, 9 August 1920, 14 August 1920, 18 August 1920, 19 August 1920; *The Sporting News*, 23 September 1920; United States Census Manuscript Schedules, City and County of Philadelphia, 1920.
19. *The Sporting News*, 24 February 1921; *Bridgeport Telegram*, 13 April 1921, 2 May 1921, 17

August 1921, 2 September 1921, 19 September 1921; http://www.baseball-reference.com/minors/player. cgi?id=lai---002wil, accessed April 24, 2009.
  20. *Philadelphia Inquirer*, 17 October 1921.
  21. *Ibid.*, 23 April 1922, 24 April 1922, 2 May 1922, 6 May 1922, 7 May 1922, 12 May 1922, 17 June 1922, 4 July 1922, 8 July 1922, 13 July 1922, 22 July 1922, 25 July 1922; *Lethbridge Herald*, 13 May 1922; *Trenton Evening Times*, 11 July 1922.
  22. *Delaware County Daily Times*, 17 July 1962; *Chester Times*, 20 April 1923, 28 July 1923, 5 March 1938; *Brooklyn Eagle*, 23 April 1923, 16 July 1923.
  23. *Trenton Evening Times*, 25 April 1924, 2 May 1924, 9 May 1924, 16 May 1924, 23 May 1924, 31 May 1924; *Brooklyn Eagle*, 5 May 1924.
  24. *Trenton Evening Times*, 2 June 1924, 12 June 1924, 27 June 1924, 30 June 1924, 3 July 1924, 7 July 1924, 14 July 1924.
  25. *Ibid.*, 7 October 1924.
  26. *Brooklyn Eagle*, 20 April 1925, 18 May 1925, 6 July 1925, 27 July 1925, 31 August 1925; *Chicago Defender*, 1 May 1926, 23 July 1927; *New York Times*, 13 October 1927.
  27. *Chester Times*, 3 November 1927, 17 January 1928; *New York Times*, 10 January 1928; *Hagerstown Daily Mail*, 16 January 1928; *Uniontown Morning Herald*, 20 January 1928; *Seattle Times*, 26 January 1928; *Lethbridge Herald*, 9 February 1928; *Gettysburg Times*, 14 January 1928; *Los Angeles Times*, 28 February 1928.
  28. Lank Leonard, "Buck Lai to Get Trial," *Trenton Evening Times*, 16 February 1928.
  29. *Ibid.*
  30. *Ibid.*
  31. *Ibid.*
  32. *New Castle News*, 9 March 1928.
  33. *Washington Post*, 13 March 1928; *New York Times*, 14 March 1928, 15 March 1928; *Massillon Evening Independent*, 13 March 1928; *Circleville Herald*, 13 April 1928.
  34. *New York Times*, 15 March 1928; *Appleton Post Crescent*, 15 March 1928.
  35. *New York Times*, 13 April 1928, 16 April 1928; *The Sporting News*, 26 April 1928; *Zanesville Signal*, 28 March 1928; *Trenton Evening Times*, 11 April 1928, 7 May 1928; *Brooklyn Eagle*, 4 May 1928; *Berkshire Evening Eagle*, 19 February 1952; http://www.baseball-reference.com/minors/player. cgi?id=lai---002wil, accessed April 24, 2009.
  36. William Carlson Smith, *Americans in Process* (New York: Arno Press, 1970), 114.
  37. Email correspondence from Mary Lai, December 2, 2009; *Trenton Evening Times*, 7 July 1928; *Brooklyn Eagle*, 23 July 1928; *New York Times*, 13 October 1928.
  38. *Brooklyn Eagle*, 23 June 1930; *New York Times*, 24 July 1930; *Trenton Evening Times*, 7 April 1930, 3 July 1930.
  39. *Brooklyn Eagle*, 6 July 1931.
  40. *Ibid.*, 1 May 1933, 22 May 1933, 24 September 1932, 22 September 1933; *Middletown Times Herald*, 24 July 1933.
  41. Ben Gould, "Max Rosner, Who Operated Legendary Bushwick, Dies," *The Sporting News*, 9 December 1953; Thomas Barthel, *Baseball's Peerless Semipros: The Brooklyn Bushwicks of Dexter Park* (Haworth, NJ: St. Johann Press, 2009).
  42. *The Sporting News*, 18 January 1934.
  43. *Brooklyn Eagle*, 7 May 1934, 13 August 1934, 20 August 1934, 23 August 1934, 20 September 1934; *New York Times*, 18 October 1934.
  44. *Bridgeport Telegram*, 20 December 1921; *Philadelphia Inquirer*, 6 January 1922.
  45. *Gettysburg Times*, 26 January 1932, 1 February 1932.
  46. *Frederick Daily News*, 2 February 1932; *Rochester Democrat and Chronicle*, 12 March 1932; *Trenton Evening Times*, 4 November 1932, 11 November 1932.
  47. *Washington Post*, 28 January 1934.
  48. James Murphy, "Buck Lai Bringing All-Star Nine from Hawaii in Semipro War," *Brooklyn Eagle*, 14 February 1935.
  49. *Ibid.*
  50. *Ibid.*; 17 February 1935; *Honolulu Advertiser*, 3 March 1935.
  51. Stannard, *Honor Killing*.
  52. *Honolulu Advertiser*, 3 March 1935, 5 March 1935.
  53. *Ibid.*, 22 March 1935; United States Census Bureau, Manuscript Census Schedules, City and County of Honolulu, 1930; Island of Hawaii, 1930.
  54. *Honolulu Advertiser*, 24 March 1935, 30 March 1935, 31 March 1935, 1 April 1935; United States Census Bureau, Manuscript Census Schedules, City and County of Honolulu, 1930.
  55. *Honolulu Advertiser*, 7 April 1935, 15 April 1935, 20 April 1935.
  56. Rod Ohira, "Hawai'i All-Star recalls 1935 Tour," *Honolulu Advertiser*, 8 April 2002, www. honoluluadvertiser.com.
  57. *Connelsville Daily Courier*, 21 March 1935; *Emporia Gazette*, 20 May 1935; *Brooklyn Eagle*, 17 May 1935; *Moberly Monitor-Index*, 25 May 1935, 27 May 1935; *Jefferson City News and Tribune*, 26 May 1935; *Chicago Tribune*, 1 June 1935.
  58. *Syracuse Daily Herald*, 7 August 1935, 10 August 1935; *Oswego Palladium-Times*, 10 August 1935; United States Census Bureau, Manuscript Census Schedules, City and County of Honolulu, 1930.
  59. *Helena Independent*, 13 September 1935; *Chicago Tribune*, 19 November 1935; *The Sporting News*, 28 November 1935.
  60. *Chester Times*, 19 June 1935, 21 June 1935, 22 June 1935, 5 July 1935, 26 August 1935.
  61. *Honolulu Star-Bulletin*, 3 March 1936, 13 March 1936, 7 April 1936, 22 April 1936, 2 May 1936, 12 May 1936.

62. *Ibid.*, 2 May 1936, 12 May 1936.
63. *Helena Independent*, 24 May 1936.
64. *Ibid.*, 26 May 1936, 27 May 1936.
65. *Elyria Chronicle Telegram*, 2 June 1936, 4 June 1936, 5 June 1936.
66. *Hartford Courant*, 9 July 1936.
67. *Big Spring Daily Herald*, 5 April 1937.
68. *Ada Evening News*, 16 May 1937, 20 May 1937.
69. *Newark Advocate and American Tribune*, 9 June 1937.
70. *Clearfield Progress*, 26 June 1937.
71. *Hammond Times*, 21 August 1937.
72. *Brooklyn Eagle*, 12 July 1937; *Fresno Bee*, 14 May 1936, 16 May 1936; *Lubbock Avalanche Journal*, 16 May 1937.
73. *Chester Times*, 1 July 1939, 16 August 1941: *Brooklyn Eagle*, 7 August 1941; United States Draft Registration Cards, World War II, www.ancestry.com, accessed September 5, 2008.
74. *Reno Evening Gazette*, 12 January 1945; *Gettysburg Compiler*, 20 January 1945; *The Sporting News*, 18 January 1945.
75. Harold Burr, "No. 1 Boy in Big Times," *Brooklyn Eagle*, 21 January 1945.
76. *Ibid.*
77. *Chester Times*, 5 August 1939; *Delaware County Herald Times*, 28 October 1969; Telephone Conversation with Mary Lai, March 7, 2008; *New York Times*, 7 March 1939, 16 April 1941.
78. www.northeasternconference.org, June 22, 2003; Telephone Conversation with Mary Lai, March 7, 2008.
79. *Brooklyn Eagle*, 15 October 1947.
80. *Ibid.*, May 19, 1950, 22.
81. Harold Burr, "Hitler Spoilsport in Buck Lai Jr.'s Life," *Brooklyn Eagle*, 7 January 1955.
82. *Berkshire Evening Eagle*, 19 February 1952, 31 July 1952, 2 August 1952, 9 August 1952, 8 October 1956; *Washington Post*, 9 February 1952; *Traverse City Record Eagle*, 6 December 1955.
83. *Berkshire Evening Eagle*, 8 October 1956; *Delaware County Daily* Times, 8 March 1961.
84. Baseball On-Line, http://www.baseballlibrary.com/ballplayers/player.php?name=Buck_Lai _1894, accessed July 18, 2011; Telephone Conversation with Mary Lai, March 7, 2008.

Epilogue

1. Clifford Geertz, *The Interpretation of Cultures* (New York: Basic Books, 1977).
2. C.L.R. James, *Beyond a Boundary* (New York: Random House, 2005).
3. Andrew D. Morris, *Colonial Project, National Game: A History of Baseball in Taiwan* (Berkeley: University of California Press, 2011), 5.
4. James Clifford, *Routes: Travel and Translation in the Late Twentieth Century* (Cambridge, MA: Harvard University Press, 1997); Mary Louise Pratt, *Imperial Eyes: Studies in Travel Writing and Transculturation*, (New York: Routledge, 1992); Edward Said, *Culture and Imperialism*, (New York: Vintage, 1994); Joel S. Franks, *Crossing Sidelines, Crossing Cultures: Sport and Asian Pacific American Cultural Citizenship* (Lanham, MD: University Press of America, 2000).
5. Okihiro, *Island World*; Buck, *Paradise Remade*; Forbes, *Introducing Bert Williams*, 21.
6. Lanctot, *Fair Dealing*.
7. Elaine Kim, "Preface," *Charlie Chan is Dead: An Anthology of Contemporary Asian American Fiction*, ed. Jessica Hagedorn (New York: Penguin Books, 1993); Ronald Takaki, *Strangers*, chapter one.

Bibliography

Archives and Special Collections

Long Island University Library, Special Collections, Brookville, NY.
National Baseball Hall of Fame and Museum Library, Cooperstown, NY.
Occidental College Library, Special Collections, Los Angeles, CA.
Seton Hall University Library, Special Collections, South Orange, NJ.
University of Arizona Library, Special Collections, Tucson, AZ.
University of Hawai'i Library, Special Collections, Honolulu, HI.

Interviews

Lai, Mary. Email Correspondence, December 2, 2009.
_____. Telephone Conversation, March 7, 2008.
Yamashiro, Andrew, Jr. Telephone Conversation, April 11, 2009.
_____. Personal Interview, June 22, 2009, San José, CA.

Annuals and Reports

Honolulu City Directory, 1937–1938.
Letter from the Attorney General transmitting in response to Senate Resolution No. 134 certain information relative to law enforcement in the Territory of Hawai'i, April 4, 1932. Referred to the Committee on Territories and Insular Affairs and ordered to be printed, with illustrations. Truncated title. Date: 1932-04-04; Publication: Serial Set Vol. No. 9511, Session Vol. No.13; Honolulu City Directory, 1937–1938, www.ancestry.com, accessed March 28, 2009.
Pacific Mail Steamship Company, Oath to Inward Passenger List, www.ancestry.com, accessed July 30, 2009.
Passenger Manifest, S.S. Matsonia, March 14, 1916, www.ancestry.com, accessed March 18, 2007.
Ship's Manifest, S.S. Honolulan, March 3, 1914, www.ancestry.com, accessed June 2, 2009.
Ship's Manifest of Alien Passengers from US Insular Possessions, S.S. Manao, March 2, 1915, www.ancestry.com, accessed March 9, 2005.
Social Security Death Index, www.ancestry.com, accessed October 16, 2007.

Spalding's Official College Baseball Annual, 1913, ed. by Edward B. Moss. New York: American Sports Publishing, 1913.
Spalding's Baseball Guide 1918, ed. John Foster. New York: American Sports Publishing, 1918.
United States Census Bureau. Manuscript Census Schedules, County of Cook and City of Chicago, 1910.
_____. Manuscript Census Schedules, Island of Hawaii, 1930.
_____. Manuscript Census Schedules, Island of Maui, 1900.
_____. Manuscript Census Schedules, Nazareth, Pennsylvania, Northampton County, 1920.
_____. Manuscript Census Schedules, New York City, 1920.
_____. Manuscript Census Schedules, Penns Grove, Salem County, New Jersey, 1920.
_____. Manuscript Census Schedules of the City and County of Honolulu, 1900, 1910, 1920, 1930.
United States Draft Registration Cards, World War I, www.ancestry.com, accessed September 28, 2004; October 13, 2005; February 17, 2007; August 7, 2007; October 21, 2007.
United States Draft Registration Cards, World War II, www.ancestry.com, accessed October 21, 2007; September 5, 2008.
University of Arizona Desert Yearbook, 1914–1915.

Thesis

Kaulukukui, Thomas. "The Development of Competitive, Team Sports," MA Thesis: University of Hawai'i, 1941.

Internet

Bill Inman, Baseball-Reference.com, http://www.baseball-reference.com/minors/player.cgi?id=inman-002wil, accessed April 4, 2009; April 6, 2009; April 24, 2009.
Chun Kan Yen, World War I Service Record, Hawaii State Archives Digital Collections, http://archives1.dags.Hawai'i.gov/gsdl/collect/worldwa2/index/assoc/HASH75ba/fe3261f7.dir/Chun%20Kan%20Yen.jpg, accessed November 13, 2008.
Diamond Angle, www.diamondangle.com, accessed January 7, 1998; May 7, 2002; November 26, 2002.
F. L. Akana, World War I Service Record, Hawaii State Archives Digital Collections, http://archives1.dags.Hawai'i.gov/gsdl/collect/worldwa2/index/assoc/HASH01ca/b6847a33.dir/Akana%20F%20Lang.jpg, accessed November 13, 2009.
Hawaii Medical Library, www.hml.org, accessed March 31, 2003.
Lions Club of Honolulu Charter Members, www.honolululions.org/charter_members.asp, accessed June 24, 2009.
Northeastern Conference, www.northeasternconference.org, June 22, 2003.

Newspapers and Magazines

Aberdeen Daily American
Ada Evening News
Albany Evening Journal
Amsterdam Evening Recorder
Anaconda Standard
Appleton Post Crescent
Arizona Life
Atlanta Constitution
Auburn Citizen
Baltimore Afro-American
Baseball Magazine
Bennington Evening Banner
Berkshire Evening Eagle
Big Spring Herald
Boston Daily Globe

Boston Journal
Bridgeport Telegram
Brooklyn Eagle
Brownsville Daily Bulletin
Cedar Rapids Evening Gazette
Cedar Rapids Republican
Charlotte Observer
Chester Times
Chicago Defender
Chicago Tribune
Chinese Students' Monthly
Circleview Herald
Clearfield Progress
Cleburne Morning News
Cleveland Plain-Dealer
Colorado Springs Gazette
Commerce Journal
Connelsville Daily Courier
Coshocton Daily Times
Daily Californian
Daily Commonwealth
Daily Northwestern
Daily Palo Alto
Dallas Morning News
Decatur Review
Delaware County Times
Des Moines Daily News
Duluth News-Tribune
Eau Claire Leader
Edwardsville Intelligencer
Elyria Chronicle Telegram
Elyria Evening Telegram
Emporia Gazette
Fort Wayne News
Fort Wayne Sentinel
Fort Worth Star-Telegram
Frederick Daily News
Frederick Post
Freeman
Fresno Bee
Galveston Daily News
Gettysburg Compiler
Gettysburg Star and Sentinel
Gettysburg Times
Hagerstown Daily Mail
Hagerstown Morning Herald
Hammond Times
Hartford Courant
Hawaii Herald
Hawaiian Star
Helena Independent
Honolulu Advertiser
Honolulu Independent
Honolulu Record
Honolulu Star-Bulletin
Idaho Daily Statesman
Indiana Gazette
Indiana Weekly Messenger
Indianapolis Evening Gazette
Indianapolis Star
Iowa City Daily Press
Jackson City Patriot
Jefferson City News and Tribune
Kalamazoo News
Kansas City Star
Kokomo Tribune
Lethbridge Herald
Lexington Herald
Lima Daily News
Lincoln News
Loganport Daily Tribune
Los Angeles Times
Lowell Sun
Lubbock Avalanche Journal
Macon Telegraph
Marshall Evening Gazette
Massilon Evening Independent
Miami Herald
Middletown Daily-Times Press
Middletown Times Herald
Moberly Monitor-Index
Muscatine Journal
Nevada State Journal
New Castle News
New London Day
Newark Advocate
Newark Advocate and American Tribune
Newark News
New York Age
New York Sun
New York Times
New York Tribune
North Adams Transcript
Oakland Enquirer
Oakland Tribune
Occidental
Oelwein Daily Register
Ogden Examiner
Oswego Palladium-Times
Pacific Commercial Advertiser
Paradise of the Pacific
Pawtucket Times
Philadelphia Inquirer
Philadelphia Public Ledger
Portland Oregonian
Portsmouth Daily Times
Poughkeepsie Eagle News
Racine Journal-News
Reno Evening Gazette
Rochester Democrat and Chronicle
Sacramento Bee
Salt Lake Evening Telegram
Salt Lake Herald Republican
San Antonio Light
San Francisco Call
San Francisco Chronicle
San Francisco Examiner
San Jose Mercury
Savannah Tribune
Seattle Post-Intelligencer
Seattle Times
Sheboygan Press
South Carolina State
Sporting Life
Sporting News
Stockton Daily Record
Stockton Evening Mail
Syracuse Daily Journal
Syracuse Herald
Trenton Evening Times
Tulsa World
Tuscon Citizen
Uniontown Morning Herald
Urbana Daily Courier
Utica Observer
Warren Evening Mirror
Washington Post
Zanesville Signal

Books and Articles

Almaguer, Tomás. *Racial Fault Lines: The Historical Supremacy of White Supremacy in California.* Berkeley: University of California Press, 1994.
Anderson, Benedict. *Invented Communities: Reflections on the Origins and Spread of Nationalism.* London: Verso, 1983.
Barthel, Thomas. *Baseball's Peerless Semipros: The Brooklyn Bushwicks of Dexter Park.* Haworth, NJ: St. Johann Press, 2009.
Benfrey, Christopher. "Herman Melville and John Manjiro: Toward a Wave-Theory of the Pacific," *Common-Place* V, January 2005, www.common-place.org.
Bruce, Janet. *The Kansas City Monarchs: Champions of Black Baseball.* Lawrence: University Press of Kansas, 1985.
Buck, Elizabeth. *Paradise Remade: Politics of Culture and History in Hawai'i.* Philadelphia: Temple University Press, 1993.
Buckingham, Dorothy Dee. "General Patton's Hawaiian 'Internment List.'" www.hawaiireporter.com, February 23, 2002.
Chan, Sucheng. *Asian Americans: An Interpretive History.* Boston: Twayne, 1991.
_____. *This Bittersweet Soil: The Chinese in California Agriculture.* Berkeley: University of California Press, 1986.
Cisco, Dan. *Hawai'i Sports: History, Facts and Statistics.* Honolulu: University of Hawai'i Press, 1999.
Clifford, James. *Routes: Travel and Translation in the Late Twentieth Century.* Cambridge, MA: Harvard University Press, 1997.
Cohen, Lizabeth. *Making a New Deal: Industrial Workers in Chicago.* Cambridge: Cambridge University Press, 1990.
Dunn, Betty. *Jackie Pung: Women's Golf Legend: The Thrills and Heartbreak of an LPGA Professional.* Bloomington, IN: iUniverse.com, 2005.
Dyreson, Mark. *Making the American Team: Sport, Culture and the Olympic Experience.* Urbana: University of Illinois Press, 1998.
Forbes, Camille F. *Introducing Bert Williams: Burnt Cork, Broadway, and the Story of America's First Black Star.* New York: Basic Civitas Books, 2008.
Franks, Joel S. *Asian Pacific Americans and Baseball: A History.* Jefferson, NC: McFarland, 2008.
_____. *Crossing Sidelines, Crossing Cultures: Sport and Asian Pacific American Cultural Citizenship.* Lanham, MD: University Press of America, 2000.
_____. *Hawaiian Sports in the Twentieth Century.* Lewiston, ME: Edwin Mellen Press, 2003.
_____. *Whose Baseball? The National Pastime and Cultural Diversity in California, 1859–1941.* Lanham, MD: Scarecrow Books, 2001.
Fugita, Steve. "Frederick Kinzaburo Makina." *Distinguished Asian Americans.* Edited by Hyung-chan Kim. Westport, CT: Greenwood, 1999.
Geertz, Clifford. *The Interpretation of Cultures.* New York: Basic Books, 1977.
Gyorgy, Andrew. *Race, Politics, and the Chinese Exclusion Act.* Chapel Hill: University of North Carolina Press, 1998.
Hammamoto, Darrell Y. *Monitored Peril: Asian Americans and the Politics of TV Representation.* Minneapolis: University of Minnesota Press, 1994.
Hobsbawm, Eric. *The Age of Empire.* New York: Vintage, 1989.
Hoe, S.H. "America Invaded by Oriental Foes." *Baseball Magazine.* March 1914.
James, C.L.R. *Beyond a Boundary.* New York: Random House, 2005.
Jenkins, Sally. *The Real All-Americans: The Team That Changed a Game, a People, a Nation.* New York: Doubleday, 2007.

Kim, Elaine. "Preface," *Charlie Chan Is Dead: An Anthology of Contemporary Asian American Fiction,* edited by Jessica Hagedorn. New York: Penguin Books, 1993.
Kraus, Bob. *Johnny Wilson: The First Hawaiian Democrat.* Honolulu: University of Hawai'i Press, 1994.
Lanctot, Neil. *Fair Dealing and Clean Playing: The Hilldale Club and the Development of Black Professional Baseball, 1910–1932.* Syracuse, NY: Syracuse University Press, 2007. (Originally published Jefferson, NC: McFarland, 1994.)
Lau, Luck Yee. "A Baseball Trip to the Far East." *Ka Palapala,* College Hawaii, May 1916.
Lee, Robert G. *Orientals: Asian Americans in Popular Culture.* Philadelphia: Temple University Press, 1999.
Levine, Peter. *From Ellis Island to Ebbets Field: Sport and the American Jewish Experience.* New York: Oxford University Press, 1992.
Lopez, Ian Haney. *White By Law: The Legal Construction of Race.* New York: New York University Press, 1996.
MacGregor, Davianna Pomaika'i. *Na Kua'aina.* Honolulu: University of Hawai'i Press, 2007.
Malloy, Jerry. "The 25th Infantry Takes the Field." *The National Pastime,* no. 15, (1995).
McClain, Charles. *In Search of Equality: The Chinese Struggle Against Discrimination in Nineteenth-Century America.* Berkeley: University of California Press, 1996.
Merry, Sally Engle. *Colonizing Hawai'i: The Cultural Power of Law.* Princeton, NJ: Princeton University Press, 2000.
Mills, Dorothy Seymour, and Harold Seymour. *Baseball: The People's Game.* New York: Oxford University Press, 1991.
Morris, Andrew D. *Colonial Project, National Game: A History of Baseball in Taiwan.* Berkeley: University of California Press, 2011.
Okihiro, Gary. *Cane Fires: The Anti-Japanese Movement in Hawai'i, 1865–1945.* Philadelphia: Temple University Press, 1991.
_____. *Island World: A History of Hawai'i and the United States.* Berkeley: University of California Press, 2008.
_____. *Pineapple Culture: A History of the Tropical and Temperate Zones.* Berkeley: University of California Press, 2009.
Omi, Michael, and Howard Winant. *Racial Formation in the United States: From the 1960s to the 1990s.* 2d ed. New York: Routledge, 1994.
Oriard, Michael. *Reading Football: How the Popular Press Created an American Spectacle.* Chapel Hill: University of North Carolina Press, 1998.
Osorio, Jon Kamakawiwo'ole. *Dismembering Lahui: A History of the Hawaiian Nation to 1887.* Honolulu: University of Hawai'i Press, 2002.
Peiss, Kathy. *Cheap Amusements: Working Women and Leisure in Turn-of-the-Century New York.* Philadelphia: Temple University Press, 1986.
Pfaelzer, Jean. *Driven Out: The Forgotten War Against Chinese Americans.* New York: Random House, 2007.
Pratt, Mary Louise. *Imperial Eyes: Studies in Travel Writing and Transculturation.* New York: Routledge, 1992.
Reaves, Joseph A. *Taking in a Game: A History of Baseball in Asia.* Lincoln: University of Nebraska Press, 2002.
Riess, Steven. *Touching Base: Professional Baseball and American Culture in the Progressive Era.* Westport, CT: Greenwood Press, 1980.
Roberts, Randy. *Papa Jack: Jack Johnson and The Era of White Hopes.* New York: Free Press, 1985.
Rogin, Michael. *Black Face, White Noise: Jewish Immigrants in the Hollywood Melting Pot.* Berkeley: University of California Press, 1996.

Rosenzweig, Roy. *Eight Hours for What We Will: Workers and Leisure in an Industrial City, 1870–1920.* Cambridge: Cambridge University Press, 1983.

Rydell, Robert. *All the World's a Fair: Visions of Empire at American International Expositions, 1876–1916.* Chicago: University of Chicago Press, 1987.

Said, Edward. *Culture and Imperialism.* New York: Vintage, 1994.

———. *Orientalism.* New York: Vintage, 1979.

Saxton, Alexander. *The Indispensable Enemy: Labor and the Anti-Chinese Movement in California.* Berkeley: University of California Press, 1971.

Seymour, Harold, and Dorothy Seymour Mills. *Baseball: The Early Years.* New York: Oxford University Press, 1960.

Siddell, John, ed. *Men of Hawaii: Being a Biographical Reference Library, Complete and Authentic of the Men of Note and Substantial Achievement in the Hawaiian Islands.* v. 1, Honolulu: Honolulu Star-Bulletin, Ltd., 1917.

Silva, Noenoe. *Aloha Betrayed: Native Hawaiian Resistance to American Colonialism.* Durham, NC: Duke University Press, 2004.

Smith, William Carlson. *Americans in Process.* New York: Arno Press, 1970.

Spalding, Albert G. *America's National Pastime.* Lincoln: University of Nebraska Press, 1992.

Spalding, John E. *Sacramento Senators and Solons.* Manhattan, KS: Ag Press, 1995.

Stannard, David. *Honor Killing; Race, Rape, and Clarence Darrow's Spectacular Last Case.* New York: Penguin, 2005.

Sussman, Warren. *Culture as History.* New York: Pantheon, 1984.

Takaki, Ronald. *Pau Hana: Plantation Life and Labor in Hawai'i, 1835–1920.* Honolulu: University of Hawai'i Press, 1983.

———. *Strangers from a Different Shore: A History of Asian Americans.* Boston: Little, Brown, 1989.

Tamura, Eileen H. *Americanization, Acculturation, and Ethnic Identify: The Nisei Generation in Hawaii.* Champagne: University of Illinois Press, 1994.

Tchen, John Kuo Wei. *New York Before Chinatown: Orientalism and the Shaping of American Culture, 1776–1882.* Baltimore: Johns Hopkins University Press, 1999.

Trachtenberg, Alan. *The Incorporation of America: Culture and Society in the Gilded Age.* New York: Hill and Wang, 1982.

Tygiel, Jules. *Past Time.* New York: Oxford University Press, 2000.

Voigt, David. *American Baseball. Vol. 1: From Gentlemen's Sport to the Commissioner System.* University Park: Penn State University Press, 1979.

Ziegler, Mark. "James Vincent Jamison, Jr.: Blue Ridge League President, 1916–1918, 1920–1930." *The National Pastime.* no. 39 (2009).

Index

Page numbers in ***bold italics*** indicate illustrations.

Aberfoyle Manufacturing Company Baseball Club 189
Akana, Albert 46, 58, 61, 66, 67, 68, 95, ***96***, 105, 108, 109, 228
Akana, F.L. 27
Akana, Lang 2, 6, 38, 42, 46, 52–53, 54, 84, 92, 95, 97, 98, 99, 100, 115, 116, 118–***119***, 120–121, 123–125, 129, 155, 158, 159, 169, 170, 172, 176, 193–194, 224, 228; *see also* Akana, F.L
Akina, Clement 92
All Chinese Collegians of Shanghai Basketball Team 210
Aloha Hawaiian Stars Basketball Team 210–211
Apau, Kau 2, 29, 36, 37, 41, 44, 45, 50, 52, 61, 67, 70, 73, 75, 76, 81, 82, 88, 91, 92, 95, 100, 102, 103, 105, 107, 109, 110, 111, 113, 114, 115, 117, 127, 128, 131, 136, 137–138, 139, 140, 142–143, 144, 146, 147, 148, 150, 152, 156, 163, 165, 166, 168, 169, 170, 175, 183, 190–***191***, 224, 228, 229
Apau, William 98, 117
Arakawa, Wallace 213
Asahi Baseball Club 116
Asam, Alex 35, 45, 47, 48, 52, 56–57, 98
Austin College 164
Ayau, Vernon 2, 37, 45, 53, 63, 67, 74, 75, 80, 83, ***85***, 86, 90, 95, 96, 104, 106, 111, 117, 128, 129, 130–131, 141, 147, 150, 154, 155, 158, 159, 160, 162, 164, 168, 171, 172, 174, 174–183, 187, 190, ***193***, 194, 224, ***225***, 228
Aylett, Jimmy 128, 152, 155, ***193***, ***225***

Bacharach Giants 168, 182, 185, 189, 192
Baird, Tom 217
Baker, Frank 189
Bancroft, Dave 178
Bates College 145
Baum, A.G. 117
Baumgartner, Stan 209
Baylor University 137–138
Bee, Clair 220
Beloit College 47
Bender, "Chief" 41, 80, 119, 210
Bethany College 139
Bethlehem Steel Company Baseball Club 191–192
Bethlehem Steel Company Baseball League 198–199
Bezdek, Hugo 200
Blue Ridge League 183–184
Bo, George 155, 163, 164
Boston Braves 32, 198
Bridgeport Americans 199–203, 220
Bronx Athletics 80
Brooklyn Bushwicks 112, 114, 145, 148, 150, 166, 169, 181, 185, 189, 197, 200, 204, 205, 208–211
Brooklyn Dodgers 76, 81, 88, 209, 221–222
Brooklyn Royal Giants 165, 181, 185, 209
Brown University 145–146, 166
Buck, Pearl 219
Buck Lai's Hawaiian All-Stars 212–219
Bucknell University 147, 165
Bush, George 128, 136, 146, 149, 156, 224; *see also* Bo, George

Calvo, Jacinto 178
Camden Athletic Club 109–110, 167
Carlisle Institution 24
Chan, Charlie 219
Chance, Frank 33
Chang, Wah Kai 141
Chester Baseball Club 182, 189, 191, 204, 215

250

Index

Chester Shipbuilding Company Baseball Club 181
Chicago American Giants 18, 86, 182
Chicago Cubs 33
Chicago White Sox 118–120, 121, 124, 125–127, 220
Chillingsworth, Henry 83–84, 212
Chin, Yen 9, *128*, 156, *157*, 159, 166, 172
Chinese Alohas Baseball Club 29
Chinese Athletic Club 28, 31, 35, 37, 38, 40, 42
Chinese Athletic Union Baseball Club 96, 98, 99, 115–118, 132
Chinese Exclusion Law (1882) 14, 21, 57
Chinese National Society 80
Chinese Students Alliance 89
Chong, W. Tin 99, 116, 132, 153
Chun, Kan Yen 8, 41, 50, 54, 68, 71, 73, 74, 75, 76, 77, 80, 81, 83, 89, 92, 95–96, 97, 103, 105, 106, 107, 109, 110, 117, 129, 133, 153, 155, 156, 158–159, 160, 170, 172, 175–176–177, 192, 212, 224
Chung, Mon Yen 57
Chung Wah Merchants' Association 87
Cincinnati Reds 127
Cobb, Ty 17, 18, 47, 170, 219
Cohen, Andy 206
Colgate University 147
College of Hawai'i 67, 151, 153
Columbia University *96*, 108–109
Comstock Cheney Company 166
Concordia Seminary 140
Consumer Culture 14–19, 25
Corbett, James 198
Corley Catholic Club 208
Cozy Baseball Club 100
Creole Hawaiian 11–12
Crescent Athletic Club (New York City) 85
Crisfield Crabbers Baseball Club (Maryland) 192
Cuban Stars 209
Cypress Hills Baseball Club 77, 109, 114, 149

Danbury Baseball Club 77, 79
Dean, Dizzy 210
Dean, Paul 210
Delaware University 192
Delaware Valley League 189, 197
Delco Basketball Team 210
DePauw University 141–142
Desha, Alex 98
Detroit Tigers 34, 80, 170
Dexter Park 58, 109, 114, 149, 205, 209, 210, 211, 218, 219
Dihigo, Martin 209
Dismukes, Dizzy 164, 169
Donnelly, Frank 208
Doty, Roy 156, *157*, 160, 161, 163, 165, 166, 170, 175, 180
Dykes, Jimmy 184, *185*

East Chicago Giants 218
East Helena Baseball Club 216–217
East Texas Normal College 164
Eastern League 185–187, 199
Eastern Shore League 192
Ebbets, Charles 79
Ebbets Field 79
Eliot, Rowdy 177
Elyria Athletics 75
Enomoto, Kenichi 216
Ensue, Charlie 155, 169–170

Farrington, W.R. 88, 94
Fitzgerald, Justin 124
Fordham University 48–50
Foster, Rube 86, 223
Freeth, George 228
Fresno Japanese Baseball Club 218
Fullerton, Hugh 142

Geary Act (1892) 21
Gehrig, Lou 205, 209
General Electric Baseball Club 148
Genovese, Vincent *39*
Georgetown University 47–48
Glocalization 227
Gomez, Lefty 210
Goo, Francis 213–214, 215
Gottleib, Eddie 212
Green, Guy 34, 84
Griffith, Clark 219
Grimes, Ray 200

Hawaiian Islanders Baseball Club 194
Henderson, Lew *39*
Hidalgo, Manuel 219
Hilldale Baseball Club 182, 205
Ho, Kim Tong 65, 132, 133
Hoe, Henry Pan 29
Hoe, Sing Hung 8, 38, 44, 45, 46, 50, 65, 69, 70, 71, 73, 74, 79, 80, 89, 90–93, 98, 114
Hokea, Ben 193
Hong, Chack 38, 58
Honolulu Ad Club 97
Hop, Sam 37, 38, 47, 54, 58, 59, 61–62, 63, 64, 67, 70, 71, 73, 77, 86, 87–88, 89, 92, 95, 96, 97, 98, 99, 103, 104, 105, 106, 107, 113, 117, 127, 174, 195
Howard Payne College 162–163

Indiana State Normal 144
Indiana University 108
Inman, Bill 116, 156, 160, 161, 163, 164, 165, 166, 167, 170–*171*, 172, 175
"Inside baseball" 223–224
International League 208
Iowa State University 73–74, 140–141

J&J Dodson Baseball Club 192
James, Bill 124

Japanese Athletic Club 61
Jersey City Cubans 165, 168
Johnson, Jack 24–25, 62, 124
Johnson, Judy 219
Joy, Barney 32–33, 61, 97, 212

Kahanamoku, Duke 18–19, 24, *39*, 54, 158, 193, 226, 228
Kansas City Monarchs 214, 217
Kansas Normal 105
Kansas State Agricultural College 139
Kaulukukui, Tommy 213
Keio University 7, 31, 35–36, 43, 47, 52, 108
Kekoa, Luther 96, 98, 101, 102, 104, 108, 128, 132, 136–137, 141, 142, 155, 156, 158, 166, 192–*193*, 224, *225*, 229
Kendall College 122
Kentucky State University 74
Kerr, John 214, 215
Knox College (Illinois) 73
Kokomo Red Sox 141, 164
Kong, Li Hong 98
Krichell, Paul 185, 199
Kuali, Henry 68, 73, 92, 98, 128, 142, 147, 149, 172, 212
Kunihisa, Lawrence 215, 216

Lafayette University 147, 165–166
Lai, Buck 2, 3, 4, 182, 183, 186–187, 189, 196–222, 224, 228; *see also* Lai, Tin
Lai, Buck, Jr. 218, 220–222
Lai, Tin 6, 8, *9*, 35, 37, 41, 42, 43, 45, 46, 48, 50, 52, 65–66, 68, 70, 75, 76, 77, 81, 82, 89, 92, 95, 96, 97, 98, 99, 100, 111, 115, 117, 118–120, 121, 125–127, *128*, 129, 130, 131–132, 134–135, 136, *137*, 140, 142, 143, 145, 146, 147, 150, 154, 155, 156, *157*, 158, 159, 160, 161, 163, 164, 165, 166, 168, 169, 170, 171, 172, 174, 175, 181, *193*, 195, *225*
Leard, William 174, 177, 178, 179, 180
Lehigh University 145, 151, 165, 192
Lincoln Giants 55–56, 80, 151–152, 223, 228
Lit Brothers Baseball Club 190
Lloyd Athletic Club 220
Lo, Shipp 213, 216
Local culture 11–14, 223
Logan Square Baseball Club 181, 187, 189
Long Island University 2, 77, 220-
Lorain Loyon Tailors 217
Los Angeles Angels 73
Lowery, Bert 98
Luque, Dolph 210
Luther College 141

Mack, Connie 80, 219, 223
Manhattan College 73; *see also* Kansas State Agricultural College
Mark, Fred 155, 181, 197
Markham, Fred 64, 67, 68, 73, 74, 75, 76, 81, *85*, 87, 96, 97, 98, 103, 108, 128, 148, 150, 151, 156, *162*, 164, 170, 174, 175, 181–182, 183, 189–190, 197, 198, 212, 224, 228; *see also* Mark, Fred
Markham, John 81, 95
Marshall College 143
Mathewson, Christy 109
McCarthy, Jack 124, 125
McCreadie, Walter 120, 121, 123, 125, 176–177
McGraw, John 79, 88, 205–208, 209
McKinley High School 65, 219
Medwick, Joe 210
Meyers, "Chief" 34, 80, 210
Missouri School of Mines 71
Mitchell, Jackie 218
Moran, Pat 121, 197, 198
Moriyama, Chinito 64, 98, 105, 129, 155, 156, 160, 164, 166, 172, 176, 177, 224
Moriyama, Jimmy *9*, *128*, *162*; *see also* Moriyama, Chinito
Moriyama, Tom 64

Nalua, Al 213, 215, 216
New York Giants 34–35, 76, *78*, 79, 81, 148, 205–208, 209, 219
New York Yankees 182, 219
Nobriega, Ted 213
North Phillies Baseball Club 192
Northwest Steel Company Baseball Team 180
Notre Dame University *72*, 73
Nushida, Kenso 210

Oahu College 64, 65
Oahu League 60–61, 62, 99, 115–116, 117, 155
Oakland Oaks 177
Oana, Henry 210
Oberlin College 75
Occidental College 100–102
Ohio Northwestern 74
Ohio University 143
Oklahoma A&M 164
Olympic Club 158–160
Orientalism 18–19
Original Celtics basketball team 210

Pacific Coast League 117–125, 194
Pacific Northwest League 174–180
Page, Pat 31
Pan Pacific Exposition 229
Passon, Harry 211
Patton, George 188
Penn-Jersey League 204
Penn State University 76, 145
Pennsylvania Railroad League 203
Philadelphia Athletics 80, 174, 181, 189
Philadelphia Baseball Association 204
Philadelphia Phillies 121, 148, 197–199, 215, 220
Philadelphia Red Caps 199
Philadelphia Royal Giants 215
Pinelli, Babe 176

Pittsburgh Pirates 200
Polo Grounds 48, 63, 79, 88, 148
Portland Beavers 116, 118, 120–121, 124, 131, 175, 176–177
Portuguese Athletic Club 89
Poughkeepsie Cubans 168
Primitivism 18–19
Punahou School 64, 151, 156, 158, 160
Pung, Afo 213
Pung, Barney 195
Pung, En Sue 7, 8, 27, 28, 31–32, 33, 35, 37, 40, 62–63, 65, 66, 67, 70, 73, 74, 75, 76, 80, 81, 82, 83, *85*, 92, 95, 96, 97, 100, 101, 102, 103, 105, 109, 112, 114, 117, 121, 159, 161, 172, 194–195, 212–213, 224, 226; *see also* Ensue, Charlie
Pung, Hans 213
Pung, Jackie Liwai 195
Pung, Ping Kong 83, 89, 92, 105, 117

Redding, Dick 181, 209
Redlands University 131, 132
Rensselaer Polytechnic 147
Reuther, Dutch 172
Rice Institute 136, *137*
Richmer Oilers 218
Ridgewood Baseball Club 50, 77, 80
Robinson, Alvin 95, 96, 102, 104, 107, 112
Robinson, Foster 61, 64, 65, 67, 68, 69, 70, 73, 75, 77, 79, 80, 81, 82, 83, 84, 88, 95, 98, 101, 104, 108, 109–110, 111, 112, 127, 128, 224
Rodriques, Walter 213
Rogan, Wilbur 156, 170, 172
Rogers, Adele 101–102
Rollins College 73
Rommel, Ed 205
Roosevelt, Teddy 24
Rosner, Max 209, 211–212, 218
Ruth, Babe 181, 205, 209, 214, 219

St. Louis Cardinals 210
St. Louis College 27, 33, 64, 158, 159, 160
St. Mary's College (California) 34, 69–70, 160
St. Mary's College (Kansas) 139
St. Mary's College (Maryland) 144, 165
St. Victor's College 141
St. Xavier's College 142
San Francisco Seals 32, 42, *171*, 178, 215
Santa Clara College 29, 160
Savitt Gems 217
Seattle Giants 174–180
Seton Hall University 50–51
Shadow Ball 229
Shafer, Artie 79
Shamrocks Baseball Club 142
Sherman Institute 34
Simmons College 161
Sisler, George 166

South Philadelphia Hebrew Association 204
South Phillies 203–204
Southwestern University 163
Speaker, Tris 219
Stanford University 34, 69, 129, 160, 161
State Hospital Grays Baseball Club 209
Stetson Athletic Club 81–82, 84, 91, 167, 168
Strawbridge and Clothier Baseball Club 82, 86, 113, 151, 166, 167, 168, 191
Strong, Nat 54, 55–56, 58, 63, 79, 80, 84, *85*, 86, 89, 107, 110, 122, 128–129, 132, 150, 165, 181, 209, 211–212, 218
Susquehanna University 146
Swan, Fred 156, 160, 161, 163, 164, 165, 166, 167, 168–169, 170, 171, 224
Syracuse University 52

Tam, Eddie 213
Taylor ABCs 164–165, 168
Temple Preparatory School 173
Terry, Bill 219
Texas Christian University 103–104, 136, 138
Thorpe, Jim 24
Toon, Ah 59
Trenton Baseball Club 189–190, 204–205
Trinity University 166
Twenty-Fifth Regiment 66, 86, 117, 155, 156, 158, 171, 228

University of Arizona 102–103, 135, 161
University of California 34, 42, 43–44, 100, 116, 117–118, 129, 194
University of Chicago 31, *37*, 46, 141
University of Cincinnati 47
University of Dallas 104
University of Illinois 75
University of Kansas 106, 140
University of Kentucky 143
University of Maine 145
University of Minnesota 74
University of Missouri 140
University of Oklahoma 138–139
University of Pennsylvania 190
University of Pittsburgh 144
University of South Dakota 141
University of Texas 136–137, 163–164, 219
University of Utah 45
University of Washington 179
University of Wisconsin 46–47, 65
Upland Baseball Club 181, 182, 189, 197

Vance, Dazzy 210
Vickery, William 213, 214
Victrix Catholic Club 112, 144
Vida, Earl 213

Walsh, Ed 201, 203
Waseda University 7, 34, 35, *37*, 43, 45, 52, 169
Weaver, Buck 124, 127

West Virginia Wesleyan College 144
Westminster College 140
Wilberforce College 143, 165
Wildwood Baseball Club 180, 181, 182, 186, 192
Williams, Bert 229
Williams, Joe 152
Williams, John B. 33–34, 94, 156, 212
Williams College 75, 76, 141, 147
Wolverton, Harry 178
World War I 190–191, 192, 196–197, 200

Yamada, Richard 213, 215
Yamashiro, Andy 2, 3, *9*, *128*, 132, 139, 148, 155, 156, *157*, 161, *162*, 163, 170, 173–174, 175, 181–188, 200, 212, 219, 224, 228; *see also* Yim, Andy
Yap, Al 128, 129, 131, 132, 135–151, 155, 166, 167, 190, 191–192, 212
Yap, E.K.C. 37, 38, 42, 43, 45, 59
Yap, Robert 31, 38, 59, 195, 229
Yee, Luck 48, 65, 67, 70, 73, 83, 88, 92, 116, 153–154, 158, 159, 169, 212, 224
Yim, Andy 146, 150, 165, 169, 191, 199
Yingling, Earl 79
Yuan, Shi-Kai 134

Zenimura, Kenichi 218